Russian Trade Policy

This book reveals the key trends in the modern Russian trade policy to provide a deeper understanding of the main challenges and barriers, possible paths and opportunities in its development.

An international team of authors investigates specific factors influencing the Russian trade policy evolution; recent trends in Russia's international trade development; and the impact of Russia's participation in the World Trade Organization on the domestic economy. Particular attention is paid to regional integration processes that involve Russia and their outcomes; as well as challenges in the remaining and building commercial relations with Russia's traditional and 'new' trade partners, taking into consideration those alienating the West and economic sanctions regimes. The analysis of key trends is combined with a special focus on selected industries and economic partners of Russia. The book contains a variety of case studies investigating the ways in which political and business actors adapt to the transformation of Russian trade policy, how Russia participates in the WTO dispute settlement mechanism, and what the driving forces and outputs are for the national economic agents. Finally, the authors consider what the reasonable expectations might be regarding the future prospects of Russian trade policy.

The book presents a unique, comprehensive and multidimensional analysis of modern Russian trade policy. Filling an important gap in the existing literature, this book will be of value to all those interested in Russia's economic development path.

Sergei F. Sutyrin is a Professor and World Economy Department Head at Saint Petersburg State University, WTO Chair Holder since 2010.

Olga Y. Trofimenko, Candidate of Economic Science (PhD), is an Associate Professor at the World Economy Department of Saint Petersburg State University.

Alexandra G. Koval, Candidate of Economic Science (PhD), is an Associate Professor at the World Economy Department of Saint Petersburg State University.

Routledge Studies in the European Economy

Economic Crisis and Structural Reforms in Southern Europe
Policy Lessons
Edited by Paulo Manasse and Dimitris Katsikas

Crisis in the European Monetary Union
A Core-Periphery Perspective
Giuseppe Celi, Andrea Ginzberg, Dario Guarascio and Annamaria Simonazzi

Rethinking Economic and Monetary Union in Europe
A Post-Keynesian Alternative
Philip B. Whyman

Central and Eastern Europe in the EU
Challenges and Perspectives Under Crisis Conditions
Edited by Christian Schweiger and Anna Visvizi

Greek Employment Relations in Crisis
Problems, Challenges and Prospects
Edited by Horen Voskeritsian, Panos Kapotas and Christina Niforou

Centrally Planned Economies
Theory and Practice in Socialist Czechoslovakia
Edited by Libor Žídek

SME Finance and the Economic Crisis
The Case of Greece
Alina Hyz

Russian Trade Policy
Achievements, Challenges and Prospects
Edited by Sergei F. Sutyrin, Olga Y. Trofimenko and Alexandra G. Koval

For a full list of titles in this series, please visit: www.routledge.com/series/SE0431

Russian Trade Policy

Achievements, Challenges and Prospects

Edited by Sergei F. Sutyrin, Olga Y. Trofimenko and Alexandra G. Koval

Routledge
Taylor & Francis Group
LONDON AND NEW YORK

First published 2019 by Routledge

2 Park Square, Milton Park, Abingdon, Oxon, OX14 4RN
605 Third Avenue, New York, NY 10017

Routledge is an imprint of the Taylor & Francis Group, an informa business

First issued in paperback 2020

British Library Cataloguing-in-Publication Data
A catalogue record for this book is available from the British Library

Library of Congress Cataloging-in-Publication Data
Names: Sutyrin, S. F., editor. | Trofimenko, Olga, editor. | Koval, Alexandra, editor.
Title: Russian trade policy : achievements, challenges and prospects / edited by Sergei Sutyrin, Olga Trofimenko and Alexandra Koval.
Description: Abingdon, Oxon ; New York, NY : Routledge, 2019. | Series: Routledge studies in the European economy | Includes index.
Identifiers: LCCN 2019008074 | ISBN 9781138614499 (hardback)
Subjects: LCSH: Russia (Federation)—Commercial policy. | Russia (Federation)—Foreign economic relations.
Classification: LCC HF1558.2 .R8697 2019 | DDC 382/.30947—dc23
LC record available at https://lccn.loc.gov/2019008074

ISBN: 978-1-138-61449-9 (hbk)
ISBN: 978-0-367-72860-1 (pbk)

Typeset in Times New Roman
by Apex CoVantage, LLC

Contents

Figures

Tables

Contributors

Alexis Dantas, DsC is a Professor and Vice-Director of the Faculty of Economic Science (FCE) at the State University of Rio de Janeiro (UERJ). He has authored or co-authored many articles and book chapters. His main research interests include Latin American Studies, Integration Processes and Trade Policy of Brazil. He coordinates the Nucleus of Studies of America (NUCLEAS), promoting Conferences, Congresses, Courses relating to Latin American issues.

Antonia Diakantoni is a Counsellor in the WTO Trade Monitoring Section of the Trade Policies Review Division. Before joining the WTO, she was employed by the European Commission in the Directorate-General for Environment and by the Free University of Brussels (ULB) in the area of Economic modelling and Statistics. Ms. Diakantoni holds a Masters in Applied Mathematics in Management from the ULB and a Bachelor of Science in Mathematics from the University of Patras (Greece).

Maryana A. Gubina, Candidate of Economic Science (PhD) is an Associate Professor at the World Economy department of Saint Petersburg State University. She has authored or co-authored nearly 40 papers and book chapters. Her main research interests include various dimensions of India's involvement in the global economy, Russian-Indian economic relations, International Trade and Public Health. She was a visiting researcher at the Helsinki University. She has participated in the WTO Chair programme.

Jeffrey K. Hass received an AB in chemistry from Harvard University and an MA and PhD in sociology from Princeton University. He works on post-socialist institutional and organizational change, including political trajectories and organizational fields. His other major project is political economy, power, and survival practices in war, in particular regarding the Blockade of Leningrad. His books include: *Economic Sociology*; *Power, Culture, and Economic Change in Russia*; *Rethinking the Post-Soviet Experience*; and *Rethinking the Post-Socialist Experience.*

Norio Horie is a Professor of the Center for Far Eastern Studies, University of Toyama, Japan. He was awarded the Japan Consortium for Area Studies Award in 2011. He is a leading researcher in Japan on Sino-Russian relationship, especially on cross-border migration between China and Russia. His research focuses on labour in Russia ranging from human resource management to labour migration issues in Russia with trans-disciplinary approaches.

Tatiana M. Isachenko is a Doctor of Economics, Full Professor, Department of International Economic Relations and Foreign Economic Ties, Moscow State Institute of International Relations (MGIMO-University). She is an author and co-author of more than 80 publications, including books, papers, and electronic publications. Her area of research and teaching is Trade Policy and Multilateral Trading System. Prof. Isachenko is a member of Editorial Board of several Russian and international journals and a member of the Parliamentary Expert Committee on International markets, trade and economic cooperation.

Teemu Itälinna, Master of Science (Economics) and Master of Arts (Social Sciences) has worked at the Pan-European Institute (PEI) at the Turku School of Economics, University of Turku, since 2017. His main research interests include the Baltic Sea region maritime sector and the internationalization of state-owned enterprises.

Irina A. Korgun, Candidate of Economic Science (PhD), is an expert in Korea's economic development and trade. Currently working in the business sector, she has previously built her academic career serving as an Assistant Professor at Hankuk University of Foreign Studies, Seoul. She has participated in several international grant projects concerning trade and development in North-East Asia and has published research works on various aspects of Korea's economic development and trade policy.

Alexandra G. Koval, Candidate of Economic Science (PhD) is an Associate Professor at the World Economy department of Saint Petersburg State University. She has authored or co-authored nearly 80 articles and book chapters. Her main research interests include trade policy developments in Russia and Latin America and Russian–Latin American economic relations. She was a visiting researcher at various universities and think tanks in Europe, Latin America and Asia. Dr. Koval has participated in the WTO Chair programme and coordinated the EU Marie Curie programme "Power and Region in a Multipolar Order" at St. Petersburg State University.

Kari Liuhto began working as a Professor at the Lappeenranta University of Technology in 1997. In 2003, he was invited to hold a tenure professorship in International Business at the Turku School of Economics, Finland. In addition to the professorship, he is Director of the Pan-European Institute (PEI) and Director of the Centrum Balticum Foundation.

Nikita A. Lomagin is an academic director of the ENERPO programme at European University in St. Petersburg and Professor of the World Economy Department at St. Petersburg State University. He was post-doctoral fellow at the Davis Center for Russian Studies at Harvard and researcher at Kennan Institute, University of Michigan Law School, Finnish Institute for international relations and GSPIA. He earned his doctorate in history at St. Petersburg

Institute of History of the Russian Academy of Sciences and holds a diploma in law from St. Petersburg State University. He is the author of several monographs on the history of the Second World War and contributed chapters to a number of collective volumes on Russian foreign policy.

Peter Pedersen is the Head of the Trade Monitoring Section in the Trade Policies Review Division at the WTO. He has authored or co-authored several articles and papers on transparency and institutional reform issues facing the multilateral trading system. Prior to joining the WTO he worked at the Institute for Transition Economies at Copenhagen Business School. He was a Visiting Fellow and Associate Professor at the Institute for International Trade at Adelaide University. Mr. Pedersen holds a Master of Science in Economics from Copenhagen Business School and a Master of Philosophy in International Relations from University of Cambridge.

Liudmila V. Popova, Candidate of Economic Science (PhD) is an Associate Professor at the World Economy department of Saint Petersburg State University. She is an author of about 80 publications including monographs. Her main research interests include China's trade policy and Russian–Chinese economic relations. She was a visiting researcher at Renmin University of China, Tohoku University (Japan), and University of Helsinki. She participated in the WTO Chair programme.

Vladimir G. Sherov-Ignatev, Candidate of Economic Science (PhD) is an Associate Professor at the World Economy department of Saint Petersburg State University. Dr. Sherov-Ignatev is an author of one monograph, and he has authored or co-authored up to 60 articles and book or textbook chapters. His research interests concentrate on regional trade agreements with the special emphasis on customs unions. He has been invited as a visiting lecturer to several universities in Belarus, China, and Germany. He participated in a number of international projects, including in the WTO Chair programme.

Maarten Smeets is the Head of Section at the Institute for Training and Technical Co-operation (ITTC) in the WTO, Geneva, leading the WTO Chairs Programme and WTO's cooperation with academia. He has held senior positions in the Trade Directorate of the OECD (Paris) and at the Ministry of Economic Affairs, Netherlands. He holds a Ph.D. from the Faculty of Law at Maastricht University, a master's degree in economics, finance, and international trade from Tilburg University, and higher degrees from the Graduate Institute in Geneva and the Ecole Nationale Nationale d'Administration (ENA), Paris. He is a senior visiting fellow at a leading think tank in the Netherlands, Clingendael Institute (Den Haag) and a fellow from Salzburg Seminar (Austria). He is a frequent lecturer at universities and training institutes around the world, including the UN in New York (UNITAR) and the IDLO in Rome.

Sergei F. Sutyrin is a Professor and World Economy Department Head at St. Petersburg State University, WTO Chair holder since 2010. In addition to his professorship at SPSU he has delivered lectures in several universities in Finland, Germany, and Japan. Research interests of Prof. Sutyrin include Russian foreign economic relations, international trading systems, and global governance. He is an author of more than 250 books, pamphlets, and articles in different fields of economic theory. Sutyrin has been involved in many research and educational projects funded in particular by EU, DAAD, CIDA, and the International Trading Center.

Dmitry I. Tonkov is a First Secretary at the Permanent Mission of the Russian Federation to the WTO and an external Ph.D. candidate, Department of World Economy, Faculty of Economics, St. Petersburg State University. Previously he served in expert and managerial roles at the Department for Trade Negotiations, Ministry of Economic Development of the Russian Federation. Areas of research interest: trade and industrial policy, subsidies, and trade remedies.

Olga Y. Trofimenko, Candidate of Economic Science (Ph.D.) is an Associate Professor at the World Economy department of Saint Petersburg State University. She is author or co-author of more than 60 papers and book chapters. She also was a co-editor of some monograph and conference proceedings. She was invited as a visiting lecturer to various universities. Research interests concentrate on global governance, international trade rules, and foreign direct investments. She is a coordinator of various academic and research projects at SPSU, including the WTO Chairs project and Jean Monnet – European module.

Olesya V. Veredyuk, Candidate of Economic Science (Ph.D.) is an Associate Professor at the Department of Economic Theory, St. Petersburg State University. She has authored or co-authored nearly 30 papers (including in English and Chinese languages). Her main research interests are labour economics and the Russian labour market. She was an expert at the ILO project, a visiting researcher at Freie Universität Berlin (Germany), University of Jyväskylä (Finland), a coordinator of the first Saint Petersburg International Youth Labour Forum.

Zhou Weidi, Dr. of Economics, is a Professor and a Vice Dean of School of Economics & Business Administration, Central Normal University of China. He obtained his Ph.D. in Theoretical Economy from Zhejizng University (China) in 2010. In recent years, he has presided or participated in more than 10 research projects and has about 40 publications (including books) in domestic and foreign journals.

Introduction

Alexandra G. Koval and Olga Y. Trofimenko

From the beginning of the twenty-first century, the Russian Federation has significantly transformed its trade policy. The focal point in Russia's trade liberalization was its accession to the WTO in 2012. Another significant step was the establishment of the EAEU following lengthy attempts to boost the integration process within the post-Soviet space. Despite some fears, these developments created rather positive expectations regarding the country's economic prospects. However, the events in Crimea and Ukraine in 2014 have led to a vicious circle of sanctions challenging the Russian development path and influencing its trade patterns.

Substantial trade policy transformation began in Russia in the 1990s, but the main focus of the book is national trade policy evolution in the twenty-first century. It is clear that many existing patterns and challenges of the current stage of the national trade policy development refer back to the Soviet Union collapse and the rapid switch from a planned to a market economy. There is a substantial amount of studies analysing that period of transformation, but this book attempts to address later issues of trade policy evolution.

Russia has steadily enhanced its role in international trade. In 2001, it accounted for nearly 1.6 percent of the world's commodity export, and 0.7 percent of the import. By 2013, these figures had substantially increased to 2.8 percent and 1.7 percent, respectively. The sanctions, as well as an economic downturn of the Russian economy, negatively impacted trade. In 2017, Russia's share of the world export was estimated to be 2 percent, with imports at 1.3 percent. However, a slight recovery was observed during 2016–2017, with Russia's exports and imports increasing by 26 and 25 percent, respectively. Russia is currently among the top 20 exporters and importers on international commodity markets. The country plays a crucial role in the world's exports of energy and raw materials. In 2017, Russia ranked first in exports of mineral fuels and fertilizers (with shares of 10.7 and 14.1 percent, respectively), second for exports of nickel and cereals (10.7 and 7.3 percent), fifth for exports of wood, iron and steel, and aluminium (5.8, 5 and 3.9 percent). Existing political tensions and sanctions undermined Russia's opportunities for international cooperation, and this is reflected in the trade of certain goods and services and in FDI inflows. The sanctions created advantages for some domestic industries, but others suffer and rely on a substantial government support. Future prospects in trade dynamics and the country's economic development are not clear, piquing the research interest of the book's authors.

Internal problems and the challenges arising from outside the country have forced the national government to find solutions based on certain priorities. The goal of the book is to reveal the cornerstone trends of the modern Russian trade policy, thus providing a more clear understanding of the main challenges and barriers, and the possible paths and opportunities for its development. The objectives of the book are to investigate:

- the main specific factors influencing the evolution of Russian trade policy;
- how Russian trade has developed over the last two decades;
- how Russia's participation in the WTO and regional integration processes has impacted the domestic economy and foreign trade;
- how sanctions have influenced Russian trade and its commodity and geographical composition;
- challenges in the development of Russian commercial relations with its traditional and "new" trade partners;
- how political and business actors adopt to the transformation of Russian trade policy;
- reasonable expectations regarding future prospects for Russian trade.

Taking all these angles into consideration, the book presents a comprehensive multidimensional analysis of modern Russian trade policy, which has yet to appear in the literature. An international team of authors offers independent thoughts with regard to the issues under investigation.

The idea of the book was generated by the editorial team of the World Economy Department of St. Petersburg State University. Its roots went back to the participation of Sergei F. Sutyrin, Olga Y. Trofimenko, and Alexandra G. Koval at the WTO Chairs Programme launched in 2009. St. Petersburg State University is the only institution in Russia and other post-Soviet states that has been acknowledged by the WTO as a think tank conducting research and other activities on trade-related issues. The WTO Chairs Programme has given significant incentives for deeper studies on Russian trade policy and developing high-level expertise in this field, as well as enhancing academic networking worldwide.

The book considers results of research completed by the international team of 20 experts from Brazil, China, Finland, Japan, Russia, Switzerland, and the USA. The authors express independent opinions on the hot topic of modern debates about Russian trade in the context of the turbulent geopolitical environment. Their analyses are based on classical trade theories, the political economy of trade, institutional theories and theoretical foundations of international business. Such a multidisciplinary approach has presented a comprehensive view on the studied phenomenon.

The book is structured as follows: in Chapter 1, Peter Pedersen and Antonia Diakantoni reveal contemporary global trends in trade policy and highlight, in particular, the variety of trade-restriction measures applied by the WTO members after the world financial crisis of 2008–2009. The main challenge for modern commercial relations continues to come from increasing protectionist pressures, especially in the form of trade remedies as well as measures justified by national security issues, which both negatively influence trade flows.

Taking into account the rise of geopolitical rhetoric in the international trading system, Alexandra G. Koval and Sergei F. Sutyrin investigate how transformation in Russia's perception of global governance has affected its trade patterns. In Chapter 2, they underline how the Russian Federation, as a rule co-maker/co-keeper, attempts to conduct a more sophisticated and diversified trade policy.

In Chapter 3, Nikita A. Lomagin and Jeffrey K. Hass analyse state–market interplay in the Russian trade of hydrocarbons and agricultural products. They compare *dirigisme* in the oil and gas sector, which encourages exports and integration into the global market, with corporate capitalism in agriculture focused mainly on the domestic market and recently supported by the import substitution policy in response to sanctions.

Chapter 4 explains the controversial way in which sanctions are today being used as an attractive political tool. In this study, Maarten Smeets evaluates the effects of sanctions on Russian trade and presents sanctions as a lose–lose game.

In Chapter 5, Sergei F. Sutyrin, Maryana A. Gubina, and Olga Y. Trofimenko assess the consequences of WTO accession for recently acceded members (RAMs), analysing their key macroeconomic indicators. The results show that WTO accession has a rather limited impact on the development of most RAMs. The Russian economy is no exception.

Chapter 6 explores the trade dynamics with the EAEU. Vladimir G. Sherov-Ignatev points out that Russia has significant economic reasons for the development of regional integration, which at the same time is characterized by a high level of asymmetry.

Chapter 7 is devoted to analyzing economic, political, and legal backgrounds of Russia–EU trade. In her study, Tatiana M. Isachenko reveals key challenges and future prospects of Russian commercial cooperation with the EU.

In Chapter 8, Kari Liuhto and Teemu Itälinna examine the development of Russian–Finnish food trade under the EU–Russia sanctions. Using case studies, they consider the adaptation strategies of foreign companies to the changing business environment in Russia.

In Chapter 9, Liudmila V. Popova and Zhou Weidi concentrate on studying Russia's turn towards Asia, based on the analysis of trends in Russian–Chinese trade and the calculation of trade intensity, trade specification, and intra-industry trade indexes. They argue that sanctions have not only substantially encouraged Russian trade flows with China, but also caused changes in the commodity structure of trade while increasing Russian food exports to the Chinese market.

In Chapter 10, Irina A. Korgun explores the impact of sanctions on Russian–South Korean trade. She argues that both sides have demonstrated willingness to find ways to maintain cooperation and extend it despite economic uncertainties. On the basis of Hyundai's case, she discovers the main challenges in the development of business cooperation between countries under modern conditions.

Alexandra G. Koval and Alexis Dantas investigate the main dimensions, trends, and challenges in Russian–Brazilian trade relations. In Chapter 11, they aim to identify whether state visits and state-to-state cooperation under BRICS and other institutional frameworks enhance Russian–Brazilian trade.

Chapter 12 deals with development of the Russian automotive industry and the dilemma between import substitution and export-led industrialization. Dmitry I. Tonkov examines the industrial policies applied in this sector before and after the accession of the Russian Federation to the WTO.

After the WTO accession, Russia has adopted its policy to the rules and norms of the multilateral trading system in various trade-related fields. In Chapter 13, Norio Horie and Olesya V. Veredyuk discuss prospects for liberalization of the temporary movement of natural persons in the framework of GATS Mode 4.

In Chapter 14, Olga Y. Trofimenko analyses the key challenges Russia faces while participating in the WTO dispute settlement system. To date, Russia has participated in 16 WTO disputes as a complainant and a respondent, and this substantial amount of cases allows conclusions to be drawn regarding challenges, preferences, and opportunities of utilizing this mechanism.

In Chapter 15, Sergei F. Sutyrin makes some concluding remarks while also suggesting certain perspectives for future studies.

The contemporary geopolitical and economic situation further encourages the editors and contributors to continue their studies and research cooperation with the Russian and foreign experts for improved understanding of the development of the international trading system and Russia's role. The relevance of this research is confirmed by the interest of not only academia but also business and media as well as research funds. The manuscript development was supported by the Russian Foundation for Basic Research (RFBR) No. 17–02–00688 "Transformation of Russian Foreign Economic Policy in a Changing Geopolitics".

On behalf of the editors, we would like to thank all the authors for their contributions and enthusiastic participation in the publication. The book endeavours to open a modern substantive discussion on Russian involvement in the international trading system. We hope that our work will inspire other researchers to continue this study.

1 Trade monitoring – a global perspective on trade policy trends

Peter Pedersen and Antonia Diakantoni[1]

Introduction

In October 2008, during the immediate aftermath of the outbreak of the global financial crisis and amidst widespread fears of a protectionist spiral akin to the Great Depression of the 1930s, the Director-General of the WTO established a Secretariat Task Force to monitor the trade-related developments associated with the crisis. Although trade was not at the root of the crisis, the significance of this rapid institutional response by the multilateral trading system was evident as two Trade Monitoring Reports in early 2009 confirmed that international trade had fallen dramatically.

In early April, the G20 Leaders meeting in London called on the WTO, together with other international bodies, to monitor and report publicly on the G20 adherence to resisting protectionism and promoting global trade and investment. This call followed up on an earlier commitment by the G20 to reject protectionism, refrain from raising new barriers to trade and investment or implement measures inconsistent with the WTO.

Since 2009, the WTO trade monitoring exercise has continued to provide G20 economies, in addition to all WTO Members, with regular updates on the latest trends in the implementation of trade measures as well as important developments in trade policy-making more generally. On some levels the news has not been good. Annual growth of international trade since 2008 has been subdued and has underlined a weakening in the relationship between trade and GDP growth. While trade has typically grown in recent decades at 1.5 times faster than GDP, latterly the ratio has slipped towards 1:1. Conversely, a protectionist backlash failed to materialize even during the most difficult years of the crisis. Nevertheless, and perhaps somewhat ironic given the evidence of a steadily recovering world economy, the tone of the trade debate has turned increasingly negative more recently with hostile protectionist rhetoric and the strategic application of trade policy dominating the headlines.

This chapter aims to provide the reader with an introduction to the WTO trade monitoring exercise and to the origins of the transparency platform upon which it rests. The chapter will also seek to provide an overview of selected trends and developments identified by the monitoring exercise since 2009, including trade measures taken by the Russian Federation. Finally, the chapter will address some of the challenges facing the WTO monitoring exercise as an institutional platform for transparency and accountability as it enters its tenth year.

Theoretical background and methodology

At the heart of the WTO trade monitoring exercise and the Trade Policies Review (TPR) Mechanism mandate to which it is anchored, lies the notion of transparency and the idea that an international intergovernmental organization can provide a constructive platform for a peer review amongst the membership of trade issues in general and trade policies in particular. In providing the WTO, and prior to that the GATT, with the mandate to create a peer review platform Members implicitly acknowledged the usefulness of such an exercise to ensure their accountability with respect to WTO rules. The G20 Declarations at the end of 2008 and in early 2009 were explicit examples of this. Collins-Williams and Wolfe (2010), Wolfe and Halle (2011), and Najam and Halle (2010) provide important perspectives and examples of the accountability issues facing international organizations. In a Member-driven organization such as the WTO, holding the membership accountable represents a particular set of challenges, especially in the context of a Secretariat-led exercise such as the regular trade monitoring. Collins-Williams and Wolfe (2010) points to the sensitivity among Members surrounding an activist Secretariat at the very beginning of the monitoring exercise. Interestingly, although this sensitivity did not initially result in the imposition of constraints on the Secretariat, since 2011 the pendulum has swung decisively in the direction of greater Member scrutiny of the trade monitoring exercise. Pendulum swings between Members and the WTO Secretariat are not uncommon and have happened on several occasions and in several areas over the past two decades, including on issues such as the relationship with non-governmental organizations and on institutional coherence with other intergovernmental organizations.

The benefits of market openness and the cost of protectionism have been widely studied and there is general agreement that going from a situation of trade to no trade reduces welfare overall. Irwin (2011) provides an interesting perspective on the import drop and income loss in the United States as a result of the 1930 Smoot-Hawley Law. In the context of the 2008 global financial crisis, most commentators referenced the Great Depression and the beggar-thy-neighbour policies, which sent the world economy tumbling. At the outset of the crisis, therefore, many considered that there was a real possibility that countries would resort to protectionist policies as a result of domestic pressures. However, although the WTO trade monitoring exercise has not detected such a turn of events when it comes to the implementation of trade-restrictive policies, other observers of the global trading system have. For example, Evenett and Fritz (2015) report significant increases in protectionist trade policies, in particular in 2009 and again since 2012. The variations in the numbers and conclusions of various monitoring exercises are generally a result of different methodologies. This discussion is, however, beyond the scope of this chapter. Collins-Williams and Wolfe (2010) and the Swedish National Board of Trade (2016) both provide important insights into the use and merits of different methodologies in trade surveillance.

The methodology behind the trade monitoring mechanism in general, and the Trade Monitoring Reports in particular, reflects not only the Secretariat mandate to collect and present information, but also the close involvement of WTO Members in the exercise. The WTO Secretariat prepares four Trade Monitoring Reports per year, i.e. two for the full WTO membership and two for the G20 economies. The report on G20 trade measures is circulated together with a report on G20 investment measures prepared by the OECD and UNCTAD. The data collection and analysis for the WTO-wide reports constitute the basis for the G20 Trade Monitoring Reports and methodologically both reports are now almost identical.

There are two major approaches to collecting information for the reports: by requesting information from WTO Members and through an independent Secretariat research process. These approaches are complementary and are characterized by a close collaboration between the Secretariat and WTO Members. In March and in September, the Director-General makes a formal request to all Members and Observers for information on measures that have been implemented and have an impact on the international trading environment. The request specifies the precise period and the types of measures covered by the forthcoming monitoring report. It also provides an illustrative list of measures affecting trade in goods, services, intellectual property and general economic support; and expected deadlines for submissions. Members are given one month to reply. In parallel, an ongoing process of data collection is conducted by the Trade Monitoring Section of the Trade Policies Review Division (TPRD). The Secretariat screens a range of public sources for information, including national laws, agreements, resolutions, decrees, amendments, executive orders published on Government websites such as ministries, customs offices, central banks, regional secretariats, or through other international organizations' websites or reports. Customs notices, press websites or press reports and releases are also screened for relevant information. Notifications to the WTO are used together with measures directly received from Members and Observers.

Information and measures obtained are then returned to the relevant Members and Observers for verification. Subsequently, the Secretariat collates a final list of measures for further analysis and interpretation. The data on trade in goods are divided and analyzed by three categories, i.e. measures facilitating trade, trade remedy actions, and other trade and trade-related measures (with possible trade-restrictive effect). The number of newly implemented measures and their trade coverage are then compared to previous periods. Services measures are categorized according to sector and mode of supply in a separate annex and analyzed in-depth in the Report. Measures that have not been verified by the respective Member are included in the reports as "recorded, but non-confirmed information". The intellectual property section of the reports has so far focused on the analysis of the principal trends affecting trade in intellectual property. Publication of the Trade Monitoring Reports takes place in June and November, respectively, and the reports are then discussed by delegations at dedicated Trade Policy

Review Body (TPRB) meetings. The current procedure establishes an annual formal meeting in December and an informal meeting in July. The reports as well as the meetings attract considerable attention from Members, Observers, and the media. The G20 Reports are generally circulated ahead of important meetings of that group, e.g. trade ministers' meetings or Leaders' Summits.

Trade surveillance in the GATT

The internal trade monitoring Task Force established by the Director-General (DG) in October 2008 (WTO 2008) was by no means the first time that the Secretariat had responded to a specific trade surveillance challenge. For example, in the uncertain global economic environment in the late 1970s and early 1980s, the GATT Contracting Parties discussed the need to seek enhanced adherence to existing trade rules. In November 1979, as part of the Tokyo Round of trade negotiations, these talks resulted in the adoption of the Understanding Regarding Notification, Consultation, Dispute Settlement and Surveillance (Further – Understanding). Included in this document, was a decision "to conduct a regular and systematic review of developments in the trading system" (GATT 1979), which formally marked the beginning of periodic reviews of trade policy changes. It was subsequently agreed that a Secretariat background note would facilitate such discussions.

The first Secretariat note, circulated in October 1980 (GATT 1980), covered developments in trade policies and related matters over a six-month period and reviewed compliance by Contracting Parties with notification obligations. However, merely listing submissions of notifications failed to provide much insight into actual compliance and to correct for this, the Secretariat's notes from 1983 also included information that was not based on notifications. Importantly, the Secretariat's notes deliberately refrained from suggesting whether particular actions conformed to GATT obligations, reserving those judgements for the GATT Contracting Parties (GATT 1983).

Discussions among the Contracting Parties on further improvements to the functioning of the GATT continued throughout this period and the issues of enhanced surveillance, more publicity and peer reviews gained traction as necessary tools to contribute to better adherence to the rules. In 1985, a central proposal by the Leutwiler Group (Trade Policies for a Better Future: The Leutwiler Report, GATT, and the Uruguay 1987)[2] to work towards greater transparency of trade policies related to the idea that all Contracting Parties should be subject to regular reviews. This notion of enhanced surveillance was subsequently brought into the GATT framework by the creation of the negotiating Group on the Functioning of the GATT system (FOGS) at the launch of the Uruguay Round in 1986 (Pedersen 2011).

Amongst the FOGS Group significant outcomes was the emergence of the Trade Policy Review Mechanism (TPRM). Provisionally introduced in 1989, the TPRM was confirmed by Annex 3 of the Marrakesh Agreement Establishing the WTO. The TPRM also incorporated an annual overview by the DG of recent trade policy developments, which would become the vehicle for the WTO Trade Monitoring Reports from 2009 onwards.

Trade monitoring in the WTO

The onset of the global financial crisis in September 2008 triggered the search for a trade monitoring mechanism within the multilateral trading system. Less than one month later, in October, DG Pascal Lamy established a Secretariat Task Force to advise him on the trade implications of the financial crisis and on the trade measures that were implemented in this context. The work of the Task Force was initially meant to be purely internal, but a number of delegations encouraged DG Lamy to report in writing to the membership.

The first WTO monitoring reports were circulated to WTO Members in January and April of 2009 and contained the first stock-takes with respect to trade-related developments since the outbreak of the financial crisis (WTO 2009b). Introducing the reports and responding to concerns regarding the initiative, DG Lamy reiterated the need for it to be Member-driven and "carried out by, and for the benefit of the whole membership" (WTO 2009a). At the core of this reference was the participation of delegations both in providing information to the Secretariat and in the verification of measures found through other sources.

The trade monitoring exercise has featured in several consultative processes since 2009, including as part of the regular TPRM Appraisals, and there has been consistent support for its continuation and strengthening. At the Eighth Ministerial Conference in December 2011 Ministers provided an unambiguous endorsement of the trade monitoring mechanism (WTO 2011a, 2011b).

In 2012, a series of informal consultations by the Chairman of the TPRB took place to follow up on the 2011 Ministerial Decision on trade monitoring "to continue discussing the strengthening of the monitoring exercise of trade and trade-related measures on the basis of Members' inputs". During these consultations it became clear that while no Member questioned the importance of the monitoring initiative from a transparency point of view, there was a general view that the exercise could be further improved and that Members were best placed to take the lead in that endeavour. The informal consultations as well as the sixth TPRM Appraisal in 2016 demonstrated that Members were in no mood to provide the Secretariat with additional flexibility on trade monitoring and were, on the contrary, seeking to rein in the exercise. While the Secretariat has tried to push for specific improvements to the exercise, many of which arguably would have fallen squarely within the existing mandate, such efforts have been pushed back by Members.

Trends and developments since 2009 – proliferation of protectionism?

The WTO trade monitoring mechanism is first and foremost a transparency exercise, which aims to shed light on the latest trends in the implementation of a broad range of policy measures that facilitate as well as restrict the flow of trade. Although the exercise covers both aspects, the focus of this section is on new trade restrictions implemented between 2009 and 2016. In addition, the section will take a closer look at trends in the application of trade remedies, general economic support measures, services, and intellectual property measures, trade concerns raised across WTO committees and the unfinished business of notifications. The section will also provide a brief overview of policy measures implemented by the Russian Federation.

The implementation of trade facilitating measures is a crucial variable in determining the direction and health of world trade and the trade monitoring exercise has been able to show that countries have consistently implemented more facilitating than trade-restrictive measures over the past ten years. Recent years have seen important trade liberalization on many levels, including through the expansion of the Information Technology Agreement, the implementation of the Trade Facilitation Agreement and through a wide range of bilateral and plurilateral trade initiatives. However, the focus here will be on the trends and developments in the implementation of trade-restrictive measures because these variables may indicate whether countries are turning inward and adopting measures that discriminate against foreign exporters. Deepening our understanding with factual information on the importance of trade restrictions, the sectors covered and the economies involved will add accuracy and perspective to the trade debate. Since the beginning of the WTO trade monitoring exercise, very limited variation has been observed in the introduction of new trade restrictions. Further, it appears that there have been no major and fundamental trade policy reversals since 2009, including in those countries most directly affected by the financial crisis. Arguably, and especially in the early stages of the crisis, several important policies to support domestic economic entities saw the light of day and various import and export related policies have subsequently undergone various transformations. However, overall there has been no indication of an imminent descent into protectionism, involving widespread resort to trade restrictions and retaliation. The multilateral trade rules under the WTO have provided a strong defence and a unique insurance policy against such a scenario. Although positive, it is equally clear that the tone of the trade debate continues to cause fear that the global economy could enter into a protectionist tailspin.

The following section provides an empirical analysis of trends in trade restrictions, based on numerical counting of the measures collected through the trade monitoring exercise and also on the trade covered by those measures. The trade coverage of a measure is calculated to be the value of annual imports of the specific product concerned from countries affected by the measure. Highly traded goods may significantly influence the estimation of the trade coverage. Although the numerical counting has shown a limited variation of new trade-restrictive measures introduced per month by WTO Members, the corresponding volume of trade covered by those measures shows a significant decrease since 2015. Similarly, the number of initiations of trade remedy investigations during that same period appeared to be somewhat stable. In contrast the trade covered by the trade remedy investigations reveals a significant increase since 2015, suggesting a shift in the type of trade measures applied by WTO Members.

Trade restrictions since 2009

WTO Members have implemented a range of new trade restrictions[3] every year since the beginning of the monitoring exercise. From 2009 to 2016, 15 new trade-restrictive measures were applied on average per month, with two peaks recorded in 2011 (19 measures) and 2015 (22 measures) as shown in Figure 1.1.[4] Around

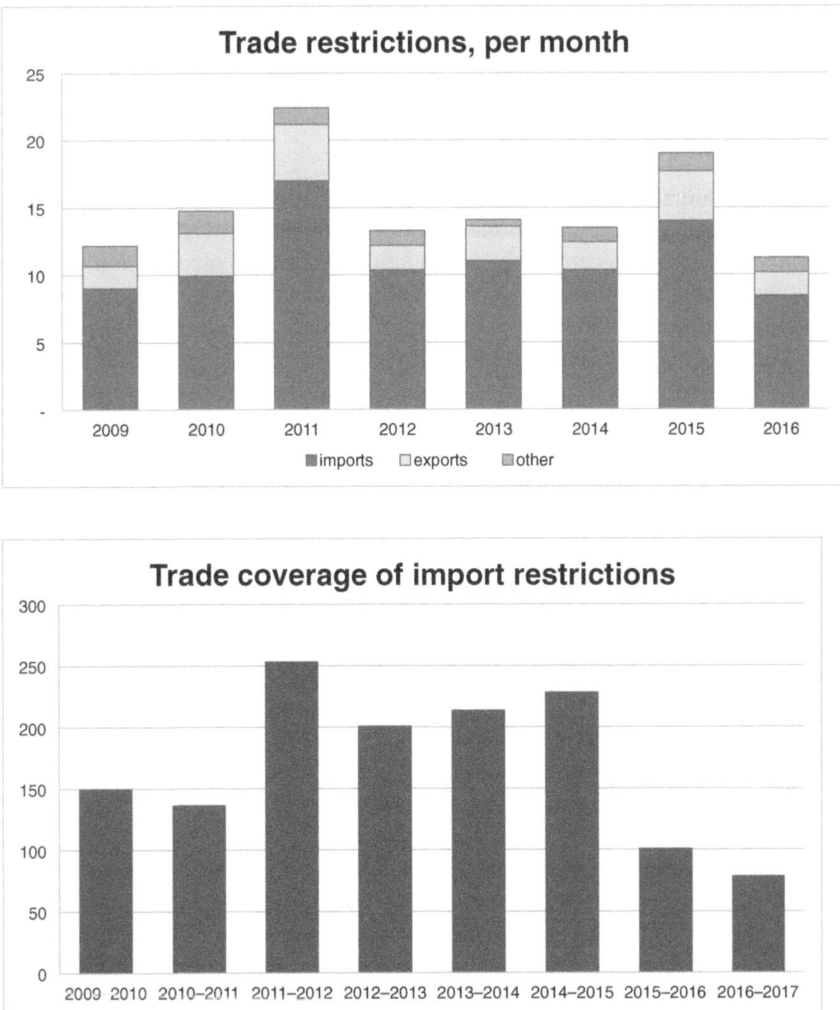

Figure 1.1 New trade-restrictive measures implemented by WTO Members and trade covered by import restrictions

75 percent of these trade restrictions applied to imports. Import measures include primarily tariff increases, but also customs procedures, quantitative restrictions, and import taxes. With respect to measures restricting exports, the majority of such measures were quantitative restrictions and export duties.

The estimated trade covered by import-restrictive measures show that they accounted for more than $200 billion of merchandise trade every year between 2011 and 2015. At 1.2–1.4 percent of world merchandise imports, this is roughly equivalent to Australia's annual merchandise imports. Since 2015, a significant decrease has been recorded in the trade covered by those restrictions. Sectoral analysis shows that the top five sectors most targeted by import-restrictive measures were iron and steel (ranking in the top five every year since 2013), followed by machinery and mechanical appliances, electrical machinery, vehicles, and parts and vegetable fats and oils.

Trade remedies

Looking simultaneously at initiations of trade remedy investigations will add some perspective on the trade policy options available to governments. The trade monitoring exercise records only the initiation of a trade remedy action and does not subsequently count the imposition of temporary or other duties so as to avoid double counting. Termination of a trade remedy measure is recorded when temporary or other duties are ended. Numerically, trade remedy investigations represent a very important share of the measures recorded by the trade monitoring exercise, even if the trade covered remains relatively small. Typically, WTO Members have initiated more trade remedy investigations compared to the number of trade remedy actions they have terminated. It is important to emphasize that the inclusion and reference to the trade remedy initiations here do not imply a categorization of them as restrictive or protectionist. The objective is to provide a factual account of their use.

The inclusion and categorization of trade remedy actions in the G20 and WTO-wide Trade Monitoring Reports has been a source of some controversy since the beginning of the monitoring exercise. The November 2012 Report included a dedicated box on the evidence of the chilling effect caused by the initiation of trade remedy investigations (WTO 2012). From 2009 to 2013, in the case of the WTO-wide Monitoring Report, and from 2009 to 2017, in the case of the G20 Report, initiations of trade remedy investigations were categorized as restrictive and terminations of trade remedy actions were considered liberalizing. This methodology was, however, considered problematic by some who firmly believe that these measures are taken to address a market distortion resulting from trade practices of entities in another trading partner. The strength of the opposition to this categorization, to a large extent, depended on whether a particular country was initiating relatively more trade remedy investigations or whether it was the target of such actions. Both sets of Monitoring Reports now provide numbers on trade remedy actions separately from other measures, these measures in a separate annex. Moreover, the Reports have shown that there has been no discernible change in the number of initiations of trade remedies coinciding with the financial crisis.

Although the number of trade remedies introduced between 2012 and 2016 does not show significant variations (Figure 1.2), the trade covered by those measures has increased significantly since 2015. Metal products, and in particular steel, are targeted by the majority of trade remedy investigations. The second most-investigated sector through a trade remedy initiation was chemical products, followed by plastics and foodstuffs. It is important, nevertheless, to note that

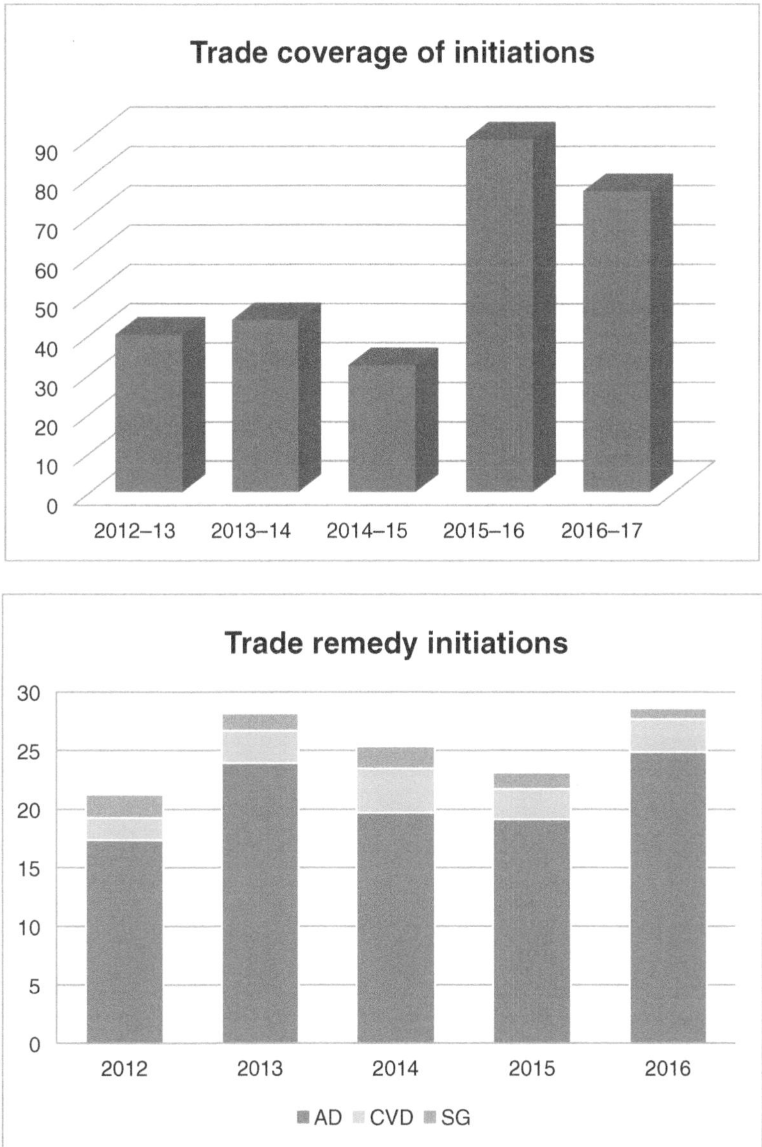

Figure 1.2 Trade remedy initiations and trade covered, WTO Members

although the majority of trade remedy initiations lead to the imposition of measures, some do not. In terms of countries affected by new investigations, China remained by far the most frequent target of investigations, followed by the Republic of Korea, India, and Turkey. Anti-dumping measures make up more than 80 percent of all trade remedy initiations.

Trade restrictions in G20 economies

Further focusing on the G20 economies adds additional perspective to the analysis of the trends in the implementation of trade restrictions. G20 economies represent around 95 percent of world trade, implying that any measure taken by a G20 member could likely have global implications. The G20 economies account for almost half of the total trade-restrictive measures implemented by all WTO Members and more than 80 percent of the estimated trade coverage. Virtually all trade-restrictive measures taken by G20 economies between 2009 and 2016 identified by the trade monitoring exercise were applied on a most favoured nation (MFN) basis.[5] Only 5 percent of G20 measures were applied to specific trading partners.

Looking at G20 MFN trade restrictions, and in particular at the number of products targeted at the Harmonized System (HS) 4-digit level,[6] the highest level of activity was recorded in 2010 and 2015, with some 720 and 1,600 products targeted respectively (Figure 1.3).

There has been considerable variation between G20 economies when it comes to the implementation of restrictions to trade. During the period 2009–2016,

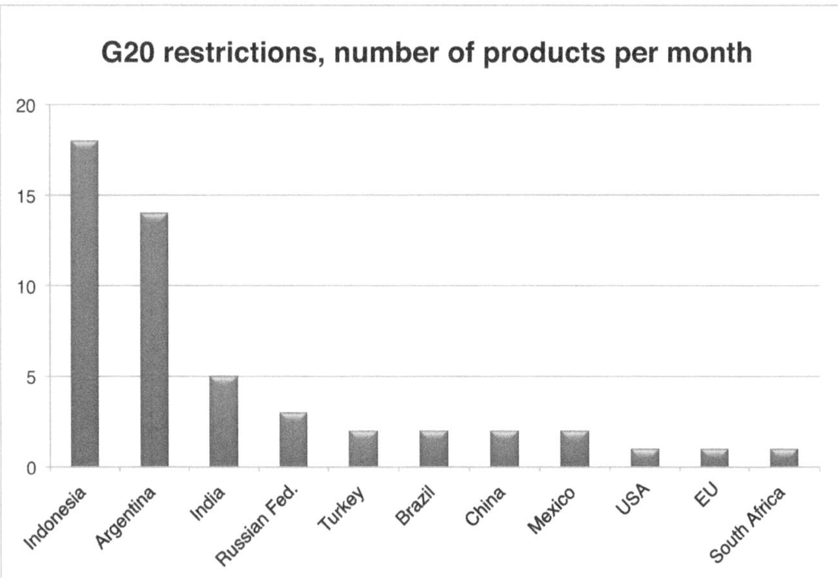

Figure 1.3 New trade-restrictive measures, G20 economies, 2009–2016

Indonesia and Argentina were among the top users of restrictive measures. Indonesia has targeted on average 18 products per month, followed by Argentina (14) and India (5). Indonesia was particularly active in 2015 and was the principal reason for the 2015 peak in G20 restrictions. Indonesian measures covered primarily minerals and metals, non-electrical machinery and textiles. Argentina was particularly active at the beginning of the monitoring exercise and again in 2016. Argentinian measures targeted mainly non-electrical machinery, textiles, and chemicals. Mexico's restrictions applied primarily to textiles, followed by minerals and metals and clothing. Turkey's focus was on minerals and metals, followed by clothing and textiles. US restrictions were mainly on oil seeds, fats and oils, followed by cereals and preparations, whereas the European Union's measures targeted minerals and metals. China implemented most of their trade restrictions on minerals and metals followed by chemicals. The Russian Federation restrictions primarily targeted non-electrical machinery followed by minerals, metals, and chemicals. Trade-restrictive measures by the Kingdom of Saudi Arabia, Canada, Australia, and the Republic of Korea were rarely recorded by the trade monitoring exercise between 2009 and 2016 and no restrictive measure has been recorded for Japan.

Overall, between 2009 and 2016, G20 economies implemented MFN restrictions targeting firstly minerals and metals, a finding that was also confirmed for the entire WTO membership. Metals, and in particular steel, was found to be the sector targeted the most by trade remedy investigations, revealing its importance for many economies. The second most targeted sector by G20 trade restrictions was non-electrical machinery, followed by chemicals and textiles (Figure 1.4).

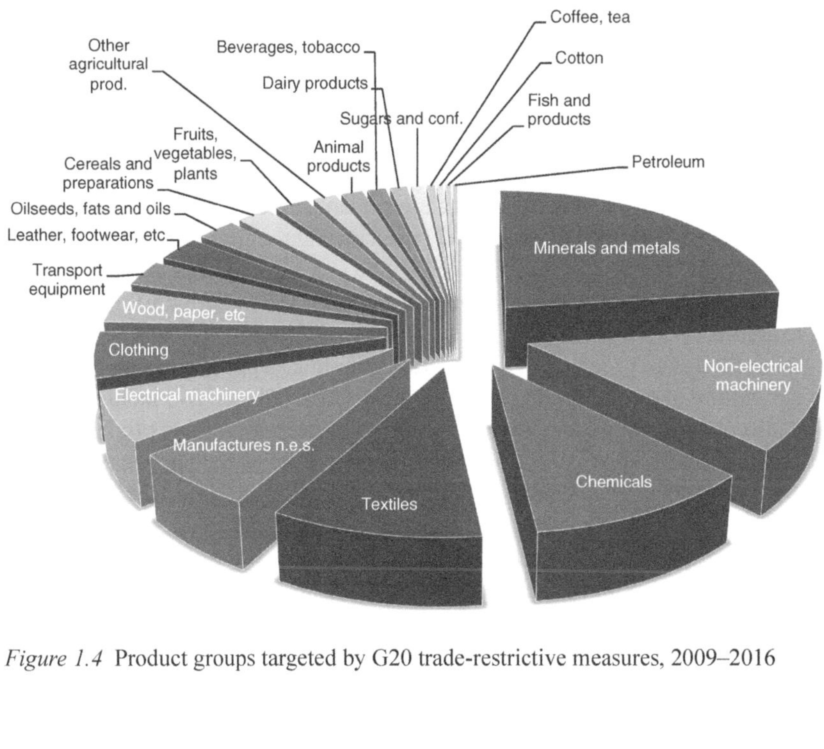

Figure 1.4 Product groups targeted by G20 trade-restrictive measures, 2009–2016

With respect to G20 trade restrictions applied to specific trading partners, textiles was found to be the main sector targeted, followed by minerals and metals, fruits, vegetables, and plants.

General economic support measures

WTO Members have also used general economic support measures to provide assistance to or promote specific sectors of their economies. These measures cover stimulus packages, state aid, dedicated financial support to specific sectors or any sector-specific incentives, loans, loan guarantees, transfers, preferential credit lines, investment insurances, export credit/insurance, and tax reductions/rebates.

General economic support measures and various subsidies or subsidy programmes may affect trade or distort competition as certain economic sectors or activities are treated more favourably than others. Many of these would have a negative impact on trade, but for some the trade impact is hard to evaluate. Since the beginning of the monitoring exercise, it has proved very difficult to obtain information on general economic support measures from Members. In particular since 2015, the number of WTO Members that have volunteered information on such measures has been disappointingly low. This does not necessarily indicate a decline in these policies, but may suggest that countries are less transparent about them.

Analysis of the general economic support measures captured by the monitoring exercise during the period October 2008–October 2016 showed that a quarter of these measures were introduced in direct response to the financial crisis. Overall, multi-sector or economy-wide stimulus packages constitute the bulk of general economic support measures introduced by WTO Members since October 2008 (Figure 1.5). Multi-sector measures, the first recipient of general economic support measures, have traditionally been very broad and can cover, simultaneously and under one programme, a diverse range of sectors from agriculture and forestry to medical and shipbuilding. These measures, together with the banking and financial sectors, which received a significant share of the general economic support in 2008–2009, were extensively used during the first three years after the financial crisis. The rise in the number of state subsidy schemes at the beginning of the crisis constituted one of the main reasons for the initiation of the monitoring exercise.

The second largest recipient of general economic support measures has been the agriculture and food sectors covering a variety of objectives, including long-term improvements in productivity, incentive packages through tax breaks and preferential credit lines. WTO Members have provided regular support to the automotive sector since the beginning of the monitoring exercise. SMEs have also been the beneficiaries of economic support measures, with aid schemes, credit guarantee programmes, incentive packages and improved access to investment and capital representing the more prevalent assistance provided. Other sectors, which have received general economic support include the energy and the transport sectors.

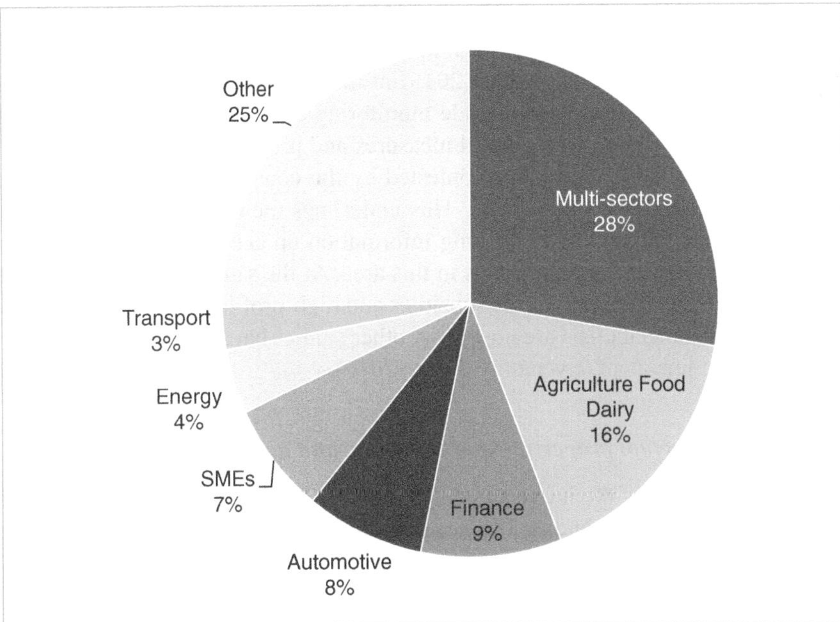

Figure 1.5 Sectors covered by general economic support measures, October 2008–October 2016

It is important to note that the numerical counting of general economic support measures does not provide any indication of the extent of these measures or their potential impact. In the various stimulus packages recorded by the trade monitoring exercise, from direct grants to a specific manufacturer to the development or restructuring of particular industrial sector, governmental expenditures ranged from less than a million to hundreds of billions of US$. In particular, the banking and financial sectors received a very significant share of the general economic support, especially in 2008–2009. Panetta et al. (2009) indicate that between September 2008 and June 2009 the financial resources provided by governments to support the banking system amounted to €5 trillion (more than 6 trillion US$) in 11 countries: Australia, Canada, France, Germany, Italy, Japan, Netherlands, Spain, Switzerland, the United Kingdom, and the United States.

From the information gathered on general economic support measures, it appears that these have been mostly temporary in character. This is especially the case for those general economic support measures that were introduced in 2008–2010 in response to the financial crisis. Nevertheless, despite the initial indication of termination dates it seems that several support measures have been extended, sometimes indefinitely, without official notification thereof.

Based on available information, the general economic support measures that have been reduced or eliminated, aside from the financial and credit sectors are mostly found in the energy, food, and agriculture sectors. One such example is the reduction in 2015–2016 by several countries of various fuel price support schemes, likely in response to the fall in the price of oil.

As mentioned previously, since 2015 information provided on general economic support measures for the trade monitoring exercise has been disappointingly incomplete. Moreover, several measures and programmes identified by the Secretariat have been vigorously contested by the country in question and have had to be omitted from the reports. This underlines the challenges faced by the Secretariat in collecting and verifying information on general economic support measures and in reporting on trends in this area. At the same time, it is clear that although the large economy-wide subsidies and high-profile bail-outs of the early years of the financial crisis are now rarer, other studies have shown that state subsidies remain prevalent (Evenett and Fritz 2017).

Services, intellectual property, trade concerns, and notifications

Although the bulk of the interest generated by the Trade Monitoring Reports has focused on trends surrounding the implementation of trade-restrictive measures, other issues have gained profile in the reports due to their importance in the global economy. These include trade-in-services measures, intellectual property (IP) measures, non-tariff measures, trade concerns, and compliance with notification obligations. The following section will briefly address the principal trends in each of these areas.

Trade in services has grown in importance in the Trade Monitoring Reports over the years. Although services measures are verified with Members, they are treated separately and are not included in the headline numbers on restrictive or facilitating measures. Several new trade-in-services measures, some horizontal in nature and some affecting a variety of services sectors, have been introduced by WTO Members since the beginning of the trade monitoring exercise. The majority of these measures provided for additional liberalization or have been aimed at strengthening or clarifying regulatory frameworks. However, a number of services measures implemented also appeared to be trade-restrictive.[7] Several sectors were covered by the implementation of new services measures, such as the air transport, construction, distribution, finance, postal, maritime transport, and telecommunications sectors, as well as the supply of services through the movement of natural persons.

Developments in the area of Trade-Related Aspects of Intellectual Property Rights show that the relation between IP and trade has further strengthened. The entry into force of the Protocol Amending the TRIPS Agreement on January 23, 2017 was an important milestone addressing public health needs of developing and least-developed country Members. Technological innovation and the need to protect and enforce intellectual property rights in the digital economy are consolidating the importance of IP for trade and economic development and diversification.

Non-tariff measures (NTMs) remain an increasingly important concern in international trade. In particular, business has been drawing attention to such behind-the-border measures as causing real and often unjustified obstacles to trade. For example, in 2017 the B20, the business representatives from the G20 economies, published a survey which showed that differences in regulatory standards, technical barriers to trade measures and IP rights were identified by individual businesses as the most distortive trade measures (B20 2017).

At the outset, it is important to emphasize that WTO Members have the right to apply sanitary and phytosanitary (SPS) or technical barriers to trade (TBT) measures as provided under these agreements. In excess of 3,000 SPS and TBT notifications are received annually by the WTO. Although an increased number of such notifications does not automatically imply a greater use of protectionist measures, but rather enhanced transparency, many generate intensive discussions in the SPS and TBT Committees. SPS and TBT measures are described and analyzed in great detail in separate sections in the Monitoring Reports, but the Reports do not make a judgement on whether or not these measures conform to WTO rules. The increasing concern regarding the use of discriminatory behind-the-border measures is also reflected in the growing number of specific trade concerns (STCs)[8] raised in both the SPS and TBT Committees. While the majority of STCs have been raised at one or two Committee meetings, around 12 STCs have been raised more than five times in the SPS Committee and some 30 in the TBT Committee since the creation of the WTO in 1995, indicating more serious and persistent concerns. STCs have increased over the years and their trend shows a marked correlation with the number of notifications. While STCs may involve simple requests for additional information for clarification to questions on the consistency of measures with the respective agreements, they may also reflect increasing and more complex trade frictions. On the other hand, the fact that the number of STCs has been growing may also suggest that WTO Members see the SPS and TBT Committees as useful fora in which trade concerns may be resolved non-litigiously.

In recent years, an increasing number of trade concerns, other than those within SPS and TBT, have been raised across various WTO bodies. These trade concerns have neither the status nor the procedural framework of the STCs raised in the SPS and TBT Committees, but they provide an interesting snapshot of the sort of trade issues that are at the forefront of discussions at the WTO. Moreover, several such concerns were raised simultaneously in multiple WTO bodies, which may suggest that they increasingly involve highly complex and cross-cutting issues. It may also provide an indication that WTO Members are soliciting multiple platforms within the WTO committee structure to address various aspects of such trade concerns. From a systemic point of view, this is significant because of the increased transparency it brings, but also because it demonstrates that Members are actively using the WTO committees to constructively engage trading partners on potential areas of trade friction. Over the past few years several trade concerns raised in various WTO bodies have specifically referred to measures taken under the security exceptions mentioned in Article XXI of the GATT.

Transparency in trade and in trade policy-making is fundamental for allowing economic agents to make informed decisions. This, in turn, permits markets to operate more efficiently. Notifications are the primary instrument for ensuring transparency in the multilateral trading system and the end-of-year WTO-wide Trade Monitoring Report includes a general stock-take on notifications across the WTO. Historically, the compliance and timeliness of Members' notifications to the WTO has been problematic and has clearly illustrated that, with a few exceptions, compliance with notification requirements of the various WTO Agreements leaves much to be desired.

The lack of compliance with notification obligations across WTO bodies is problematic for several reasons. One such reason is that it undermines individual agreements and more generally the operation of the multilateral trading system. There are different reasons for the low compliance with many notification requirements, an important one being the lack of capacity of many WTO Members. Improving the notification record across the WTO will continue to be a significant collective challenge in the immediate future.

The Russian Federation and WTO trade monitoring

The information recorded by the trade monitoring exercise, shows that the Russian Federation implemented, directly or through the Eurasian Customs Union, 65 trade restrictions before its accession to the WTO on August 22, 2012 and 38 trade restrictions thereafter. The main sectors targeted by those restrictions were minerals and metals, chemicals, and non-electrical machinery products. The Russian Federation has also introduced a number of general economic support measures, representing roughly 4 percent of all such measures recorded by the monitoring exercise. Even if this low percentage is genuine or reflects underreporting, it does not provide any indication regarding the extent of these measures, nor their potential impact.

Since 2014, the Russian Federation has faced a number of economic measures in the form of targeted sanctions related to tensions with the Ukraine. Those restrictions were adopted mainly by Australia, Canada, the European Union, and the United States. The Russian Federation responded with countermeasures against a number of countries, including a total ban on food imports from the Australia, Canada, the European Union, Norway, and the United States.

From 2009 to 2016, the trade monitoring exercise captured 25 trade remedy initiations of investigations initiated mostly by the Eurasian Customs Union (and subsequently by the EAEU). Of these actions 17 were anti-dumping investigations. The Russian Federation's activity regarding trade remedies initiations was stable before and after its accession to the WTO, with 13 trade remedies initiated before and 12 after the accession date. The Russian Federation was the subject of 43 initiations of trade remedy investigations during the same period. The majority (31) were initiated after the Russian accession to the WTO. The Russian Federation is involved in a number of disputes in the WTO, in six cases as complainant, in eight cases as respondent and in 40 cases as third party.

In 2016, the first Trade Policy Review of the Russian Federation took place and provided Members with the opportunity to learn about developments in the Russian Federation's economic and trade policies since its accession and to review the country's participation in the multilateral trading system as a Member of the WTO (WTO 2016).

WTO trade monitoring – challenges

The WTO monitoring exercise faces a number of significant challenges as it transitions from its emergency post-financial crisis status to becoming another tool in the transparency toolbox of the multilateral trading system. What is common to all of these challenges is the extent of the willingness of WTO Members to actively promote and contribute to transparency.

Ensuring and maintaining significant participation in the trade monitoring exercise is a key challenge. Approximately 50 percent of Members, representing more than 95 percent of world imports, have regularly participated – either by voluntarily submitting input or by responding to the request for verification. As the only horizontal and regular transparency exercise within the multilateral trading system ensuring high participation will continue to require significant efforts on the part of both the Secretariat and Members.

The stakeholder relationship between the Secretariat and Members is fundamental to the credibility and sustainability of the trade monitoring exercise. However, as consultations on the exercise have demonstrated, it also represents a very real constraint. In a Member-driven institution such as the WTO it remains a significant and continuous challenge for the Secretariat to push for the ability to report independently but within its mandate, on the one hand, and, on the other, maintain a productive stakeholder relationship with the membership. Both are crucial from a credibility point of view.

The substantive coverage of measures by the monitoring exercise in general, and in the Reports in particular, has evolved since 2009. Continue to broaden the coverage of the trade monitoring exercise represents a big challenge as the trade agenda of the twenty-first century moves forward. Deepening and crystallizing the analysis provided in the monitoring exercise, which currently remains mostly at a global and aggregated level, would likely provide interesting information on the impact of specific measures for particular countries, regions, and sectors. Expanding the coverage of the monitoring exercise is closely linked to the nature and evolution of the stakeholder relationship with the membership and with Members' commitment to transparency.

Remaining relevant to the outside world, in particular business, is another significant challenge. It will be important to continue to explore ways to improve transparency and predictability, which would benefit those doing business in the global economy. Similarly, exploring ways in which business could contribute to the trade monitoring exercise could possibly open up an additional source of information.

Conclusion

The creation of the WTO Secretariat Task Force on the trade implications of the crisis less than one month after the collapse of Lehman Brothers in September

2008 and the circulation of the first Trade Monitoring Report to WTO Members in early January 2009 were important systemic events within the multilateral trading system. Above all, they underscored the recognition in the WTO that the crisis could have a significant negative impact on global trade flows and that the WTO was ideally placed to provide the platform for an ongoing, up-to-date and transparent monitoring of trade-related measures. It was also clear that such a platform had to be firmly based on existing mandates to avoid drawn-out negotiations which, almost inevitably, would have resulted in lost credibility for the multilateral trading system.

Regular trade monitoring by the Secretariat had already been a feature under the GATT and subsequently became solidly anchored in the WTO's TPR Mechanism. Under both regimes it was fundamental that the transparency provided by the Trade Monitoring Reports rested on the direct and active participation of countries, as well as on the ability of the Secretariat to independently search for and report objectively on relevant trade developments. The stakeholder relationship between Members and the WTO Secretariat is crucial to the credibility of the trade monitoring exercise as an additional tool in the WTO's transparency toolbox. But it may also become a constraint when Members interpret their commitment to transparency selectively. This tension has been evident since the beginning of the current monitoring effort and as the emergency of the financial crisis has faded.

Since 2009, the monitoring exercise has seen only limited evidence of countries rushing towards protectionist trade policies. There has been slippage and discrimination, but overall trade-restrictive measures generally have been taken within the rules of the multilateral trading system and the commitments of individual Members. The numerical count of new trade restrictions and of the initiation of trade remedy investigations has shown moderate variation since 2009. However, since 2015, the trade covered by new trade restrictions has decreased significantly while that covered by trade remedy initiations has increased substantially. This may suggest a more strategic application of certain types of trade measures that may be more direct or confrontational. Unsurprisingly, metal products, and in particular steel, are the sectors primarily targeted by new trade restrictions and by the overwhelming majority of trade remedy initiations. However, it is broadly recognized that the WTO and its rules have provided a strong defence and a solid insurance policy against protectionist policies gaining the upper hand.

Nevertheless, there are many reasons why vigilance and caution are required. Behind-the-border non-tariff measures, many of which are perfectly legal under the WTO, are increasingly placed in the spotlight for creating real discrimination in the marketplace. The financial and fiscal stimulus packages that were introduced early in the crisis mostly favoured the restoration of trade growth globally. The general economic support measures seen today may be less eye-popping and comprehensive, but they often contain elements – such as state aid, other subsidies and "buy/lend/invest/hire local" conditions – that favour domestic goods and services at the expense of imports. There is no evidence that countries have backed away from the use of such measures, with the past couple of years showing that countries are both less transparent in this regard and often unwilling to allow the Trade Monitoring Reports to cover them.

One factor helping to contain protectionist pressures has been greater public scrutiny of trade policies and there is little doubt that the drive for greater transparency in trade policy-making is irreversible. Protectionist rhetoric is one thing; actual implementation of beggar-thy-neighbour policies is another. Over the past couple of years, the WTO trade monitoring exercise has reported on a significant negative turn in the tone of the trade debate. The use of national security as a justification for specific trade actions and the application very specific and targeted "smart" sanctions are also very much part of the recent trade discourse. All of these are of systemic concern. While it is clear that the incremental accumulation of trade restrictions and their negative impact on the effectiveness of policies to boost demand remain of serious concern, the more recent shift to a more adversarial approach to international trade relations poses perhaps the more significant risk to the multilateral trading system. The risk that governments will cede ground to protectionist pressures remains very real.

Notes

1 The authors are WTO Secretariat staff members. Any views expressed here are those of the authors and should not be attributed to Members of the WTO or to the WTO Secretariat. The authors are grateful to Carlos Perez de Castillo, Amalia Mkhitaryan, and Alvaro Rivero for their inputs, to Willy Alfaro, Arne Klau, and Mark Koulen for their constructive comments and to Anna Treadwell and Jean-Marie McAdams for the editing.
2 The Report was prepared by a group of seven eminent and independent persons. In 1983 GATT DG Arthur Dunkel appointed the group to identify and address the challenges affecting the international trading system. The group was chaired by Mr. Fritz Leutwiler, Chairman of the Swiss National Bank and President of the Bank for international settlements. Members of the group were public and private professionals in the financial and trade sectors.
3 Trade remedies, SPS, and TBT measures as well as general economic support, services and IP measures are not included in this sub-section, but are addressed separately.
4 It is important to recognize that the numerical counting of measures, while an indication of overall activity, presents only a partial picture. The inclusion of trade coverage calculations provides some additional perspective. A trade impact analysis was undertaken for the June 2013 G20 report, but despite the comprehensive and resource-intensive nature of this exercise, its findings did not substantially change the overall conclusions of the report. Arguably, a focus on the discriminatory intent of specific trade measures would provide insight into protectionist tendencies, but such an approach would be controversial in the context of the WTO monitoring exercise.
5 MFN measures are applied to all WTO members.
6 Only measures containing HS codes were included in the analysis and the product codes were cut/expanded to four digits of the HS nomenclature. Customs unions' measures were also included.
7 For example, Indonesia's insurances schemes or Tanzania's electronic and postal communications measures, introduced both in 2016.
8 A specific trade concern is a specific trade complaint raised by Members in the SPS or TBT Committees in relation to an SPS or a TBT measures maintained by another Member.

Bibliography

B20 2017, *Rolling Back Protectionism*, viewed 30 November 2018, www.b20germany.org/priorities/trade-investment/ti-dossier/trade-investment-article/news/rolling-back-protectionism/

Collins-Williams, T and Wolfe, R 2010, 'Transparency as a Trade Policy Tool: The WTO's Cloudy Windows', *World Trade Review*, vol. 9, no. 4, pp. 551–581.

Evenett, S and Fritz, J 2015, *The Tide Turns? Trade, Protectionism, and Slowing Global Growth*, Centre for European Policy Research, London.

Evenett, S and Fritz, J 2017, *Europe Fettered – The Impact of Crisis-era Trade Distortions on Exports From the European Union*, Centre for European Policy Research, London.

GATT 1979, *Understanding Regarding Notification, Consultation, Dispute Settlement and Surveillance*, BISD 26S/210, 28 November 1979, viewed 30 November 2018, www.wto.org/english/docs_e/legal_e/tokyo_notif_e.pdf

GATT 1980, *Notification and Surveillance*, Note by the Secretariat C/W/349, 31 October, viewed 30 November 2018, https://docs.wto.org/gattdocs/q/GG/C/W349.PDF

GATT 1983, *Minutes of Meeting*, C/M/169, 10 August, viewed 30 November 2018, https://docs.wto.org/gattdocs/q/GG/C/M169.PDF

Irwin, D 2011, *Peddling Protectionism: Smoot-Hawley and the Great Depression*, Princeton University Press, Oxford and Princeton.

Najam, A and Halle, M 2010, 'Global Environmental Governance: The Challenge of Accountability', in: *Sustainable Development Insights*, Boston University, Frederick S. Pardee Center for the Study of the Longer-Range Future, Boston.

Panetta, F, Faeh, T, Grande, G, Ho, C, King, M, Levy, A, Signoretti, F, Taboga, M and Zaghini, A 2009, *An Assessment of Financial Sector Rescue Programmes*, BIS Papers, no. 48, viewed 30 November 2018, www.bancaditalia.it/pubblicazioni/qef/2009-0047/QEF_47.pdf

Pedersen, P 2011, *The Case for Creating a Working Party on the Functioning of the WTO*, WTO Staff Working Paper, no. ERSD-2011-16.

Swedish National Board of Trade 2016, *Protectionism in the 21st Century*, viewed 30 November 2018, www.kommers.se/Documents/dokumentarkiv/publikationer/2016/Protectionism%20in%20the%2021st%20Century_webb.pdf

Trade Policies for a Better Future: The Leutwiler Report, GATT, and the Uruguay 1987, Martinus Nijhoff Publishers, Dordrecht, Boston, Lancaster.

Wolfe, R and Halle, M 2011, *Did the Protectionist Dog Bark? Transparency, Accountability, and the WTO During the Global Financial Crisis*, viewed 30 November 2018, www.iisd.org/pdf/2011/protectionist_dog_bark.pdf

WTO 2008, *Lamy Creates WTO Task Force on Financial Crisis*, viewed 30 November 2018, www.wto.org/english/news_e/news08_e/tnc_chair_report_oct08_e.htm

WTO 2009a, *Lamy: "We Must Remain Extremely Vigilant"*, viewed 30 November 2018, www.wto.org/english/news_e/news09_e/tpr_09feb09_e.htm

WTO 2009b, *Report to the TPRB From the Director-General on the Financial and Economic Crisis and Trade-Related Developments*, WT/TPR/OV/W/1, viewed 30 November 2018, https://docs.wto.org/dol2fe/Pages/FE_Search/FE_S_S009-DP.aspx?language=E&CatalogueIdList=87914,77232,73793,102343,69653&CurrentCatalogueIdIndex=2&FullTextHash=&HasEnglishRecord=True&HasFrenchRecord=True&HasSpanishRecord=True

WTO 2011a, *Eighth Ministerial Conference, Geneva, Chairman's Concluding Statement, 15–17 December 2011*, WT/MIN(11)/11, viewed 30 November 2018, https://docs.wto.org/

dol2fe/Pages/FE_Search/FE_S_S009-DP.aspx?language=E&CatalogueIdList=235010, 234868,234792,234737,129935,97672,30873,96729&CurrentCatalogueIdIndex=6& FullTextHash=&HasEnglishRecord=True&HasFrenchRecord=True&HasSpanishReco rd=True

WTO 2011b, *Trade Policy Review Mechanism*, Decision of 17 December 2011, WT/L/ 848, viewed 30 November 2018, https://docs.wto.org/dol2fe/Pages/SS/directdoc.aspx? filename=t:/wt/l/848.doc

WTO 2012, *Overview of Developments in the International Trading Environment*, Annual Report by the Director-General, WT/TPR/OV/15, viewed 30 November 2018, https://docs. wto.org/dol2fe/Pages/FE_Search/FE_S_S006.aspx?Query=(((%40Symbol%3dWT% 2fTPR%2fOV%2f*+NOT+%40Symbol%3dWT%2fTPR%2fOV%2fW*)+AND+% 40DocumentType%3dReport))&Language=ENGLISH&Context=QuerySearch&btsTy pe=&SourcePage=FE_B_007&languageUIChanged=true#

WTO 2016, *Trade Policy Review Report, Russian Federation*, WT/TPR/S/345, viewed 30 November 2018, www.wto.org/english/tratop_e/tpr_e/s345_e.pdf

WTO 2018, *Trade Monitoring Database*, viewed 30 November 2018, http://tmdb.wto.org/ SearchMeasures.aspx?lang=en-US

2 Transformation of the Russian trade policy facing the geopolitical challenges

Alexandra G. Koval and Sergei F. Sutyrin

Introduction

Modern global governance faces financial and economic turbulence and a shift in the balance of power that affects the development of the international trading system and national trade policies. The rise of new players – emerging economies – has, on the one hand, led to a tense relationship between developed and developing countries. On the other hand, it has revealed the imbalance in international regulation, and the necessity of reforms.

BRICS states are nowadays considered as the major emerging powers, which challenge the traditional Western leaders. The BRICS aim to develop the multipolar order and take certain places in the changing world (Davydov 2008). However, the performance of emerging powers shows a considerable gap between their aspirations and their ability to reach their goal (Schrim 2012). Nevertheless, their intention to influence the development of international economic relations in general and international trading system in particular leads to the conflict of interests between new and old powers reflecting on their trade patterns. By any means, it is obvious that the emerging powers increase their role in the global trade governance (Hopewell 2017).

The Russian Federation as a BRICS member has a unique position taking into account its historical background. Being a superpower in the past century, Russia seems to be re-emerging on the global arena. It has significantly changed its perception of global governance since the collapse of the USSR. Nowadays Russia has increasingly challenged the international order and changed its foreign economic policy (Kanet 2018). Trade policy as a constituent part of economic policy has been respectively transformed. The sanctions approved by both Western states and Russia under the "Ukrainian crisis" are vivid examples of a changing global political environment that has trade-related implications.

Since the trade policy covers trade relations conducted at the several levels, namely bilateral, regional, and multilateral ones, the state under changing geopolitical terms tends to re-balance its trade regulation among mentioned levels. For instance, the modern geopoliticization of trade negotiations leads to the increase of regional agreements and strengthening the relationship of emerging powers with neighbouring states (Mitachi 2015). In the case of Russia, an evident reference is a development of the Eurasian Economic Union. Moreover, in order to deal with sanctions and to find an alternative to the Western economic institutions in the contemporary geopolitical context, Russia likely considers the BRICS as a cornerstone of foreign policy development (Aalto and Forsberg 2016), which will involve the development of an economic relationship. Notably, cooperation within the BRICS is already one of the top discussions in Russian society, both in research and business (Toloraya 2015).

The aim of the chapter is to reveal the interdependence between the Russian geopolitical position and its trade policy in a historical retrospect. The authors examine the evolving role of the Russian state in the global governance from the USSR to today and its impact on the different levels of trade policy: bilateral relations with the main trading partners as well as Russia's participation in the regional trade agreements and the multilateral trading system. The analysis of the trade policy transformation is verified by the dynamics of trade flows whether the changing political attitude highly affects Russia's trade structure.

The main question addressed is to what extent does the Russian perception of global governance influence its actual trade pattern. In the next section, the authors identify the gap in the literature linking the studies on Russia's re-emergence in the global economic governance, on the one hand, and its trade policy development, on the other hand. The empirical part explores the evolution of Russia's geopolitical positions affecting its trade policy focus. The final section presents conclusions clarifying the modern trends in the Russian trade policy and the challenges it faces.

Theoretical background

The transformation of trade policy is almost always contentious. The priorities of the domestic actors and national economic situation, the nature of prevailing ties with core partners and the global trends all together affect the implementation of the foreign economic policy and trade policy as its integral part. Moreover, policies are rarely based on the economic theory alone, but rather on the political economy (Kerr and Gaisford 2007). The combination of economic and political sciences in the studies of international trade policy provides the possibility to expand the analytical toolbox (Odell 1990); however, today still much of economics does not refer to politics and vice versa.

One of the main reasons for the shift from international economics to the political economy in the investigations on trade policy already in the 1980–1990s was an expansion of the, relatively weak in an economic sense, influence countries had up to the level comparable to that of the largest powers (Richardson 1990). The re-balance of powers at the beginning of twenty-first century as well as the rise of multipolarity resulted in a significant impact of geopolitics on trade policies. In particular, a slowdown of multilateral talks under the World Trade Organization (WTO) has demonstrated the political context of trade negotiations (Laidi 2008).

An emergence of the mega-regional integration projects such as Transatlantic Trade and Investment Partnership (TTIP) and Trans-Pacific Partnership (TTP) has made the dependence of the modern trade policy on geopolitics even more noticeable (Dieter 2014). The most recent discussions on the US-China trade war and extended sanctions against Russia have also vividly demonstrated the increasing interconnections between economics and politics. Moreover, new plurililateral initiatives such as Trade in Services Agreement (TiSA) are primarily introduced by developed nations and represent the certain retreat from multilateral negotiations within the WTO. The majority of plurilateral talks does not involve BRICS and so far demonstrate the division between old and re-emerging powers. The shortfall of international political leadership is one of the most important dimensions of international trade policy in particular and global economic governance in general (Deese 2014).

The bulk of studies in the field of international economic relations considers emerging powers as the drivers of modern global developments, mostly focusing on BRICS (Hurrell 2006; Kingah and Quiliconi 2015). Russia as a BRICS member has been also in the focus of research (Jacobs and Van Rossem 2014; Lo and Hiscock 2014); however, some experts either debate its emerging status (Macfarlane 2006) or do not include the country in their analysis (Narlikar 2013). One of the main reasons for separating Russia from the research of emerging powers is a historical context. Taking into account the heritage of the USSR, Russia in global governance is analysed within the context of a re-emerging global power (Hedenskog et al. 2005; Kanet 2007; Makarychev and Morozov 2011).

Another reason for studying Russia separately is that the country is not considered as a part of the "North-South" dialectics or the "South–South" cooperation (Nayyar 2016). After the collapse of the USSR, Russia searched for its new place on the global arena and initially intended to be closer to the Western world. However, Russian policies have been frequently misinterpreted in the West and, finally, Russia has decided to capitalize on its power in order to compensate for a mistreatment from the Western states (Tsygankov 2009).

The Russian Federation has repeatedly been considered in the context of the "West and Non-West" relationship (Martynov 2015); although some Russian experts indicate the hazards of such a distinction for the analysis and further implications (Baranovsky and Ivanova 2015). The point is that while presenting Russia in opposition to the "West", respective experts tend to oversimplify the complexity of modern international relations. Indeed, on the one hand, in many instances culturally, politically, and economically Russia was and still is an integral part of Europe. On the other hand, "non-West" appears to be extremely heterogeneous and any direct or indirect attempts to ignore this diversity seriously distort the assessments made regarding Russian society, and its economic and political systems. Hence, incorrect perceptions – if accepted and widely disseminated – could result in biased conclusions and wrong political decisions.

However, the majority of Russian scholars emphasize the decline of the power of Western states, in particular resulting in erosion of traditional institutions of the global governance (Dynkin and Ivanova 2014). Therefore, there is an urgent need to reform these international institutions, including the WTO (Gromyko 2013). One should take into consideration that the mainstream represented by Russian politicians and researchers does not propose to replace totally the existing order with a completely new one. At the same time, Russian experts tend to argue that the new global order is ultimately unavoidable and the leading nations, including Western states in general, the USA or EU in particular, as well as China and Russia, are responsible for the scenario to establish this new order (IMEMO 2016).

The rising scholarly attention is also given to the development of regional subsystems (Torkunov 2013). Russia is perceived as an unconditional leader in the post-Soviet space while former Soviet republics have no chance for the economic development without Eurasian cooperation even when intending to be closer to the Western states (Bordachev 2013). Therefore, some scholars consider Russia as a Eurasian power (Kanet and Piet 2014). The establishment of the Eurasian economic union (EAEU) on January 1, 2015 on the basis of the Customs Union between Russia, Belarus, and Kazakhstan has especially strengthened the interregional ties in the post-Soviet space. The later accession of the Kyrgyz Republic and Armenia to the EAEU and the rising scope of its regulation have enhanced the leading role of Russia in the region.

The most recent discussion in the Russian academic field focuses on reorientation of national foreign policy towards Asia (Korolev 2016). The Western sanctions and Russian anti-sanctions have encouraged Russia's turn to the East, mainly to China (Mikheev et al. 2015). In this context, the BRICS could be considered as a platform for strengthening Russian–Chinese as well as Russian–Indian relations. Notably, the BRICS might help to balance power not only between developed and developing countries, but also between China and other emerging powers.

Russia could be interested in the BRICS not only because it seeks its own niche in the global governance, but also for purely economic reasons. Some international relations scholars argue that in the case of Western sanctions, the BRICS will gradually replace Europe vice versa of various goods (Lukin 2015). Such arguments seem to be too ambitious if one analyses Russian-BRICS cooperation not from the political, but from the economic perspective (Koval and Trofimenko 2017).

So far, there are a variety of studies on Russia's participation in the global governance and international trading system from a political point of view. In economics, the majority of scholars analyse either general trends in foreign trade and other forms of commercial cooperation between the Russian Federation and its partners (Balandina and Spartak 2017; Rasoulinezhad 2018; Obolensky 2018) or trade policy from the perspective of the application of various trade policy instruments regulated by the multilateral and regional trade agreements (Gerasimenko 2012; Isachenko 2013). In both cases, a significant geopolitical factor is largely under-investigated, while the main reason for a changing economic policy of Russia is the search of new opportunities in case of rising competition under the geopolitical tension (Medvedev 2015).

Thereby, there is a certain gap in the publications, which examine the linkages between, on the one hand: the geopolitical situation, Russian political aspirations, and its role in the global governance, and on the other hand, the effects of these issues on trade policy and trade flows. Considering the modern rise of geopolitics in international trade, the author's effort to examine the transformation of

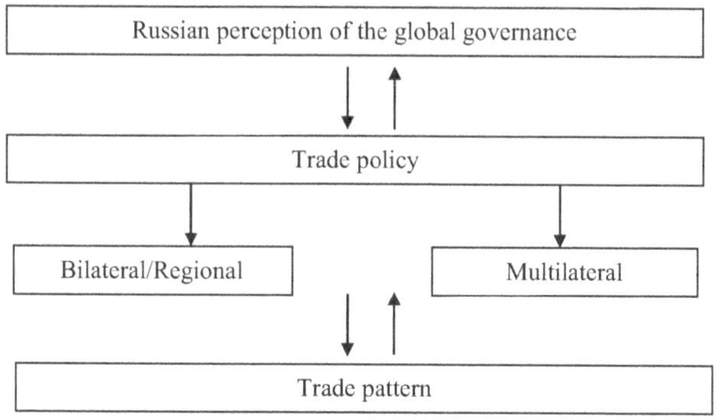

Figure 2.1 The concept of geopolitics-trade analysis

trade policy from a perspective of the international political economy. For this purpose, the chapter explores the way Russia's perception of the global governance has evolved and an impact this evolution has had on the trade policy (Figure 2.1). The latter is analysed at bilateral/regional and multilateral levels. One might argue that Russia also could change its trade instruments unilaterally. However, the country's membership in regional and multilateral agreements tends to impose a substantial limitation on the scope of unilateral decisions. The trade policy also affects a trade structure as well as any trade pattern constrains possible changes in the trade policy.

Could one claim that nowadays Russia's geopolitical goals ultimately predefine trade policy of the country? The answer is not so evident and straightforward.

Research findings

The USSR for a long period of time perceived itself as an alternative to Western capitalism that ultimately was doomed, being unable to compete with "an advanced socialist social-economic system". Under the circumstances, the Soviet Union, especially after the end of the Second World War, tried to introduce and to promote totally new rules of the game in international relations. In their turn, the Western states also mostly considered the Soviet system in comparison with their own as an entirely different one, challenging and even threatening. Therefore, foreign strategy was antagonistic from both sides, Soviet and Western. In addition to that, one should take into consideration two important features of the Soviet economy: a) an enormous internal market, and b) an extremely high level of the monopolization with a substantial number of industries/markets entirely dominated by one to three huge enterprises that mainly delivered their products to the domestic consumers. Under the circumstances, both the scale and the scope of USSR's foreign trade were relatively modest. In their turn the national trade relations were totally dependent on the political and ideological perceptions. The main focus of the USSR's foreign commerce was on the members of the "Soviet bloc". As for the interaction with the Western economies, on top of its relatively modest scale, trade with them was frequently perceived as a tool to oppose one country to another in their common attitude towards the USSR. Trade was perceived as an instrument of the geopolitical competition rather than of the economic cooperation (Behrman 1959).

Within the framework of its "alternative model" self-perception, the Soviet Union, while conducting international commercial collaboration, ultimately relied upon a non-market mechanism. In particular, foreign trade state monopoly constituted one of the key integral principles for the centrally planned economy. A respective ministry was in charge of the economic components of basically all the contracts between domestic and foreign partners. One could sensibly argue that under the circumstances a notion of "trade policy" in its conventional Western market sense did not apply to the Soviet regulatory system. This provided yet another explanation of the USSR's deliberate decision not to participate in the GATT, as well as in the Bretton-Woods institutions in general. From that perspective the Soviet Union in its attitude towards the international economic system might be considered as a "rule breaker". Indeed, the country intended to promote the new "socialist" pattern of international commercial cooperation instead of the old one intrinsic to "the capitalism".

After the disintegration of the Soviet Union in 1991, the Russian Federation launched a process of the radical changes ultimately aimed at the destruction of the major pillars of the Soviet system and introduction of what was advertised as the "universal" principles of a "contemporary civilization". In fact, Russian transformation was totally based on the Western norms and fundamentals. One might sensibly argue that the country deliberately accepted the role of "rule taker", completely adopting Western perception of the global governance. The dramatic shift in Russia's self-perception, demonstrated by the predominance of a "shock therapy" approach in adjusting the national economy to the "ultimate truth" of the Western model of economic development, was largely supported by the collapse of the USSR.

In terms of the foreign trade flows these developments resulted in a set of significant consequences. Firstly, the geographical structure of Russian foreign trade during a very short period experienced the substantial changes. In 1989, nearly 70 percent of the Russian Soviet Federal Socialist Republic deliveries went to Ukraine, Belarus, Kazakhstan, and other republics of the USSR. In comparison, by 1994, the share of the Commonwealth of Independent States (CIS) countries in the Russian foreign trade turnover was only 24 percent. Moreover, Russia severely reduced its commercial cooperation with the developing countries of Latin America, Asia, and Africa. For instance, Russian trade with Latin America decreased from billions to millions of US dollars after the collapse of the USSR (Koval 2009). On top of that, the development of foreign trade focused on the substitution of a large variety of the goods produced in Russia for the foreign ones mainly originating from the developed countries. This was due to the fact that the majority of Russian citizens in 1990s had a strong perception that almost any product made abroad was *paribus ceteris* of better quality than the domestic one.

Secondly, the Russian export industrial structure experienced an evident deterioration. The share of raw materials such as mineral products, metals, and timber in the Russian deliveries substantially increased while the share of machines and transport units declined. The national economy was characterized by a clear focus on the selling of natural resources and growing dependence on the imports of high value-added products. Statistical data clearly demonstrate (Table 2.1) that after the collapse of the USSR a share of mineral products, metals and wood in the national export has never been less than 74 percent.

Thirdly, within the framework of the largely misleading goal of "Russia's integration into the global economy", the domestic economic agents did their best to expand as much as possible external commercial relations. In particular, a forced export phenomenon became a very significant factor (in a sense even a unique factor), which facilitated Russian deliveries to the rest of the world. The point was that many Russian enterprises sold their products abroad literally in order to survive. The domestic customers had no money to pay for the deliveries. The foreign customers, especially European ones, who paid for the products they bought, from that crucial, albeit in a sense short-term perspective, appeared to be then top priority clients, despite the fact that the prices they offered hardly covered expenses or even inflicted losses for the Russian manufacturers.

All in all, the above-mentioned developments generated a variety of negative repercussions for the Russian economy. They included, in particular, a negative elasticity of foreign trade on GDP and industrial production. Indeed, during 1993–1996 the latter contracted almost two-fold against the background of an impressive expansion of both Russian export and import. The breakdown of trade relations between the former Soviet republics substantially contributed to the economic crisis accounting (according to some estimates) for 60 percent of the overall GDP contraction (Sutyrin 1996). The extraordinary rise of poverty in the country as well as the growth of an inequality among social stratum and regions could also be largely attributed to the same reasons. It was not by chance that several leading international experts at that time assessed the results of Russian transformation as a failure (Stiglitz 2002).

The attitude of the Russian Federation to the global order started to change at the beginning of the twenty-first century. By that time the economic contraction

Table 2.1 Commodity structure of Russian exports, 1990–2017

	1990	*1993*	*1995*	*1998*	*2000*	*2003*	*2005*	*2008*	*2011*	*2014*	*2017*
Mineral products	45.5	52.8	42.0	42.8	53.8	58.4	65.0	69.8	70.3	70.2	60.4
Metal and precious stones	12.9	19.0	26.1	27.6	21.7	13.8	14.2	13.2	11.1	8.1	10.4
Wood and pulp products	4.4	3.8	5.6	4.9	4.3	4.2	3.5	2.5	2.1	2.3	3.3
Machines and transport units	17.6	6.9	9.9	11.4	8.8	8.5	5.3	4.9	4.5	5.0	7.9

Source: Federal Customs Service of the Russian Federation (2018).

experienced by the country from 1992 ultimately exploded in the notorious August 1998 crisis. All these developments clearly demonstrated a fiasco of the implemented transformation model in general, the enormous vulnerability of the national economy vis-à-vis various external shocks in particular. The new Russian president and his team focused their policies on the national integrity, and prioritized the national interests.

In 2000–2007, Russia demonstrated the positive results in its economic performance, in particular an annual GDP growth rate varied from 5.4 to 8.5 percent; the unemployment level contracted from 9.9 down to 6.1 percent. The positive trend in the behaviour of major macroeconomic indicators in combination with the growth of world oil as well as other hydrocarbon prices, helped the Russian Federation to strengthen its national position on the global energy market and – more generally – to promote its international image and influence. The country began to play a more significant role in some international institutions. In particular, Russia joined the G7, converting later into the G8. More than that, the decision made to hold the G8 2006 summit in St. Petersburg became one of the symbols of a changing Russian role in the global governance. Regarding the international trading system, the process of Russia's accession to the WTO intensified at that time.

As for the actual foreign trade performance, both export and import flows experienced an impressive expansion, clearly demonstrating the enhancing interest of the foreign companies in developing their trade cooperation with the Russian partners. This expansion was interrupted by the Great Recession of 2008–2009 and its follow-up in combination with a variety of economic and geopolitical factors influencing the Russian external collaboration in a negative way (Figure 2.2).

In addition to that, trade with the CIS countries gradually lost its relative significance. Table 2.2 clearly demonstrates the trend.

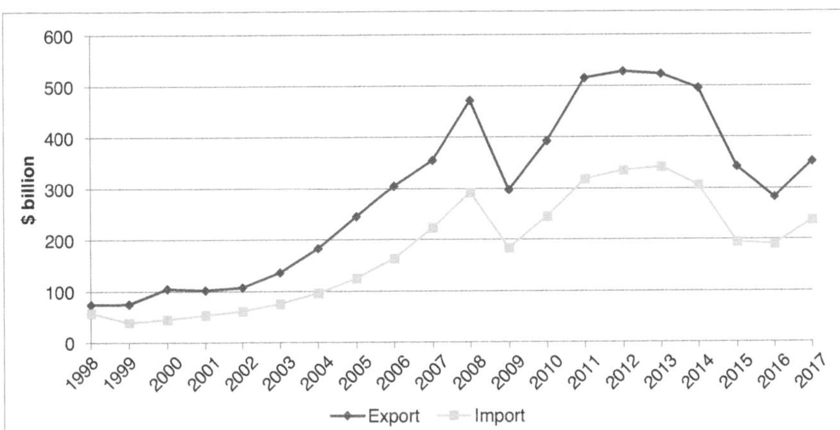

Figure 2.2 Russian merchandise foreign trade, 1998–2017

Source: Federal Customs Service of the Russian Federation (2018).

Table 2.2 Share of the CIS-trade in overall Russian foreign trade, 1997–2017

	1997	*1999*	*2001*	*2003*	*2005*	*2007*	*2009*	*2012*	*2013*	*2014*	*2015*	*2016*	*2017*
Export	19.5	14.7	14.4	15.3	13.8	15.9	15.5	14.8	14.9	13.7	13.0	13.2	13.4
Import	26.7	27.7	26.9	23.0	17.4	14.9	13.0	12.9	13.6	11.8	11.4	10.8	10.8

Source: Federal Customs Service of the Russian Federation (2018).

In 2008–2013, the Russian perception of the global governance and its own role in the process went through a serious reconsideration. That resulted from the following reasons. Firstly, the Great Recession of 2008–2009 clearly evidenced a failure of the Western states in their traditional function of defining the international "rules of the game" and securing an effective universal enforcement of the latter. It is not by chance that the G20 and the BRICS came on stage actively participating in the regulation of the global economic development. Secondly, there was a significant growth in the Russian economy in 2000–2007 that demonstrated the economic potential and power of the country and whipped up Russian ambitions on the global arena. Moreover, in 2008 the Concept of the Foreign Policy of the Russian Federation was revised reflecting the intention to diversify the country's cooperation linkages (Kremlin 2008).

On top of the above-mentioned factors, Russian relations with the West became tenser as a result of the "color revolutions" in Georgia and Ukraine. Compounding this, the Russian leadership focused on strengthening and institutionalizing relations with its neighbouring partners, Belarus and Kazakhstan, establishing the Customs Union (Sutyrin et al. 2012). Thereby, the process of Russia's accession to the WTO was partly interrupted. The Russian Federation tried to promote its regional leadership before being involved more deeply in the international trade component of the global governance.

In August 2012 Russia finally became a full-fledged member of the WTO. Being a newcomer the country took some time to adjust to its acquired status. During the Bali Ministerial conference in 2014, Russian delegation mainly observed trade negotiations and discussions. At the same time, one should take into consideration the active participation of the country in the WTO Dispute settlement mechanism. In contrast to the unofficial tradition of the so called 2–3 years "honeymoon" for the newly acceding members, as early as July 2013, the first two disputes were initiated against Russia by the EU and Japan. The latter in its turn initiated a dispute against EU in December 2013. By September 2018 the Russian Federation has participated as a complainant in seven disputes, as a respondent in nine disputes, and as a third party in 47 disputes (WTO 2018a).

In general, Russia has tried to enhance its involvement in the process of global governance. The EAEU, BRICS, WTO, APEC, etc. might be named as the most significant evidences. It goes without saying that in this way there are certain objective and subjective barriers. In particular, one could argue that Russia's search for a bigger role in the global governance via Eurasian leadership and BRICS cooperation, does not have the proper economic basis, making these strategies more a weakness than a strength (Johnson and Kostem 2016). Nevertheless, some positive results are still achieved. From the point of view of the authors, Russia's strategic goal – to be one of global "rule co-makers" – is both correctly defined and feasible. In 2013, in the Foreign Policy Concept, Russia demonstrated that the state perceived itself as a re-emerging power in the multipolar order: "The ability of the West to dominate world economy and politics continues to diminish. The global power and development potential is now more dispersed and is shifting to the East, primarily to the Asia-Pacific region. The emergence of new global economic and political actors with Western countries trying to preserve their traditional positions enhances global competition, which is manifested in growing instability in international relations" (Ministry of Foreign Affairs of Russia 2013). Nevertheless, the aforementioned changes in national foreign strategy did not so far result in any comprehensive radical changes of the Russian foreign trade flows.

The Ukrainian crisis and sanctions against Russia in 2014 have enhanced the confrontation between Western and emerging powers and forced Russia to promote its positioning in the global governance. The vicious circle of sanctions and contra-sanctions measures in the past four years has motivated the Russian government, on the one hand, to diversify further its political as well as economic relations and, on the other hand, to reinforce its leadership in the Eurasian region.

On January 1, 2015, the Customs Union between Russia, Belarus, and Kazakhstan was transformed into the Eurasian Economic Union. Thus, Russia aimed to strengthen its presence in the post-Soviet space via the EAEU development. The latter has two major dimensions: in depth – towards a level of integration higher than in the overwhelming majority of existing regional agreements, except the EU; and in breadth – with an accession of new members such as Kirgizstan and Armenia.

In addition to the above-discussed focus on the post-Soviet space, a more comprehensive diversification of Russian foreign trade relations (in order to become less dependent on the Western states) is currently perceived as one of the key trade policy priorities. Intensification of the trade relations with other BRICS countries logically enough is among the primarily targets. Meanwhile in spite of a certain contraction, the EU is still a leading partner for Russia accounting in 2017 for 42.2 percent of the total foreign trade turnover. Of course, one could also observe the remarkable gradual increase in the Chinese share up to 14.9 percent in 2017. As for the other BRICS states, their role in the Russian trade remains relatively insignificant (Table 2.3).

Table 2.3 Share of selected partners in Russian merchandised foreign trade turnover, 2008–2017

	2008	*2009*	*2011*	*2013*	*2014*	*2015*	*2016*	*2017*
EU	52.1	50.3	48	49.6	48.2	44.8	42.8	42.2
China	7.6	8.4	10.2	10.5	11.3	12.1	14.1	14.9
USA	3.7	3.9	3.8	3.3	3.7	4.0	4.3	4.0
Brazil	0.9	1.0	0.8	0.7	0.8	0.9	0.9	0.9
India	0.9	1.6	1.1	1.2	1.2	1.5	1.6	1.6
South Africa	0.1	0.1	0.1	0.1	0.1	0.2	0.2	0.1

Source: Federal Customs Service of the Russian Federation (2018).

In the latest edition of the Russian Foreign Policy Concept (Ministry of Foreign Affairs of Russia 2016), there is a certain focus on the expansion of cooperation within RIC (Russia, India, and China) alongside BRICS. The document also claims that "Russia views strengthening its positions in the Asia-Pacific Region and stepping up relations with its States as a foreign policy area of strategic importance". Some recent publications declare that Russia turns to Asia or makes a "pivot to the East" (Fortescue 2016; Rozman 2018). However, a reorientation in Russian trade towards Asia seems to be just one part of the more strategic view on the needs to transform and to diversify the national trade policy (Koval et al. 2018). However, it is an uneasy task taking into account that the trade policy of the BRICS states seems not to be tangibly converging (Pioch 2017).

More than that, Russian export to the BRICS states consists mainly of the raw materials and there is a limited space for any substantial product diversification. Nowadays the transformation of existing trade patterns is not an easy task. The restructuring of trade relations after the collapse of USSR was possible largely due to the total destruction of Soviet cooperation links. In the contemporary world, current global value chains (GVCs) make such changes very difficult. GVCs as the international join-up production arrangements changed the political and economic landscape (Fung 2013). Modern production involves inputs from a number of the countries that lead to the rise of an interdependence between the states. With the predominance of GVCs in the economic systems of many countries, the world moved much closer to the model of a global community. Under the circumstances, elimination of these connections is extremely problematic. On the one hand, the participation of Russia in global value chains is relatively low in spite of quite a high dependency on an energy supply to the leading partners (Sutyrin et al. 2014). The different interests of national companies involving at various stages of GVCs impede the radical changes in national trade policy. At the same time, the supply-chain trade in general is highly regionalized (Baldwin 2012). This is not the case for the EAEU and Russia. The Western states and some emerging powers have already developed very sustainable value chains and it is not easy to re-orient them or to find a competitive niche for a new player.

Moreover, in a comparison with the developed countries, the BRICS states demonstrate a different pattern in negotiating and establishing the regional trade agreements (RTAs). This is not that much related to merely the number of RTAs. For instance, the EU has notified the WTO of 42 agreements, the USA – 14, the BRICS countries – about 11 on average with substantial fluctuations within the group (India, China, and Russia signed 17, 15, and 12 RTAs accordingly, while South Africa and Brazil agreed on seven and six RTAs each) (WTO 2018b). The main point is that the Western countries establish RTAs with the countries all around the globe. In a contrast to that, the BRICS states mainly focus on their regions (except China). Indeed, 90 percent of all Russian RTAs was signed with the CIS states. The quantity and regional focus of RTAs concluded by the BRICS members explain why they recognize the key role of the WTO and not RTAs in the international trade regulation.

Nevertheless, RTAs and the inter-regional trade agreements such as TTIP, TTP or the plurilateral agreements such as TiSA potentially could split the world into competing blocks. In many cases, such initiatives are proposed by the Western states and do not include BRICS countries. Even if economically such mega-agreements do not cause the substantial direct damage for Russia (Sutyrin 2015), geopolitically they could lead to the fragmentation of the global governance. Therefore, Russia might try to increase its role in particular through a relatively more active participation in the WTO negotiations (Portanskiy 2017). However, neither during the Nairobi nor Buenos Aires Ministerial conferences did Russian delegation initiate any large-scale discussions and developments as well as the BRICS states didn't present any common position at the WTO. On the contrary, on several issues of the negotiations BRICS seem to express different attitudes. For instance, only Russia and China signed the Declaration in support of the Multilateral Trading System at the end of the last Ministerial conference. In general, the WTO development is largely criticized by the present American government and many other states that lead to the spread of other types of agreements. Even the Chinese initiative "One Belt – One road" demonstrates the search for the new forms of trade cooperation. The Russian Federation should take into account the complicated nature of modern international trading system in general, the potentials of wider and broader RTAs or other agreements in particular.

Thus, in 2014–2018, Russia tried to reinforce its position as a rule-co-maker/co-keeper in the context of dramatically changing geopolitical situation that encouraged its attempts to further diversification of the national trade policy. The new sanctions being introduced by the USA and some other Western states in August 2018 most probably would encourage Russia to promote its position in the global economic governance, including the extra efforts to spread its regional influence and to intensify its relations with China and other non-Western countries.

Conclusion

Our retrospective analysis of the impact of the Russian/Soviet perception and involvement in the global governance on a national foreign trade, allows us to introduce at least three substantially different patterns that have dominated during the consequent time periods. With a certain (hopefully acceptable) level of simplification these patterns might be called "rule breaker", "rule taker", and "rule co-maker/co-keeper". The first one was typical for the most part of the Soviet era; the second one characterized the way "new Russia" performed in the 1990s; finally the third one applies to the last ten to 15 years. The summarized information on the above-mentioned patterns and their major features is presented in Table 2.4.

What might one expect in a foreseeable future? Leaving aside the possibility of a large-scale tragic geopolitical crisis, the authors consider the following scenario as the most likely one. The Russian Federation will try not merely to secure but rather promote as much as possible the pattern of "rule co-maker/co-keeper". It is this very pattern that largely corresponds to the economic capacity of the country

Table 2.4 Russian/Soviet perception of global governance and its effects on trade policy

Global governance perception pattern	*Time-frame*	*Trade policy*	*Regional focus*	*Participation in the GATT/WTO system*
'Rule breaker'	'Soviet era'	didn't exist	Soviet bloc	deliberate non-participation
'Rule taker'	1990s	ad hoc	EU	launch of negotiations on accession
'Rule co-maker/ co-keeper'	Early 2000s–2013	more comprehensive/ sophisticated	EU, some attempts to diversify	completion of accession, full-fledged membership
	2014–onwards	more sophisticated with geopolitically motivated trade measures	EU, strong geopolitically motivated attempts to diversify towards BRICS (mostly China) and EAEU	support of multilateral trading system, non-participation in plulilateral talks

Source: Compiled by the authors.

as well as to some basic trends in seeking appropriate balances between the major powers of the modern multipolar world.

Under the circumstances, Russian trade policy will aim at achieving some kind of an optimal combination of two partly alternative models in the process of trade liberalization. They are: (1) the multilateral approach within the framework of the WTO system, G20 and similar global arrangements; and (2) the regional approach with a focus on negotiating and establishing of the various RTAs in many instances challenging the universal rules of international trading system. It seems important to acknowledge that ultimately advocating the trade promoting liberalization both the models do not totally outlaw a whole set of instruments intended for the support of domestic economic agents. More than that – and this is very significant for the Russian Federation due to a variety of factors including the geopolitical ones – the above-mentioned instruments provide necessary flexibility for almost any viable national trade policy.

As for the actual Russian trade flows, the authors tend to argue that their interconnection with a trade policy designed by the national regulators and implemented by the respective government agencies is relatively complicated. Of course, this is true for the other countries as well. Nevertheless, in the specific Russian case, one should take into consideration at least two significant factors. On the one hand, the process of policy-making and policy implementation by definition is a very time consuming one. The policy maker needs to reconcile the interests of various stakeholders. The resulting time gap constitutes an additional source of uncertainty for the domestic as well as for the foreign economic agents. On the other hand, in the process of trade policy implementation, the messages sent by the policy maker could be misunderstood. More than that, in the case of a conflict of interests between the economic actors and the policy maker, the former makes deliberate steps to avoid and to evade "prescriptions" of the latter. In other words, certain components of trade policy could be either partly or totally neutralized.

Meanwhile, taking all the above-mentioned into consideration, the authors with respect to the future developments in Russian foreign trade flows would indicate the following most probable trends:

- Firstly, the total foreign trade turnover in volume terms will fluctuate largely in line with an overall economic performance. In other words, one might expect in the case of both export and import a positive elasticity on the GDP, typical for the bulk of other national economies. More than that, according to some kind of universal trend of the last several decades, foreign trade turnover dispute settlement demonstrate higher volatility than GDP or industrial production.
- Secondly, the growth rate of export deliveries in value terms will, as previously, largely depend on fluctuations in the world oil prices. Their "ups" and "downs" should also seriously influence value of the Russian imports.
- Thirdly, the commodity structure of exports will experience a gradual (albeit modest) diversification via growing share of the industrial goods with higher value added. An expansion in export of services also might contribute to this diversification.
- And lastly, one could expect a gradual but modest diversification of geographical structure of the foreign trade, with less focus than previously on a relative small number of the leading trading partners.

Bibliography

Aalto, P and Forsberg, T 2016, 'The Structuration of Russia's Geo-economy Under Economic Sanctions', *Asia Europe Journal*, vol. 14, no. 2, pp. 221–237.

Balandina, GV and Spartak, AN 2017, 'Perspektivy i ogranichenija uchastija Rossii v regional'nyh i global'nyh cepochkah stoimosti', *Rossijskij vneshnejekonomicheskij vestnik*, no. 11, pp. 3–16.

Baldwin, R 2012, *WTO 2.0: Global Governance of Supply-Chain Trade*, CEPR Policy Insight, no. 64, viewed 20 September 2018, https://cepr.org/sites/default/files/policy_insights/PolicyInsight64.pdf

Baranovsky, VG and Ivanova, NI (eds.) 2015, *Global'noe upravlenie: vozmozhnosti i riski*, IMEMO RAN, Moscow.

Behrman, JN 1959, 'Trade Duel', *Challenge*, vol. 7, no. 9, pp. 47–51.

Bordachev, T 2013, *Eurasian Union: Integration for the Sake of Sovereignty*, viewed 20 September 2018, http://valdaiclub.com/opinion/highlights/eurasian_union_integration_for_the_sake_of_sovereignty/

Davydov, V 2008, 'The Role of Brazil, Russia, India & China (BRICS) in Reconstruction of the International Order', *Megatrend Review*, vol. 5, no. 1, pp. 85–97.

Deese, DA (ed.) 2014, *Handbook of International Political Economy of Trade*, Edward Elgar, Cheltenham and Northampton.

Dieter, H 2014, *The Return of Geopolitics: Trade Policy in the Era of TTIP and TPP*, Friedrich-Ebert-Stiftung, Berlin.
Dynkin, AA and Ivanova, NI 2014, *Global'naja perestrojka*, IMEMO RAN, Moscow.
Federal Customs Service of the Russian Federation 2018, viewed 20 September 2018, http://customs.ru/index.php?option=com_content&view=article&id=13858&Itemid=2095
Fortescue, S 2016, 'Russia's Economic Prospects in the Asia Pacific Region', *Journal of Eurasian Studies*, vol. 7, no. 1, pp. 49–59.
Fung, VK 2013, 'Governance Through Partnership in a Changing World', in: DK Elms and P Low (eds.) *Global Value Chains in a Changing World*, World Trade Organization, viewed 20 September 2018, www.wto.org/english/res_e/booksp_e/aid4tradeglobalvalue13_e.pdf
Gerasimenko, D 2012, 'Russia's Commercial Policy, 2008–11: Modernization, Crisis, and the WTO Accession', *Oxford Review of Economic Policy*, vol. 28, no. 2, pp. 301–323.
Gromyko, AA (ed.) 2013, *Global'noe upravlenie v XXI veke: innovacionnye podhody*, Institute of Europe RAN, Moscow.
Hedenskog, J, Konnander, V, Nygren, B, Oldberg, I and Pursiainen, C (eds.) 2005, *Russia as a Great Power: Dimensions of Security Under Putin*, Routledge, Abingdon.
Hopewell, K 2017, 'The BRICS – Merely a Fable? Emerging Power Alliances in Global Trade Governance', *International Affairs*, vol. 93, no. 6, pp. 1377–1396.
Hurrell, A 2006, 'Hegemony, Liberalism, and Global Order: What Space for Would-be Great Powers?', *International Affairs*, vol. 82, no. 1, pp. 1–19.
IMEMO 2016, 'Global'naja sistema na perelome: puti k novoj normal'nosti', *Mirovaya ekonomika i mezhdunarodnye otnosheniya*, vol. 60, no. 8, pp. 5–25.
Isachenko, TM 2013, 'The Trade Policy of Russia: Latest Developments and Main Priorities', *Rivista di Studi Politici Internazionali Nuova Serie*, vol. 80, no. 3, pp. 347–360.
Jacobs, LM and Van Rossem, R 2014, 'The BRIC Phantom: A Comparative Analysis of the BRICs as a Category of Rising Powers', *Journal of Policy Modelling*, no. 36, pp. 547–566.
Johnson, J and Kostem, S 2016, 'Frustrated Leadership: Russia's Economic Alternative to the West', *Global Policy*, vol. 7, no. 2, pp. 207–216.
Kanet, RE (ed.) 2007, *Russia: Re-emerging Great Power*, Palgrave Macmillan, London.
Kanet, RE 2018, 'Russia and Global Governance: The Challenge to the Existing Liberal Order', *International Politics*, vol. 55, no. 2, pp. 177–188.
Kanet, RE and Piet, R (eds.) 2014, *Shifting Priorities in Russia's Foreign and Security Policy*, Ashgate, Surrey and Burlington.
Kerr, WA and Gaisford, JD 2007, *Handbook on International Trade Policy*, Edward Elgar, Cheltenham and Northampton.
Kingah, S and Quiliconi, C (eds.) 2015, *Global and Regional Leadership of BRICS Countries*, Springer, Cham.
Korolev, A 2016, 'Russia's Reorientation to Asia: Causes and Strategic Implications', *Pacific Affairs*, vol. 89, no. 1, pp. 53–73.
Koval, AG 2009, 'Perspektivi razvitiya torgovo-ekonomicheskih otnosheniy Rossii so stranami Latinskoy Ameriki v usloviyah finansovogo krizisa', *Vestnik Sankt-Peterburgskogo universiteta. Seriya 5: Ekonomika*, no. 3, pp. 94–104.
Koval, AG, Popova, LV and Sutyrin, SF 2018, 'Transformation of the Russian Trade Policy: Pivot to Asia, Focus on China', in: *Research on the Economic Development of Russia in 2017*, Renmin University of China, Beijing.
Koval, AG and Trofimenko, OY 2017, 'Rol' BRIKS vo vneshnetorgovoj politike Rossii', *Mezhdunarodnaja jekonomika*, no. 10, pp. 20–29.

Kremlin 2008, *Koncepcija vneshnej politiki Rossijskoj Federacii*, viewed 20 September 2018, http://kremlin.ru/acts/news/785

Laidi, Z 2008, 'How Trade Became Geopolitics', *World Policy Journal*, vol. 25, no. 2, pp. 55–61.

Lo, VI and Hiscock, M (eds.) 2014, *The Rise of the BRICS in the Global Political Economy: Changing Paradigms*? Edward Elgar, Cheltenham and Northampton.

Lukin, A 2015, 'Konsolidacija nezapadnogo mira na fone ukrainskogo krizisa: Rossija i Kitaj, ShOS i BRIKS', *Mezhdunarodnaja zhizn'*, no. 2, pp. 72–91.

Macfarlane, N 2006, 'The "R" in the BRICS: Is Russia an Emerging Power?', *International Affairs*, no. 82, pp. 41–57.

Makarychev, A and Morozov, V 2011, 'Multilateralism, Multipolarity, and Beyond: A Menu of Russia's Policy Strategies', *Global Governance: A Review of Multilateralism and International Organizations*, vol. 17, no. 3, pp. 353–373.

Martynov, BF 2015, *Zapad i ne-Zapad: proshloe, nastojashhee . . . budushhee*? ILA RAN, Moscow.

Medvedev, D 2015, 'A New Reality: Russia and Global Challenges', *Russian Journal of Economics*, vol. 1, no. 2, pp. 109–129.

Mikheev, V, Lukonin, S and Lukonina, Y 2015, 'Kitaj – Rossija: kogda jemocii umestny?', *Mirovaya ekonomika i mezhdunarodnye otnosheniya*, no. 2, pp. 5–13.

Ministry of Foreign Affairs of Russia 2013, *Concept of the Foreign Policy of the Russian Federation*, viewed 20 September 2018, www.mid.ru/foreign_policy/official_documents/-/asset_publisher/CptICkB6BZ29/content/id/122186?p_p_id=101_INSTANCE_CptICkB6BZ29&_101_INSTANCE_CptICkB6BZ29_languageId=en_GB

Ministry of Foreign Affairs of Russia 2016, *Foreign Policy Concept of the Russian Federation*, viewed 20 September 2018, www.mid.ru/foreign_policy/news/-/asset_publisher/cKNonkJE02Bw/content/id/2542248?p_p_id=101_INSTANCE_cKNonkJE02Bw&_101_INSTANCE_cKNonkJE02Bw_languageId=en_GB

Mitachi, T 2015, 'The Geopoliticization of Trade Talks', in: *Geo-economics: Seven Challenges to Globalization*, World Economic Forum, viewed 20 September 2018, www3.weforum.org/docs/WEF_Geo-economics_7_Challenges_Globalization_2015_report.pdf

Narlikar, A 2013, 'Negotiating the Rise of New Powers', *International Affairs*, vol. 89, no. 3, pp. 561–576.

Nayyar, D 2016, 'BRICS, Developing Countries and Global Governance', *Third World Quarterly*, vol. 37, no. 4, pp. 575–591.

Obolensky, VP 2018, 'Vneshnjaja torgovlja Rossii: priroda pod#emov i spadov', *Rossijskij vneshnejekonomicheskij vestnik*, no. 3, pp. 24–32.

Odell, JS 1990, 'Understanding International Trade Policies: An Emerging Synthesis', *World Politics*, vol. 43, no. 1, pp. 139–167.

Pioch, M 2017, 'BRICS in Trade Clusters: The Prospects of Convergent Trade Policies of Large Emerging Economies', *St Petersburg University Journal of Economic Studies*, vol. 33, no. 2, pp. 282–302.

Portanskiy, A 2017, 'Ot Bretton-Vudsa do Bujenos-Ajresa', *Torgovaja Politico*, vol. 11, no. 3, pp. 32–45.

Rasoulinezhad, E 2018, 'A New Evidence From the Effects of Russia's WTO Accession on Its Foreign Trade', *Eurasian Economic Review*, vol. 8, no. 1, pp. 73–92.

Richardson, DJ 1990, 'The Political Economy of Strategic Trade Policy', *International Organization*, vol. 44, no. 1, pp. 107–135.

Rozman, G 2018, 'The Russian Pivot to Asia', in: G Rozman and S Radchenko (eds.) *International Relations and Asia's Northern Tier*, Asan-Palgrave Macmillan Series, Palgrave, Singapore.

Schrim, SA 2012, 'Leaders in Need of Followers: Emerging Powers in Global Governance', in: E Fels, JF Kremer and K Kronenberg (eds.) *Power in the 21st Century, International Security and International Political Economy in a Changing World*, Springer-Verlag, Berlin and Heidelberg.

Stiglitz, JE 2002, *Globalization and Its Discontents*, W. W. Norton, New York and London.

Sutyrin, SF 1996, 'Problems and Prospects of Economic Reintegration Within the CIS', *Review of Economies in Transition*, no. 1, pp. 29–43.

Sutyrin, SF 2015, 'TTIP: A Russian Perspective', in: MS Akman, SJ Evenett and P Low (eds.) *Catalyst? TTIP's Impact on the Rest*, CEPR Press, viewed 20 September 2018, https://voxeu.org/system/files/epublication/TTIP_23march.pdf

Sutyrin, SF, Koval, AG and Trofimenko, OY 2014, 'Integrating Into the Multilateral Trading System and Global Value Chains: The Case of Russia', in: M Jansen, MS Jallab and M Smeets (eds.) *Connecting to Global Markets: Challenges and Opportunities: Case Studies Presented by WTO Chair-holders*, World Trade Organization, Geneva.

Sutyrin, SF, Lomagin, NA, Sherov-Ignatiev, VG, Trofimenko, OY, Kapustkin, VI, Nazarova, MV and Lisitsyn, NE 2012, *Russia's Accession to the WTO: Major Commitments, Possible Implications*, International Trade Centre, Geneva, viewed 20 September 2018, www.intracen.org/uploadedFiles/Russia%20WTO%20Accession%20English.pdf

Toloraya, G (ed.) 2015, *VII BRICS Academic Forum*, National Committee on BRICS Research, Moscow.

Torkunov, AV 2013, 'Mezhdunarodnye otnoshenija v postkrizisnom mire: vzgljad iz Rossii', *Vestnik MGIMO-Universiteta*, vol. 30, no. 3, pp. 8–11.

Tsygankov, AP 2009, 'Russia in Global Governance: Multipolarity or Multilateralism?', in: D Lesage and P Vercauteren (eds.) *Contemporary Global Governance: Multipolarity vs New Discourses on Global Governance*, Peter Lang, Brussels.

WTO 2018a, *Dispute Settlement*, viewed 20 September 2018, www.wto.org/english/tratop_e/dispu_e/dispu_by_country_e.htm

WTO 2018b, *Regional Trade Agreements Information System*, viewed 20 September 2018, http://rtais.wto.org/UI/PublicMaintainRTAHome.aspx

3 States and *dirigisme* versus markets

Hydrocarbons, agriculture, and Russia's trade policy, 1991–2017

Nikita A. Lomagin and Jeffrey K. Hass

Introduction: political economy of post-Soviet trade

When COMECON and the USSR fell apart as a political-economic bloc and as a unified country, respectively, many post-Soviet enterprises suddenly found themselves cut adrift from former trading partners. Institutional reforms in 1992 in Russia proper left them in an economic liminal state, uncertain not only of future exchange relations or open markets, but also of uncertainty about their very statuses as enterprises and about the rules of the business game. Structures and rules in flux compelled desperate attempts to find a certain source of supplies and income – especially as state-centered relations remained but were under duress, and fields of market actors had yet to emerge or were small and underdeveloped. Yet fields of exchange in flux also provided opportunities to make new relations and even to shape the contours of post-Soviet relations of trade and production. How Russian patterns of trade – structures, successes and failures, and future prospects – got from there to here still deserves rigorous and creative analysis, and in this chapter we take some tentative steps in this direction by embedding policies in domestic and international political fields. This is an important claim on our part, which we draw from decades of work in political economy and economic sociology: policies and trade reflect politics as much, if not more, than market forces and interests. Yet how this operates is not mechanistic or straightforward, and rather than elucidate a mechanistic theory, we follow the example of Max Weber and suggest "signposts", or important social forces that can contingently interact and shape trade and its policies. Rather than enumerate various policies of foreign and domestic trade, we explore dialectical relations between political context (political economy), policies, and outcomes. We do not deny that policies matter, but we reject both the simplistic notion that one can understand economics by positing policies alone, and the notion that the contents of policies and their implementation exist in a vacuum.

Economics is never devoid of politics, as post-socialism (along with economic history) revealed. This was clearly the case for reconstructing trade relations in the 1990s, in the wake of Soviet institutional collapse, and then again in the 2000s, after the 1998 ruble crisis and a new regime and political economy coming to power. Certainly, much of the effort by business actors was oriented to making sales – but business actors also orient strategies to considerations of peers' actions to generate legitimacy as well as monetary profit or market share (Fligstein 1990). And in post-socialist Russia, taking for granted market institutions was a mistake Russians themselves did not make – not only did they face the challenge of reconstructing institutions, but they also had the opportunity to shape those institutions for their own benefit (or lose out to others able to do so). Another sin of omission is taking for granted and oversimplifying dynamics of *organizing* economic activity (North 1990). Usual mainstream models in economics take for granted the genesis of organizational forms within and between firms, as these should reflect a regression to an efficient and profitable norm. One model of bilateral international trade, the gravity model (Tinbergen 1962), considers distance and size of economy of trading countries – but "size" carries a lot of weight, including organization. Ultimately, much economic analysis harkens back to David Ricardo's claims that comparative advantage shapes relative costs of trade and shapes relations and priorities. If institutions matter, they provide basic foundations (property rights, contract); otherwise, they potentially interfere with the workings of the market.

Using hydrocarbons and agriculture as our cases, we make the following argument about policy and trade, in which domestic and global politics matter as much or more than markets. Firstly, the kinds of policies that emerge are in part a function of state structures and political relations. State structure affects the capacity (or lack thereof) of political elites to shape the economy (including traders and trade). State structure also affects the capacity of other elites to gain access to policy-making (Skocpol 1992). Political relations involve networks and alliances between different elite actors – in our case, how organized elites of different sectors were (e.g. so as to influence elections or the like), and whether elites of different sectors had access to state elites, in particular their links to "clans" in Boris Yeltsin's Kremlin of the 1990s and to Vladimir Putin's *siloviki* of the 2000s. Secondly, we argue that earlier fundamental reforms shaped future paths for trade and trade policies. In particular, privatization broke apart the agricultural sector, kept gas under state control, and left oil in a middle ground split between private oligarchs and state ownership. This affected state capacity and political relations as noted earlier, as well as creating variation in incentives for different trade policies (e.g. defending hydrocarbons over agriculture early on). Thirdly, we note how trade policies are embedded not only in these domestic political contexts, but also in geopolitics. In gas and oil, Russia had an important competitive advantage vis-à-vis other global actors, providing an incentive to maintain state leverage over this sector. Oil and gas provided income for the state and a source of soft power, and gas also provided important leverage at home, in the form of cheap heating for citizens. The agricultural sector enjoyed no such advantages. However, the politics after the 2014 events in Crimea and Ukraine, especially Western sanctions, altered how state elites viewed agriculture, leading to import substitution policies – moving agricultural trade closer to that of hydrocarbons.

In sum, politics shaped policies, which in turn was made possible because the state retained its olympian position even after Boris Yeltsin's market reforms. The politics of state power and status in domestic politics and economics, and in geopolitics, meant policies profited the state. This does not mean markets were meaningless, as we will see for both cases – but markets did not predominate in decision-making, either. To make this argument, we pull back from a focus on a list of individual trade policies, to look at the entire picture.

Crafting markets, relations, and practices: fields of politics and trade

Any study of policies risks incompleteness, given the various important variables, dynamics, and levels of analysis involved: not only concrete actors and interests, political institutions of authority and access, and broader fields of political rules and practices (domestically and geopolitically). Further, while technical specifics of policies might change over time, general logics shift more slowly in the absence of dramatic shocks and even then sometimes still persist (Dobbin 1994). Hence, we limit ourselves to providing a brief glimpse of *variation* in the evolution and structure of relations and policies of post-Soviet trade.

That businesses orient to markets is not surprising, and usual market suspects (especially comparative advantage) cannot be entirely discounted when making sense of trade relations and practices. However, that actors construct those markets – in post-Soviet Russia, they had to – complicates the issue, especially for mainstream economic theory. New Institutional Economics does point out that institutions are crucial for structuring economies and performance, although efficiency and profit still take centre stage and politics is often epiphenomenal. How are we to make sense of how economies are structured, especially in a case such as Russia's? The majority of empirical cases (and theoretical references) are relatively stable capitalist systems, in which property rights, contract, state structures (including relatively robust procedures to enforce the law and resolve disputes), currencies, and the like are settled and in place. These institutional foundations are crucial to New Institutional Economics: firms can develop governance structures to fit their contexts because they can invoke property rights, contract, and a working state to ground organizational forms. What of a case, such as post-Soviet Russia's, when this background was *coevolving* alongside governance structures and decision-making about trading?

The most important institution is the state, a nerve centre of power. That state elites' interests do not align entirely with those of business should not surprise us; political economy of trade should be a starting point for analysis. Yet many analyses leave aside politics as a separate sphere of institutions (e.g. as in the gravity model of trade). Institutionalist economics, such as Positive Political Economy (Alt and Shepsle 1990), implicitly or explicitly sees state involvement in the economy as negative, skewing any analysis of the political economy of trade. Yet eliding power deprives us of understanding how and why particular economic trade relations take root. For its part, usual political economy adds power and presumes actors' interests might not be cooperative and shaped by institutional position, rather than assumed to be some vague, acontextual utility function. Comparative studies of Latin America and East Asia in the 1990s revealed the importance of state structures and capacity, state-business relations, and global economic and geopolitical positions for organizational forms and institutional relations across countries (Wade 2003; Haggard 1990; Evans 1995). This literature takes seriously Max Weber's claim that states compete with markets. While businesses try to optimize profits and market positions, political elites and state actors try to optimize resources and positions of power (which might require capital but are not reducible to capital). States might seek to shape trade to realize interests (e.g. lobbying and favouring particular clients), realizing geopolitical interests or needs, or shaping the economic for the (perceived) better interests of society.

Interestingly, while state-centered and institutional analyses did recover other institutions and practices that mainstream economics elided (and continues to elide), there was still an interesting overlap between critics and the object of their critiques. East Asian strategies of states "helping" markets were lauded as successful, while Latin American import substitution was seen as a failure (Haggard 1990). This was partly due to populist and corporatist domestic politics that threw up obstacles to effective use of economic resources, as well as bad decisions that came home to roost by the 1980s (e.g. taking on massive debt in the hopes of future economic gains to offset those debts). However, comparisons between the two regions suggested that states do, and likely should, play a role in economies – but that states should leave much of the hard work up to private business. Post-Soviet Russia offers us an opportunity to revisit this debate. Firstly, the 1990s was the age of "shock therapy", and even if reality did not quite match the prescriptions of Jeffrey Sachs and his colleagues, the 1990s was a wager on private elites taking the economy out of the state's hands – at the least to avoid a return to a communist-style command economy, and at best achieving a "primitive accumulation of capital" that would be invested in domestic growth. Needless to say, the results of that experiment were underwhelming, although one wonders whether that experiment was given enough time and a fair shot. After 2000, Vladimir Putin's new political economy brought the state back into the economy, especially in the commanding heights of sectors considered to be of strategic importance, especially hydrocarbons and military production. After Crimea became a part of Russia and ensuing Western sanctions, Putin's government implemented policies of "import substitution" (*importozameshenie*) to grow some domestic sectors in a tit-for-tat versus the West (including agriculture). In real time, as it were, we have the opportunity to revisit dynamics similar to those that took place in Latin America, and we can assess what might drive state policies, and what effects these can have.

Assessing the political economy of fields of trade

On remaking post-Soviet trade, the tradition of political economy would have us look at the position, capacity, and coherence of state institutions, and interests of state and political elites, and of relevant business actors (those with sufficient resources and interests to lobby the state). Business elites would focus as much on political profit as on business profit, i.e. securing policies and alliances among political elites to guard and advance their interests in the political sphere, to help them gain advantages in the business sphere. This can include subsidies or tax breaks, favourable regulatory policies, and so on. Political economy does face the same challenge as mainstream economies and New Institutional Economics: namely, the issue of state reformation simultaneously with remaking business institutions and practices. However, the issue here is not so intractable, as political elites will be scrambling just like business elites to remake state structures. In political economy, a *dialectical* process between economic and business groups and interests is always in operation: one shapes the other, so that even moments of institutional equilibrium are never too far from being challenged. For post-Soviet Russia, the key to making sense of trade is to look for groups and their respective interests and resources, legal and other institutional tools available to different parties, and the contingencies of inter-elite negotiations and rivalries (not all of which need be governed by hard-nosed interests alone).

Our approach is to compare two sectors with potential for development and trade (domestic and foreign), and correlate their histories with their position in fields of domestic politics and foreign geopolitics. Our hypothesis is that contingencies of domestic and global politics (as well as markets) shaped the relations between the state and different sectors, and thus the health of domestic and foreign trade for these sectors. We perform our analysis for two sets of actors in two different sectors: *agriculture* and *hydrocarbons*. While both were potentially oriented to domestic *and* international markets simultaneously, each leaned more in one direction than the other. Hydrocarbon companies oriented more to export markets, because there was greater demand and wealth to be had. Agribusinesses, on the other hand, would face stiffer competition from the global market both abroad and at home, and had demand inside the domestic market.

We see two important sets of actors and lobbies pulling trade policies in two directions: protection to boost domestic production, accompanied by reorienting imports from those states that did not impose sanctions on Russia (agriculture), and integration into the global market (hydrocarbons). Which would win might depend on each lobby's capacity – money, networks, political representation – and on state capacity to resist or co-opt these collective actors. For hydrocarbons, politics played a crucial role. The gas sector was shielded from reforms, including privatization and export of dry gas. The state retained control over this sector and a near-monopoly via Gazprom. However, this politics involved delivering cheap gas for domestic consumption, constraining gas development in fields remote from export pipelines. While the oil sector was reformed and mostly privatized, the state regained capacity under Vladimir Putin. The spike in oil prices in the 2000s made oil a tool of soft power, although one the state did not directly control; oil trade and gains were driven more by the market than was the case for gas. For agriculture, the lack of powerful lobbies in the Kremlin meant less state investment or protection, and agriculture could not be a geopolitical tool or growth engine at home.[1] However, sanctions in 2014 provided an important stimulus for import substitution policies (although food security issue has been an issue since 2010), so that elite investment could increase and shape future development of domestic agricultural trade, with foreign trade still questionable at present.

Politics meets markets: hydrocarbon *dirigisme*

The significance of oil and gas for Russia's political economy is clear, but the quality of its significance remains disputed. Are oil and gas an addiction that encouraged rent-seeking and led Russia to flirt with a Dutch disease and contributed to Russia's authoritarian turn (Karl 1997; Fish 2005; Goldman 2008; Ross 2012)? Potential and real oil and gas revenues have complicated Russia's politics and political economy (Douglas 2015; Gustafson 2012). Additionally, there are questions about effectiveness given its centrality to political power: Luong and Weinthal (2010) insist on contingencies in the construction of petrostates; particular ownership structures and tax policies can mitigate the hydrocarbon curse. Miller (2018, pp. 41–48) argues that Russian economic policy, including its energy sector, has been well designed and effectively executed, enabling Putin to project power at home and abroad and to reclaim state power once lost to oligarchs.

In terms of energy content, Russia produces about as much gas as oil – a little over 500 million tons of oil equivalent each year – but the markets differ. Firstly, in energy terms, gas yields less value than oil. Secondly, whereas Russia exports three-quarters of its oil output (CEIC 2018), it consumes nearly two-thirds of its gas output, much at prices below export parity (artificially low).[2] In terms of money earned, Russia's oil exports generate over four times the revenue of gas exports. Thus, one could say that oil pays the bills abroad, and gas subsidizes the economy at home. This shows that the structure and politics of Russian gas and oil have followed different paths (Miller 2018, pp. 48–56) – and both have differed from the path of agricultural trade. For Russia's energy strategy, much existing work has focused on strategic or market perspectives. In the "realist" school, large corporations are adjuncts to, or instruments of, state policy and are mentioned in passing. After the attack on Khodorkovskii in 2004, the former approach has dominated: energy was, is, and will be Russian leaders' best weapon (Goldman 2008; Ross 2012; Stuhlberg 2007). As Balzer (2005) observed over a decade ago, even before becoming Yeltsin's heir, Vladimir Putin argued for state control of the commanding heights of Russia's energy sector. An alternative perspective accepts the decisive role of the state but adds that energy policy is made largely by powerful national energy companies (NECs) pursuing corporate and commercial interests (Gustafson 2012; Luong and Weinthal 2010; Strange 2000; Lomagin 2015, pp. 137–141, 159–159). As well, much academic work, as well as political and media coverage, views the Russian energy sector (especially gas) from the perspective of European energy security, especially supply dependency. Our analysis takes a dialectical approach, avoiding *de facto* favouring one over the other.

Oil and gas: an overview

Russia's proven oil reserves total approximately 109.5 billion barrels, which equates to nearly 6.4 percent of the total global reserves. The country's proven gas reserves are the largest in the world, roughly 32 trillion cubic meters (17.3 percent of total global reserves), enough for approximately 80 years at current production rates (here and further in this section, see Josefson and Rotar 2018). The majority of reserves are in Siberia, with the Yamburg, Urengoy, and Medvezhye fields alone accounting for more than 40 percent of production. Despite declines in natural gas production in 2014 (down 4.3 percent) and 2015 (down 1.5 percent), Russia remains the world's second largest gas producer, behind the United States, and its top exporter. Oil made up 22 percent of Russia's primary energy consumption in 2016, and natural gas accounted for 52.2 percent. The vast majority of Russian gas is shipped via pipelines, but in 2016 the country produced nearly 15 billion cubic meters of liquefied natural gas (LNG), all produced by the Sakhalin II project and exported. Launched in late 2013, Yamal LNG is one of the largest and most complex LNG projects in the world. With partners Total, CNPC, and the Silk Road Fund, Novatek is developing the enormous South Tambey gas field. The project aims to tap natural gas reserves totaling more than 4 billion barrels of oil equivalent. To do so, more than 200 wells have been drilled and three LNG trains built, each with a capacity of 5.5 million metric tons (Yamal LNG 2018). Potential future LNG sites are in the Russian Arctic and the Baltic Sea. In general, Russian NECs are the key pillars of the Russian economy. Table 3.1 illustrates this point from the prospective of oil and gas exports.

In 2016, around 8.1 million barrels of oil and oil products were shipped abroad daily (5.1 million of this was crude oil, 3 million was refined products). In 2017, this amount increased by 8.1 percent. While more than 85 percent of all crude exports are pumped through state monopoly Transneft's pipelines, the share of seaborne shipments remains strong despite global reduction. Around 68 percent of all gas exports are shipped to Europe, with Germany and Turkey accounting for approximately 50 percent and 25 percent respectively. In 2016, Russia became China's biggest crude oil supplier for the first time. In 2017 aggregate volumes reached almost 24.5 million cubic meters, 9.5 percent more than in 2016. Of the liquefied gas produced by Sakhalin II, 65.5 percent went to Japan, 17 percent to South Korea, 12 percent to Taiwan, and small amounts to China. During the first two months of 2018 the export of LNG by Sakhalin II grew by 2.5 percent in comparison with the same period of 2017. This said, in overall terms, the Russian

Table 3.1 Significance of oil and gas exports to the Russian economy (pre-sanction period), 2013

Export Revenues	*US$ billion*	*Percent of GDP*	*Percent of Export Revenues*
Crude oil exports	174	8	33
Oil products exports	109	5	21
Total oil exports	283	14	54
Natural gas pipeline exports	67	3	13
LNG exports	6	0	1
Total natural gas exports	73	3	14
Total oil and natural gas exports	356	17	68

Source: Compiled from data in Bordoff and Houser (2014).

domestic oil and gas sector has been facing more challenging times in recent years due to the low oil prices and limited access to financing due to international sanctions. In 2017, total oil and gas export declined, mostly due to relatively low prices on hydrocarbons. This said, state policy for oil and gas has focused on maintaining the current production levels and supporting state companies.

Structure of the field: state, market, and hydrocarbon trade

While oil and gas export revenues grew from US$28 billion in 1998 to US$143 billion in 2005, oligarchs who controlled Russia's oil output minimized taxes paid and tried (but failed) to turn this wealth into political power (Gustafson 2012, pp. 187–188). In contrast, Soviet citizens did not experience the usual hallmarks of capitalist oil booms, such as increasing inequality or destabilizing influxes of petrodollars. Socialist hydrocarbon income did not rival the power of the state, and oil did not occupy the same status position in the USSR as in capitalist oil producers (Douglas 2015). While Russia's oil sector did experience privatization and diversification in 1990s, in the Putin years the trend has been increasing concentration of oil assets in the hands of state-owned enterprises: for example, Rosneft's acquisition of Iuganskneftegaz from Iukos, TNK-BP's assets, and Bashneft (Russia's sixth-largest oil company at the time). Such state-owned companies as Rosneft, Gazprom, and Gazprom Neft accounted for about half of all oil production. In natural gas, Gazprom dominates as a *de facto* monopoly (on Gazprom's structure, see Mitrova 2014). Gazprom controls more than 70 percent of Russia's gas reserves and supplies two-thirds of Russia's domestic natural gas. In contrast, the second largest producer, private company Novatek produced 62 billion cubic meters of gas in 2017, versus Gazprom's output of 471 billion cubic meters. The state also dominates transportation of oil and gas. Transneft controls transportation of oil, Transnefteprodukt transportation of petroleum products, and Gazprom-owned Unified Gas Supply System (UGSS) transportation of natural gas. The Ministry of Energy approves quarterly schedules that detail the precise volume of oil each producer can pump through the Transneft system. Once access rights are allocated, oil producers generally cannot increase their allotted capacity in the export pipeline system, although they have limited flexibility to alter delivery routes. Oil and gas are mostly sold under direct transactional agreements, subject to regulations established by Federal law No. 325-FZ.

However, state control is not limited to direct ownership or controlling transportation. Equally significant are regulatory policies that make the state the final arbiter in questions about rights to resources.[3] Official state policy objectives, as set out in the Energy Strategy of Russia until 2030, include transitioning to energy efficiency and transforming production of energy – although since these objectives were set in 2009, the state has tended to lose sight of them. While crude oil prices are not regulated, prices for gasoline, natural gas, and oil transportation are. Gas produced by Gazprom and its subsidiaries is subject to wholesale price regulation. Independent producers, who account for only a relatively small share of total production, are not subject to regulation. However, certain consumers (such as residential consumers) are entitled to fixed retail gas prices. The regulated prices are established by the Federal Service for Tariffs. Tax policies, on the surface, encourage the search for and development of oil reserves. For onshore and offshore oil and gas exploration and production, there are two kinds of regimes. The first is a "tax-royalty" regime, grounded in the federal law "On Subsoil" (February 21, 1992) and subsequent regulations. The second regime involves production sharing (from the December 30, 1995 law, "On Production Sharing Agreements"). In practice, these tax regimes have hindered further development in extraction. The Mineral Extraction Tax and export tax – geared more to short-term gain rather than longer-term development – make further investment in necessary new technologies unfeasible, in contrast to a possible profit-based tax that the state has dismissed (Mitrova 2014). This reflects a rent-seeking logic by the state vis-à-vis hydrocarbon trade.

Licensing for extraction is also closely regulated and gives the state various advantages. For oil, licensing is administered by the Ministry of Natural Resources and Ecology; the Federal Agency for Subsoil Use (Rosnedra) is responsible for issuing, suspending, and revoking subsoil use licenses, and for approving development plans. The Federal Service for Supervision of the Use of Nature (Rosprirodnadzor) oversees compliance with legislation on subsoil use. The Federal Environmental, Industrial and Nuclear Supervision Service (Rostekhnadzor) issues mining allotments that determine deposit boundaries, safety certificates, and operating licenses. Russian law also requires a foreign investor to obtain prior consent from the Governmental Commission, chaired by the Russian prime minister, if a foreign investor wants to acquire control over a company holding a subsoil use license for a deposit of federal significance (i.e. recoverable oil reserves of 70 million tons or more, or gas reserves of 50 billion cubic meters or more, and underneath land designated for defence or security). For deposits on the continental shelf, existing laws basically limit activity to Gazprom and Rosneft.

The politics of gas markets: state interests and structured trade

We now come to the crux of this particular field of trade: the dance between market and political actors and forces. Potential gains from participating in global hydrocarbon markets provides both political and market opportunities for Russia's hydrocarbon companies, especially those state-owned. That Russia continues to export means its hydrocarbon companies were embedded in global market relations. One hypothesis is that global forces of supply and demand, and of competition (but also possible collusion), would compel particular corporate strategies and structures, whether from competitive pressures or from field pressures to conform to common corporate practices (Fligstein 1990, 2001). Alternatively, we might expect market forces to compel Russian companies to find niches so as to reduce exposure to competitive and market pressures (Hannan and Freeman 1989).

However, such hypotheses are grounded in theories developed from market-oriented economies, in particular the American economy, in which the state sets parameters of legal economic behaviour but otherwise does not participate actively *in* the economy. Comparative studies in political economy have long noted variation in states' roles in national economies: from state ownership and support of monopolies in French *dirigisme*, to one-time state ownership but current support for market relations in Great Britain, to state support both for market competition and social foundations to support healthy economic performance (German ordoliberalism). While theoretically states might be distant actors in state-owned enterprises, delegating strategic decision-making to managers and profiting (or losing) from their decisions, the temptation to use such assets for political ends is often quite great, as Latin American countries discovered in the decades of important substitution between the 1930s and 1980s (Haggard 1990). State strategies might include using state-owned enterprises as cash cows (if they are profitable), as sources of employment and other goods for citizens, and as insulation from global economic shocks (one original impetus for import substitution industrialization in Latin America after the Great Depression). We can add that states can also use state-owned enterprises as tools in geopolitical competition: this has a historical pedigree, as we see with mercantilism in England and the use of National Champions in France.

The mix of private and state-owned oil companies has meant some diversity in strategies for developing capacity, and Russia is constrained to an extent by the structures of the global oil market in which OPEC plays a leading role. The geopolitics of oil, in other words, revolve in part around collective decisions of this particular cartel that can constrain Russia's freedom to act. But in 2017, cartel and some non-OPEC oil producers led by Russia made a deal known as OPEC-plus (on new OPEC strategy see Hickin 2017) in order to effect production cuts by 1.8 million barrels per day (bpd) and raise oil prices. Primarily Russia's state oil companies Rosneft and Gazprom Neft as well as private Lukoil reduced production by 300 000 bpd with OPEC for the first time. However, they have been pushing for a clear message on how to exit cuts so the market does not flip into a deficit too soon, and prices do not rally too fast and rival US shale firms do not boost output further. In this respect, Russia needs much lower oil prices to balance its budget than OPEC's leader Saudi Arabia, which is preparing a stock market listing for national energy champion Aramco and would hence benefit from pricier crude (Lawler et al. 2018). In May 2018 with oil at about US$80 per barrel, Russia and OPEC not only reached their goal but also established a high level of trust to ensure that this deal would be long lasting through new forms of cooperation including, *inter alia*, "measuring market stability", consultations, etc. The impending return of American sanctions aimed at Iran's oil exports, along with the radical decline of oil production in Venezuela, offer the opportunity for Russia and other producers to raise output while the group as a whole remains within its overall target. Thus, being a price-taker on the global oil market, Russia has substantially changed her oil diplomacy and achieved some tangible results in negotiations with the key OPEC member state, Saudi Arabia. Contrary to the Cold War era, when OPEC, led by the Saudis, substantially contributed to the demise of Soviet power, especially after invasion of Afghanistan, it seems that Russia's deep involvement in the Syrian crisis did not prevent OPEC states from finding a common denominator with Russia. Oil (or interest in keeping oil prices stable and high) now closely binds former foes.

In contrast, if oil has a mix of state and private actors and interests pursuing both market and geopolitical goals, the state and politics are more central in the gas sector. Natural gas accounts for over half of domestic energy consumption, used in homes (cooking, heating) and electricity production (Mitrova 2014). For this reason, gas prices are important to public mood – indeed, the Russian government has been resistant since the 1990s to raise gas prices too much so as to avoid popular discontent. Additionally, Gazprom invested in non-gas projects of more value to the Russian state, e.g. infrastructure work for the Sochi Olympics in 2014 and the 2018 World Cup.

Additionally, foreign trade in natural gas began with market incentives but gained a geopolitical logic over time. In the 1990s, as Boris Yeltsin's Russia and the West seemed to be coming closer diplomatically, Russian supply of gas to Europe seemed an economically logical policy, an evolution from earlier Soviet supply to Europe.[4] Readily available Russian gas could replace coal, nuclear, and oil for ecological and geopolitical reasons. In particular, Germany and Turkey were quite willing to import Russian gas, because the price was competitive, transportation was easy via pipelines (some begun in the Soviet era), and until the Ukrainian "Orange Revolution", Europeans considered Russia a noteworthy partner. This deepened European dependence on Russian gas. However, relations between Russia and the European Union began to sour after 2004, and European businesses began to react negatively to asymmetries in market access – for example, Gazprom had easier access to investment in European markets and share ownership in European firms than vice versa. Even if Putin did not openly wield gas as a tool of soft power, European leaders knew of their dependence on Russian gas. Even though European gas purchases have been important for Gazprom income, European perceptions of energy security shifted. But growing concern about climate change supports the earlier appreciation for Russian gas which is viewed as rather a clean energy source.

Political tensions over the 2014 Ukrainian crisis and continuing disputes between Kiev and Moscow over Ukrainian gas debts led the European Commission to perform a "stress test" to estimate the effects on 38 European countries of Russia ending its supply of gas for six months. Bulgaria, Finland, and Estonia would be hit the hardest (losing three-quarters to all of their gas), with Latvia and Croatia the least harmed.[5] This drew yet more attention to the geopolitics of gas. As well, the hydrocarbon boom in the United States (e.g. from fracking) and growing potential for shipping LNG have promised competition to Gazprom, especially in Europe, thus reducing its global market and geopolitical positions. Finally, Europe's efforts to liberalize its energy markets and to integrate its energy grid, Russia's accession to the WTO, and the emergence of smaller, independent Russian companies producing gas have called into question Gazprom's reliance on long-term contracts, oil-indexed prices, and the use of pipelines. This said, American LNG will not free Europe from Russian gas any time soon, and Russia will remain Europe's dominant gas supplier for the foreseeable future – more than 30 percent of gas continues to come from Russia, and much American and other LNG might go to Asia rather than Europe (Bordoff and Houser 2014). Other political strategies might limit Gazprom's trade and soft power potential in Europe. New EU legislation (the "third energy package") will limit the operations of Gazprom and its subsidiaries in Europe. In September 2012 the European Commission opened investigations into whether Gazprom was abusing its market position. This has involved Gazprom's activities in Bulgaria, the Czech Republic, Estonia, Hungary, Latvia, Lithuania, Poland, and Slovakia. As well, some WTO members (primarily from the EU) question Russia's high export tariffs on oil and gas exports, as well as dual pricing on the world and domestic markets. Finally, sanctions following the crises over Ukraine in 2014 have undercut Russian oil and gas sales. Novatek, Russia's No. 2 gas producer, was put on the Western sanctions list, limiting its ability to raise funds in Western markets. Novatek leads the aforementioned multibillion Yamal LNG project in the Russian Arctic, which is expected to more than double Russia's share of the global liquefied natural gas market.

Russian hydrocarbon trade, which looked quite promising in the 2000s, faces challenges. While gas exports to Europe in 2017 was at its highest since the 1970s (194.4 billion cubic meters) and the price of oil has been slowly increasing (Gazprom export 2018), the country's reliance on hydrocarbon exports became patently clear when the prices of both had dropped earlier and the Russian economy stagnated, with growth in 2017 half the global average and structural deformations revealed. Further, the effect of geopolitics in the European market, and the post-2014 sanction regime and worsening relations with the West, have also made it difficult to obtain investment while also providing incentives for those countries to find new supplies of hydrocarbons or energy. However, post-2014 geopolitics have added yet another wrinkle to hydrocarbon trade: a pivot to Asian markets. Indeed, the concept of "energy diplomacy" in Russian academic and political discourse first became fashionable when oil prices were high in the 2000s. This new approach, combined with Vladimir Putin's December 2005 declaration that Russia should become "an energy superpower", led analysts to conceptualize Russia's energy strategy as motivated by a geopolitical calculus (Milov 2006, p. 3). Russia's elite can create energy alliances with China to reduce the impact of sanctions and to provide the foundation for future interdependence and relations.[6] Export tariffs on Russia's hydrocarbons and its products are still kept high[7] – for crude oil about 65 percent, for natural gas 30 percent, and for gasoline 90 percent (Sutyrin et al. 2012; WTO 2011).

Membership in the WTO did not entail serious implications for the business of Gazprom. State regulation of gas tariffs in Russia was preserved even upon accession of Russia to this organization (entry to equal return prices were not planned earlier than in 2015 and it did not happen by now), whereas relations between Gazprom and Russian consumers are arranged in the form of "standard commercial contracts" as it has been before. Initially export contracts of Gazprom, which gave the monopolist about 50 percent of its proceeds, were not affected as well. No special commitments on abolishment of export duties on pipeline gas were stipulated in the Agreement on WTO Accession. The desire of the WTO to limit the export duty on LNG from Russia (21 percent, but not more than €40 per ton) is no longer urgent as at present export duties on Gazprom LNG from Sakhalin are not applied (instead, product-sharing agreement is used). As for a new Yamal LNG project, the Government has already made a decision to establish zero export duty. But potential competition with American LNG in Europe might affect export strategy of Russian energy companies. According to government plans, export duties might shrink gradually, and in parallel domestic prices on gasoline and natural gas would rise in order to bridge the gap between profits made by oil companies and Gazprom respectively on external and domestic markets and keep competitiveness of Russian energy goods. At the same time, in order to avoid deficit of gasoline, kerosene, and diesel on the domestic market, the government has reserved the right to increase export duties up to 90 percent on these products (Kremlin 2018).

Corporate capitalism? The political economy of agricultural trade

If oil and gas reveal that the determinants of trade can be as much political as economic, the case of agriculture and trade makes a similar point – except in this case, by the relatively lower level of state involvement until 2014, at which point continent geopolitics shifted the nature of trade. For reasons of space, our discussion of trade in the agricultural sector will be more concise.

Agriculture presents a puzzle: After almost a century of painful and dramatic agricultural experiments resulted in starvation (1930s) and later dependency on import of foreign grain and other basic basic foodstuffs, Russia is potentially self-sufficient and becoming an increasingly important food exporter. Agriculture is one of the fastest growing non-hydrocarbon sectors in Russia, with a growth rate of 2.4 percent over the last 15 years. In 2005, the Putin government identified agriculture as a national priority to receive more funding (available thanks to the post-2000 petrodollar windfall), which led to federal programmes to revive agribusiness. After nearly a decade of discussion, the Medvedev government approved a "Food Security Doctrine" on February 1, 2010, that aimed to develop agriculture and fisheries and in general to respond to sudden shifts in international and domestic food markets, so as to guarantee a reliable supply of domestically produced food for the population and to participate effectively in international cooperation on food security. The doctrine identified risks to and mechanisms for Russian food security, and it set threshold values for domestic production of particular food products: no less than 95 percent domestic production of grain, 80 percent for sugar, 80 percent for vegetable oil, 85 percent for meat, 90 percent for milk, 80 percent for fish, and 95 percent for potatoes (Kremlin 2010). Joining the WTO meant the possibility of foreign competition, although overall Russian agriculture was protected through the transition period – albeit some producers of pork and meat had serious concerns (Nazarova 2013). More troubling was the sudden change in the geopolitical climate and global economy. The year 2014 was hard on Russia due to multiple challenges: a crash in the global price of oil, geopolitical pressures, and Western sanctions. GDP dropped by 0.6 percent, the ruble lost value nearly half its value, inflation spiked, and the stock market tumbled. Russia's economy suffered another recession between 2015 and 2017, which led to a 0.2 percent decrease in GDP for 2016. Russian agriculture did not avoid sharing economic pain: production dropped from US$86.4 billion annual during 2008–2010, to around US$60.0 billion (much due to ruble devaluation) in 2015–2017. Yet over the 2015–2017 period, growth was at 3.5 percent per year, and in 2017 agriculture counted for 4.4 percent of GDP (in contrast to 3.8 percent before 2012) (World Bank 2017). Some oligarchs, such as Potanin, Deripaska, Abramovich, and the Magamedov brothers (who at present are under arrest for fraud and other crimes), turned their attention to agriculture. The politics of sanctions and counter-sanctions in 2014 and after helped this sector: between 2014 and 2016, imports of food products declined from US$60 billion to US$20 billion, while exports reached US$20.5 billion in 2017 – almost a sevenfold increase from US$3 billion in 2005.

Russia could become a powerhouse for agricultural trade. Yet who will drive the direction of development for agricultural trade – smaller private farmers, agricultural oligarchs, or the state, or some combination of these actors? If the record from the past is any guide, and if we properly extrapolate from recent years, the state will not be absent, but its role will be different, and private elites will dominate this sector – resulting in a field of trade closer to corporate capitalism than *dirigisme*.

Structure of the field: corporations, farmers, and a relatively distance state

This sector is split between smaller farmholdings and larger businesses. A substantial share of agricultural output is produced by household plots. This includes mostly labor-intensive products, such as potatoes, vegetables, meat, and milk: approximately 50 percent of meat and milk is produced by small farms, as is around 60 percent of wool and 25 percent of eggs. Overall, however, agribusiness predominates: agricultural enterprises account for 45.7 percent of total agricultural output, versus 7.5 percent from private farms and individual entrepreneurs. Grain makes up 16.4 percent of Russia's gross agricultural production, for US$14.2 billion annually. Grain crops constitute about 60 percent of cultivated land. The share of grain in gross agricultural production declined in 2009–2010 after peaking in 2008, when the grain harvest was 108.2 million tons. This increased again, with 2017 bringing a record harvest of 134.1 million tons (World Bank 2017). This said, according to former Minister for Agriculture Nikolai Fedorov, 19.87 million hectares of agricultural land (of 56 million) are in the hands of individual and corporate entities but not in use, including 11.4 million hectares of arable land. By using this land at the same level of productivity, Russia could double grain output (Federation Council of the Russian Federation 2016).

One scenario might be redistribution of land to large holding companies controlled by regional elites or oligarchs diversifying holdings. The Table 3.2 provides

Table 3.2 Top companies in Russian agribusiness and trade

Company • *Owner(s); size; headquarters*	*Specialization*	*Revenue, rubles*	*Foreign investors*	*Markets/interests*	*Access to Power*
Commonwealth • Alexander and Natalia Lutsenko; 2,500 employees; Svetly, Kaliningrad	Proteins and oils from vegetable and animal materials; export of grain	149 billion (2016)	IFC; Mitsui & Co	Russia; EU; Middle East; Brazil, Paraguay	Governor of Kaliningrad; Indirectly via first vice-prime-minister Igor Shuvalov
Miratorg • Alexander and Viktor Linnik; 21,000 employees; Moscow region	Meat and meat processing, ready meals. Largest pork producer (12% of market)	112 billion (2016). Largest investor in Russian agribusiness	Brazil	Russia and EEU. Planned capacity of 4 million pigs per year. Aggressive approach to private farmers	Since 2008, by Government's decree belongs to 295 national systemically important economic institutions. Operates in 13 regions
EFKO Group • Valery Kustov and partners; 14.500 employees; Voronezh	Specialty oils, mayonnaise, vegetable oil, ketchup, soap	2016: 107 billion rubles	Mubadala Development Company (UAE) and their partners	Russia, EEU	Since 2015, belongs to national important economic institutions Operates in five regions
PJSC "Cherkizovo Group" • Igor Babayev, sons Sergey and Evgeny Mikhailov; 22.800 employees; Moscow	Meat and meat processing. Largest poultry and meat producer, second largest pork producer	2017: 90.5 billion rubles	Listed at LSE	Russia and EEU	Regions where operates
Rusagro Group LLC • Vadim Moshkovich (senator 2006–14) and family; 13,362 employees; Moscow	Sugar, cereals, meat, oils	2016: 84 billion rubles	Listed at LSE	Russia, EEU	Federal and regional governments

(*Continued*)

Table 3.2 (Continued)

Company • *Owner(s); size; headquarters*	*Specialization*	*Revenue, rubles*	*Foreign investors*	*Markets/interests*	*Access to Power*
Agro-Belogorye • Vladimir Zotov; 8500 employees; Belgorod	Meat processing. Fourth largest pork producer in Russia (1.43 million pigs, 2016).	2017: 67 billion rubles		Russia and EEU	Member of Belgorod regional duma and former head of Economic department of Belgorod Administration
Aston • Vadim Vikulov; 4300 employees; Rostov-on-Don	Vegetable oil, food ingredients, cereals	2016: 57 billion rubles.		Russia and EEU	Known for support of ROChs and sport
LLC Reef Trading House • Petr Khodykin; 2500 employees; Rostov-on-Don	Purchase and sale of agricultural products. 2.8 million tons of grain exported	2015: 50 billion rubles		Russia, EEU, Middle East	
Prodimex Group • Igor Khudokormov; Moscow region	Cereals, sugar (produces 22.5% of Russian sugar). Owns 570,000 hectares of land	2016: 63.8 billion rubles		Russia, EEU, far abroad	

Sources: Osipov (2015), Sudrugestvo (2016), Agroinvestor (2018), Kostyrev (2017), and RIF (2018).

information on top companies. Most are vertically integrated and operate in South and Central Russia. Half belong to a privileged group of "nationally important economic institutions", a status guaranteeing state support in case of need. All behave aggressively to expand business at the expense of small and medium size companies – they employ administrative tools for mergers and acquisitions, and only a few are listed on the London Stock Exchange. Another common feature for most companies is direct access to local authorities and the federal government. Finally, except for grain producers, top companies focus on markets in Russia and the Eurasian Economic Union (EEU). Farmers and others in the agricultural sector say that then acting minister Aleksandr Tkachev lobbied in support of the interests of his family and his company, Agrocomplex – after this, former governor of the Krasnodar region received his post, Agrocomplex bought competitors at a frantic pace. In 2018, Agrocomplex bought a sugar plant for ₽10 billion, and later purchased the Pavlovsk and Tikhoretskii sugar factories and the sugar firm Crystal. (Let us add that the minister's relatives bought 75 percent of the Tambov sugar company [TSC].) The Russian Antimonopoly service did not find any violations in these deals despite the fact that there is a threat of monopolization of the market. The concentration in Tkachev's hands of such a number of powerful plants made his family the fifth largest producer of sugar in Russia (RBC 2017).

The initial delay in agricultural recovery from the Soviet period and 1990s was due, in part, to lack of initiative from the state to support or enforcement of the restructuring of ownership, organization, and trade in this sector. The Agrarian lobby was among the weaker groups in the Duma and in the system of informal Kremlin "clans" in the 1990s. As a result, the sector was not as defended as, say, Gazprom and the gas sector, either from oligarch predation or foreign competition. However, agrarian interests were not without allies. The main goal of agrarian actors from 1993 to 2003 was to maintain or increase state support and to write off debts.

In 1998, under Prime Minister Evgeny Primakov, the Agrarian lobby succeeded in the passing of the federal law "On price parity for agricultural and industrial goods for agribusiness and proper compensation". This provided for writing off all debts to federal budget and all extrabudgetary funds accumulated by farmers before January 1, 1999; forgiving debts for fuel and electricity accumulated up to July 1999; introducing a 5 percent discount on energy; and requiring the Central Bank to provide agribusiness with ₽12 billion worth of loans for five years at a quarter of formal refinancing rate. However, Boris Yeltsin vetoed this proposal, and the project was eventually abandoned in 2002.

In the wake of failures to protect the sector, the Agrarian Party began to cooperate with United Russia in 2004 and dismissed its earlier project of building "agrarian socialism". In 2008, the Agrarian Party was dissolved, with most of its members joining United Russia, but in 2012 reemerged. To prevent open conflict with United Russia, other proponents created an alternative party under the leadership of Olga Bashmachnikova from the Association of Farmers and Agri-Cooperatives of Russia. This Association was founded in 1990 and uniting 68 regional organizations with more than 93,000 farming households and agricultural cooperatives, offered amendments to federal laws to protect the sector (AKKOR 2018). Alas, a change in electoral law in 2015 led the Agrarian Party not to participate in elections and to support Putin in 2018, in part because he had supported subsidies for farmers. Pavel Grudinin, one of the most successful businessmen in this sector, became the Communist Party's presidential nominee for the 2018 elections. He had taken over a state-run strawberry farm in 1995 and privatized it as a social enterprise that reportedly pays its workers significantly higher wages than other farms and provides them with modern apartments and health care, as well as parks and subsidies for their children (RBC 2018). This said, Grudinin received less than 12 percent of the vote.

As the Russian elite does not believe Western sanctions will end soon, and counter-sanctions will remain in place for some time, Russian agriculture can grow not only because of less competition and state subsidies for import substitution – some in new fields such as aquaculture – but also because millions of hectares of land remain unused and thus a source for investment and profit. For these reasons, Russian agricultural trade policy is mostly inward looking. Exports have been growing mostly for grain. At the same time, actors in this sector are interested in foreign investment to aid further modernization of infrastructure (more than 40 percent of which is outdated), innovations, and access to foreign markets, possibly including Europe, Asia (China), Africa, and the Middle East (TASS 2018). Further, according to the 2016 all-Russia agricultural census, over the last ten years the number of farming households has dropped by 38.7 percent, from 285,100 to 174,600. This is due to inadequate state support and aggressive competitive policies by corporations. According to communists and agrarians, there is a high risk of oligopolies emerging in the field in crucial regions, followed by further degradation of Russia's provinces and rising unemployment. Finally, Russian agribusiness indebtedness is almost equal to turnover. The situation has been improving for small companies since 2018 because of the new system of short-term loans at 5 percent interest, for which the Ministry of Agriculture covers the margin with the market rate. Should Russian agribusiness profit sufficiently from its defended position in the Russian market and invest profits wisely, there might be an even better possibility for expanding into foreign markets – geopolitics notwithstanding.[8] Meanwhile, there is consensus among smaller farmholdings and larger businesses: both welcome the state's decision to maintain the counter-sanction regime until the end of 2018 and preferably longer. In a sense, their dream came true, as the Russian government now protects its agricultural sector against Western competitors more than any other time in the post-Soviet period. This said, we should not overstate effects of all trade policies: the extensive use of various NTBs vis-à-vis Georgian wine and mineral water, as well as milk products from Belarus, made little difference for Russian producers and consumers, and seemed to be politically motivated (Lomagin 2017, pp. 98–101).

Contrasting outcomes and state structure

In the end, hydrocarbon actors and their lobby won the day. Agribusiness cannot be said to have "lost", given the potential for profit from domestic sales given the size of the country and the regime of counter-sanctions, a novel form of protectionism and indirect form of subsidy. At the same time, the agricultural sector did not get its way until geopolitics provided a powerful enough opportunity: support for agribusiness was more *accidental* than planned.

How can we explain variation in outcomes? State support did not depend on electoral constituencies. Agribusiness could potentially mobilize electoral support in the so-called Red Zone (agrarian regions) and was not the same target as hydrocarbon elites, even if the latter contributed to a burst of economic growth in the first half of the 2000s: the government gained more currency from this than oil or gas companies, and there is no evidence to the contrary. Even in the 1990s, agricultural business and trade had less to do with "democracy" and more to do with Kremlin clans and proximity to Boris Yeltsin's administration, which had the greatest say over privatization and other economic policies. Agribusiness in the 1990s faced a two-sided disadvantage: it was a backward-looking, defensive association of elites and organizations at a time when Yegor Gaidar and his allies were looking to break socialism, and when Gaidar et al. had Yeltsi's ear. While the hydrocarbon sector was also not well reformed in the 1990s, the oligarchs were more interested in that sector, and these were reformers' natural allies: younger, oriented to finance and some form of capitalism, they were the (relatively) "sober and strong" on whom Yegor Gaidar, Anatoly Chubais, and other reformers had placed their bets. That is, networks were important, but there were plenty of network relations around Yeltsin's Kremlin; what mattered was the interests and ideology of those closest to power. In the 1990s, Gazprom remained a state monopoly because Viktor Chernomyrdin could protect it; part of the oil sector was privatized because there was no one powerful enough to defend it. On the other hand, hydrocarbon elites were not as "Soviet" as those in agriculture, and so were treated as innocuous.

Under Putin, the story changed somewhat. Hydrocarbons were a hot commodity, and the state regained some control over oil and retained control over the gas sector. Agriculture, on the other hand, was left to those oligarchs and other elites who toed the Putin party line, as well as to smaller but politically less powerful actors. The failure of the agrarian lobby in the 1990s meant they were not much of a force to be reckoned with. After 2014, food security became a more important political topic, such that the state turned to protection and subsidies. However, this did not mean "agriculture" as a set of actors with a shared collective identity and interests gained political capital. This field remains fragmented between corporate entities and smaller landholders, and it is not as important to the global economy – and thus to the Russian state's geopolitical interests as oil and gas. For this reason, the state has not actively reshaped this field, as it has for oil and gas and to the benefit of the state and elite allies in that field.

We should also not ignore the global market and geopolitics, which have been important in our narrative. Russia had a more favourable factor endowment in the 2000s and benefited from hydrocarbon prices. Combined with the politics of privatization, the state could use Gazprom and natural gas for soft politics abroad and popular patronage at home. This is clear from the evidence: natural gas trade in Russia is a handmaiden of politics, first and foremost, from subsidies to the population to legislation that protects gas fields and trade for Gazprom. Until 2014, agricultural trade faced some foreign competition and did not have nearly the same presence in the global market because of underinvestment. Whether important substitution can change this remains to be seen; certainly corporatization of agricultural production and trade means at least an improved position in the domestic market, but breaking out into the global market will require much more investment in production, marketing, and the like – a function of know-how as much as of money. Oil has been in the middle, its trade shaped by politics and market. Given that some major Russian players have been private for some time (e.g. Lukoil) and that the global oil market has major players itself (from OPEC to the United States), the Russian state has been able to gain from oil income but has not been able to use oil trade so freely for soft power. As a result, the state has had to use a soft touch oil trade.

Russian trade in agriculture and hydrocarbons has been shaped by politics and markets, with the former gaining ground after 2014. Can Russia avoid the pitfalls of import substitution and state-owned enterprises? Oil and gas remain sources of income, and agricultural exports have increased – as of this writing (July 5, 2018), the Dmitrii Patrushev reported that grain exports for July 2017–18 were 52.4 million tons, a 49 percent increase over the previous same period (Rambler 2018). Yet short-term gains do not always translate into longer-term trends, and so the lessons of Latin America still provide a warning to politicians and scholars alike. Short-term gain is possible, but over time states can become addicted to the gains of state ownership and protection. If the state needs to restructure hydrocarbon firms, then Russian employees might lose jobs and Russians themselves might lose some advantages, such as relatively cheap natural gas. Agricultural trade might ultimately become competitive on the world market – but will this make Russia another world breadbasket (like the United States) or more dependent on those very global markets (as Latin America learned repeatedly in the twentieth century)? The advantage of the market is that private actors, not political elites, become a major target of public ire during hard times, and the state can use private enterprise as a political scapegoat. This is not so when the state is deeply involved in trade. Further, private actors have narrower interests and incentives; restructuring, no easy task, is less complicated because business elites answer to the market and to investors, not a broader public that might vote, or at the least confers legitimacy. State protection can work, but not in all circumstances (Evans 1995). Finally, the kind of *dirigisme* Putin is pursuing requires a state techocracy with requisite skills and capacity to act. It is far from clear that Russia has the skilled and autonomous technocracy that even Mexico had in the 1980s and 1990s (not to speak of France). The Mexican Miracle and French Miracle of the 1950s gave way to stagnation (and in Mexico to crisis by the 1980s). Will we witness – if we are not already witnessing – a repeat of history, as *dirigisme* without nuance drags down the state and the economy?

Notes

1 Note that the new Minister of Agriculture is Dmitrii Patrushev, the older son of Nikolai Patrushev, a former FSB director and Secretary of the National Security Council. This

might mean that agribusiness finally has a powerful representative inside the Kremlin, and, in an expansion of *dirigisme*, that petrodollars could flow into the sector to help develop its position at home and in the global market, especially vis-à-vis Eurasia and Africa.

2 There is a debate among economists, and between Russia and its main market, the European Union, over the appropriate basis for pricing Russian gas: export netback parity versus long run marginal cost. EU authorities use the former benchmark, and anything lower is an unwarranted subsidy to Russian domestic consumers and manufacturers. Many on the Russian side argue that the second benchmark recognizes the value of Russia's abundant gas resources, which Russian consumers should be allowed to enjoy (Gustafson 2012, p. 503; for the WTO dispute on this issue see Bohanes and Markitanova 2015).

3 Sources for this discussion on regulation of transportation are from the Russian government's own sites: www.pravo.gov.ru (official portal for legal information); www.supcourt.ru (Supreme Court of the Russian Federation); www.garant.ru/ http://english.garant.ru/about (Garant, a legal information system that provides a database of Russian legal acts); www.consultant.ru (the largest Russian service network with a database of Russian legal acts). See also Josefson and Rotar (2018).

4 After 1973, the USSR seemed a more reliable partner for hydrocarbon trade than Arab countries, who used an oil embargo to punish the West for supporting Israel. In the late 1970s Soviet leaders entered into negotiations with firms from Western Europe and the United States to develop the Urengoi natural gas field in Siberia, the largest gas field in the world. Negotiations centered on building an enormous pipeline that would stretch from Siberia to the Soviet–Czech border. In return for participation in the project, West European countries were to receive large and secure supplies of Soviet natural gas for 25 years, amounting to about one-third of their natural gas needs. The US$30 billion project was viewed as the biggest East–West trade deal in history.

5 Note that this might overstate negative impacts, as the EU could also buy LNG on the global market, create, and then use gas reserves, turn to Norway, and even invest in other fuel sources, e.g. biomass.

6 However, the Asian pivot could also lock Russian into dependency on Chinese demand, while China could play off other suppliers against Russia. Thus, the pivot is a potential double-edged sword. Chinese demand might also maintain the predominance of hydrocarbon trade and income for the Russian economy.

7 The only exception is LNG, which is exported without export duties.

8 Note that agricultural products are not on the radar for sanctions, at the moment.

Bibliography

Agroinvestor 2018, *Agro-Belegore*, viewed 6 June 2018, www.agroinvestor.ru/companies/a-z/agro-belogore/

AKKOR 2018, *Ob Assotsiatsii*, viewed 6 June 2018, www.akkor.ru/about.html

Alt, J and Shepsle, K 1990, *Perspectives on Positive Political Economy*, Cambridge University Press, New York.

Balzer, H 2005, 'The Putin Thesis and Russian Foreign Policy,' *Post-Soviet Affairs*, vol. 21, no. 3, pp. 210–225.

Bohanes, J and Markitanova, A 2015, 'A Few Reflections on DS474 and the Intersection of Russia's Domestic Energy Policies and the EU's Anti-dumping Cost Replacement Methodology', *Vestnik SPbGU. Serie 5*, no. 2, pp. 72–89.

Bordoff, J and Houser, T 2014, *American Gas to the Rescue? The Impact of US LNG Exports on European Security and Russian Foreign Policy*, Center on Global Energy Policy, Columbia University, viewed 6 June 2018, http://energypolicy.columbia.edu/sites/default/files/CGEP_American%20Gas%20to%20the%20Rescue%3F.pdf

CEIC 2018, *Russia Crude Oil: Exports 1995–2017*, viewed 6 June 2018, www.ceicdata.com/en/indicator/russia/crude-oil-exports

Dobbin, F 1994, *Forging Industrial Policy*, Cambridge University Press, New York.

Douglas, R 2015, *The Depth of Russia: Oil, Power, and Culture After Socialism*, Cornell University Press, Ithaca.

Evans, P 1995, *Embedded Autonomy*, Princeton University Press, Princeton.

Federation Council of the Russian Federation 2016, 'Obespechenie prodovolstvennoi bezopasnosti Rossiiskoi Federatsii', *Analaticheskii vestnik*, no. 34 (633), viewed 6 June 2018, http://council.gov.ru/media/files/d7AyThMfOHGKnaLJUoATIt3pvjU2HazD.pdf

Fish, MS 2005, *Democracy Derailed in Russia: The Failure of Open Politics*, Cambridge University Press, New York.

Fligstein, N 1990, *The Transformation of Corporate Control*, Harvard University Press, Cambridge.

Fligstein, N 2001, *The Architecture of Markets*, Princeton University Press, Princeton.

Gazprom export 2018, *Gas Supplies to Europe*, viewed 6 June 2018, www.gazpromexport.ru/en/statistics/

Goldman, MI 2008, *Petrostate. Putin, Power, and the New Russia*, Oxford University Press, New York.

Gustafson, T 2012, *Wheel of Fortune: The Battle for Oil and Power in Russia*, Harvard University Press, Cambridge.

Haggard, S 1990, *Pathways From the Periphery*, Cornell University Press, Ithaca.

Hannan, M and Freeman, J 1989, *Organizational Ecology*, Harvard University Press, Cambridge.

Hickin, P 2017, *OPEC-Plus: Old Strategies, New Manifesto – Fuel for Thought*, viewed 6 June 2018, http://blogs.platts.com/2017/06/05/opec-plus-old-strategies-new-manifesto/

Josefson, J and Rotar, A 2018, *Oil and Gas Regulation in the Russian Federation: Overview*, Thomson Reuters Practical Law, viewed 6 June 2018, https://uk.practicallaw.thomsonreuters.com/0-527-3028?transitionType=Default&contextData=(sc.Default)&firstPage=true

Karl, TL 1997, *Paradox of Plenty: Oil Booms and Petrostates*, University of California Press, Berkeley.

Kostyrev, A 2017, *Prodimeks' meshaet sakhar s molokom*, Kommersant, December 22, viewed 6 June 2018, www.kommersant.ru/doc/3503512

Kremlin 2010, *Utverzhdena Doktrina prodovol'stvennoj bezopasnosti Rossijskoj Federacii*, viewed 6 June 2018, http://kremlin.ru/events/president/news/6752

Kremlin 2018, *Direct Line With Vladimir Putin*, 7 June, viewed 6 June 2018, http://en.kremlin.ru/events/president/news/57692

Lawler, A, El Gamal, R and Nasralla, S 2018, 'OPEC, Russia Agree Oil Cut Extension to End of 2018', *Reuters*, viewed 6 June 2018, www.reuters.com/article/us-opec-meeting/opec-russia-agree-oil-cut-extension-to-end-of-2018-idUSKBN1DU0WW

Lomagin, N 2015, 'Foreign Policy Preferences of Russia's Energy Sector: A Shift to Asia?', in: M Sussex and RE Kanet (eds.) *Russia, Eurasia and the New Geopolitics of Energy: Confrontation and Consolidation*, Palgrave Macmillan, London.

Lomagin, N 2017, 'A Cold Peace Between Russia and the West: Did Geo-Economics Fail?', in: RE Kanet (ed.) *The Russian Challenge to the European Security Environment*, Palgrave Macmillan, London.

Luong, PJ and Weinthal, E 2010, *Oil Is Not a Curse*, Cambridge University Press, Cambridge.

Miller, C 2018, *Putinomics: Power and Money in Resurgent Russia*, University of North Carolina Press, Chapel Hill.

Milov, V 2006, 'The Rise of Energy as a Political Tool', *EU-Russia Review*, no. 1, May, EU–Russia Centre, Brussels.

Mitrova, T 2014, 'The Political and Economic Importance of Gas in Russia', in: J Henderson and S Pirani (eds.) *The Russian Gas Matrix: How Markets Are Driving Change*, Oxford Institute for Energy Studies, Oxford.

Nazarova, MV 2013, APK Rossii: problem i perspektivy razvitiia v usloviiakh prisoedineniia v VTO', in: SF Sutyrin and NA Lomagin (eds.) *Chlenstvo v VTO – novyi etap uchastiia Rossii v mezhdunarodnoi torgovoi sisteme*, Izdatelskii tsentr Ekonomicheskogo Fakulteta SPbGU, St. Petersburg.

North, D 1990, *Institutions, Institutional Change, and Economic Performance*, Cambridge University Press, New York.

Osipov, A 2015, 'Postroil rynok', *Agroinvestor*, July 2015, viewed 20 July 2018, www.agroinvestor.ru/companies/article/16683-postroil-rynok/

Rambler 2018, *Minsel'hoz mozhet peresmotret' prognoz po urozhaju zerna*, July 6, viewed 20 July 2018, https://news.rambler.ru/business/40269228/?utm_content=rnews&utm_medium=read_more&utm_source=copylink

RBC 2017, *Kompania semji ministra Tkacheva stala piatoi po proizvodstvu sakhara v Rossii*, June 7, viewed 20 July 2018, www.rbc.ru/business/07/06/2017/593740bc9a794700b5a743a1

RBC 2018, *Grudinin pokazal khudshii dlia KPRF rezultat na vyborakh prezidenta*, March 19, viewed 6 June 2018, www.rbc.ru/politics/19/03/2018/5aaf528d9a7947073f01bc21

RIF 2018, *Zakupka i eksport selskokhoziaistvennoi produktsii*, viewed 6 June 2018, https://rif-rostov.ru/

Ross, M 2012, *The Oil Curse: Howe Petroleum Wealth Shapes the Development of Nations*, Princeton University Press, Princeton.

Skocpol, T 1992, *Protecting Soldiers and Mothers*, Harvard University Press, Cambridge.

Strange, S 2000 'States, Firms and Diplomacy', in: *International Political Economy. Perspectives on Global Power and Wealth*, 4th edition, Routledge, Abingdon.

Stulberg, AN 2007, *Well-Oil Diplomacy: Strategic Manuipulation and Russia's Energy Statecraft in Eurasia*, State University of New York Press, Albany.

Sudrugestvo 2016, 'GK 'Sodruzhestvo' otkrylo docherniuiu kompaniiu v turtsii', *Sodrugestvo*, February 1, viewed 6 June 2018, www.sodrugestvo.ru/news/

Sutyrin, SF, Lomagin, NA, Sherov-Ignatiev, VG, Trofimenko, OY, Kapustkin, VI, Nazarova, MV and Lisitsyn, NE 2012, *Russia's Accession to the WTO: Major Commitments, Possible Implications*, International Trade Centre, Geneva, viewed 6 June 2018, www.intracen.org/uploadedFiles/Russia%20WTO%20Accession%20English.pdf

TASS 2018, *Innovatsii v selskom khoziaistve i zaniatost v agrarnom sektore: v poiske balansa*, March 26, viewed 6 June 2018, http://tass.ru/pmef-2017/articles/4273445

Tinbergen, J 1962, *Shaping the World Economy: Suggestions for an International Economic Policy*, The Twentieth Century Fund, New York.

Wade, R 2003, *Governing the Market: Economic Theory and the Role of Government in East Asian Industrialization*, Princeton University Press, Princeton.

World Bank 2017, 'Russia's Recovery – How Strong Are Its Shoots?', *Russia Economic Report*, no. 38, November, viewed 6 June 2018, https://openknowledge.worldbank.org/bitstream/handle/10986/28930/30-11-2017-17-58-52-forwebNovFINALRERENGfull.pdf?sequence=7&isAllowed=y

WTO 2011, *Report of the Working Party on the Accession of the Russian Federation, Commitments on Goods. PART V – Export Duties*, WT/ACC/RUS/70/Add.1, viewed 6 June 2018, www.wto.org/english/tratop_e/schedules_e/rus.zip

Yamal LNG 2018, viewed 6 June 2018, http://yamallng.ru/en/project/about/

4 The theory and practice of economic sanctions

Maarten Smeets[1]

Introduction

The number of sanction episodes seems to be on the rise and sanctions have increasingly gained in popularity in recent years despite the fact that the literature does not present conclusive evidence that economic sanctions are an effective policy instrument. The objectives of the sanction episodes vary and range from merely being an expression of dissatisfaction to demanding a change of policies in the targeted country. The higher the level of ambition and change envisaged, the more difficult it is to achieve. This is particularly so when economic sanctions are taken by countries individually. Even when the sanctions are backed by groups of countries collectively and ideally are covered by a decision taken by the United Nations, thus giving them the strongest international and diplomatic support and legitimacy, their success is far from being assured. The time it generally takes to align governments in support of the sanctions and reach agreement on the measures involved, often gives the target country ample opportunities to build alliances with "sanction busters" and find alternative outlets for its goods and services, thus undermining the effectiveness of the sanctions. Given that the literature and evidence shows that the rate of success is very limited, why were economic sanctions applied against the Russian Federation in its territory dispute with Ukraine?

The main objective of this chapter is to review how economic sanctions are meant to work from an analytical perspective and the challenges encountered in making sanctions an effective trade policy tool. It does not include views or take a position on the merits and/or legitimacy of the actions taken by any of the parties. Following a review of how economic sanctions are meant to work in theory, the practice will be analysed with specific reference to sanctions applied against the Russian Federation. It will be argued that given the difficulties to make sanctions effective, they should mainly be seen as tools complementing diplomatic and other forms of pressure put on the target country and are a confirmation that the countries involved in the sanction episode are serious about their request and walk the talk.

How economic sanctions are meant to work: the theory

There is quite a bit of literature on economic sanctions, but as will be argued below, the practice differs considerably from the theory. There is a tension between sanctions and the fundamental objectives of the WTO: the WTO's principle aim is to liberalize trade, whereas the direct purpose of economic sanctions is to restrict trade and such mostly for non-economic reasons. Sanctions are precisely meant to deprive countries of economic gains that can be obtained through trade. In a WTO context, the notion of sanctions is also often associated with retaliatory action resulting from the conclusion of a WTO dispute settlement process: according to the dispute settlement procedures in the WTO a party to a dispute may be authorized to withdraw concessions in order to compensate for losses suffered resulting from an unjustified trade action. The (authorized) retaliatory action resulting from WTO trade disputes follows the logic of maintaining or rather restoring a balance in rights and obligations between members when these are affected by a country applying policies inconsistent with the WTO. These issues will not be addressed.

Also, the economic and trade sanctions are mostly justified under the security exceptions and more specifically Article XXI and Article XIV bis of the GATS when services trade is involved.[2] The purpose of this chapter is not to address the legality of the sanctions under WTO rules and which were addressed in earlier writings (Smeets 2000). It is up to the WTO Members to decide on the legality of economic sanctions in the WTO and interpret the rules and WTO provisions through the Dispute settlement procedures and there may soon again be an opportunity to do so.[3] The main objective of this analysis is to assess the effects of economic and trade sanctions resulting from political decisions to act against another country and which policies or actions are being contested.

The economic theory of sanctions is largely based on a number of stylistic assumptions with regard to trade and how it can be affected by sanctions and which often don't reflect the realities. As will be seen, it also doesn't take account of human behaviour and responses, including by the leaders of countries that are facing the sanctions and which can seriously undermine the effectiveness of sanctions. So, what does the theory tell us and what are the realities?

Hufbauer, Schott, and Elliott argue that economic sanctions have only a very limited capacity to serve their intended objectives (Hufbauer et al. 2007). Overall their track record is poor. To the extent that they work, the time span for the actual impact is very short. These views are broadly supported by van Bergeijk and van Marrewijk (Bergeijk and van Marrewijk 1994). In earlier writings I have expressed reservations about the effectiveness of economic sanctions as a policy instrument and questioned their use in specific cases (Smeets 1990, 1994, 2000). Yet they continue to be a popular policy tool. The effectiveness of sanctions is further reduced today due to a growing interdependency between markets and a "shrinking world". It becomes hard to single out products that can effectively hurt the country being sanctioned and without repercussions for countries taking these punitive measures. All these aspects merit further consideration.

What are economic sanctions? Generally speaking they cover trade-restricting policies between sovereign nations, including so-called "boycotts" and "embargoes". Boycotts are generally associated with the refusal to purchase goods and services from a supplier, and embargoes imply that no goods and services will be supplied to the buyer.[4] The scope of sanctions naturally varies with each case and can include a policy to completely isolate a country and break off economic and trade relations and which is perhaps the most difficult to accomplish. Rare are the cases where a full embargo was imposed with the purpose of cutting off all economic and trade relations with a specific country. The United States tried this with Cuba for over half a century, but didn't succeed despite Cuba's vulnerability as an island nation and its geographic proximity to the United States' mainland. Cuba's vulnerability was further increased given its geographical distance from its main ally, the former Soviet Union, and its markets of supply. The sanctions have now mostly come to an end, without having achieved their objective.[5] The economic sanctions taken against North Korea are also far ranging and were further strengthened by the United States late February 2018. It was found that the sanctions are not watertight, with trade continuing between North Korea and some trading partners in one way or another (Collins et al. 2018; Manson 2018). Some time back, countries tried to isolate South Africa for many decades in order to end the Apartheid regime and which eventually ended, but it remains questionable what the contribution of the economic sanctions per se was, given that the sanctions were largely circumvented.[6]

The mechanism through which economic sanctions are believed to achieve their ultimate objectives from an economics perspective is based on a reversal of the international trade theories developed by D. Ricardo (1817) 200 years ago, who introduced the notion of trade and specialization and which assume that world economic welfare is maximized under conditions of free trade. The theories of economic sanctions are mostly associated with the Swedish economists Ohlin (1929) and Hecksher (1919) who reversed Ricardo's theory. The key element in Ricardo's theory is that different goods require different factor proportions, and different countries have different relative factor endowments. Countries will tend to have a comparative advantage in producing goods that use their most abundant factors more intensively, for this reason each country will end up exporting its abundant-factor goods in exchange for imported goods that use scarce factors intensively. Trade therefore is not a "zero-sum game" in which one side gains only what the other loses. The whole world gains from trade and both sides are at least as well off with some trade as with no trade.

What follows from the theory is that any limitation of trade, and in particular the protection of individual markets through an increase in tariffs or applying direct import restrictions through quota, will ipso facto reduce the general welfare level. The theory of economic warfare developed by Kemp in essence is based on a reversal of the Heckscher-Ohlin theory (Kemp 1964). An embargo will create a supply shock and a boycott will isolate the target country from the world market. A net welfare loss will be the result. Depending on the relative balance of powers between the countries involved and the importance of their economic interaction (large versus small country), the imposing party can explicitly depress the income and welfare level of the target country to an unacceptably low level. The weaker party will face deteriorating terms of trade and it is expected that it will be forced to comply.

One weakness in the theory is that it is essentially based on a two-good and two-country model, which suggests a strong interdependence between the two economies prior to the sanctions and hence vulnerability. The reality is different, as the world is dynamic and highly interdependent, with increasingly complex trade ties between all countries. These new realities result from the rapid growth of trade *per se*, globalization, the emergence of global production networks and a splitting up of the production process. Obviously, a correct description of trade requires a multi-good and multi-country model, with complex interrelations, both through trade and investment, subsidiaries, cross-stockholding of companies and so on, which make things a lot more complicated. Ideally, all these factors would need to be included in the equation.

The simplified approach also means that a critical condition for sanctions to be successful is already fulfilled. It assumes that the target country has little scope to escape from the sanctions, as it depends on the other good. The growing interdependency of markets and the emergence of Global Value Chains (GVCs), the increased role of services trade, e-commerce, and the role of Foreign Direct Investment (FDI) as an alternative way to penetrate markets complicate matters. In addition, sanctions are often circumvented by engaging in trade with third parties refusing to abide by them. The economic sanctions can even have the reverse effect; leaders using the sanctions as an explanation for the lower levels of growth and welfare, instead of failing economic policies. It can lead to them digging in their heels and resisting the sanctions even more, thus making it even harder to achieve the set objectives. A good illustration is presented in the sanctions that were applied against Iraq, where Saddam Hussein was even more determined than ever before to resist the outside pressures and eventually leading to a military intervention.

Recognizing the limitations and shortcomings in the classical literature on sanctions and building on several studies that were undertaken in this field, Sajjad Farayi Dizaji and van Bergeijk (2013) developed a dynamic model of sanctions taking into account various situations and leading to different scenarios. They establish that "firstly, the social impact of economic sanctions may well extend beyond the sanction episode and, secondly, that the deterioration during the initial phase will exceed the improvement during the recovery that sets in either in the second phase or when the sanction is terminated" (Dizaji and van Bergeijk 2013, p. 734). They conclude that "the costs of imposing sanctions exceed the benefits of lifting sanctions".

Given the increased interdependence and the close network of economic, trade, and investment relations among Western countries, economic sanctions are increasingly less likely to work. The large variety of sources of supply and the mobility of capital seem to facilitate the replacement of goods and services by other suppliers. Production processes have internationalized through the investment decisions of multinational corporations. In addition, trade is increasingly characterized by intra-industry or even intra-firm trade as opposed to inter-industry trade, which makes it hard to find a particular good that can be adequately singled out for sanctions.[7] This reasoning applies to a lesser extent to trade with developing countries, which often have a less diversified production and export package and would thus seem to be more vulnerable. Even then, it turns out to be difficult to effectively apply sanctions.

In the past much attention was given to the significance of strategic goods in trade, which can be of crucial importance in economic warfare. It was felt that countries would be particularly vulnerable if they were to be deprived access to strategic goods, thus creating a bottleneck in an economy. This was tested after WWII with regard to East–West trade during the Cold War and more specifically in relation to the former Soviet Union. The Coordinating Committee for Multilateral Export Controls (CoCom), created shortly after WWII was meant to prevent the Soviet Union and China from obtaining technological goods and material that had strategic significance. CoCom was abolished in 1994, following the easing of the East–West tension in 1989. There is no evidence that CoCom prevented the two countries from developing their economic potential due to the measures taken with regard to strategic goods. The discussions thus seem to have become largely hypothetical in the context of sanctions: Iran and North Korea have been able to develop their domestic nuclear activities despite the fact that the technology was supposedly not freely available on the markets.

On the question of the duration of sanctions and their short-term effects compared to the longer run, the research undertaken by Hufbauer et al. (2007) also shows that economic sanctions lose much of their effectiveness after the first and second year, which accounts for 55 percent of successful sanction episodes, followed by a steep decline. Dizaji's and van Bergeijk's empirical analysis establishes that economic sanctions can be successful in the first two years following the implementation of sanctions. They found "strong and consistent evidence for an initially significant economic impact of sanctions that wanes at the end of the simulation period for government consumption per capita, imports per capita, gross capital formation per capita and GDP per capita" (Dizaji and van Bergeijk 2013, p. 728). Accordingly, the likelihood of compliance by the targeted country decreases significantly after that time.

Another important element to be kept in mind in sanction episodes is the fact the sanctions will generally imply economic costs not only to the target, but also to the countries that initiate the sanctions through the loss of business contracts and a reduction or interruption in trade (depending on the scale of the sanctions). These costs will have to be borne by the consumer and taxpayer, which will be ready to accept this if they believe in the cause and the achievement of the objectives. The costs for the sender can be considerable and undermine both the economic rationale and the political willingness to engage in the sanctions.

As the target country is more likely to become less rather than more vulnerable to the sanctions with time, this again underscores the need for a speedy implementation of sanctions and in order to prevent the target country from organizing its resistance to the sanctions and thus undermining their efficacy. The target country can build up stocks, and take diplomatic steps to create an alliance with friendly countries and develop an import-substituting industry, or divert its trade to new trading partners. The position and role of third parties and their involvement in the sanction episode is of critical importance. "Sanction busters" can create loopholes in the sanctions and thus undermine their effectiveness. The role of alliances (with third parties) in sanction situations has been studied by Early, who researched 96 episodes of sanctions imposed by the United States over a 50-year period. The behaviour of third parties and their willingness to bust sanctions will largely depend on the economic gains they are likely to obtain (Early 2012). The target country on its side will do everything necessary to diminish the economic dependence of the sender.

It is thus crucial that the countries taking the economic sanctions decide swiftly and implement their decisions abruptly and to the fullest extent possible. While this seems to be obvious, in practice it is a difficult condition to fulfil, particularly when several countries are involved in the sanctions episode and more specifically when the sanctions are taken under the aegis of the United Nations. It is often extremely difficult to reach common agreement on the necessity for and the extent of the sanctions to be applied. There will always be countries dragging their feet and taking the economic benefits of sanctions by engaging in friendly relations with the target country in return for business contracts.

Furthermore, there are other considerations to bear in mind when using sanctions as a trade policy tool. While it would a priori seem that the effectiveness of economic sanctions largely depends on the vulnerability of the country undergoing the sanctions and the instruments available in the sanction campaign, the effectiveness of sanctions is never guaranteed. One explanation is that economic sanctions are an economic instrument that aims to achieve political objectives. Not only is it challenging as political objectives may shift, but it can equally be hard to assess the contribution of the sanctions in order to achieve a specific outcome ("attribution"). As I will argue below, in the case of Russia, the rapid fall of oil prices on world markets are likely to have had a deeper effect on the Russian economy than the sanctions. At the same time, this never was part of the sanctions' plan and cannot be influenced by the countries taking the sanctions.

Finally, but no less important, is the absence of clearly defined and specific objectives of many sanction episodes with the logical consequence that sanctions often stay in place for longer than necessary. The related problem is that in the absence of clearly specified objectives it becomes unclear when to lift sanctions without losing face and more specifically if the objectives have not been achieved. The more specific the objectives of the sanctions are defined, the easier it becomes to assess when the target has been achieved, thus allowing for a lifting of the sanctions.

Despite the weaknesses of sanctions and the lack of their effectiveness, it is definitely a preferable policy tool if it contributes to averting armed conflict, but the two often go hand in hand and sanctions are not always given enough time to be effective. Sanctions can (at least in the first instance) provide an alternative for military warfare. At the same time, governments are not always willing to allow time for sanctions to bite. One example is the intervention in Iraq in 1990, with initial sanctions put in place and then quickly followed by military intervention, thus overriding the economic sanctions per se. Iraq was generally viewed as providing almost perfect conditions for sanctions to work, but they were not given the time to do so. A similar situation occurred with the former Yugoslavia (as it was then known) in the 1980s, where armed interference complemented the economic sanctions that had been put in place. It would seem that other, mainly political factors, provided overriding arguments to use military force in both cases, irrespective of the question whether the sanctions would bite or not.

In the case of Iraq, the invasion in Kuwait gave political leaders an opportunity to get rid of Saddam Hussain. In the case of Yugoslavia, a new geopolitical balance was in the process of being established and at the same time NATO countries decided to intervene to halt what was referred to as acts of genocide in the region. The relationship between sanctions and armed conflict is studied by Erikson and Wallensteen, who provide insights into their interaction and the role of the United Nations and how it complements the goals of sanctions (Rikson and Wallensteen 2015). As, however, in both cases the sanctions were not given the time they needed to be effective, it is hard to know what would have happened without military intervention.

In the case of disputed territories by the Ukraine and the Russian Federation, the Western leaders decided to abstain from military intervention and focus on the economic and political sanctions, albeit more selectively than applying them on a full scale (Bond et al. 2015). Both the German Chancellor and American President have excluded military intervention, which could have escalated matters.

Given the weak track record of sanctions, why then would countries continue resorting to economic sanctions? They are generally recognized to be a more powerful expression of disagreement than making purely political declarations. Sanctions are meant to give teeth to these declarations and leaders want to walk the talk. It shows the domestic electorate that politicians take responsibility and do not sit on their hands and watch "evil" taking place without acting. Nevertheless, it remains uncertain to what extent they really can bite. It is thus believed that economic sanctions are a powerful foreign policy instrument instead of being a trade policy tool. Other measures may prove more effective than economic measures, including boycotting sports events (e.g. Olympic Games). Of course several measures can be taken simultaneously, thus building cumulative effects.

The practice: sanctions taken against the Russian Federation

Following actions by the Russian Federation reclaiming territories in Ukraine both the United States and the European Union responded with economic sanctions. A brief account of the chronology and content of the sanctions put in place by the US administration is provided by Nelson (2017). The economic and trade sanctions taken against Russia included a mixed bag of economic, financial, and diplomatic sanctions. Sports sanctions are also a popular ingredient in sanction episodes and where applied in 1980 when the US decided to boycott the Olympic Games in Russia. It threatened to repeat that action for the Winter Olympics at Sochi in 2014. The President of the European Council at the time, Herman van Rompuy, said in March 2014 "Sanctions are not a question of retaliation, they are a policy tool. Not a goal in themselves, but a means to an end. Our goal is to stop Russian action against Ukraine, to restore Ukraine's sovereignty – and to achieve this we need a negotiated solution" (Nelson 2017, p. 3). This shows again that the sanctions were meant to be a complementary policy tool and not the sole measure taken to achieve its objectives.

Nelson points out that "Canada, France; Germany, Italy, Japan, the United Kingdom and the United States have suspended (Russia's) participation in the G-8 and instead convened as the G-7, of which Russia is not a member, for the first time since the late 1990s" (Nelson 2017, p. 6). The simple fact of excluding Russia from the G-8 sends a strong political signal, as it was considered a major step when Russia joined the G-8 in the first place, in recognition of the role it plays on the world economic and political scene. At the same time imposing sanctions can put leaders in a delicate situation, which is the case in Germany, as the strongest European and economic partner of Russia. The position of Germany's Chancellor is of critical importance and according to Bond et al. "much will turn on whether Angela Merkel maintains her firm line: she has invested a lot in her relationship with Putin" (Bond et al. 2015, p. 16).

The sanctions include the freezing of assets for individuals and specific entities, restrictions on financial transactions with Russian firms, restrictions on oil-related products as well as on dual-use exports. Further insights are provided by Portansky (2014) who explains what measures were put in place, starting as early as March 2014 and followed by a tightening of the sanctions in April and later during the summer. Russian political leaders thus were specifically targeted by using "smart sanctions" in the belief that this would hurt the most (The Economist 2018). The sanctions thus affected a number of high-ranking Russian officials and politicians, forbidding them to enter the United States and freezing their assets and property abroad. The authors of a study prepared by the Graduate Institute of International and Development Studies in Geneva provide a detailed historical account of the sanction episode (Moret et al. 2016). It also provides insights into the costs endured by Russia and the sanctioning powers.

The sanctions affected trust in Russia and according to Portansky (2014) "resulted in capital flight and a worsening investment climate that was never particularly good". Russia witnessed a serious decline of its economy and hence its currency, the ruble, which lost nearly 50 percent of its value in 2014. This decline was caused by many factors and cannot be attributed to the sanctions per se. According to Bond et al. (2015, p. 11), "German Gref, a former minister has indicated that sanctions are having a major effect on the bank's ability to borrow money". Separately, specific market conditions can be of critical importance in sanction episodes and this applies again to the Russian Federation: the international oil market collapsed shortly after the sanctions were put in place against Russia. This was a coincidence and considerably strengthened the impact of the sanctions and the likelihood that they would contribute to their goal. The oil prices dropped to extremely low levels, hitting a low of nearly 30 US dollars in early January 2016, as opposed to well above 100 US dollars earlier in 2014. Oil and gas prices are closely linked and increase and decline in parallel. The drop in oil prices is explained by several factors unrelated to the sanctions, including the continued economic recession, thus lowering the economic demand worldwide and the rapid growth of oil production and development in the United States, which has become a net exporter of oil and gas. In addition, the OPEC decided to stick to its policy to maintain the (high) levels of oil production. The implications of these developments are worrisome for economic growth perspectives and created major budget imbalances, as well as capital outflows.

The former Russian Finance Minister Alexei Kudrin warned that the sanctions could depress the Russian economy by as much as 1–1.5 percent of GDP, which he considered "not to be disastrous for the economy" (Portansky 2014). These observations were made well before the drop in oil prices, thus underestimating the real cost to the Russian economy. Hence, the economic impact has been much more important than initially anticipated. The purchasing power of the citizens has been reduced and many goods previously accessible are no longer available, with little or no domestic substitutes available.

The vulnerability of the Russian economy is also evidenced by Sutyrin et al. (2014) who argue that, irrespective of a sanctions perspective, Russia's structural dimension has remained mostly unchanged since the 1990s, with similar patterns of trade. The Russian economy is not that diversified and therefore theoretically more vulnerable to sanctions. The authors argue that the economy is highly dependent on the importation of goods and supplies for both consumption and production. Russia is also not well-connected to GVCs and continues to be highly dependent on the export of raw materials and base products. They observe that Russian exports mainly consist of mineral products, which represent a share of nearly 70 percent of exports. Sutyrin et al. thus suggest that Russia needs to diversify its production and increase its efforts to link to GVCs. This would not only be beneficial to the Russian economy globally, but more diversity automatically diminishes the economy's vulnerability. A similar point is made by Vladimir Mau (2014), who argues that Russia faces structural problems and needs economic liberalization, which would provide the necessary modernization for institutional growth and modernize the welfare state.

Bond, Odendahl, and Rankin explain how the EU and Russia are economically intertwined and the extent to which the EU and Russia depend on each other (Bond et al. 2015).

According to their calculations, the EU is a far more important trading partner for Russia than the other way round. Based on total trade (exports and imports), the EU is roughly five times more important to Russia than vice versa. The EU buys more than half of Russian exports, equivalent to almost 10 percent of Russia's economic output (Bond et al. 2015, p. 5).

Given the trade dependency of the EU in its relation with Russia, the sanctions backfired in several ways as a result of the retaliatory actions by Russia. In the agricultural sector European farmers have been hit hard by Russia's ban on imports of fruit, vegetables, meat, dairy, fish, and other foodstuffs. The close interdependency between the two economies is also explained by Nelson (2017), who argues that Russia has a power of retaliation as well as alternative sources of supply and for the outlet of its goods, including China.

Separately, Russia has the power to deprive the West from important energy supplies and more specifically from gas, on which the European countries are highly dependent. According to the EU Commission, the sanctions are likely to have reduced the EU's economic growth in 2014 by 0–3 percent points and 0.4 percent in 2015 (Bond et al. 2015, p. 12). According to the Graduate Institute, EU exports to Russia fell by 12.1 percent and Russia exports to the EU dropped by 13.5 percent with a fall in total trade value from €326 billion to €285 billion and can mainly be attributed to a reduction in gas and oil prices (Moret et al. 2016, p. 12). At the political level, the talks on Russia's accession to the OECD were interrupted and Russia's de facto membership of the G-7 suspended, as was indicated earlier.

It was argued earlier that sanctions are often seen as a policy instrument that is used for domestic (political) consumption. In the country imposing sanctions, the leadership may show its determination and capacity to act, but this argument can work both ways depending on the determination and the power of the target country to resist and take countermeasures. It seems that the Russian leadership has largely managed to attribute the difficult economic situation that the country is experiencing to the sanctions. According to various reports, the Russian President Putin became more popular since the military intervention and benefits from large and broad support. He is capitalizing on the sanctions and Russia is reported to have managed to portray the situation as the "Great Patriotic War" (Bond et al. 2015, p. 11). In other words, there seems to be some form of cohesion building, thus leading to a natural resistance against the sanctions and undermining their efficacy.

Separately, and according to the study by the Graduate Institute, Russia is on a path of substituting the EU as a key trading partner and diversifying its trade by seeking closer relations with other countries for obtaining technology and finance and for trading agricultural goods and selling its oil (Moret et al. 2016, p. 23). The study refers to countries like China, India, Brazil, and Turkey, alongside Argentina, Belarus, and Chile. In the medium to longer term, this means that the Russian dependency of foreign goods and services for domestic consumption and its supply of goods and services to foreign markets will change. These effects are likely to be felt much harder by Russia's traditional and geographically nearby trading partners then the United States, which has a rather insignificant share of trade with Russia (Moret et al. 2017). The study also notes that some countries have not joined the coalition of countries applying the sanctions, including South Korea. According to Nelson (2017, p. 13), "In October 2014, Russia and China completed approximately 40 agreements related to finance and technology. Russia is also reportedly turning to Brazil and other Latin American countries for food imports to compensate for losses resulting from its ban on agricultural imports from other countries". On the side of the coalition, weaknesses can be found too and a growing reluctance to renew the sanctions given the forgone market opportunities. Hence, building a coalition is one thing, keeping it together another. The chain can only be as strong as the weakest link and the chain is being tested.

Given that the sanctions have been in place for some four years, and the inverse relationship that was established between the duration of sanctions and their effectiveness, the likelihood that they will bite is decreasing. It seems highly unlikely that Russia will give up its claim on territories in Ukraine. The question then is what next? Bond et al. suggest that the "West certainly needs to re-evaluate collectively how far its sanctions are achieving their objectives. If it concludes that they are ineffective or only partly effective, the EU, US and other countries which have imposed sanctions on Russia have several alternatives".

The suggestions include the following five options:

> i They can leave sanctions in place, in the expectation that their effect will grow over time, and because they want them to give a permanent political signal that annexing territory is unactable.
> ii They can lift sanctions and return to business as usual.
> iii They can maintain the objectives but adjust the sanctions.
> iv They can maintain the sanctions but adjust the objectives.
> v They can adjust both sanctions and objectives.
>
> (Bond et al. 2015, p. 17)

The option that will be chosen remains open for now, but the analysis has shown that keeping sanctions in place with the expectation that in the longer run they will work is not realistic and not supported by the evidence. At some point a decision would need to be taken with regard to the duration and scope of the sanctions and eventually lifting them.

Conclusion

While the use of economic sanctions can politically be an attractive policy tool, their effectiveness is arguable. How much do they really contribute to achieving the policy changes that are mostly the purpose of the measures put in place? If they are ineffective and perhaps even costly, what then would be the reason for countries to apply economic sanctions? It is argued in this chapter that sanctions show a willingness and even determination by governments to act and go beyond mere rhetoric. Governments are willing to walk the talk, no matter the costs. Indeed, it was shown that they seem a priori a powerful instrument and generate economic costs, but it was argued that these costs work both ways. In addition, there are generally third parties willing to take advantage of the situation and break the sanctions. It may lead to a change in trade partners and the creation of new alliances and thus adding to the costs to at least one of the parties. Given the ways in which trade has evolved over time, including the globalization of production and the growing interdependency of trade relations between nations, the effectiveness of economic sanctions is reduced even further.

Given the weak history of economic sanctions episodes, it is argued that they are hardly applied in isolation and complement other measures, including diplomacy. Given the combination of various measures put in place, it becomes even harder to assess the effectiveness of economic sanctions per se. In addition, other economic and/or external factors may kick in, unrelated to the sanctions per se, complicating the analysis even further in assessing the contribution of the sanctions to the eventual resolution of the conflict. In some cases they are not given the time to work and are overtaken by military action.

Russia was found to be economically vulnerable given the limited diversification of its economy and a high dependency on raw materials. It was argued that while the sanctions have produced economic hardship this pain was also caused by other external and unrelated factors. Indeed, and due to a number of coinciding circumstances, the Russian economy was affected by drastically lower oil prices, a decline in the currency, capital flight and a reduction in its GDP. Yet, there is no indication that the sanctions will lead to the ending of the crisis and tensions with the Ukraine. It was argued that the main sender (the EU) is also affected by the sanctions it imposed and that the coalition supporting the sanctions is being weakened.

In conclusion, there is general agreement that economic sanctions are always preferable to warfare, but the measures come at a cost, and they are not one-sided: those taking the sanctions may end up shooting themselves in the foot.

Notes

1 This contribution is written in the author's personal capacity and builds on analysis, contained in a WTO Economic Research and Statistics Divisions staff working paper in March 2018 (Smeets 2018). Any views expressed in the analysis are his and cannot be attributed to the WTO Secretariat.

2 GATT 1994, Article XXI, states that "Nothing in this Agreement shall be construed (b) to prevent any contracting party from taking any action which it considers necessary for the protection of its essential security interests (iii) taken in time of war or any other emergency in international relations; or (c) to prevent any contracting party from taking any action in pursuance of its obligations under the United Nations Charter for the maintenance of international peace and security". These provisions find their mirror image in Art. XIV bis GATS.

3 Qatar most recently brought a case against Bahrain and Saudi Arabia, in which it contests the restrictions imposed by the two countries with regard to trade in goods and services and trade-related aspects of intellectual property rights (DS527 and DS528).

4 The origin of boycotts according to dictionary.com is related to Charles C. Boycott (1832–97), an English estate manager in Ireland against whom nonviolent coercive tactics were used in 1880.

5 The US President Barack Obama and the Cuban President Raul Castro made a joint statement to that effect before Christmas 2014. Diplomatic relations between the two countries resumed in the summer of 2015.

6 Apartheid ended, but few would argue that this resulted from the sanctions imposed on South Africa per se. The sanctions added to the pressures, but it is generally held that a rapid evolution in domestic politics and more specifically the role of Nelson Mandela (later President) were largely determined in the transition from a white minority to a black majority government in South Africa and the logical ending of apartheid.

7 The difficulty of identifying products for retaliatory purposes is also apparent when it comes to authorized retaliation in the context of the dispute settlement body.

Bibliography

Bergeijk, PAG and Van Marrewijk, C 1994, 'Economic Sanctions: A Hidden Cost of the New World Order', in: M Chatterij, A Rima and H Jager (eds.) *Economics of International Security: Essays in Honour of Jan Tinbergen*, Mac Millan, London.

Bond, I, Odendahl, C and Rankin, J 2015, 'Frozen: The Politics and Economics of Sanctions Against Russia', *Centre for European Reform*, viewed 29 June 2018, www.cer.eu/sites/default/files/publications/attachments/pdf/2015/frozen_sanctions-10787.pdf

Collins, K, Cohen, Z, Borak, D and Merica, D 2018, 'Trump Announces New North Korea Sanctions', *CNN*, 24 February, viewed 29 June 2018, https://edition.cnn.com/2018/02/23/politics/donald-trump-north-korea-sanctions/index.html

Dizaji, SF and van Bergeijk, P 2013, 'Potential Early Phase Success and Ultimate Failure of Economic Sanctions: A VAR Approach With an Application to Iran', *Journal of Peace Research*, vol. 50, no. 6, pp. 721–736.

Early, B 2012, 'Alliances and Trade With Sanctioned States, a Study of US Economic Sanctions, 1950–2000', *Journal of Conflict Resolution*, vol. 56, no. 3, pp. 547–572.

The Economist 2018, 'Sanctions on Russia, Copy and Paste', February 3.

Hecksher, EF 1919, 'The Effects of Trade on the Distribution of Income', *Economic Tidskrift*, pp. 497–512.

Hufbauer, GC, Schott, JJ, Elliott, KA and Oegg, B 2007, *Economic Sanctions Reconsidered: History and Current Policy*, 3rd edition, Peterson Institute, Washington, DC.

Kemp, MC 1964, *The Pure Theory of International Trade*, Prentice Hall Inc., New Jersey.

Manson, K 2018, 'US Sanctions 27 Shipping Companies for Ties With North Korea', *Financial Times*, 23 February, viewed 29 June 2018, www.ft.com/content/666e7710-18ab-11e8-9376-4a6390addb44

Mau, V 2014, 'Russia Needs Reforms, Not a Sanctions War', *Global Affairs*, no. 3, viewed 29 June 2018, https://eng.globalaffairs.ru/book/Russia-needs-reforms-not-a-sanctions-war-17006

Moret, E, Biersteker, T, Giumelli, F, Poretla, C, Veber, M, Jarosz, D and Bobocea, C 2016, *The New Deterrent? International Sanctions Against Russia Over the Ukraine Crisis; Impacts, Costs and Further Action*, PSIG, Geneva.

Moret, E, Giumelli, F and Bastiat-Jarosz, D 2017, *Sanctions on Russia: Impacts and Economic Costs on the United States*, PSIG, Geneva.

Nelson, R 2017, *US Sanctions on Russia's Economy*, US Congressional Research Service, viewed 29 June 2018, https://fas.org/sgp/crs/row/R43895.pdf

Ohlin, B 1929, 'The Reparations Problem: A Discussion; Transfer Difficulties, Real and Imagined', *The Economic Journal*, no. 39, pp. 172–183.

Portansky, A 2014, 'Sanctions Pushing to Decline, a New Reality for the Russian Economy', *Global Affairs*, no. 3, viewed 29 June 2018, https://eng.globalaffairs.ru/number/Sanctions-Pushing-to-Decline-16992

Ricardo, D 1817, *On the Principles of Political Economy and Taxation*, John Murray, London.

Rikson, M and Wallensteen, P 2015, 'Targeting Sanctions and Ending Armed Conflicts: First Steps Towards a New Research Agenda', *International Affairs*, vol. 91, no. 6, pp. 1387–1398.

Smeets, M 1990, 'Economic Sanctions Against Iraq: The Ideal Case?', *Journal of World Trade*, vol. 24, no. 6, pp. 105–120.

Smeets, M 1994, 'Economic Sanctions Against Iraq', in: H Blumberg and C French (eds.) *Lessons From the Gulf War: Social Science Findings*, University Press of America, Lanham.

Smeets, M 2000, 'Conflicting Goals: Economic Sanctions and the WTO', *Global Policy Dialogue*, vol. 2, no. 3, pp. 119–129.

Smeets, M 2018, 'Can economic sanctions be effective?' WTO Staff Working Paper ERSD-2018–03, 15 March 2018.

Sutyrin, SF, Koval, AG and Trofimenko, OY 2014, 'Integrating Into the Multilateral Trading System and Global Value Chains: The Case of Russia', in: M Jansen, MS Jallab and M Smeets (eds.) *Connecting to Global Markets. Challenges and Opportunities: Case Studies Presented by WTO Chair-holders*, World Trade Organization, Geneva.

5 Impact of the WTO accession on acceding countries

Analysis of key macroeconomic indicators

Sergei F. Sutyrin, Olga Y. Trofimenko, and Maryana A. Gubina

Introduction

Accession to the World Trade Organization (WTO) is a very important trade policy decision made by countries that were not signatories to the General Agreement on Tariffs and Trade (GATT). Indeed, as a rule, specific economic and political circumstances within such states dictated non-participation in the GATT system. For example, the Council for Mutual Economic Assistance (CMEA), once the principal trade framework for the countries of Central and Eastern Europe, subjected those economies to its central planning and seriously limited free international trade operations. Many developing countries were busy with their internal economic problems, and GATT participation was at the bottom of their political and economic agenda. At the same time, the CMEA system collapsed and many countries came to understand that the GATT/WTO requirements regulated the bulk of international trade. Their wish to influence the development of new trade rules (among other arguments) forced these countries to initiate negotiations toward full participation in that network.

Joining the WTO system became more difficult than had been the case at its creation. A rather simple process under the GATT, which in some cases required no negotiations or vote of approval from members and no expectation that acceding countries would make any formal commitments beyond maintaining existing levels of economic liberalization (Davis and Wilf 2013), became more demanding. A "higher accession price" resulted from concession imbalances, along with severe terms of accession (including the WTO-plus requirements) and long and rather complicated accession procedures. Therefore, finding a compromise and agreeing on appropriate individual participation conditions had always challenged negotiators. Quite often within a society of a candidate nation, an intensive discussion of the impact of WTO membership on the domestic economy accompanied the accession process. For example, during an 18-year history of accession to the WTO, Russian academic journals and mass media frequently presented directly opposite predictions regarding possible repercussions of prospective WTO membership (Mikhailenko and Gruzdov 2012). In contrast, the overwhelming majority of foreign experts shared relatively optimistic views, arguing that even assuming certain potential losses, the Russian economy should gain from WTO accession

(World Bank 2012; Tarr 2007). Most of the fears and expectations never became a reality. At the same time, serious disagreements remain about the impact of WTO accession and membership on the Russian economy, and one could argue that they will most probably continue for at least several years (Sutyrin and Kolesov 2017). Moreover, from time to time, some politicians in Russia and other WTO members announce the idea of leaving the organization. In addition, the WTO faces many challenges at the moment, promoting discussions on institutional reforms of this organization and their design. In both developed and developing countries, governments also tend to be rather defensive toward globalization as the cause of economic realities on the ground, including high levels of job loss (Smeets 2017).

The purpose of the chapter is to discover whether WTO accession has had a negative or a positive effect on countries that have joined the organization since its establishment. Findings will support the development of trade-policy recommendations for countries still in the process of accession, as well as for recently and very recently acceded members (RAMs and VRAMs).

Methodology of the study

From 1996 until August 2018, 36 countries had already joined the WTO (WTO 2018a). One might sensibly argue that to a greater or a lesser extent, all of them felt the impact of accession on a variety of macroeconomic indicators. Of course, these countries are very diverse in terms of their size, geography, location, involvement in international trade, and level of economic development. In terms of a research sample, this diversity could constitute an advantage over more homogeneous samples. Indeed, if after their accession a substantial majority of these economies experienced roughly the same pattern of development in terms of a specific indicator, their diversity would make a convincing argument in favour of a causal relationship between WTO accession and the effect on the indicator. At the same time, the existence of different patterns clearly indicates that no general trend applies to these countries. The circumstances would require a more profound cluster analysis to make any meaningful generalizations valid for a certain group of countries (e.g. transitional, post-transitional, landlocked).

To achieve the study's goal, the authors use the approach initially introduced by Sutyrin and Kolesov (2015), who observed and compared the dynamics of key macroeconomic indicators for 29 non-GATT contracting parties using the "floating time-frame" approach. They observed the data for two years before and after accession to the WTO between 1995 and 2012.

These countries demonstrate very diverse patterns in development of trade and trade-related economic indicators after accession, compared with the pre-accession period. The countries under review experienced amazingly large differences in average annual growth rates. Sutyrin and Kolesov (2015) also show that less than half of the countries under review demonstrate uniformity in the dynamics of all selected indicators.

In the present study, the authors also investigate trends of key macroeconomic indicators for RAMs and VRAMs, but there are two main differences in approach.

Firstly, the chosen period for this analysis is three years before their WTO accession and three years after, due to the assumption that some accession consequences cannot be seen in the short run due to the existence of transition periods for liberalization in various sectors.

Secondly, the present study not only analyses the data for individual economies, but generalizes the results for various country groups. Such an approach allows broader conclusions with regard to different types of WTO members. For this purpose, the authors use the World Bank (WB) classification of economies by income, regardless of the fact that the WTO distinguishes only three: developed, developing, and least developed (LDCs).[1] This approach presents itself with the understanding that in the WTO, a country might self-assess as a developing country regardless of the level of its economic performance. As a result, it might expect less severe terms of accession than those for developed countries, and even special differential treatment envisaged in the WTO agreements.[2] The World Bank classification of countries is more accurate in measuring economic status.

Accordingly, all sample states were combined into four groups (World Bank 2018):

- high-income economies (HIE): eight (Chinese Taipei, Croatia, Estonia, Latvia, Lithuania, Oman, Panama, and Saudi Arabia);
- upper-middle-income economies (UMIE): eleven (Albania, Armenia, Bulgaria, China, Ecuador, Jordan, Montenegro, Russian Federation, Samoa, FYR of Macedonia, and Tonga);
- lower-middle-income economies (LMIE): ten (Cabo Verde, Cambodia, Georgia, Kyrgyzstan, Lao PDR, Moldova, Mongolia, Ukraine, Vanuatu, and Vietnam);
- low-income economies (LIE): three (Democratic Republic of the Congo, Nepal, and Tajikistan).

To have comparable series, Yemen, Seychelles, Kazakhstan, Liberia, and Afghanistan were not included in the analysis because necessary information is missing, as there is no data for these countries for three years after accession.[3]

Considering that countries officially joined the WTO in different months of respective years and that macroeconomic indicators for the analysis are statistically presented on an annual basis, the authors take (by analogy with Sutyrin and Kolesov 2015) a half year as a "border line" to distinguish between pre- and post-accession periods. Therefore, for the countries acceding to the WTO during January–June, these months together with the rest are taken for the first post-accession year. In contrast to that, for the countries with accession dated in July–December, the whole of that year is taken for the last pre-accession year.

In the present study, the authors present results for the following indicators:

- Merchandise export plus export of services X (m+s) average annual growth rate: Available statistics do not support a widely shared belief that trade in services tends to grow faster than merchandise trade. According to the WTO during the period of 2000–2006, average annual global growth rate was 10 percent for the former, and 11 percent for the latter (WTO 2007, p. 6). During the period 2005–2013, these two components of world export demonstrated the same dynamics – average annual growth of 8 percent (WTO 2014, p. 25). Nevertheless, assuming that at the moment, both scope and scale of services traded internationally are much less than those traded in the domestic market, existing untapped reserves for export of services expansion look really impressive;

- Merchandise import plus import of services M (m+s) average annual growth rate: Among possible threats of the WTO accession for the "newcomers" fast growth of import resulting in redistribution of market share in favour of foreign manufacturers as well as service providers arguably has the highest rank;
- Nominal GDP average annual growth rate: From the very beginning of its existence to the present day, official documents of GATT/WTO system have constantly emphasized that international trade is not an ultimate goal, but rather an important instrument of economic development. Liberalization of trade policies and respective expansion of trade flows among the countries should contribute to more balanced global economic growth and performance, narrowing the gap between wealthy and less prosperous members of the international community;
- Real GDP (in constant 2010 prices) average annual growth rate: Due to various reasons, level of inflation in the group under review tends to differ substantially between countries. Influenced by some global trends, this level also fluctuated within the framework of the almost two-decade time span investigated;
- FDI inflows average annual growth rate: Accession to the WTO is widely perceived as a factor stimulating inward FDI. Expansion of investment inflows might result from a more transparent and predictable business environment in newly acceding countries, as well as better protection of intellectual property rights associated with the provisions of an Agreement on Trade-Related Intellectual Property Rights (TRIPS). In particular, in Russia's case, many potential investors during the 1990s and 2000s had named serious concerns regarding security of their intellectual property as a barrier to FDI. As a substantial share of global FDI goes to services sectors, one might expect that liberalization steps taken by acceding countries under the General Agreement on Trade in services (GATS) might also influence FDI growth.

In other words, the authors focus on relative indicators in order to assess either as "positive" or as "negative" the developments of individual national economies after their accession to the WTO. More specifically, the question is: How did rate of growth (calculated as a geometrical mean) influence the status of the WTO member? Under the circumstances, "positive" dynamics in average annual growth rates means one of the following:

- higher rate of growth;
- slowdown of contraction;
- shift from contraction to growth.

In its turn, "negative" dynamics in average annual growth rates means one of the three following options:

- lower rate of growth;
- higher rate of contraction;
- shift from growth to contraction.

Taken alone, data on changes of economic indicators might lead to wrong conclusions. Better or worse dynamics might depend upon global trends in certain periods of time. Therefore, the authors also determine correlations between indicators: X(m+s) average annual growth rate in sample countries before/after the WTO accession and the world X(m+s) average annual growth rate; M(m+s) average annual growth rate in sample countries before/after the WTO accession and the world M(m+s) average annual growth rate; nominal GDP average annual growth rate in sample countries before/after the WTO accession and the world nominal GDP average annual growth rate; real GDP average annual growth rate in sample countries before/after the WTO accession and the world real GDP average annual growth rate; and individual countries' inward FDI growth rates before/after the WTO accession and world FDI growth rates. To ensure as much consistency and comparability as possible, most of the data are from the same source, namely the UNCTAD statistical database (UNCTAD 2018). GDP data for most countries was collected using BMP5 methodology, and for countries acceded after 2008, BMP6.

In addition to generalized analysis of countries' performance before and after their WTO accession, the authors pay particular attention to relevant economic indicators of the Russian Federation. The results might provide an overall assessment of its membership in the organization.

Results of the analysis

Average annual X(m+s) growth rate

Average annual export of goods and services growth rate before and after the WTO accession for all sample-countries groups shows "negative" dynamics (9.67 and 8.27 percent correspondingly). In high-, upper-middle-, and low-middle-income countries, an average annual growth rate has declined. In low-income economies, it was "negative" (Table 5.1). However, some individual countries showed outstanding results. The most significant increase in average annual growth rate was observed in Lithuania (−1 percent before and 25 percent after). On the contrary, Saudi Arabia has lost significantly in the average annual X(m+s) growth rate, but this is primarily due to the fall in oil prices, and not as a result of the WTO accession.

All in all, "positive" dynamics of various magnitudes in X(m+s) average annual growth rate took place in only 12 economies out of 32. These were: China, Chinese Taipei, Croatia, Estonia, Georgia, Jordan, Kyrgyzstan, Lithuania, the Former Yugoslav Republic of Macedonia (FYROM), Moldova, Nepal, and Tonga.

These results are slightly different from findings of Sutyrin and Kolesov (2015). They showed "positive" dynamics for 14 countries out of 29. But in a three-year period, Bulgaria, Democratic Republic of the Congo, Latvia, and Samoa moved to a group of countries with a "negative" trend. On the contrary, Chinese Taipei and Georgia showed better performance (Appendix 5.1).

Average annual merchandise and service export growth rates in the Russian Federation before and after the WTO accession was 20 percent and −17 percent respectively (Appendix 5.1). A sharp reduction after the accession can be explained mainly by the decline of oil prices in 2012–2016 and volumes of oil exports in 2013–2014 (Figure 5.1).

Table 5.1 Export of goods and services average annual growth rates before and after the WTO accession (percent)

Before	*After*	*Before*	*After*
High-income economies 10.62	10.32	Lower-middle income economies 9.67	8.43
Upper-middle income economies 11.07	9.64	Low-income economies 1.99	−2.81

Source: Authors' calculations of data from UNCTAD (2018).

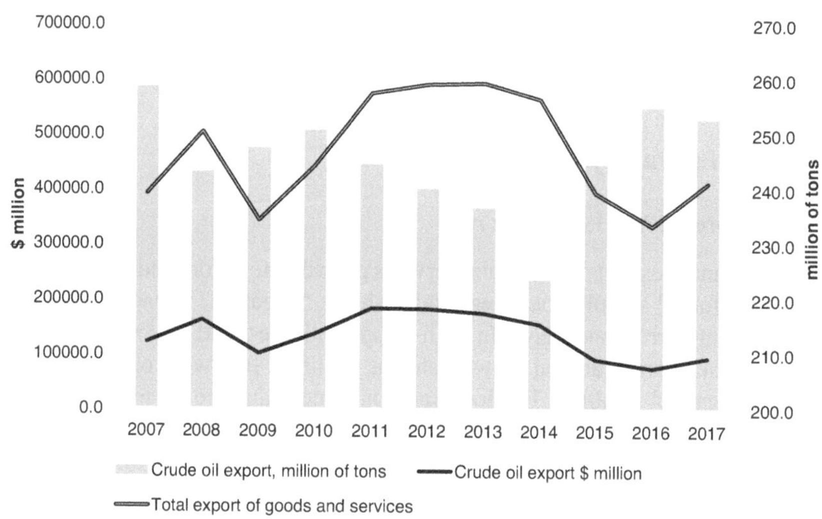

Figure 5.1 Total merchandise export and export of crude oil by the Russian Federation, 2007–2017

Source: CBR (2018).

The correlation coefficient between total export revenues and crude oil export of Russia in value terms equals to 0.93. So the above-mentioned assumption about the importance of oil exports for the overall country's export revenues should be valid.

Comparison of average annual X(m+s) growth rate for sample countries with the world average annual X(m+s) growth rates

We compare average annual X(m+s) growth rates for individual countries with the world average annual X(m+s) growth rates for the same periods (Appendix 5.6). The analysis shows a low correlation between these indicators before the WTO accession (0.38). On the contrary, after the accession, the relationship is stronger (correlation coefficient equals to 0.73). This supports an idea that the WTO membership creates better export opportunities.

Average annual M(m+s) growth rate

In general, the results show that average annual M(m+s) growth rate declines for all countries' groups (Table 5.2). This contradicts with the general assumption that after the WTO accession import increases due to liberalization steps. This is not a surprise, as acceding countries could negotiate higher levels of protection. In addition, developing and least developed members enjoy special and differential treatment (SDT).[4]

All in all "positive" dynamics of various magnitudes in M (m+s) annual growth rate took place in 14 economies out of 32 – the results of Sutyrin and Kolesov (2015) were 15 economies out of 29. These were Armenia, Bulgaria, Cambodia, Chinese Taipei, Croatia, Estonia, Georgia, Jordan, Lithuania, The Former Yugoslav Republic of Macedonia (FYROM), Moldova, Montenegro, Nepal, and Oman. China, Democratic Republic of the Congo, Mongolia, Saudi Arabia, Vanuatu, and Vietnam moved to a group with the lower M(x+s) average annual growth rate (Appendix 5.2).

In the Russian Federation after the WTO accession, one could observe "negative" trends in import growth regardless of trade liberalization steps according to country's obligations (Appendix 5.2). The key reasons for that are quite obvious:

Table 5.2 Import of goods and services average annual growth rates before and after the WTO accession (percent)

Before	*After*	*Before*	*After*
High-income economies		Lower-middle income economies	
6.22	3.98	11.97	10.54
Upper-middle income economies		Low-income economies	
9.27	6.38	13.07	−1.52

Source: Authors' calculations of data from UNCTAD (2018).

sharp depreciation of national currency and various bans on import within the "anti-sanction" regime.

Comparison of M(m+s) average annual growth rate for sample countries with the world average annual M(m+s) growth rate

Sample countries demonstrate moderate correlation between individual countries' average annual import growth rates and world imports dynamics before joining the WTO (0.56) and stronger after (0.72) (Appendix 5.6). Therefore, one might argue that after the WTO accession, member states perform closer to the general international dynamics.

Nominal GDP average annual growth rate

"Positive" dynamics of nominal GDP average annual growth was shown by high- and low-income economies, while upper-middle-income and low-income countries demonstrated a decline (rather modest). After the accession, a nominal GDP average annual growth rate for selected country groups fluctuated between 1.36 percent and 11.80 percent in the case of low-income and high-income countries correspondingly (Table 5.3).

Individual-country performance can be found in Appendix 5.3. All in all, "positive" dynamics of various magnitudes in average annual growth rate for this indicator took place in 18 economies out of 32. Sutyrin and Kolesov (2015) found affirmative results for 17 countries out of 29. These were Albania, Armenia, Bulgaria, Cambodia, China, Chinese Taipei, Croatia, Democratic Republic of the Congo, Estonia, Georgia, Jordan, Kyrgyzstan, Lithuania, The Former Yugoslav Republic of Macedonia (FYROM), Moldova, Nepal, Oman, and Tonga. While Georgia left "the club" of countries with the "negative" dynamics of nominal GDP, Vanuatu and Vietnam worsened their rates in the three-year time period.

The nominal GDP average annual growth rate in Russia was −18 percent three years after the accession (Appendix 5.3). It is much worse than for other counties of the upper-middle-income group. That resulted from the fact that in 2015 Russian ruble lost almost half of its value vis-à-vis USD.[5]

Table 5.3 Nominal GDP average annual growth rates before and after the WTO accession (percent)

Before	*After*	*Before*	*After*
High-income economies 6.54	11.80	Lower-middle income economies 9.89	7.91
Upper-middle income economies 7.46	6.85	Low-income economies 0.27	1.36

Source: Authors' calculations of data from UNCTAD (2018).

Comparison of nominal GDP annual average growth rate for sample countries with the world nominal GDP average annual growth rate

Sample countries demonstrate weak correlation between individual countries' average annual nominal GDP growth rates and world respective dynamics before joining the WTO (0.45) and stronger after (0.71) (Appendix 5.6). One might assume that a higher correlation after the accession is connected to greater dependence between X(m+s) average annual growth rate and respective international data. But this phenomenon needs further investigation.

Real GDP average annual growth rate

A "positive" dynamic in the real GDP average annual growth rate was observed in high- and upper-middle-income economies. In contrast, "negative" dynamics were experienced by lower-middle and low-income countries (Table 5.4).

Appendix 5.4 contains data for the real GDP average annual growth rates for individual economies. The indicator fluctuated within the range of −4 percent in the case of Congo and Ukraine and 13 percent in the case of Armenia. A previous study pointed out all the different most "losing" and "winning" countries: – 14.8 percent for Chinese Taipei and 10.8 percent for Cambodia (Sutyrin and Kolesov 2015). All in all "positive" dynamics of various magnitudes in annual growth rate for this indicator took place in 19 cases out of 32 (13 cases out of 26 in the previous study). These were Armenia, Bulgaria, Cambodia, China, Chinese Taipei, Croatia, Estonia, Georgia, Jordan, Latvia, Lithuania, the Former Yugoslav Republic of Macedonia (FYROM), Moldova, Montenegro, Nepal, Samoa, Tajikistan, Tonga, and Vanuatu. New in this list were Armenia, Chinese Taipei, Montenegro, Nepal, Samoa, Tajikistan, Tonga, and Vanuatu. Kyrgyzstan and Saudi Arabia left the list of countries with the "positive" dynamics of Real GDP growth.

By analogy with the nominal GDP average annual growth rate, the real GDP average annual growth rate was "negative" in Russia three years after the accession at −1 percent mainly due to depreciation of national currency (Appendix 5.4). This is contrary to trends for upper-middle-income countries.

Table 5.4 Real GDP average annual growth rate before and after the WTO accession (percent)

Before	*After*	*Before*	*After*
High-income economies		Lower-middle income economies	
4.21	4.33	5.69	4.43
Upper-middle income		Low-income economies	
3.38	4.22	2.42	1.88

Source: Authors' calculations of data from UNCTAD (2018).

Comparison of real GDP average annual growth rate for sample countries with the world real GDP average annual growth rate

Sample countries demonstrate no correlation between individual countries real GDP average annual growth rates and world respective dynamics before and after joining the WTO (0.15 and 0.22 respectively (Appendix 5.6). One might argue that the WTO membership had no influcnce on economic growth in selected countries in the short term.

Inward FDI average annual growth rate

In three country groups under investigation, an inward FDI average annual growth rate declined after the WTO accession. The sharpest reduction can be observed for the upper-middle income countries group (3.6 times), for economies with high income (2 times) and low-middle (1.3 times). Low-income economies demonstrated a substantial positive dynamics of the indicator (6.7 times) (Table 5.5).

The FDI average annual growth rates fluctuated within the range of −52 percent in the case of Kyrgyz Republic and 181 percent in the case of Oman. The latter demonstrated substantial changes in the indicator (average annual growth rate of 8 percent before and above-mentioned impressive increase after the accession).

All in all, "positive" dynamics can be found for 14 countries out of 32. These are Armenia, Cambodia, China, Estonia, Georgia, Lao PDR, Lithuania, Moldova, Mongolia, Montenegro, Nepal, Oman, Samoa, and Tonga (Appendix 5.5). In contrast, a two-year perception of this indicator showed "positive" dynamics for Croatia, Estonia, and Moldova and "negative" dynamics for five countries: Cabo Verde, Montenegro, Panama, Russia, and Ukraine.

Comparison of inward FDI average annual growth rate for sample countries with the world inward FDI average annual growth rate

The correlation between individual countries' inward FDIs average annual growth rate and relevant global trends is negligible (Appendix 5.6). This means that the WTO membership did not have a direct effect on FDI inflows for sample countries.

As for the Russian Federation, the flow of direct investments from abroad dried up and declined substantially, and this process does not meet a general perception

Table 5.5 Inward FDI average annual growth rate before and after the WTO accession (percent)

Before	*After*	*Before*	*After*
High-income economies		Lower-middle income economies	
61.87	28.67	17.34	13.36
Upper-middle income economies		Low-income economies	
27.05	7.53	7.11	47.70

Source: Authors' calculations of data from UNCTAD (2018).

that the WTO accession might facilitate FDI inflows. Similarly to some previous indicators, the reasons for foreign direct investment downsizing are mainly non-WTO issues. As Sutyrin and Trofimenko (2017) argued, the FDI fall in 2014 was the result of two simultaneously existing and interconnected factors: institutional (general worsening of Russian image worldwide, political tensions influencing companies' performance) and economic (decrease of oil prices, depreciation of Russian Ruble, market shrinking, inflation and federal budget deficit). Moreover, expectations of foreign investors regarding the prospects of the Russian market, at least in the short term, tended to prevent new FDI.

Conclusion

The analysis of available data for all 32 non-GATT contracting parties that successfully acceded to the WTO between 1996 and 2013 demonstrates very diverse patterns in development of trade and trade-related (presumably accession-dependent) economic indicators after accession, in comparison with the pre-accession period. In general, the countries under review experienced an amazingly large difference of average annual growth rates. These results align with conclusions of Sutyrin and Kolesov (2015).

The analysis confirmed very small differences between the number of countries that experienced "positive" and "negative" dynamics (Appendix 5.6). A summary of "positive" and "negative" changes in the dynamics of selected indicators for sample country groups is presented in Table 5.6. Remarkably, none of the groups presented showed "positive" dynamics in all indicators under investigation. Moreover, X(m+s) average annual growth rates were "negative" for all country groups under investigation.

The analysis shows that "positive" dynamics could be observed for high-income economies in the case of M(m+s), nominal and real GDP average annual growth rates. Low-income countries showed "positive" dynamics in nominal GDP and

Table 5.6 Summary on "positive" and "negative" changes in dynamics of selected indicators for country groups, classified by income after their accession to the WTO

"Positive" dynamics	*"Negative" dynamics*
X(m+s)	
	HIE, UMIE, LMIE, LIE
M(m+s)	
HIE	UMIE, LMIE, LIE
Nominal GDP	
HIE, LIE	UMIE, LMIE
Real GDP	
HIE, UMIE	LMIE, LIE
Inward FDI	
LIE	HIE, UMIE, LMIE

inward FDI average annual growth rates, while upper-middle-income economies in real GPD average annual growth rate only. Lower-middle income countries demonstrate "negative" trends for all selected indicators. Such poor performance can be explained by relatively demanding liberalization obligations taken by some countries from this group (e.g. Ukraine and Kyrgyz Republic), the 2008–2009 economic crisis impact (e.g. Ukraine and Vietnam), strong dominance of raw materials and/or low value-added products in export, as well as price fluctuations on major export goods (Cambodia, Lao PDR, Mongolia, and Vietnam).

As the group of low-income economies under investigation contains just three countries and, therefore, a very low number of observations, reasonable conclusions most probably cannot be made for this country group.

As for individual economies, only four countries from the sample (Estonia, Georgia, Lithuania, and Moldova) showed "positive" results after the WTO accession in all comparisons. Meanwhile, Russian Federation, Ukraine, Saudi Arabia, Ecuador, Cabo Verde, Vietnam, and Panama have "negative" dynamics after the WTO accession in all indicators (Appendix 5A.7). But these pessimistic results could be explained by many other reasons, rather than the WTO accession – namely, economic sanctions, and national currency depreciation in the case of Russia, decline of international oil prices in the case of Russia and Saudi Arabia; world economic crisis in the case of Ukraine, Panama, and Ecuador.[6] All in all, a correlation analysis shows a very low dependence of selected indicators' dynamics for individual countries before the WTO accession with corresponding international data. In contrast, after the accession a substantial correlation can be found in the case of X(m+s), M(m+s), and nominal GDP average annual growth rates and corresponding global dynamics. Real GDP and inward FDI average annual growth rates for selected countries showed no correlation with corresponding international data and therefore one can argue that the WTO accession has a very low impact on these indicators, at least in the short run.

The analysis shows that the accession within a two-year period before and after the accession generated "positive" average annual growth rates in all five indicators for eight countries (namely, China, Croatia, Democratic Republic of the Congo, Estonia, Jordan, the Former Yugoslav Republic of Macedonia (FYROM), Moldova, and Vietnam) and "negative" rates for six (namely Cabo Verde, Montenegro, Oman, Panama, Russian Federation, and Ukraine) (Sutyrin and Kolesov 2015). Assessing a three-year period gives slightly different results: all "positive changes" in four WTO members (Estonia, Georgia, Lithuania, and Moldova), and "negative" in seven (Cabo Verde, Ecuador, Panama, Russian Federation, Saudi Arabia, Ukraine, and Vietnam).

All in all, comparing two- and three-year periods of selected countries' performances before and after their WTO accession, one can hardly find a general trend. Some indicators changed the pattern from "negative" to "positive" and the reverse. Some countries constantly showed "positive" (China, Estonia, and Moldova) and "negative" (Cabo Verde, Panama, and Ukraine) dynamics. Considering the extremely high level of diversity typical for these countries further, a more profound cluster type of analysis would be needed to make any meaningful generalizations valid for certain groups of economies.

The Russian Federation also demonstrated "negative" average annual growth rates for all selected indicators both in two- and three-year assessments. This reveals patterns similar to LMIEs and LIEs. The authors argue, though, that the WTO accession is not the determining factor among those influencing such performance.

While assessing the impact of the WTO accession using the selected approach one has to take into consideration that it has its own limitations. Firstly, the analysis shows what happened with selected indicators *after*, but not *due to* the WTO accession. Several aspects make it difficult to distinguish the effect of the WTO accession from other external and internal factors. Accession/membership is far from being the only "international factor" that really matters in influencing the performance of national economies. Countries might be very sensitive (if not quite vulnerable) to various negative and positive external shocks. At this very moment, uncertainty regarding prospects of global economic growth, fluctuations in oil prices, and exchange rates and economic sanctions (in the case of the Russian Federation) are among the most significant external factors influencing the way national economies operate. To partially overcome the influence of international factors, the authors compare changes in export/import growth of acceded countries with international trends.

Secondly, even though joining the WTO means that countries agree to respect all the WTO rules (i.e. equal conditions for all), the agreements *per se* contain different provisions for developed and developing countries, including those classified as "least developed". Sample countries joining the WTO have different status as either "developed" or "developing".

Thirdly, accession conditions substantially vary from country to country and depend on many factors, including the candidate's bargaining power, speed of accession, lobbying of national stakeholders, and received requests from the WTO members who are interested in specific trade policy measures of an acceding country. Therefore, among sample countries, one could find different levels of concessions: from rather liberal market access terms for goods, in the case of Kyrgyzstan and (to a certain extent) Ukraine, to more moderate terms for other members. For example, Nepal managed to secure one of the highest bound rates among RAMs[7] (WTO 2018b). Among differences in bound rates there are distinctions in transition periods, e.g. for selected products[8] or tariff rate quotas. Applied rates also vary, and in some cases they are far below the bound levels. One could find many differences in services as well. For example, the Russian Federation must authorize operations for direct affiliates of foreign insurance companies nine years after accession (WTO 2018c), while the Ukraine has no limitation on Mode 3 (commercial presence) in life and non-life insurance (neither in market access, nor in national treatment) (WTO 2018e). In addition, the amount of services sectors and sub-sectors excluding from liberalization is different for the WTO members under investigation. All in all, peculiarities of the accession terms of sample countries cannot be addressed by a single chapter.

Fourth, the proposition that accession to the WTO should most probably have different repercussions for various national economic actors (companies, industries, or regions) hardly requires any serious justification. Some of these actors would ultimately gain, while others would lose. Assessing results of accession from the point of view of a specific company, industry, or region should produce different conclusions.[9] Even assuming the possibility of an isolated study of the accession effect, predicting exactly how domestic producers would operate under new economic conditions would still be very difficult. Meanwhile, many things depend precisely on that (Sutyrin and Trofimenko 2013). As this study is not country-specific, it overlooks consequences of accession for specific industries, as well as behaviour of domestic economic agents.

Finally, the study neglects measures taken by national trade policy-makers within the framework of global economic disturbances. Possible discrepancies mentioned above, could be considered later as a part of cluster analysis, if necessary.

Regardless of its limitations, a chosen approach can enable judgement of whether acceding countries face rapid import growth and export expansion, as well as changes in GDP growth. In addition, a sufficiently large number of observations demonstrating similar results might turn "post-hoc" types of relations (i.e. events that took place after accession to the WTO but not necessarily the result of the accession) into causal (i.e. due to the accession) links.

Notes

1 A group of LDCs is defined using the United Nations classification of countries. The basic criteria for inclusion require that certain thresholds should be met with regard to per capita GNI, a human-assets index and an economic-vulnerability index.
2 For example, Chinese Taipei declared itself as a developing country upon joining the WTO in 2002, regardless of the fact that it belonged to a group of high-income economies, according to the World Bank. The territory, though, had never applied for a special and differential treatment, and only recently decided to give up its developing economy status in the WTO, trying to distinguish itself from mainland China (Ihara 2018).
3 Yemen joined the WTO in 2014, Seychelles and Kazakhstan in 2015, Liberia and Afghanistan in 2016.
4 The special provisions under the SDT include: longer time periods for implementing agreements and commitments, measures to increase trading opportunities for developing countries, provisions requiring all WTO members to safeguard the trade interests of developing countries, support to help developing countries build the capacity to carry out WTO work, handle disputes, and implement technical standards and provisions related to least-developed country (LDC) Members. Some of these measures might reduce import flows (WTO 2018d).
5 The country's nominal GDP taken for comparison is calculated in US dollars.
6 Ecuador raised its applied tariffs after the WTO accession; this could also be one of the reasons for the economic slowdown.
7 For example, a bound rate for HS 010410 – sheep a bound rate of Nepal is 60 percent.
8 In case of Russian Federation implementation period for pork is eight years, and seven years for motor cars, helicopters, and civil aircraft.
9 Quite frequently opinions based upon some specific observations tend to predefine general appraisals of certain processes and developments.

Bibliography

CBR 2018, *Export of Crude Oil by the Russian Federation*, viewed 22 December 2018, www.cbr.ru/vfs/statistics/credit_statistics/trade/crude_oil.xls

Davis, C and Wilf, M 2013, *Joining the Club: Accession to the GATT/WTO*, Princeton University, Princeton.

Ihara, K 2018, 'Taiwan Quits "Developing Economy" Status in WTO With Eye on China', *Nikkei Asian Review*, October 17, viewed 22 December 2018, https://asia.nikkei.com/Politics/Taiwan-quits-developing-economy-status-in-WTO-with-eye-on-China

Mikhailenko, A and Gruzdov, S 2012, *Rossia v VTO: Tri Scenario*, Orbita-M, Moscow.

Smeets, M 2017, *The WTO Multilateral Trading System in a Globalizing World: Challenges and Opportunities*, Dissertation to obtain the degree of Doctor at Maastricht University, viewed 28 December 2018, https://cris.maastrichtuniversity.nl/portal/en/persons/maarten-smeets(231b0634-065d-4661-9fd7-641cb162c814)/publications.html

Sutyrin, S and Kolesov, D 2015, *Impact of Accession to the WTO on Russian Economy: Analysis of International Background*, Foreign Economic Relations and Regional Growth in North East Asia: Russia's WTO Accession and Its Effects, HIER Discussion Paper Series, no. 44, Tokyo, pp. 1–20.

Sutyrin, S and Kolesov, D 2017, 'Stoila li igra svech? (Razmyshlenija po povodu pjatiletnej godovshhiny prisoedinenija Rossii k VTO)', *Torgovaja Politika*, vol. 11, no. 3, pp. 19–31.

Sutyrin, S and Trofimenko, O 2013, 'Russia's Accession to the WTO: Possible Impact on Competitiveness of Domestic Companies', *Baltic Sea Policy Briefing*, no. 2, viewed 22 December 2018, www.centrumbalticum.org/files/1903/BSR_policy_briefing_2_2013.pdf

Sutyrin, S and Trofimenko, O 2017, 'Do Formal Institutions Really Matter for Foreign Direct Investments to the Russian Federation? Case of FDI Flows From the European Union to Russia', in: K Liuhto, SF Sutyrin and JF Blanchard (eds.) *The Russian Economy and Foreign Direct Investment*, Routledge, London and New York.

Tarr, D 2007, 'Russian Accession to the WTO: An Assessment', *Eurasian Geography and Economics*, vol. 48, no. 3, pp. 306–319.

UNCTAD 2018, viewed 28 December 2018, http://unctadstat.unctad.org/wds/TableViewer/tableView.aspx

World Bank 2012, *Doklad of economike Rossii*, no. 27, April, viewed 28 December 2018, www-wds.worldbank.org/external/default/WDSContentServer/WDSP/IB/2012/04/30/000333038_20120430013430/Rendered/PDF/682760RUSSIAN007920B0RER0270russian.pdf

World Bank 2018, *World Bank Country and Lending Groups*, viewed 28 December 2018, https://datahelpdesk.worldbank.org/knowledgebase/articles/906519-world-bank-country-and-lending-groups

WTO 2007, World Trade Report. Six decades of multilateral trade cooperation: What have we learnt? Geneva, p. 6.

WTO 2014, World Trade Report. Trade and development: recent trends and the role of the WTO. Geneva, p. 25.

WTO 2018a, *Members and Observers*, viewed 28 December 2018, www.wto.org/english/thewto_e/whatis_e/tif_e/org6_e.htm

WTO 2018b, *Nepal and the WTO*, viewed 28 December 2018, www.wto.org/english/thewto_e/countries_e/nepal_e.htm

WTO 2018c, *Russian Federation and the WTO*, viewed 28 December 2018, www.wto.org/english/thewto_e/countries_e/russia_e.htm

WTO 2018d, *Special and Differential Treatment Provisions*, viewed 28 December 2018, www.wto.org/english/tratop_e/devel_e/dev_special_differential_provisions_e.htm

WTO 2018e, *Ukraine and the WTO 2018*, viewed 28 December 2018, www.wto.org/english/thewto_e/countries_e/ukraine_e.htm

Appendices

Appendix 5A.1

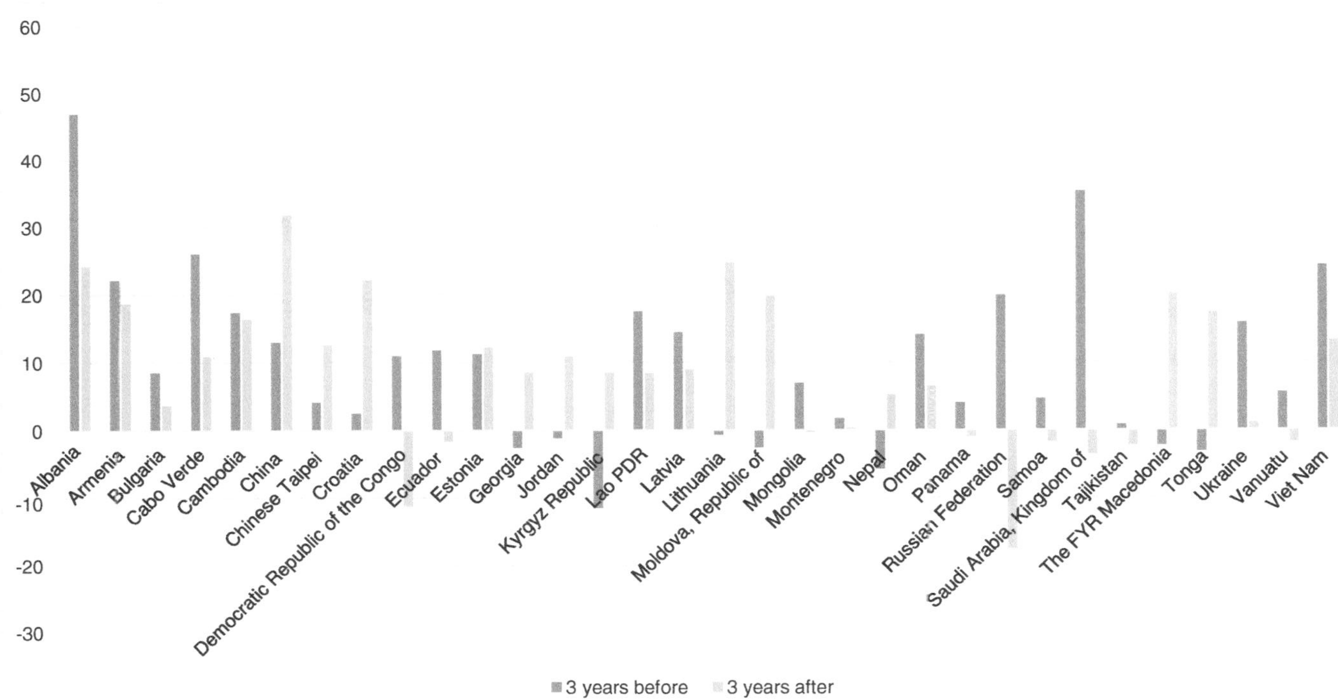

Figure 5A.1 Dynamics of exports of goods and services before and after WTO accession

Note: There are two exceptions: for Kyrgyzstan the data is just one year before and one year after, for Georgia – two years before and two years after. This is due to the lack of comparable data on their export three years before the accession.

Source: UNCTAD (2018).

Appendix 5A.2

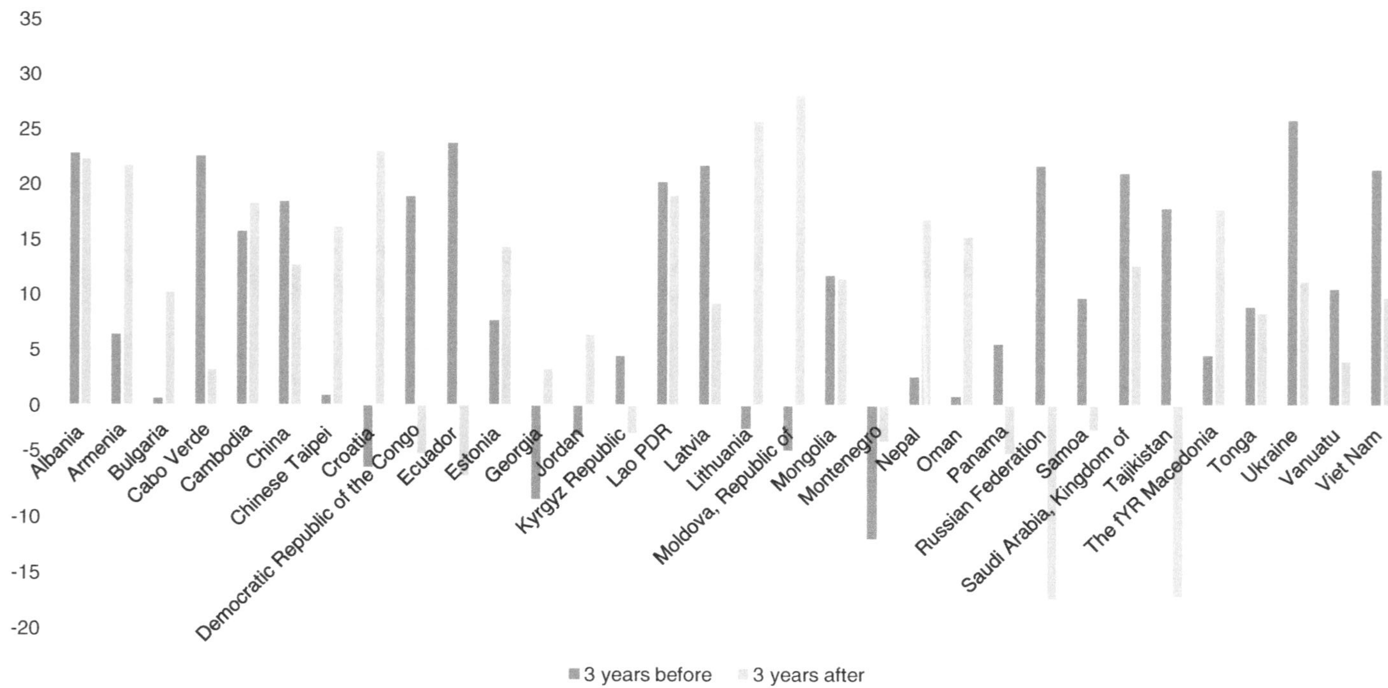

Figure 5A.2 Dynamics of imports of goods and services before and after WTO accession

Note: There are two exceptions: for Kyrgyzstan the data is just one year before and one year after, for Georgia – two years before and two years after. This is due to the lack of comparable data on their export three years before the accession.

Source: UNCTAD (2018).

Appendix 5A.3

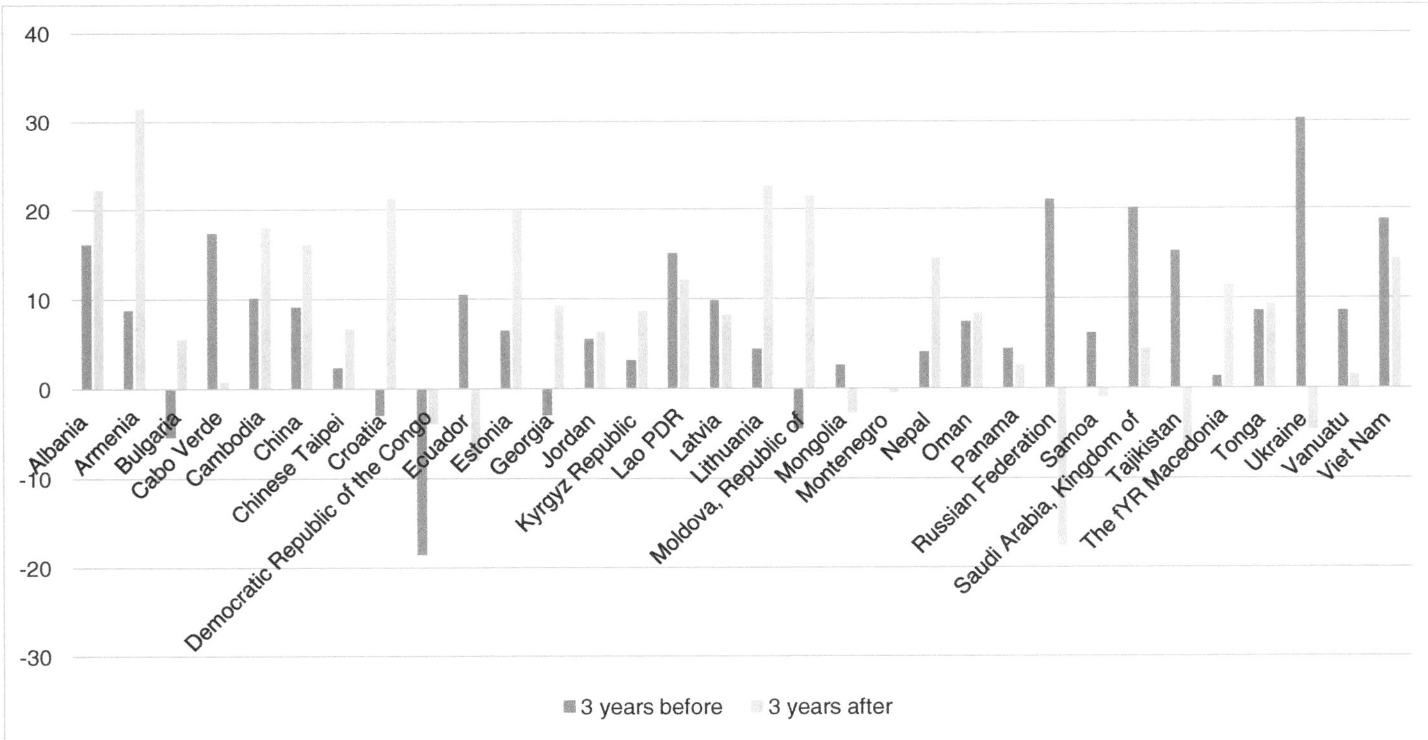

Figure 5A.3 Dynamics of nominal GDP in the countries before and after WTO accession

Source: UNCTAD (2018).

Appendix 5A.4

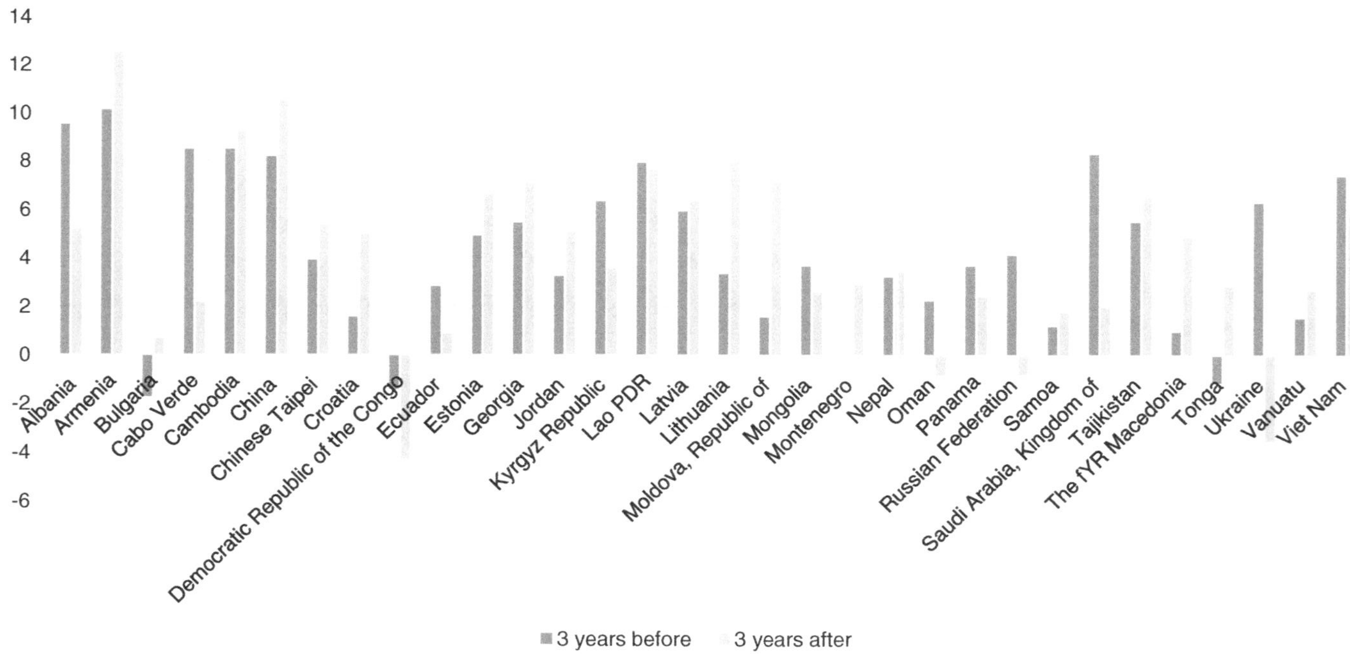

Figure 5A.4 Dynamics of real GDP (at constant prices 2010) in the countries before and after WTO accession

Source: UNCTAD (2018).

Appendix 5A.5

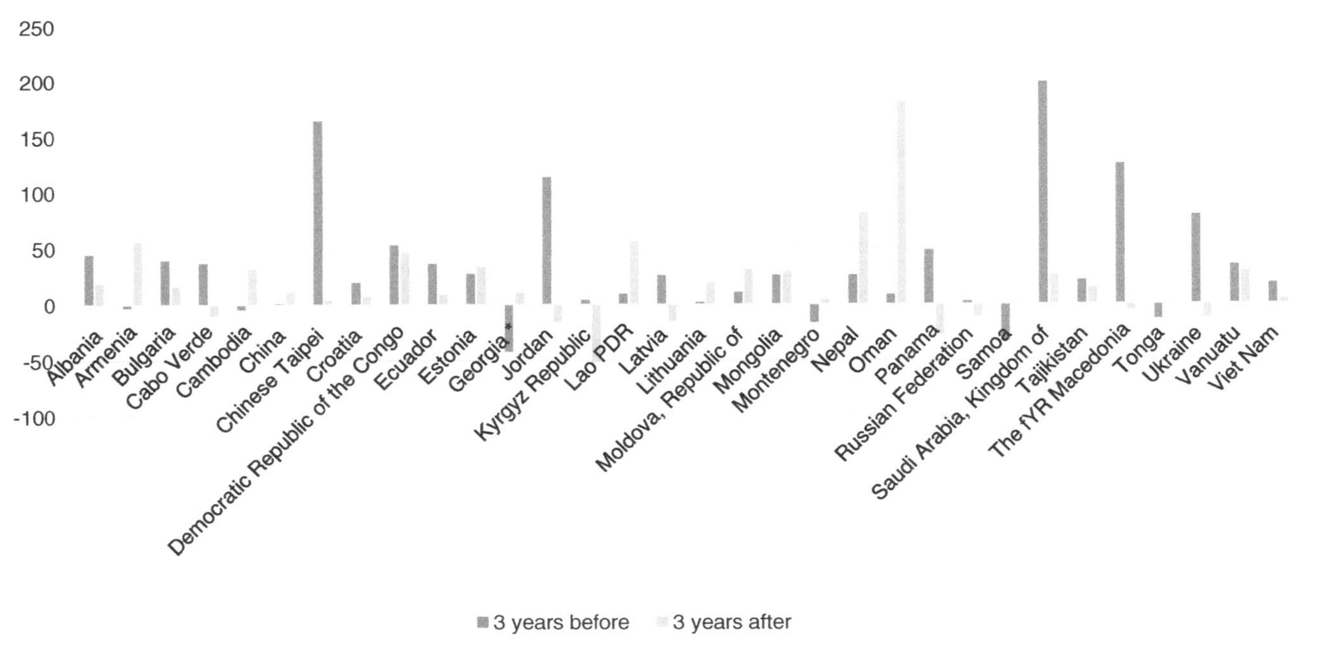

Figure 5A.5 Dynamics of inward FDI flow in the countries before and after WTO accession

Note: Georgia: analysis of inward FDI growth rate contains only two years before and after its WTO accession, as there is no data on 1996.

The fYR Macedonia: analysis of inward FDI growth rate contains only two years before and after its WTO accession, as there is no data on 2004.

Source: UNCTAD (2018).

Appendix 5A.6

Table 5A.1 Dynamics of key macroeconomic indicators of selected countries before and after the WTO accession and corresponding global data

Indicator	*Dynamics of exports of goods and services and corresponding world export growth rates*				*Dynamics of imports of goods and services and corresponding world import growth rates*				*Dynamics of nominal GDP in the country and corresponding global GDP growth rates*				*Dynamics of real GDP (at constant prices 2010) in the country and corresponding global real GDP growth rates*				*Dynamics of inward FDI flow in the country and corresponding global inward FDI flow growth rates*			
	Xm+s average annual growth rate in the country before and after WTO accession		*Xm+s average annual growth rate in the World*		*Mm+s average annual growth rate in the country before and after WTO accession*		*Xm+s average annual growth in the World*		*Nominal GDP average annual growth rate in the country before and after WTO accession*		*Nominal GDP average annual growth rate in the World*		*GDP at constant prices (2010) average annual growth rate in the country before and after WTO accession*		*GDP at constant prices (2010) average annual growth rate in the World*		*FDI inflow average annual growth rate in the country before and after WTO accession*		*FDI inflow average annual growth rate in the World*	
Country	**before**	**after**	**before**	**after**	**before**	**after**	**before**	**after**	**before**	**after**	**before**	**after**	**before**	**after**	**before**	**after**	**before**	**after**	**before**	**after**
Albania	47	24	4	14	23	22	5	13	16	22	2	10	10	5	3	3	44	19	182	−10
Armenia	22	19	4	17	6	22	4	16	9	32	2	10	10	13	3	4	−3	56	−45	155
Bulgaria	8	4	12	4	1	10	12	5	−5	6	7	2	−2	1	3	3	40	16	77	182
Cabo Verde	26	11	15	12	23	3	15	12	17	1	10	8	8	2	3	3	37	−10	57	34
Cambodia	17	16	14	15	16	18	13	15	10	18	10	10	8	9	3	3	−4	32	−10	57
China	13	32	4	17	18	13	4	17	9	16	2	11	8	10	3	4	1	11	12	61
Chinese Taipei	4	13	4	17	1	16	4	17	2	7	2	11	4	5	3	4	165	4	12	61
Croatia	2	22	4	14	−6	23	5	13	−3	21	2	10	2	5	3	3	20	8	182	−10
Democratic Republic of the Congo	11	−11	12	4	19	−4	12	5	−19	−4	7	2	−1	−4	3	3	53	46	77	182
Ecuador	12	−2	10	2	24	−6	10	2	11	−8	6	1	3	1	3	3	36	9	110	177
Estonia	11	12	2	6	8	14	2	5	7	20	1	5	5	7	3	2	27	33	177	−59
Georgia	−3	8	1	0	−8	3	1	0	−3	9	1	5	5	7	3	2	−42	11	124	−57
Jordan	−1	11	2	6	−3	6	2	5	6	6	1	5	3	5	3	2	114	−16	177	−59
Kyrgyz Republic	−12	9	−2	11	4	−3	0	4	3	9	0	2	6	4	3	6	4	−52	102	−45

Lao PDR	17	8	4	−2	20	19	4	−2	15	12	5	0	8	8	2	3	10	56	6	22
Latvia	14	9	3	4	22	9	3	4	10	8	0	2	6	6	3	6	26	−15	102	−45
Lithuania	−1	25	4	14	−2	26	5	13	4	23	2	10	3	8	3	3	2	20	182	−10
Moldova, Republic of	−3	20	4	17	−4	28	4	17	−4	22	2	11	2	7	3	4	11	31	12	61
Mongolia	7	0	12	4	12	11	12	5	3	−3	7	2	4	3	3	3	26	29	77	182
Montenegro	2	0	4	−2	−12	−3	4	−2	0	−1	5	0	0	3	2	3	−17	4	6	22
Nepal	−6	5	6	15	3	17	5	15	4	15	5	10	3	3	2	4	26	82	−59	173
Oman	14	7	4	14	1	15	5	13	7	8	2	10	2	−1	3	3	8	181	182	−10
Panama	4	−1	9	4	6	−4	9	4	4	3	4	2	4	2	3	3	48	−27	89	12
Russian Federation	20	−17	13	−4	22	−17	13	−4	21	−18	8	−1	4	−1	3	3	3	−11	34	31
Samoa	5	−2	4	−2	10	−2	4	−2	6	−1	5	0	1	2	2	3	−33	1	6	22
Saudi Arabia, Kingdom of	35	−4	17	2	21	13	17	2	20	4	11	5	8	2	4	1	199	26	61	−16
Tajikistan	1	−2	13	−4	18	−17	13	−4	15	−7	8	−1	5	7	3	3	21	15	34	31
The FYR Macedonia	−2	20	4	17	5	18	4	16	1	12	2	10	1	5	3	4	125	−5	−45	155
Tonga	−3	17	15	4	9	8	15	4	9	9	10	5	−1	3	4	2	−13	−1	173	6
Ukraine	16	1	15	4	26	11	15	4	30	−5	10	5	6	−4	4	2	79	−13	173	6
Vanuatu	6	−2	13	−4	10	4	13	−4	9	1	8	−1	2	3	3	3	35	29	34	31
Vietnam	24	13	17	3	21	10	16	3	19	14	10	4	7	6	4	1	18	5	155	−28
Correlation between countries' performance and global trends			0.38	0.73			0.56	0.72			0.45	0.71			0.15	0.22			−0.02	0.22

Note: Kyrgyzstan: analysis of exports of goods and services dynamics contains only one year before and after its WTO accession, as there is no data on 1995.

Georgia: analysis of exports of goods and services dynamics, as well as of inward FDI growth rate contains only two years before and after its WTO accession, as there is no data on 1996.

The fYR Macedonia: analysis of inward FDI growth rate contains only two years before and after its WTO accession, as there is no data on 2004.

Source: UNCTAD (2018).

Appendix 5A.7

Table 5A.2 Summary on "positive" and "negative" changes in dynamics of selected indicators for individual national economies after their accession to the WTO

"Positive" dynamics	*"Negative" dynamics*
X(m+s)	
China, Chinese Taipei, Croatia, Estonia, Georgia, Jordan, Kyrgyzstan, Lithuania, Moldova, Nepal, FYROM, Tonga	Albania, Armenia, Bulgaria, Cabo Verde, Cambodia, Democratic Republic of the Congo, Ecuador, Lao PDR, Latvia, Mongolia, Montenegro, Oman, Panama, Russia, Samoa, Saudi Arabia, Tajikistan, Ukraine, Vanuatu, Vietnam
M(m+s)	
Armenia, Bulgaria, Cambodia, Chinese Taipei, Croatia, Estonia, Georgia, Jordan, Lithuania, Moldova, Montenegro, Nepal, Oman, FYROM	Albania, Cabo Verde, China, Democratic Republic of the Congo, Ecuador, Kyrgyzstan, Lao PDR, Latvia, Mongolia, Panama, Russia, Samoa, Saudi Arabia, Tajikistan, Tonga, Ukraine, Vanuatu, Vietnam
Nominal GDP	
Albania, Armenia, Bulgaria, Cambodia, China, Chinese Taipei, Croatia, Democratic Republic of the Congo, Estonia, Georgia, Jordan, Kyrgyzstan, Lithuania, Moldova, Nepal, Oman, FYROM, Tonga	Cabo Verde, Ecuador, Lao PDR, Latvia, Mongolia, Montenegro, Panama, Russia, Samoa, Saudi Arabia, Tajikistan, Ukraine, Vanuatu, Vietnam
Real GDP	
Armenia, Bulgaria, Cambodia, China, Chinese Taipei, Croatia, Estonia, Georgia, Jordan, Latvia, Lithuania, Moldova, Montenegro, Nepal, FYROM, Samoa, Tajikistan, Tonga, Vanuatu	Albania, Cabo Verde, Democratic Republic of the Congo, Ecuador, Kyrgyzstan, Lao PDR, Mongolia, Oman, Panama, Russia, Saudi Arabia, Ukraine, Vietnam
Inward FDI*	
Armenia, Cambodia, China, Estonia, Georgia, Lao PDR, Lithuania, Moldova, Mongolia, Montenegro, Oman, Samoa, Tonga	Albania, Bulgaria, Cabo Verde, Chinese Taipei, Croatia, Ecuador, Jordan, Kyrgyzstan, Latvia, Panama, Russia, Saudi Arabia, Tajikistan, FYROM, Ukraine, Vietnam

Note: Democratic Republic of the Congo, Nepal, and Vanuatu are excluded from the analysis: in case of these countries the data on the base period has a negative sign.

6 Eurasian economic union

The first successful Russian regional trade agreement?

Vladimir G. Sherov-Ignatev

Introduction

Contemporary trade policy can hardly be understood without analyzing national policies on Regional Trade Agreements (RTAs). More than half of global trade takes place within RTAs or preferential trade regimes, and due to the abundance of preferential agreements (both reciprocal and unilateral), members of the WTO often joked that the Most Favored Nation (MFN) principle should be renamed into Least Favored Nation principle.

Regional integration[1] is one of the defining features of the contemporary period of the development of global economy. Developing in conjunction with globalization and sometimes considered to be its integral part, regional integration has developed in waves since the end of World War II. After starting in Europe, it spread to other regions like Latin America, Africa, and South-East Asia. In the first wave, Europe established many of the ideas and principles that were to follow. In the 1990s, the boom in bilateral free trade agreements (FTA) marked the second wave of regional integration, leading to the "spaghetti bowl" of bilateral FTAs (Bhagwati 1995). Some old regional initiatives also experienced a revival; some new ones, like Mercosur, emerged as well. The second decade of the twenty-first century brought mega-regional initiatives – this marks the third wave of regional integration.

Russia, having emerged as an independent state after the break-up of the USSR, tried to understand, formulate, and construct its place and role in the integration processes. It was a difficult task due to historical, geographic, economic, and political circumstances. There are several reasons to study Russia's integration policy and behaviour. Firstly, Russia is a large country with a natural resource-dependent economy; not many articles have captured the theoretical peculiarities of building RTAs of such economies. Secondly, Russia and its partners have chosen the customs union (CU), which is currently not a popular form of RTA; it is interesting to see whether CUs have some prospects in the future. Thirdly, integration projects with Russian participation belong to an interesting class of asymmetric regional integration agreements, which have specific features. Fourth, it is a unique situation, when countries, having been part of one larger country in the past, try to arrange regional integration after a period of disintegration. Fifth,

Russian integration policy has important political implications, relating to international relations and global security.

Our goal is to explain the specifics of Russia's integration policy, the reasons and motives for the decisions taken in this context, and to assess the results and prospects of Russia's integration initiatives, namely, the Commonwealth of Independent states (CIS)[2] and Eurasian Economic Union (EAEU).[3] We show that customs unions have some advantages as a form of regional integration for commodity-exporting countries. We also demonstrate that the asymmetric nature of Russia-centered RTAs largely determines their peculiarities: mode of decision-making, economic results, and probable scenarios of future development.

The chapter is structured as follows. Firstly, we describe some regional integration theories, concentrating on the aspects that are important for investigating the peculiarities of Russia's behaviour in the field of integration activity. Secondly, we pay tribute to the methodology and data. The third section is devoted to the research findings. We provide explanations for Russia's low interest in trade liberalization with its main trade partners, EU and China; we consider the current state of the CIS and analyse the EAEU as the key Russian integration project, its peculiarities, achievements, and problems. Finally, conclusions are drawn.

Theoretical approaches for explaining peculiarities of Russian participation in regional integration projects

In this section we do not provide yet another description of the universe of regional integration theories. Instead, we concentrate on approaches, which are important and relevant for explaining the characteristics of Russia's behaviour in the field of integration. This decision was made because Russia and some of its neighbours belong to commodity-exporting countries, and because Russia becomes a dominant actor in RTAs with its participation due to its size.

Literature on the role of asymmetry in RTAs in general and in the CIS and EAEU in particular

No participants of RTAs are absolutely equal – all are different. Sometimes difference is so serious, that one can speak about the asymmetry of RTA participants. Asymmetry can exist across a range of indicators, with the most obvious being the size and level of development.

Asymmetry by the level of development is captured in the vast literature on North–South RTAs. The mainframe of the discussion is whether North–South (N–S) or South–South (S–S) RTAs are recommended for developing countries. Shiff and Winters (2003), among others, insist that N-S RTAs are better because they provide access to advanced markets, developing the technological and business culture of exporters from the South, they allow access to modern technologies and financial resources of the partners with advanced economies, they increase investment attractiveness of developing countries, and stimulate the improvement of their institutions. Stiglitz and Charlton (2007) however, believe that N-S relations tend to be unfair, and trade specialization preserves already existing conditions of the division of labour. Among the last inputs to this discussion is the paper of Kim Jae Duck (2013). This Korean scientist used a new gravity model and concluded that, "the South-South RTAs have the strongest trade creating effect in comparison to other combinations of trade agreements. Surprisingly, the North's trade creating effects are much larger than the South's by North-South trade agreement. These results imply that developed countries experience more beneficial effects on their exports than developing or less developed countries through preferential trade agreements. Customs Union has more trade creating effects than FTA" (Kim 2013).

Asymmetry by size has also attracted the attention of researchers. Chang and Xiao (2015) examine differences in welfare implications between a free trade area and a customs union for member countries with differing market sizes. They use a three-country model of trade under an oligopoly. They argue that the formation of a preferential trade agreement (either a FTA or a CU) is more likely to emerge between countries of similar market size. However, forming a CU allows for a greater degree of market size asymmetry than forming an FTA.

Generally, literature on preferential trade areas assumes that small countries gain more from economic integration than large countries because of positive scale effects and reduced trade costs. The Iceland economist Thomas Snorrason tested the hypothesis of whether the effects of economic integration differed according to the size of countries. He proved that the effects of preferential trade agreements (PTA) are lowest on the trade flows, imports, and exports of large countries and on the exports of micro countries. The effects of PTAs are greatest on the trade flows, imports, and exports of small countries. Snorrason also applied two general equilibrium models to estimate the effects of PTAs on welfare according to the country's size. Results indicate that the welfare gains are asymmetric and depend on the sizes of countries; small countries are the largest relative gainers from economic integration, followed by medium-sized countries (Snorrason 2012).

CUs are famous for the challenges they produce when setting a common external tariff (CET). Asymmetry of the size of the member countries makes negotiating the CET even harder. *Ceteris paribus*, small countries tend to be more open – both functionally (measured by export/GDP or import/GDP ratios) (Natella et al. 2014) and institutionally (measured by average import tariffs); small countries also usually go further in trade facilitation measures (Amin and Haidar 2013). This behaviour stems from the absence of a large variety of industries. Vice versa, large countries have more industries to protect.[4] Thus, large CU members may be more interested in higher tariffs. Taking into account their greater bargaining power, we may expect higher import tariffs resulting from negotiations on the CET in asymmetric customs unions.

Mazhikeyev and Edwards (2015) apply the CGE modelling approach to assess the impact of asymmetry and symmetry in bargaining in deeper Eurasian regional integration. The authors conclude that if there were equal treatment of members of the new integration block, the members would likely benefit from the gains and positive externalities of deeper integration in the future. However, if we take account of the Russian bargaining power and future asymmetric treatment of smaller countries like Kazakhstan, Belarus, and others, they are less likely to receive expected gains (Mazhikeyev and Edwards 2015). The regional integration would be successful if gains are distributed fairly.

Russian researcher A. Libman claims that the degree of asymmetry in bilateral RTA is higher than in multilateral ones, concluding that for post-Soviet countries the multilateral agreement may be more beneficial from the point of view of bargaining power (Libman 2009). We must note that such an assertion is not universal. In the 1990s, an attempt to arrange a free trade agreement among CIS countries was unsuccessful. Due to the different requests on exemptions from free trade regimes, the first CISFTA has been replaced by a small spaghetti bowl of bilateral FTAs. The current version of CISFTA was arranged in 2011 by a smaller number of countries.

We shall base our own input to the analysis of asymmetric RTA on the well-known dichotomy of the two sides of regional integration. There are many synonyms, used to distinguish the two sides of regional economic integration. One side is described using terms such as functional, de facto, real, corporate, market-driven integration, and regionalization. The other is described with words such as institutional, de-jure, government-driven, politically driven integration, and regionalism. The first group of terms focuses on the business interaction between national economies, while the second group of terms highlights the government-organized activity aimed at facilitating business interaction.

This division, however, concerns aspects of integration process, but not the priorities and motives of participating countries and their governments. We dare to introduce another approach: to apply the terms "politically driven integration" and "economically driven integration" not to the means, but to the motives of integration actors. Both terms relate to the institutional integration. Thus, we distinguish *politically driven institutional integration* and *economically driven institutional integration*. Both groups of actors' motives may coexist, but one may prevail.

The two types of institutional integration can be shown throughout history. European integration in its early stages could be categorized as politically driven institutional integration, because peace, stability, and a government-led search for the chance to integrate France with Germany were the main motives for the creation of European Coal and Steel Community (ECSC) in 1951 and the Treaties of Rome in 1957. Association of South-East Asia Nations was born in 1967 for similar, primarily political reasons: to maintain stability in the region during and after several conflicts,[5] specifically when the Cultural Revolution in China reached its peak. NAFTA, however, is an example of economically driven institutional integration because economic benefits were the primary motivations for its creation.

In the case of post-USSR RTAs with Russian participation, unlike other RTAs, there is a mix of political and economic incentives for the development of institutional integration, which differs between signatories. For Russia, the economic benefits of integration with post-Soviet neighbours in relative terms are modest, due to the country size and since EU – not the CIS – is its main trade and investment partner. At the same time, Russia needs political allies, and it hopes that restored economic ties can strengthen historical and cultural ties. Smaller post-Soviet countries can gain more economically because they gain access to the larger market.

It's not always easy to find a balance between interests among partners, and the successes and failures of Eurasian integration can be explained only by taking into account the described mix of motives and goals.

Peculiarities of natural resource-rich countries and the trends and features of their policy on RTAs

Integration policy options for the countries with high concentrations of natural resources is rarely a subject of theoretical insights, though there are plenty of publications on the integration policy of resource-rich regions (Africa, Middle East, Latin America) and on the evolution of RTAs in those regions.[6] From the theoretical point of view, the most general question deserves attention: do such resource-rich countries need regional integration at all, and if yes, then which form of RTA is better for them?

Anthony Venables, head of the Oxford Centre for the Analysis of Resource Rich Economies (OxCarre), devoted an article to alternative trade policy scenarios for geographically remote resource-extracting countries and their neighbours in the region, which have fewer natural resources. Venables shows that in such situations, intraregional trade preferences contribute to a more even distribution of income, helping resource-poor countries to earn on the exports of manufactured goods and services to the resource-rich countries, which, in turn, can partially replace imports from far-away countries by the supply of goods and services from neighbours within the region. According to the estimates of Venables, resource-poor countries benefit from this kind of integration more than their neighbours in resource-rich countries (Venables 2009). He specifically cited regions in Central Africa or in Central Asia as evidence.

Most resource-exporting countries possess other industries, which are less competitive in global markets – the very product structure of exports shows this. Various manifestations of the resource curse, especially the Dutch disease, from time to time make the situation for the non-resource sectors even more difficult. According to estimates of Harding and Venables (2015), $1 worth of resource exports revenue decreases non-resource exports by 74 cents and increases imports by 23 cents. RTAs are an instrument of support for non-resource industries oriented at the national or regional market. CUs are better than FTAs in this case, since they allow additional trade creation and trade diversion effects – but only if CU are comprehensive.[7] It's interesting to note that outside Europe most CUs unite countries, which mostly export primary products, while countries of South Asia and South-East Asia, export mostly finished products and are intensively involved in global value chains, prefer FTA (Sherov-Ignatev 2014).

Literature on Russia's place in regional integration and Russia-led integration projects

Russia's integration policy for many years was not a very popular topic especially among authors writing in English probably, due to the prevalence of disintegration over integration in the post-Soviet territory.[8] However, the visible success of the CU of Belarus, Kazakhstan, and Russia as well as the EAEU compared to the previous attempts of integration among the former USSR states has attracted the attention of researchers. It's impossible to cover the whole range of relevant publications, so we shall concentrate on the main and up-to-date ones, containing most typical conclusions.

Finnish researchers Pekka Sulamaa and Mika Widgren conducted a GTAP-based (computable general equilibrium) study of probable outcomes of a potential FTA between Russia and the EU (its main trading partner) for the participants. Their conclusion was cautious: a free trade agreement with the EU is beneficial for Russia in terms of total output but not necessarily in terms of economic welfare. The main reason for this is that Russia's terms of trade would deteriorate over time since Russia gives higher trade concessions than the EU because it originally had higher import tariffs. Improved productivity in Russia would, however, make the free trade agreement with the EU advantageous (Sulamaa and Widgren 2005).

Dmitry I. Izotov, a Russian researcher, investigates the potential results of scenarios of Russian trade liberalization with the EU, Trans-Pacific Partnership (TPP) and BRICS. His approach is based on the partial equilibrium model and 2014 data. Concerning the probable effects of trade liberalization with the EU, Izotov found that both the trade creation and trade diversion effects for Russia would be more tangible than for the EU, and that trade creation would prevail. In practice it means that imports to Russia could increase by more than 30 percent, while Russia's exports are expected to grow only 3 percent. On the other hand, budget losses due to the tariffs elimination will be substantial: $26 billion (ten times more, than the loss of the EU budget). Outcomes in the case of liberalization of Russia's trade with TPP or BRICS countries would be smaller by scale, but still negative for Russia (Izotov 2017).

De Kort and Dragneva (2006) analysed the spaghetti bowl of FTAs among CIS countries and their role in the economic development of transition countries at the turn of the century. They did not foresee a consolidated "hard" multilateral framework in the short or even medium term. They made a partial mistake – more solid integration structure emerged in several years, though covering not all CIS countries.

Veronika Movchan and Michael Emerson (2018) consider two options of possible development of Eurasian integration, both leading to getting rid of the EAEU common external tariff (CET). The first option presumes that, "the exemptions currently enjoyed by Armenia, Kyrgyzstan, and Kazakhstan should be rationalized by dropping the customs union requirement of a common external tariff, which would reduce tensions within the EAEU, without hindering the process of single market integration for all four freedoms". The second suggested option is an FTA with the EU. However, this option looks unrealistic due to economic, legal, and political obstacles: Russia seems to want to continue an import substitution policy. From a political perspective, any agreement would require an acceptable settlement of the Ukraine conflict.

Approval of such suggestions would mean transitioning to an open regionalism approach. This is hardly in the political interest of Russia. Due to institutional attractiveness of the EU in the West and the economic power of China in the East, it could lead to renewed disintegration of the EAEU. From a purely economic point of view, the shift towards open regionalism would mean the restoration of customs control at internal borders and, consequently, more cumbersome border crossing and the loss of the potential trade creation effect, based on elimination of customs at mutual borders.

Another notable paper on the EAEU achievements, problems, and possible future has been published by the experts at Berlin-Economics, a think tank specializing in transition economies of Eastern Europe and the former USSR. Its experts R. Giucci and A. Mdinaradze (2017) offer well structured and rather objective analysis. The authors point at the asymmetry of EAEU as a root of its problems. (Let us note in brackets, that such asymmetry is a root of similar problems in other RTAs as well.) They point at the Russia's binary attitude to the post-Soviet countries ("for us or against us") and Russia's unilateral trade barriers regularly imposed under various pretexts against disloyal partners within the CIS. Such a policy supports disintegration, instead of integration. One more problem, mentioned by Berlin-based experts is the fact that the Eurasian Economic Commission's supranational competence is ignored by Russia as soon as important foreign policy issues are concerned. Their conclusions are mostly negative: current EAEU is a protectionist union and makes little sense for the trade policy of smaller member states. However, they give some room for a positive scenario: the potential of the EAEU could be realized if exemptions from the CET are abolished, trade barriers in internal trade including border controls are removed; competences of the EAEU Commission are strengthened and the CET reduced. Concerning the last point, we must keep in mind that when this chapter was written, the CET was already being lowered to satisfy Russia's WTO accession obligations, but that the process had not yet been completed.

Krzysztof Falkowski from the Warsaw School of Economics, Poland, examined long-term revealed comparative advantages (RCA) of four EAEU countries in line with the OECD classification of manufacturing industries based on their technology intensity. He concludes that all the EAEU countries fared the best in the medium-low-technology category, which is mostly attributable to the resources-based character of their economies. The relatively stronger competitiveness of Belarus in medium-high technology, medium-low-technology, and low-technology industries to a large extent is the consequence of low-cost processing of Russian petroleum imported at preferential prices, as well as the fact that Belarus provides a large share of exports to post-Soviet countries, especially Russia (Falkowski 2017).

Martin Russell, a researcher affiliated with the EU Parliament, believes that the relatively poor economic performance of the EAEU, including trade slump, has more to do with Russia's economic downturn than the effects of economic integration, and that prospects may improve when Russia comes out of recession (Russell 2017). The results of 2017–2018 confirm this view: mutual trade in the EAEU has seriously increased, depreciating criticism – at least for now.

Summing up the literature review, let us repeat the key conclusions. Politically driven institutional integration and economically driven institutional integration often coexist. In asymmetric RTAs economic motivation is stronger for the smaller member states, since they are the largest relative gainers from economic integration. When remote, developing, resource-rich countries arrange an RTA with resource-poor countries, the latter benefit from this kind of integration more than their neighbours in resource-rich countries. RTAs become an instrument of support for non-resource industries, oriented at the national or regional market. CUs are advantageous to FTAs in this case, since they allow additional trade creation effect, but only if CU is comprehensive, i.e. if customs control at internal borders is eliminated. Large CU members may be more interested in higher tariffs.

Concerning Russia's potential and existing RTA: RF-EU RTA make little sense for Russia. Many authors are sceptical about the future of the Eurasian integration project, but witness some potential of the EAEU, which could be realized if exemptions from the CET are abolished, CET reduced, trade barriers in internal trade including border controls are removed; competences of the EAEU Commission are strengthened, and if smaller member states are treated with respect.

Methodology and data

We use various economic criteria for the evaluation of success of the integration policy and integration projects with Russia's participation. We also consider geographic and institutional factors, affecting or determining motives of the decision-making on Russia's RTAs.

The traditional criterion for assessing the success of an integration project is *the share of mutual trade* in the total trade turnover of the trade bloc. However, it has limited applicability for the comparison of integration associations, as the share of mutual trade depends on the GDP of the association (Sherov-Ignatev and Podkorytova 2008). Nevertheless, this indicator can and should be used in dynamics.

Another similar indicator is the *intensity of trade*. This indicator compares the share of trade with the partner country or group of countries with that partner's share in world trade. Obviously, an increase in trade intensity may indicate a strengthening of mutual integration, although the impact of commodity markets on the value of this indicator is also possible. For example, the growth of prices of oil, exported mostly to the rest of the world (ROW), can decrease the share of mutual trade and the value of trade intensity. This indicator can be calculated not only for individual countries, but also for groups of countries. The intraregional trade intensity index is the ratio of intraregional trade share to the share of world trade with the region, calculated using total trade data. More than one value in the index indicates that trade flow within the region is larger than expected given the importance of the region in world trade (Anukoonwattaka and Beverelli 2013).

We use correlation to check the dependency of Russia's trade with the partner groups on oil prices. For regional associations of commodity-exporting countries, one of the most important justifications for their existence and activities is usually a higher share of non-commodity sectors in mutual trade compared to their share in exports to third countries. In this regard, the *share of non-resource sectors in mutual trade* is an important criterion for the success of such integration projects.

To assess the sustainability of asymmetric RTAs, it is important to monitor the balance of mutual trade. If mutual trade imbalances grow, there is a risk of growing contradictions within the RTA that may inhibit further integration or even call into question the existence of the trade bloc.

One of the factors which justifies an RTA is the economic complementarity of member states. A respective indicator is considered in our study. The degree of institutional rapprochement of the member states in the sphere of trade policy is assessed with the help of Doing Business indicators (Doing Business 2018).

In the next section we use the above indicators to assess the results of Russia's integration policy using the case of Russia's largest RTA: the EAEU. The *data sources* include the statistical department of the Eurasian Economic Commission (EEC), Centre of Integration Studies of the Eurasian Development Bank (CIS EDB) and standard international sources and tools: Doing Business (2018) database of the World Bank and ITC (Trade map, as the most convenient tool to get and analyse the structure and dynamics of trade, and Market Access Map), World Integrated Trade Solutions tools (WITS 2018) and Asian Development Bank (ADB), which both help to calculate trade indices. WTO, UNCTAD, and some others, including RF customs statistics are also used.

Unfortunately, we must accept challenges to the reliability of the data on Russia's trade with Belarus and Kazakhstan. Since 2011, customs statistics could not be used as a data source in these cases due to the elimination of customs on mutual borders. On a regional level it was substituted with data submitted by the firms involved in trade operations with Belarus or Kazakhstan. At the start, the new system did not work perfectly, and some companies did not submit relevant data; this is the most probable reason for the data gap in 2010–2011.

Research findings

In this section, we offer the answers to the following questions:

1 What is the place of Russia in the universe of regional and bilateral trade agreements and why has the EAEU become the most institutionally advanced among Russia's trade agreements?
2 What is the economic rationale (if any) of the choice of a customs union as a form of RTA in the case of EAEU?
3 Considering the starting period of EAEU, what are the achievements and problems of this integration project?

What is the place of Russia in the universe of regional and bilateral trade agreements and why has the EAEU become the most institutionally advanced among Russia's trade agreements?

Russia is the member of several integration agreements still in force: CIS since its foundation in 1991 (and CISFTA since 2011), Asia-Pacific Economic Cooperation (APEC) since 1998, EAEU since its foundation in 2014. As a member of the EAEU, Russia participates in a bilateral free trade agreement with Vietnam, a non-preferential trade agreement with China, and a preferential trade agreement with Iran concluded on behalf of EAEU itself.[9] Besides that, Russia has bilateral FTAs with Azerbaijan, Georgia, Turkmenistan (dating back to 1992) and Serbia (2000, in force since 2006), which are not yet incorporated into the EAEU system of trade agreements.

Russian exports to its main partners strongly correlate with oil prices. The correlation coefficients vary from 0.78 for Russian export to EAEU and Asia-Pacific Economic Cooperation (APEC) to 0.94 for export to CIS and 0.97 to the EU (Table 6.1). Russian imports from its partners also correlate with oil prices. This is not surprising because demand for imports depends on the revenues earned by exports.

The breakdown of Russian trade at first glance contradicts the breakdown of its institutional integration efforts. The EU remains Russia's main partner among the trade blocs, constituting 43.9 percent of total trade at the beginning of 2018. The EU's role in Russian trade decreased in the middle of the second decade of the twenty-first century due to the consequences of sanctions and Russian counter-sanctions in response to the Ukraine conflict. APEC countries constitute 31.2 percent, and their role grows mainly thanks to China, which became Russia's largest trading partner country. EAEU member countries contribute only 7.9 percent of Russia's trade (Figure 6.1; Table 6.1).

Taking into account this breakdown of Russia's trade, one could suggest that trade liberalization with the EU could be the most beneficial for business. This option has been considered and has been explicitly mentioned as a target for the future in the Partnership and Cooperation Agreement (PCA) between Russia and European Communities of 1994. Parties expected that FTA negotiations might begin after Russia's WTO accession. However, Russia joined the WTO only in 2012. By then, enthusiasm for liberal economic reforms largely evaporated. After the "color revolutions" in Georgia and Ukraine, the Kremlin became more suspicious of the real goals of its Western partners; the CU project was already underway to balance out Western advances.

From an economic viewpoint, an EU-RF FTA idea should be looked at with suspicion. Quantitative assessments of its probable outcome show little benefit for Russia (see the results of Sulamaa and Widgren (2005) and Izotov (2017) discussed in the first part of the chapter).

Another reason for Russia's lack of interest towards trade liberalization with the EU and China is the well-known effect of tariff escalation. Tariff escalation usually means that products with higher added value (finished consumer products) are met

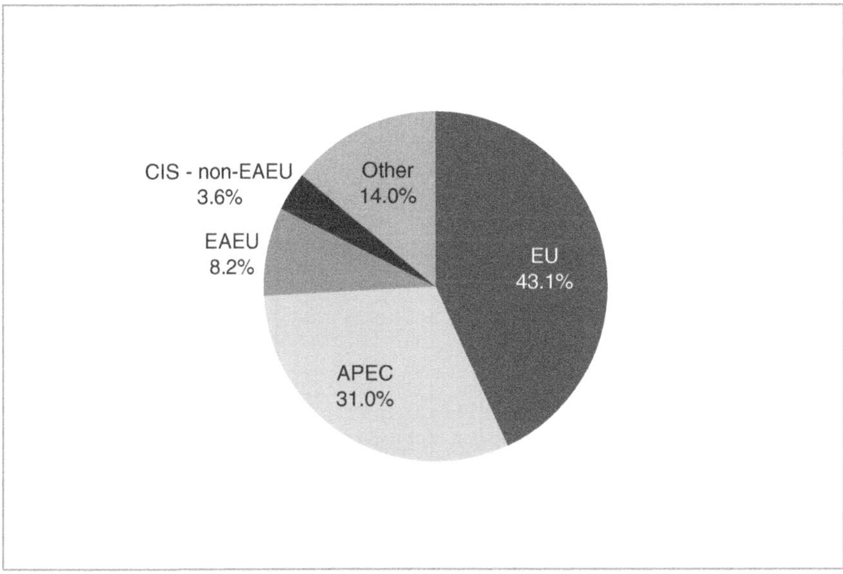

Figure 6.1 Shares of the EU, APEC, and EAEU in the RF trade, January–October 2018
Source: Federal Customs Service of the Russian Federation (2018).

by higher tariff barriers than intermediate products, while the raw materials, especially mineral products, get nearly free market access. The finished capital goods constitute an important exemption: in many developing countries such goods do not compete with the locally produced analogues and are considered important for modernization; for these reasons, such products enjoy privileged access conditions. Most often the term "tariff escalation" is used in relation to one country, but cross-country comparisons are also possible, since tariffs now differ among countries less than in previous decades. This effect is illustrated in the publications of UNCTAD (2016).

Despite the attempts to diversify its exports, Russia remains mostly the exporter of mineral products, meeting low barriers at target markets. On the other hand, Russia does import a lot of machinery and finished consumer products. Table 6.2 demonstrates the import tariff asymmetry in Russia's trade with Germany and China as of 2011. Contemporary tariffs are lower, thanks to Russia's obligations to the WTO; nevertheless, the tariff escalation is still present. Let us add that by 2015 90.8 percent of the total value of Russian non-agricultural products exported to the EU and 72.9 percent to China, entered target markets on a duty-free basis (WTO 2017, p. 144).

The idea of free trade between the EU and Russia was introduced once more in January, 2014 during the last EU–Russia summit in Brussels. Russian president Putin suggested thinking about arranging such an FTA. Evidently, it was an attempt to balance EU-Ukraine agreement, and seemed to be a more politically,

Table 6.1 The role of main country groups in Russian trade and the influence of oil prices, 2001–2017

	Share of Russian exports, percent			*Correlation of Russian exports value with oil prices, 2001–2017*	*Share of Russian imports, percent*			*Correlation of Russian imports value with oil prices, 2001–2017*
	2001	*2013*	*2017*		*2001*	*2013*	*2017*	
EU 28	54.5	45.8	44.4	0.97	44.1	42.6	35.6	0.97
APEC	15.1	18.8	24.1	0.78	18.6	34.7	40.7	0.86
CIS, including:	14.5	11.6	13.8	0.94	26.7	12.3	10.9	0.97
EAEU	6.1	3.8	4.8	0.78	14.5	6.4	7.6	0.90
Other CIS	8.4	7.8	9.0	0.94	12.2	5.9	3.3	0.94

Source: Authors' calculations of data from ITC (2018b).

Table 6.2 Import tariffs in Russia's trade with EU/Germany, China and the world in 2011 (before WTO accession) and 2015

Import tariffs, percent		*EU (Germany)*	*China*	*World*
Russian applied trade weighted (by bilateral import) import tariff for products from . . . (the country)	2011	9.1	8.8	8.6
Applied trade weighted (by bilateral imports) import tariff for products *from RF*	2011 2015 (Non-agricultural products)	0.2 (Germany) 0.4 (EU)	1.62 1.3	1.02 N/a

Sources: 1) data, derived from the Market Access Map tool of the International Trade Centre (ITC 2018b). 2) Aggregation of average import tariffs, applied in bilateral trade is available only for 2007 and 2011 (GTAP-oriented tool) from WTO Tariff Profiles (WTO 2017).

rather than economically driven step. Regardless, this initiative was met coolly and did not develop.

Russia-China trade has a similar structural imbalance (China exports mostly finished products, and Russia exports mostly fuel and other primary commodities), and Russia has not agreed to liberalize mutual trade with China despite numerous offers. However, the Agreement on Economic Partnership between China and the EAEU was signed in May, 2018. The agreement covers issues of customs procedures, intellectual property rights, government procurement, electronic commerce, inter-agency cooperation, etc., but did not presume trade liberalization per se (Agreement 2018).

Besides purely economic reasons for abstaining from free trade with the EU or China, one could guess that there are psychological factors at play as well. In these FTAs Russia would be a minor partner, and this role is neither typical, nor comfortable for this country.

The EU and China are too large to test experimental agreements, but some smaller countries could be used for this role. Before the Ukrainian crisis, the predecessor to the EAEU, the Customs Union of Belarus, Kazakhstan, and Russia (CU BKR) did negotiate an FTA with the European Free Trade Association, and in 2015 an EAEU-Vietnam FTA was arranged. It is expected, that the agreement with Vietnam will allow testing the practical effects of trade liberalization with a country with a cheap labour force. Similar negotiations are on the ride with other trading partners: Egypt, Israel, India, and South Korea. The Interim Agreement leading to formation of a free trade area with Iran is already signed. The interest of various countries wanting to arrange an FTA with the EAEU may be taken as a sign of success of the Eurasian integration project: potential FTA partners expect EAEU to be sustainable RTA worthy of dealing with.

Let us turn now towards former Soviet republics and their role in Russian regional integration policy. We shall briefly consider the CIS and more thoroughly – the EAEU.

What are the reasons for institutional integration of former Soviet republics and for the choice of a customs union as a form of RTA in the case of EAEU?

CIS countries play a relatively small role in Russian foreign trade compared to the EU and APEC. Their share of Russian exports fluctuated between 13 and 16 percent in the twenty-first century, depending on oil prices. The EAEU members now matter more in Russian trade with the CIS countries than the other members of the CIS. The conflict in Ukraine was one of the main reasons for this shift: imports from Russia halved, and exports to Russia fell four times from the pre-conflict period.

On the import side, CIS countries supplied a quarter of all goods from abroad to Russia at the beginning of the century,[10] but rising incomes, real appreciation of the Russian ruble, and an inflow of Chinese goods decreased the share of CIS countries in Russian imports two-fold from 27 percent in 2001 to 13 percent in 2009. Contraction of the CIS's role as a supplier of goods to Russia resumed after the start of the Ukrainian conflict in 2014. Until 2017, Russia imported only 11 percent of goods from CIS countries (Figure 6.2). This share can become even lower due to continual decreases of Russia-Ukraine trade, which is only slightly compensated by the growth of intra-EAEU trade in 2014–2017.

However, Russian trade relations with CIS countries remain strong and important. This is evident when we eliminate the influence of the economies' size with the help of a *trade intensity index*. The intensity of Russia's trade with EAEU countries demonstrates very high values: 13–22. The intensity of Russia's trade with Armenia and Kyrgyz Republic, who were the last to join the union, grew

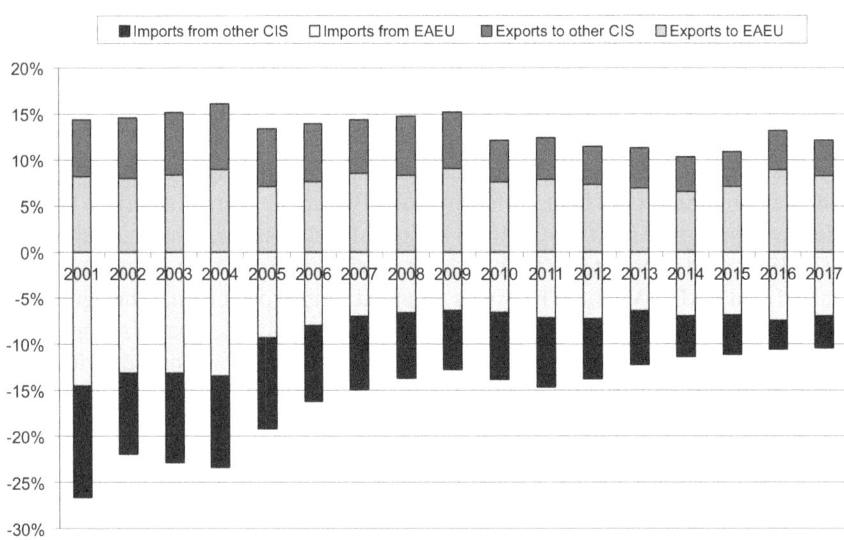

Figure 6.2 Shares of EAEU-5 and other CIS countries in Russia's exports and imports in 2001–2017

especially rapidly after their accession. Russian trade with other CIS counties is also quite intense (index varies from 3 to 11). Trade intensity index values for Russia's trade with EU and China are much lower – equal or slightly higher than 1 – a value, which could be expected, knowing their share in global trade (Figure 6.3).

Besides the high intensity of mutual trade, one more economic reason for integration of countries is their *trade complementarity*.[11] The Russian economy is relatively highly complementary with those of Belarus and Armenia and to a smaller extent – with Kyrgyzstan (Table 6.3).[12] The lowest value of this index (33.5) among Russia's EAEU partners is between Russia and Kazakhstan, which is natural, since both countries are strongly endowed with natural resources; nevertheless, complementarity exists between these economies because Russia supplies Kazakhstan with many intermediary and finished products, including machinery, which compensates for the absence of those industries in the importing country.

The de facto free trade regime between CIS countries since the moment of their birth as independent states in December 1991 was natural because there were no

Table 6.3 Trade complementarity index between Russia and its EAEU partners as for 2016

Partner	*Trade complementarity index with Russia*
Armenia	52.2
Belarus	59.8
Kazakhstan	36.5
Kyrgyzstan	43.5

Source: WITS (2018).

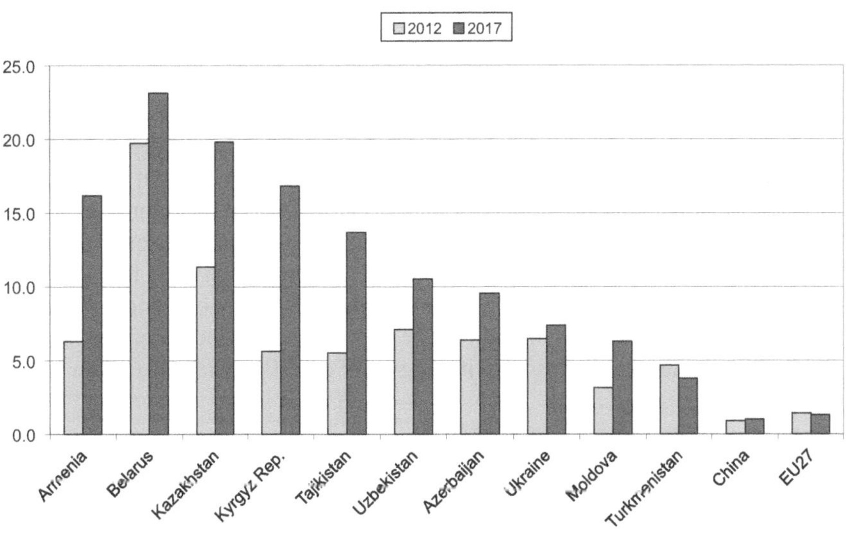

Figure 6.3 Index of trade intensity for Russia's trade with EAEU members, other CIS members, EU-27 and China, 2012–2017

technically equipped and protected borders and no customs at mutual borders. Later it was arranged de-jure. However, in the process of establishing conventional attributes of trade policy regulation and installing equipped borders, the trade regime in CIS became more cumbersome for business. According to estimates, in 2010 the border crossing procedures consisted on average of half of the total cargo transportation time between CIS countries – even in the conditions of tariff-free trade (Adyasov 2010). It was one of the arguments for arranging a customs union: a comprehensive CU allows for the elimination of customs control at internal borders, making border crossing faster, easier, and cheaper. Other arguments for the choice of a CU referenced the standard Balassa' scheme, realized in the EU.

The political cost for participant countries in choosing the CU as a form of RTA is the inability of the participants of a comprehensive CU to arrange separate FTAs with third countries and the sacrifice some of sovereign prerogatives to a supranational authority. Only the CU as a whole can negotiate with third parties. Countries with high bargaining power in a CU, like Russia, may not experience these costs, but may instead see the costs that other countries experience as a benefit to themselves. RF managed to arrange a CU (which is very close to what can be called a comprehensive CU) with the countries of the CIS, most loyal to Russia because of their common language. Russian is the most spoken language in Russia, Belarus, and even in Kazakhstan. Other factors, historical and political in the case of Armenia, and financial in the case of the Kyrzyz Republic also contributed to the formation of the CU.

Considering the motives of the CU/EAEU participants, the economic benefits are most tangible and important for the smaller countries. They get preferential access to a large market, while the major participant gets preferential access to small markets. The share of EAEU partners in Russian trade is less than 8 percent (9.6 percent of exports and 7.6 percent of imports in 2017), while Russia's share of the trade in Armenia, Belarus, Kazakhstan, and Kyrgyzstan reaches, respectively, 26.5, 51.2, 9.3, 14.7 for exports and 28.7, 65.2, 39.1, 26.4 for imports. Thus, economic motives were smaller from Russia's perspective, than from the perspective of its partners.

On the other hand, EAEU has political importance for Russia. It's members cannot sign separate FTAs with other partners, thus, Russia can keep a prevailing influence on a substantial part of the former Soviet territory and put limits to, for example, Belarus' political shift towards the EU and Kazakhstan, or Kyrgyzstan' rapprochement with China. It brings us to the conclusion that the choice of the CU as a form of economic integration was mostly politically motivated from Russia's side, and mostly economically motivated from the perspective of other participants, with the probable exception of Armenia because Armenia depends on the political and military protection of Russia in its long-lasting conflict with Azerbaijan.

Advantages, achievements, and problems of the EAEU

During the relatively short period since October 2007 when the Treaty on the Establishment of the Single Customs Territory and Formation of the Customs Union was signed, CU/EAEU made tangible advances in building and optimization of its integration institutions. Specifically, in July 2011, customs control was eliminated on the Russia–Kazakhstan border. The Eurasian Economic

Commission was arranged as a supranational regulating authority, responsible for elaborating common trading rules and later, rules for other sectors. The common customs code, common external tariff, the formula and the mechanism of collecting and distribution of import tariffs are in force. A single services market began to operate in a number of sectors identified by the EAEU member states in January 1, 2015. In value terms, those sectors add up to almost 50 percent of the total trade in services in the member states of the Union (Eurasian Economic Commission 2017b). In May 2017, a common market of medicines and medical products began to operate in the EAEU. Non-tariff barriers still exist in mutual business relations, but the systemic work on their elimination is being conducted, bringing with it positive results. In January 2018 the new customs code came into force.

Institutional advances largely explain some achievements in real integration of five national economies; though we must afford those positive changes are not far reaching yet. Russian exports to all four partners grew rapidly in 2017 from 29 to 38 percent. Overall exports of RF rose 24.8 percent, however this growth happened after the decline of mutual trade in 2013–2016, caused by the effects of the Ukrainian crisis, the depreciation of the Russian ruble (first phase of the J-effect) and low oil prices from 2013 to 2016 (Table 6.4).

One more positive feature of EAEU integration is the more diversified structure of mutual trade compared to the overall trade pattern of this trade block. In 2017, mineral products added up to 64.3 percent of EAEU exports to ROW in contrast to only 37.5 percent of mutual trade. At the same time, machinery comprised 17.9 percent of intraregional exports and only 3.4 percent of the exports to the ROW (Figure 6.4). Higher shares of processed products in mutual trade is typical for South–South customs unions (Sherov-Ignatev 2014) and has, in the case of the EAEU, two explanations: Firstly, the two largest members of the EAEU, Russia, and Kazakhstan, possess enormous mineral resources, and the need in mutual trade in this sector is limited; secondly, producers of processed products have additional competitive advantages in EAEU markets based on common standards, cheaper transportation, easier border crossing, personal connections, the price-sensitive nature of EAEU markets, and the inertia (path-dependence) of customers.

In the sphere of investments and entrepreneurship, the share of firms with Russian ownership among all foreign-owned enterprises in the EAEU countries is 34 percent. The number of firms investing in Kazakhstan has shown remarkable

Table 6.4 Growth of Russian exports to EAEU countries in 2013–2017

Importers	*Growth in exported value in 2016–2017, percent per annum*	*Growth in exported value in 2013–2017, percent per annum*	*Total imports growth of partner countries in 2013–2017, percent per annum*
Armenia	29	29	−3
Belarus	38	1	−5
Kazakhstan	31	−10	−14
Kyrgyzstan	35	−12	−9

Source: ITC (2018b).

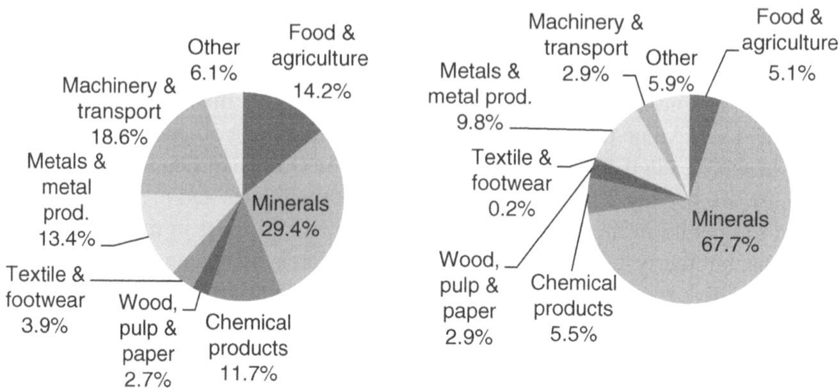

Figure 6.4 EAEU intraregional and extraregional exports by product group, January–October, 2018

Source: Eurasian Economic Commission (2018a, 2018b).

growth since 2014 (Efimova and Sherov-Ignatev 2017). Russian outward foreign direct investments (FDI) to EAEU, according to official figures add up to approximately $ 1.5 billion a year (3–7.7 percent of the total Russian outward FDI), but real figures tend to be higher due to the widespread use of offshore jurisdictions for investments deals – even by public companies. Russia is the key source of FDI in Kyrgyzstan (comprising 40–44 percent of total FDI inflow in 2014–2016) and in Belarus (30–44 percent in 2014–2017). Kazakhstani outward FDIs are fewer than Russian FDIs, but notably, the share of Kazakhstani outward FDI toward the EAEU grew from 3.8 percent in 2014 to 43 percent in 2017. This is partly due to the decline of the total amount of the FDI outflow from the country (Eurasian Economic Commission 2017c).

Thanks to preferential status for labour migrants from the EAEU countries, migrant labour has increased, reaching 1.2 million workers in 2015, most of which worked in Russia. More than 40 percent of them arrived in Russia from Kyrgyzstan and 25 percent from Armenia. After the devaluation of the Russian ruble in 2015, many Kyrgyz migrants went home, but the number of migrant workers from Belarus and Kazakhstan continued to grow.

Besides some achievements and advantages, the EAEU encounters a number of problems. Some of them can be described as the "growing pains", typical for non-mature organisms. For example, many non-tariff barriers remain in mutual business relations. Experts of the Eurasian Economic Commission are busy finding and eliminating such barriers, caused by discrepancies of national legislations. The results are not yet decisive. From 2012 to 2014, the total number of identified barriers, exemptions, and limitations reached 603. These barriers exist in many spheres such as taxation, technical standards, industrial policy, transportation, and financial markets and trade in services. Out of this number, 81 were eliminated,

27 were in the process of elimination, but most remained in place. As for 2016, figures were the following: 14 barriers, 36 exemptions and 166 limitations totalling, 216 non-tariff barriers (NTB) in mutual economic relations of five countries (Eurasian Economic Commission 2017a). Attention to the problems and attempts to solve them are visible.

Despite constant efforts to coordinate the trade regimes of EAEU countries, conditions for the participants of foreign trade remain seriously different. According to the Doing Business 2014–2018 estimates, the Trading Across Borders ranks of the five EAEU countries vary greatly, and the gap does not decrease with time. In 2015 Armenia was the best among the five countries, being only 110th, while Kazakhstan remained at one of the last, placing 185th. Since 2016, the method of index calculation has changed, and ranks changed as well. Belarus is now the best occupying the 30th place; Kazakhstan is 123rd. Trading Across Borders ranks did not improve seriously, except Russia, who jumped from 170th in 2016 to 100 in 2018 (Table 6.5). This indicator reflects not only the quality of regulating procedures, but also geographic location; importers and exporters from landlocked countries tend to suffer from longer transportation times and challenges related to border crossings. Four out of five EAEU member countries are landlocked, and Kyrgyzstan is the most remote from the ocean. However, the documentary compliance (hours) and border compliance (US$) are the main components of the method of index calculation, and it is evident that there is room for improvement in this field.

Other problems are more chronic and immanent, since they derive from the asymmetry of the EAEU country group.

One problem concerns unequal concessions during the formation of a common external tariff (CET). To reach the common level, Kazakhstan had to make its tariffs much higher, while Russia and Belarus decreased their tariffs slightly. It complicated the life of Kazakh importers and led to an increase in prices in this country for many consumer goods. This also caused trade diversion; some Chinese goods were partly crowded out from the Kazakhstani market by similar goods from Russia.

One example illustrates both the success story and the problem of the CU. The new Customs code (CC) of the EAEU, which came into force in 2018, contains many breakthrough innovations, such as the transition to mainly electronic

Table 6.5 Trading across borders ranks of the EAEU members, 2014–2018

EAEU member	*2014*	*2015*	*2016*	*2017*	*2018*
Armenia	117	110	29	48	52
Belarus	149	145	25	30	30
Kazakhstan	182	185	122	119	123
Kyrgyz Rep.	186	183	83	79	84
Russia	157	155	170	140	100

Note: Method of calculation changed in 2016.

Source: The World Bank Doing Business Reports 2014–2018 (The World Bank 2018).

declaration, the possibility of automatic customs clearance (if the risk management system does not warn about problems), and a single-window system for submitting documents. Nevertheless, the new CC has not solved the problem of abandoning the principle of residency – one of the main barriers to the free movement of goods in the EAEU (Vinokurov 2017). This means that customs clearance of goods in the EAEU is required at the country of residence of the importing firm. For example, only Belarusian firms may import to EAEU territory via Belarusian border.

The balance of Russia's trade with its EAEU partners remained positive during the second decade of the century. It is interesting to compare Russia's balance of trade in goods with the EAEU partners and with ROW in two variants: in a standard way and without mineral fuels (Chapter 27 of the HS coding system) (Figure 6.5). For Russia's trade with the ROW, the trade balance curve, which does not take into account mineral fuel trade, has a nearly mirror shape with respect to the trade balance curve for all goods: the more positive the trade balance in general, the more negative it occurs after the subtraction of mineral fuels. This phenomenon is not surprising for the country, which exports mostly oil and gas. The situation with the trade within the EAEU looks different – at least for the mineral fuels-free calculations. Since 2013 Russia's trade balance of non-fuel trade with the EAEU partners is positive and tends to improve for Russia. Meanwhile, vice versa, the balances of Russia's EAEU partners regarding trade with Russia remain negative.

Russia, being the dominant country of the trade block, tends to deal with its own problems, only occasionally recalling the existence of its minor partners-neighbours. This is a typical situation for asymmetric RTA; the US is not very

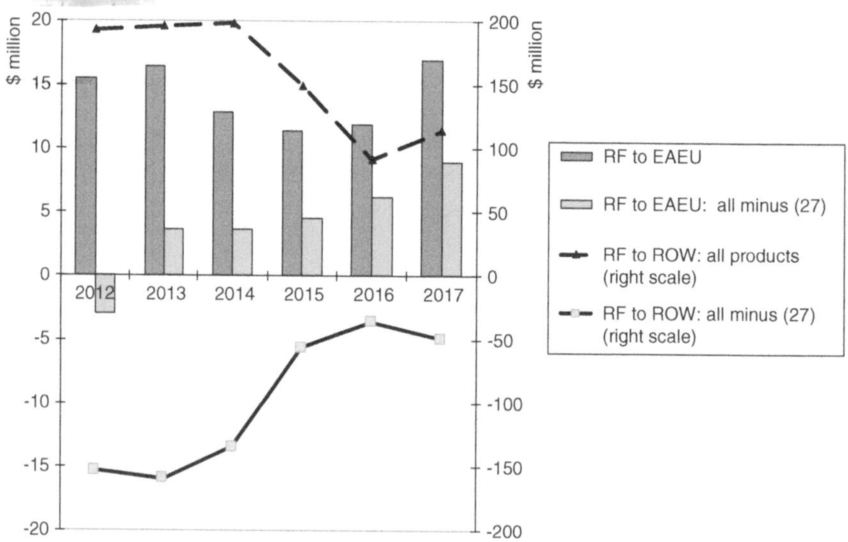

Figure 6.5 Russia's Balance of I trade with EAEU members, 2012–2017

attentive to the needs of Canada and Mexico in NAFTA, and South Africa practices double standards in its relations with its partners within the South African Customs Union (SACU). The introduction of counter-sanctions against Western countries in 2014 was not discussed in advance with the CU partners, despite the agreement on a common trade policy implemented by the EEC as a supranational body. In reality, Belarus and Kazakhstan gained some benefits when their agricultural producers substituted some of products previously imported to Russia from the EU. But this does not negate the need for collective decision-making on the issues of collective responsibility and interest.

Import substitution strategy and policy, popular in Russia nowadays, became a systemic threat to the integration process. The Russian controlling and regulating agencies often impose artificial limitations on imports of milk products from Belarus. It is widely recognized, that such moves are lobbied by Russian companies competing with Belarusian ones (Burlakova 2018). Similar things happen in other sectors as well. This Russian practice leads to doubts concerning the sense and effectiveness of the common market and the Eurasian integration project in general.

To sum up, the Eurasian integration project is grounded in economic interests, though the motives for its arrangement were not totally economic. During its short existence the EAEU gained tangible achievements, and at the same time, the asymmetry of the trade block has caused some biased decisions. For the continuation of the discussed integration project, Russia should take care of economic effectiveness of the EAEU for all member countries.

Conclusion

Our analysis helps understand why Russian leaders prefer traditional models of regional integration, and not the concept of open regionalism. The customs union as a form of integration has potential advantages for Russia and some other countries of the Eurasian Economic Union, however, the Ukrainian crisis and related events seriously limit the realization of this potential.

The choice of the CU as a form of economic integration was mostly politically motivated from Russia's perspective, and mostly economically motivated from the side of other participants. In this context we can talk about politically driven or economically driven institutional integration. However, there are important economic reasons for all member countries when they choose to create a CU. Comprehensive CUs provide opportunities for additional trade creation and a chance to increase intraregional exports of manufactured goods, which is of special importance for resources-exporting countries. The economic reasons for Russia to arrange the CU with its chosen partners include the high intensity of their mutual trade, sufficient trade complementarity and a more diversified structure of mutual trade, compared to the overall trade pattern of this trade block.

Despite the serious growth of intraregional trade in 2017–2018 and the tangible progress of integration in investments and migration, the achievements of the Eurasian integration project so far are more visible in the institutional sphere. The

Table 6.6 Main research findings. Rationale, achievements, and problems of the Eurasian Economic Union

Questions	*Aspects*	*Answers*
Why with these counties?	Formal indicators of economic reasonability	Trade complementarity index is high enough. Trade intensity index for Russia's trade with EAEU states are the highest among Russia's trade partners.
	Economic factors behind	Competitive advantages of processing industries on regional markets. Cheaper transportation, lower transaction costs thanks to neighbourhood, common infrastructure, close educational and technical standards, infrastructure, technological chains,
	Other reasons	Common language. Common history, similar mentality and mutual understanding, Bargaining power of Russia.
Why no RTA with the main trade partners?		Russian exports of mineral fuels does not meet serious barriers in partner countries. Low competitiveness of Russian manufactured products on global markets.
Why customs union?	Economic reasons	Elimination of customs control at internal borders induces additional trade creation and trade diversion effect and gives potential advantage for the manufacturing sector (to compensate its low competitiveness in the global markets by increased regional export) and for the "introvert" regions of Russia, located close to the border with Kazakhstan.
	Political reasons	CU leads to tighter integration. Comprehensive CU prevents separate FTAs of member countries with the third countries.
Visible achievements of EAEU		Easier border crossing within the EAEU. Strong growth of intraregional trade in 2017. Higher share of manufactured products in mutual trade, than in the trade with the ROW. Growth of mutual investments (Russian investments to other EAEU countries). Increased intensity of trade. Integration of the labour market.
Problems	Problems in the process of fixing	Non-tariff barriers still exist in mutual trade relations. Institutional cohesion still underway.
	Problems due to asymmetry (Russia's dominance)	Some institutional decisions are biased: dominating country does not always take into account the interests its EAEU partners.
Practical implications and recommendations		The future of the EAEU will depend on its effectiveness – in the sense of satisfying the interests of all member countries.

Eurasian economic commission conducts serious work to liberalize mutual trade and to harmonize rules. Institutional harmonization in the EAEU is far from its final stage, but the progress is visible from the dynamics of Doing Business scores and the consecutive elimination of non-tariff barriers in mutual trade. Adoption of the new Customs code lays a good basis for future intensification of business relations. The interests of various countries in arranging an FTA with the EAEU may be taken as a sign of the success of the Eurasian integration project. Potential FTA partners expect the EAEU to be a sustainable RTA, which is worthy of negotiating with.

Meanwhile, the problems and contradictions due to the asymmetry of the RTA are not easy to solve. The leading position of Russia in the EAEU often tempts Russia to make decisions without consulting its partners. The sustainability and future success of the EAEU will depend upon its ability to address the interests of all member states.

The main findings are reflected in the Table 6.6.

Notes

1 We use the term "regional integration" in a broad sense, embracing and including its aspects, known as regionalism, regionalization, regional (including bilateral) trade agreements, etc.

2 CIS was arranged in December, 1991 as a substitute to the dissolved USSR and initially consisted of 12 countries: Armenia, Azerbaijan, Belarus, Georgia, Kazakhstan, Kyrgyzstan (Kyrgyz Republic), Moldova, Russian Federation, Tajikistan, Turkmenistan, Ukraine, and Uzbekistan. Ukraine and Turkmenistan have not got full membership, since they have not signed the statute of the CIS. Georgia left the CIS in 2009after the armed conflict with Russia in 2008. The current version of CISFTA was signed in 2011 by eight countries: Armenia, Belarus, Kazakhstan, Moldova, Russian Federation, Tajikistan, Ukraine, Uzbekistan joined the CISFTA in 2013. Russia waived the free trade regime with Ukraine in 2016 when EU-Ukraine association agreement came into force.

3 The Eurasian Economic Union began functioning in 2015; its current members are Armenia, Belarus, Kazakhstan, Kyrgyzstan, and Russia. The Eurasian Economic Union (EAEU) was arranged on the foundations of its precursor, the Customs Union of Belarus, Russia, and Kazakhstan.

4 On the other hand, small, less developed economies depend on import duties as the source of budget revenues, and may keep non-zero tariffs despite having no industries to protect. Such countries maintain the high level of taxes on international trade since the tax systems in such economies are underdeveloped and they are able to generate returns primarily from easily collected indirect taxes like trade taxes (Sokolovska 2016).

5 Events of 1965 in Indonesia, Indonesia-Malaysia confrontation in 1964, Vietnam War, communist guerrillas in rural regions.

6 Publications under the aegis of Economic Commission for Africa (ECA) and Economic and Social Commission for Latin America (ECLAC) can be recommended in this context.

7 We consider CU to be comprehensive, i.e. if customs control at internal borders is eliminated. Most of the currently existing CUs are not comprehensive.

8 We must add in brackets, that the USSR-led project Council of Mutual Economic Assistance (CMEA or COMECON) attracted considerable attention of Western researchers in the 1970s to 1980s Some experts argued that the USSR itself could be regarded as a

special kind of customs union and payment union Bert van Selm (1997) or just a case of full economic integration (Sutyrin 1996).

9 The WTO RTA database is not fully relevant data source in this case. It does not include CIS-1991, the Russia–Belarus Union State and APEC, but includes the Common Economic Zone (CEZ) – the treaty of Belarus, Kazakhstan, Russia, and Ukraine of 2003, which has never been implemented. It also mentions the Russian Federation–Belarus–Kazakhstan custom union, which has been replaced by EAEU.

10 At that period the effect of the four-fold devaluation of Russian Ruble in 1998, which enforced the shift of trade direction to the suppliers of cheap products from CIS countries, was still tangible.

11 The complementarity index measures the degree to which the export pattern of one country matches the import pattern of another. The value ranges from 0 to 100. A high degree of complementarity is assumed to indicate more favourable prospects for a successful trade arrangement.

12 We do not consider trade complementarity dynamics; the history of Eurasian integration project is too short to exert influence on the economic specialization of member states. We also do not consider trade complementarity with the non-EAEU countries: it can be high, but our purpose is not to find partners with the highest complementarity index values, but rather to notify the sufficiently high level of complementarity within the EAEU.

Bibliography

Adyasov, I 2010, *Tamozhennyj soyuz: pervye itogi*, REGNUM, viewed 10 March 2018, https://regnum.ru/news/1347504.html

Agreement 2018, *Agreement on Economic and Trade Cooperation Between the Eurasian Economic Union and Its Member States, of the One Part, and the People's Republic of China, of the Other Part*, Signed in Astana 17 May, 2018, viewed 15 August 2018, www.eurasiancommission.org/en/nae/news/Pages/18-05-2017-1.aspx

Amin, M and Haidar, J 2013, *Trade Facilitation and Country Size*, World Bank Policy Research Working Paper, no. 6692, viewed 15 August 2018, https://openknowledge.worldbank.org/bitstream/handle/10986/16922/WPS6692.pdf?sequence=1&isAllowed=y

Anukoonwattaka, W and Beverelli, C 2013, *Trade Flows and Trade Policy Analysis*, Dhaka, viewed 19 August 2018, https://artnet.unescap.org/tid/projects/tradeflow-s2.pdf

Bhagwati, J 1995, 'US Trade Policy: The Infatuation With FTAs', *Columbia University Discussion Paper Series*, no. 726, pp. 1–20.

Burlakova, E 2018, 'Rossel'hoznadzor zapretil vvoz moloka iz Belorussii', *Vedomosti*, 22 February, viewed 30 May 2018, www.vedomosti.ru/business/articles/2018/02/22/751837-rosselhoznadzor-moloka

Chang, YM and Xiao, R 2015, 'Preferential Trade Agreements Between Asymmetric Countries: Free Trade Areas (With Rules of Origin) vs. Customs Unions', *Japan and the World Economy*, no. 33, pp. 28–43.

Doing Business 2018, *Reforming to Create Jobs*, The World Bank, Washington, DC.

Efimova, E and Sherov-Ignatev, V 2017, 'Russian Foreign Direct Investments in the Eurasian Economic Union', in: K Liuhto, SF Sutyrin and JF Blanchard (eds.) *The Russian Economy and Foreign Direct Investment*, Routledge, London and New York.

Eurasian Economic Commission 2017a, *Barriers, Derogations and Restrictions in the Eurasian Economic Union*, EEC Report, Moscow.

Eurasian Economic Commission 2017b, *Eurasian Economic Integration: Facts and Figure*, Eurasian Economic Commission, EEC Report, Moscow.

Eurasian Economic Commission 2017c, *Pryamye investicii v Evrazijskom ehkonomicheskom soyuze. Po operativnym dannym za 2017 god. Statisticheskij byulleten*, EEC Report, Moscow.

Eurasian Economic Commission 2018a, *Ob itogah vneshnej torgovli tovarami Evrazijskogo ehkonomicheskogo soyuza.Yanvar' – oktyabr' 2018 goda*, EEC Report, Moscow.

Eurasian Economic Commission 2018b, *Ob itogah vzaimnoj torgovli tovarami Evrazijskogo ehkonomicheskogo soyuza.Yanvar' – oktyabr' 2018 goda*, EEC Report, Moscow.

Falkowski, K 2017, 'Long-Term Comparative Advantages of the Eurasian Economic Union Member States in International Trade', *International Journal of Management and Economics*, vol. 53, no. 4, pp. 27–49.

Federal Customs Service of the Russian Federation 2018, viewed 20 April 2018, www.customs.ru/index.php?option=com_content&view=article&id=13858&Itemid=2095

Giucci, R and Mdinaradze, A 2017, *The Eurasian Economic Union – Analysis From a Trade Policy Perspective*, viewed 24 July 2018, https://berlin-economics.com/wp-content/uploads/2018-05-29_Presentation-EAEU_Moscow.pdf

Harding, T and Venables, A 2015, 'The Implications of Natural Resource Exports for Non-resource Trade', *OxCarre Research Paper*, no. 103, viewed 28 July 2018, www.economics.ox.ac.uk/materials/working_papers/4857/oxcarrerp2013103.pdf

ITC 2018a, *Market Access Map*, viewed 30 March 2018, www.macmap.org/

ITC 2018b, *Trade Map*, viewed 30 May 2018, https://trademap.org/Index.aspx

Izotov, D 2017, *Liberalizaciya torgovli Rossii so stranami Evropejskogo Soyuza, BRIKS i Transtihookeanskogo partnerstva*, viewed 24 July 2018, http://institutiones.com/general/3073-liberalizaciya-torgovli-rossii.html

Kim, JD 2013, 'The Effects of Trade Agreements *on* Trade: Asymmetric Partners and Types of Agreements', *KIET Industrial Economic Review*, 2018, vol. 13, no. 1, pp. 39–52.

Kort, J de and Dragneva, R 2006. 'Russia's Role in Fostering the CIS Trade Regime', *Leiden University Department of Economics Research Memorandum*, no. 3, viewed 19 May 2018, https://openaccess.leidenuniv.nl/bitstream/handle/1887/43253/jdk_2006_03.pdf?sequence=1

Libman, A 2009, 'Models of Economic Integration – Russian and Post-Soviet Experience', *MPRA Paper*, no. 19434, viewed 19 May 2018, https://mpra.ub.uni-muenchen.de/19434/1/MPRA_paper_19434.pdf

Mazhikeyev, A and Edwards, H 2015, 'Consequences of Asymmetric Deeper Eurasian Economic Integration', *EcoMod*, no. 8365, pp. 1–71.

Movchan, V and Emerson, M 2018, *The Eurasian Economic Union's Problematic Customs Union*, viewed 19 May 2018, www.3dcftas.eu/publications/other/eurasian-economic-union%E2%80%99s-problematic-customs-union

Natella, S, O'Sullivan, M and Keating, G 2014, *The Success of Small Countries*, Credit Suisse AG Research Institute, Zurich.

Russell, M 2017, *Eurasian Economic Union*, European Parliamentary Research Service Briefing viewed 17 July 2018, www.europarl.europa.eu/RegData/etudes/BRIE/2017/599432/EPRS_BRI(2017)599432_EN.pdf

Selm, B van 1997, *The Economics of Soviet Breakup*, Routledge, London.

Sherov-Ignatev, V 2014, 'Tamozhennye sojuzy stran – jeksporterov syr'ja kak instrument smjagchenija negativnyh jeffektov liberalizacii torgovli', *Evrazijskaja jekonomicheskaja integracija*, vol. 22, no. 1, pp. 49–63.

Sherov-Ignatev, V and Podkorytova, O 2008, 'Vneshnetorgovaya otkrytost' nacional'nyh ehkonomik i integracionnyh gruppirovok – parametry izmereniya i vozdejstvuyushchie faktory', in: *Sovremennaya sistema mirohozyajstvennyh svyazej: tendencii razvitiya i perspektivy*, Izdatel'stvo 'Evropejskij dom', St. Petersburg.

Shiff, M and Winters, A 2003, *Regional Integration and Development*, The World Bank, Washington, DC.

Snorrason, ST 2012, *Asymmetric Economic Integration: Size Characteristics of Economies, Trade Costs and Welfare*, Springer-Verlag, Berlin and Heidelberg.

Sokolovska, OV 2016, 'Trade Freedom and Revenue From Trade Taxes: A Cross-Country Analysis', *Vestnik Sankt-Peterburgskogo universiteta. Seriya 5: Ekonomika*, no. 2, pp. 52–67.

Stiglitz, J and Charlton, A 2007, *Fair Trade for All: How Trade Can Promote Development*, Oxford University Press, Oxford.

Sulamaa, P and Widgren, M 2005, 'Economic Effects of Free Trade Between the EU and Russia', *ENEPRI Working Paper*, no. 36, viewed 7 June 2018, http://aei.pitt.edu/6741/1/1220_36.pdf

Sutyrin, SF 1996, 'Problems and Prospects of Economic Reintegration Within the CIS', *Review of Economies in Transition*, no. 1, pp. 29–43.

UNCTAD 2016, *Key Statistics and Trends in Trade Policy*, viewed 30 May 2018, https://unctad.org/en/PublicationsLibrary/ditctab2016d2_en.pdf

Venables, A 2009, 'Economic Integration in Remote Resource-Rich Regions', *OxCarre Research Paper*, no. 22, viewed 7 June 2018, www.economics.ox.ac.uk/materials/working_papers/4944/oxcarrerp200922.pdf

Vinokurov, E 2017, 'Eurasian Economic Union: Current State and Preliminary Results', *Russian Journal of Economics*, vol. 3, no. 1, pp. 54–70.

WITS 2018, *World Integrated Trade Solutions Tools*, The World Bank, viewed 29 April 2018, https://wits.worldbank.org/

The World Bank 2018, *Doing Business Reports*, viewed 30 May 2018, www.doingbusiness.org/en/reports/global-reports/doing-business-2019

WTO 2017, *World Tariff Profiles*, WTO, Geneva.

7 The European context of Russian trade policy

Tatiana M. Isachenko

Introduction

For the last three decades, the European Union and Russia, as well as their economic and political ties, have been key factors in the formation of the "New Europe". As a result, the political climate and economic prosperity of the European continent largely depended – and still depends – on the state and level of their interaction. The legal base for mutual trade and economic cooperation, as well as for cooperation in many other fields, had been provided by the Partnership and Cooperation Agreement. Many additional documents were adopted that clarified strategy both by Russia and the EU towards mutual cooperation after taking into consideration current issues and the most important problems.

Russian WTO accession introduced significant challenges in Russian trade policy that opened a new stage and expanded the legal base for bilateral relations. The liberalization of trade policy attracted even more attention from Western European business to the large scale and highly segmented Russian market. The economic (financial crisis of 2008–2009) and political (confrontation in Georgia, the initiation of the Eastern Partnership, the Deep and Comprehensive Free Trade Agreement (DCFTA) between Ukraine and EU) problems blocked and negated all previous achievements and the positive effects of initial agreements, and in general brought into question the very possibility of partnership. Taking into consideration the modern features of the Russian economy and the difficulties of the economic, social, and political development, due to both internal and external factors, it is necessary to rethink the political and legal design of Russia's relations with the EU completely and to seek new relevant trade policy.

The unpredictable consequence of the Ukrainian crisis, the war in Donbas, the radically different approach of the EU and Russia to the territorial statues of Crimea – all brought the relations between two partners to a crossroads. The necessity of a new approach to Russia – EU bilateral relations follows from the fact that even with all the current political problems and trade restrictions, the EU remains Russia's main trade and investment partner. For the Russian economy, the development of economic cooperation with the EU preserves its crucial importance, hence the diversification of the trade and investment flows and the goal to overcome dependence on one partner remains a strategic task for the country. At present, the restoration of equal, transparent, mutually beneficial and stable economic ties between Russia and the EU are still a strategic priority for both sides and a prerequisite for maintaining the stability and prosperity of the Eurasian continent.

The current chapter includes a conceptual analysis of the role of trade policy in Russian economic development, as well as the trade and investment dimension of bilateral cooperation, the legal base and an overview of the main current problems. The author also tries to make some recommendations for facilitating economic cooperation on a new basis.

Methodology and conceptual basis for the analysis of the role of trade policy for Russian economic development and economic growth

Being one of the major topics of economic discussion in recent years, Russia–EU trade – and mainly its regulation – was studied at many scientific and business forums. This chapter is based on the theoretical and empirical data that serve as illustrations for the authors' ideas and conclusions. Due to the importance of the non-economic – mainly political – factors in Russia–EU relations, the author has chosen empirical-analytical methodology. The research focuses on objective knowledge and research questions. We use the existing theory as a foundation for formulating hypotheses that need to be tested. The current research is focused on explanation of the current problems and search for their solution. The goals of the current chapter are: 1) to analyse the conceptual basis of the interaction between trade and macroeconomic development as a main argument for Russia–EU trade; and 2) to define the main obstacles for the future development of cooperation and provide some recommendations. The methodology of this article suggests the discussion of problems that were anticipated and the steps taken to prevent them from occurring in future.

Trade policy plays a significant role in ensuring the effective use of external factors in the national economy and achieving the optimal openness of the national economy. The empirical research provides evidence that at all stages of economic development the key goal is to ensure a balance between the interests of domestic producers and development trends of the world market, primarily with main trade and investment partners. The competitive position of the country and its companies is highly dependent on the nature of participation in international economic cooperation. The global financial crisis of 2008–2009 and continuing negative trends in economic development demonstrate that only flexible systemic measures make it possible to overcome or mitigate crisis tendencies, and these measures play a special role in trade policy and regulation of the most sensitive markets. The political crisis of the last four years provided evidence of the use of trade policy as a tool of economic diplomacy that does not necessarily benefit the domestic industries of all countries, but rather aims at the economic and political leadership of some of them. The practice of many countries in the world has proved the direct connection between the implementation of macroeconomic reforms and trade policy. There is also a feedback effect, because under the conditions of a stable economy, the efficiency of using foreign economic regulation tools is increasing. This could serve as the main reason for deep analysis of trade policy issues in Russia–EU bilateral relations.

In the theoretical literature, views on the relationship between trade and macroeconomic policies differ and have undergone significant evolution. To a large extent, this is due to a change in the type of trade policy pursued and the relationship between protectionism and free trade. Starting from the first economic theories developed by Smith and Riccardo, economic theory concentrated on the static and dynamic effects of trade, including more and more factors that influence the choice of a foreign market access mode. Since that time the role of trade and trade policy in development and economic growth was and still is an important theoretical issue. Later elaborated theories by Swedish economists Heckscher and Ohlin in the 1930s and American economist Leontief in the mid-1950s significantly improved the concept, including factors examining: 1) the production of various commodities factors used in different proportions; and 2) the relative provision of the production factor variations.

The neoclassic theoretical concept provides a better understanding of Russia's specialization in the global economy. In particular, on the basis of the above-mentioned theory we could argue that natural resources play a significant role if their use is supported by intensive investment. In the case of Russia, this assumption proved absolutely true, and with the lack of financial resources and technology the extraction industry could not be effective and the export of primary mineral commodities could decline. This explains the dependence of Russia on trade and investments from the EU that was, is, and could be the partner most interested in cooperation with Russia in the energy sector and other fields. This theoretical background could also justify the trade policy pursued by the government and its impact on the international specialization of Russia, which could involve restriction of imports and stimulation of domestic production and exports of those industries that heavily use basic production factors, as reflected in Russian development patterns.

Another important contribution to the study of the effects of international trade and its regulation on economic development was made by Swedish economist Myrdal in 1956 (Myrdal 1956). He believed that among the characteristics that are relevant to the development of an economy are political and social forces, such as the historical traditions of production activity, national cohesion, religions and ideologies, and economic, social and political powers, and groups of interest. Contemporary development provides the best evidence how the ideological and political factors play a crucial role in the modern trade policy of Russia and its relations with the EU. He also stipulated that in the short term, international trade and economic cooperation with foreign nations could have positive effects of diffusion on developing countries,[1] but in the long term the negative effects remain because they stimulated a production of primary goods – and that in fact happened in Russia.

Later, justifying the competitive advantages of nations as a competitive diamond, Porter (1990) explained the role of the state in the use of the advantages of the external environment and attracting investments for the development of the national economy. The main conclusion of the research – that traditional comparative advantages, such as the availability of natural resources and cheap labour, are no longer the main sources of benefit – could be directly applied to Russian economic development and its trade policy priorities towards all partners, mainly the EU. According to Porter main attention should be paid to the competitive advantages of companies in a global economic environment and the industry within which the company operates, because it is there that competitors producing similar products are concentrated. This allows designing the company's strategy for the world market and the optimal mode of cooperation with foreign companies, and could also serve as theoretical justification for global value chains proliferation. Special attention is paid to the consideration of foreign trade regulation regarding inclusion of sensitive industries into global value chains: effective tariff protection, customs regulation, trade facilitation, participation in preferential trade agreements with third countries, etc. In the Russia–EU trade framework, Russia has the potential to expand participation in regional and global value chains, but its implementation requires institutional and regulatory adjustment at the national and supranational levels.

Many clarifications and corrections to the classic Riccardian comparative advantages theory were provided by Bhagwati. He was the first to add the demand of social groups with different income as a factor of international trade and thus explained the different levels of involvement in international cooperation. As proof of the theory, internal demand is a crucial factor for bilateral Russia–EU trade since both markets mutually complement each other and allow Russia and the EU to meet demand in necessary goods and services. For Russia the investigation of the demand is important for improvement of trade structure (Bhagwati et al. 1998). Later on, he introduced the price ratio element and transportation cost in the study of international trade, concluding that two countries are effective in mutual trade if they export different goods, which is valid for Russia–EU trade. Another argument for the importance of bilateral trade is transportation cost. The supply of energy exports from Russia to the EU remains extremely important for both partners, despite the EU's natural desire to avoid a high level of dependence on one supplier. Modern economic theory provides even more evidence of the relationship between trade and economic development of the country. In his new theory, Krugman went beyond traditional views on international trade and analyzed the advantages of economy of scale, overcoming the limitations of the Ricardian concept of comparative advantage and the theory of factor proportions of Heckscher-Ohlin in explaining some modern phenomena of international trade along with comparative advantages. In his research, inter-sectoral and intra-industry exchanges receive equal status and the systematic development of the entire macroeconomic development is linked to the openness of the national economy (Krugman et al. 2014).

The contemporary world is characterized by deep and dynamic changes; at any time, however, main concepts and theoretical bases prove to be important justifications of trade policy instruments used in relation with main partners.

Trade and investment dimension of Russia–EU cooperation

During its entire history, Russia has long been not only an active participant in the formation of European and world markets, but also a leader in the export of certain goods and commodities, especially in the late nineteenth to early twentieth centuries. Significant changes occurred in the second half of the nineteenth century, when Russia became a major consumer of industrial products and a European supplier of food and raw materials. Later, after the socialist regime was established and the country transitioned to a socialist economic system, traditional trade flows were significantly disrupted.

Nevertheless, even during the 70 years of the existence of two different world economic systems, Russia, as a part of the USSR, and European countries were linked by quite close trade and economic relations. The social and economic transformation in Russian society and economy in the 1990s have made it possible to develop the Russian economy in compliance with the main free market requirements and gave a significant rise to the hope that bilateral cooperation could be brought to a fundamentally new level. In turn, the enlargement of the European Union in 2004, 2007, and 2013 also contributed to the new EU approach to relations with Russia in the trade, economic, cultural, and humanitarian spheres since some of the new EU members had been historically dependent on the Russian market and the market of the former USSR, both in terms of exports and imports, whether a part of the USSR (Baltic states) or COMECON.[2]

Despite the heterogeneity and strong specificity of the national economy developing, Russian markets were, and still are, of great interest to European suppliers of goods and services. The comprehensive expansion of bilateral trade is – and should be – of mutual interest for both parties regarding investment attraction, development of the Russian banking sector, the judiciary, security, energy, education, science, and technology. Russia, in the framework of mutually beneficial cooperation, strives to obtain modern technologies and R&D achievements, modernization of the national economy, and its deeper integration into the world economic system.

Nevertheless, despite close historical ties and mutual interest, at present bilateral cooperation is to a large extent subject to the negative impact of the rapidly changing political conjuncture and crisis phenomena in the world economy. The need for a comprehensive analysis and revision of the existing problems of relations between Russia and the EU was repeatedly noted by both domestic and foreign scientists and analysts, including Emerson (2006), Cameron (2009), Borko (2010), Butorina (Butorina and Borko 2006), Entin and Entina (2015), Kaveshnikov (2010), Sutyrin and Trofimenko (2017), and T. Isachenko (2013), and others. During the last few years, a broad discussion on the modernization of cooperation between Russia and the EU and its emergence to a new progressive level of interaction became the subject of many conferences and expert meetings, primarily concerning the removal of sanctions, and possibly other restrictions, and strengthening the innovative component of a mutually beneficial partnership.

This, however, found a certain lack of support at the governmental level from both sides. As strategic partners in the 2000s the EU and Russia invested a lot of effort in expanding and strengthening political and economic ties in every possible way. As far as bilateral trade is concerned, in 2004–2013 Russia was still the fourth most important trade partner of the European Union (ahead of the US and China), while for Russia the EU remained the main trading partner, accounting for about 52 percent in 2010 (now 43 percent) of foreign trade in comparison. A decline in both exports and imports was recorded due, inter alia, to trade restrictions and the slowdown of the Russian economy. In 2014, bilateral trade decreased to US$377.53 billion; Russian exports amounted to US$259.05 billion, and imports – US$118.48 billion (Federal Customs Service of the Russian Federation 2018). By the end of 2015, there was a sharp reduction in bilateral trade by almost 40 percent to US$235.82 billion. In 2016, the trade turnover fell again (but not as significantly as in previous years) down to US$200.39 billion comprising the percentage share mentioned above.

Available statistical data for 2017 record an increase in bilateral trade: in comparison with 2016, turnover grew by almost 30 percent. Russian exports reached US$145 billion (an increase of 20 percent), and imports –US$86 billion (an increase of 9.4 percent) (European Commission 2018). According to Eurostat data, the period since 2007 was characterized by obvious instability of bilateral trade, partially due to the vulnerability of general world economic development, and partially due to bilateral conflict. The bilateral trade policy measures, i.e. the Russian counter-sanctions and food embargo, became the main reasons for the very modest increase in European exports to Russia.

Analysis of bilateral trade commodity structure provides evidence for the well-known problem of the obvious imbalance between exports and imports that has been maintained since Soviet times. Using its rich natural resources, Russia supplies raw materials (the share of fuel and energy products in the structure of Russian exports in 2015 was about 66 percent) for the industrialized countries of Europe and consumes finished products from various commodity groups. Russian exports represent one-third of the oil supply to the EU and almost a quarter of the coal products (Table 7.1). This could serve as an example of mutual interest and a platform for deepening partnership in the energy sector, which also contributes to the development of energy security and the formation of mutually beneficial principles for the operation of energy markets throughout the Eurasian continent (Kaveshnikov 2010).

Under modern conditions, ensuring the sustainability of supplies in the energy sector is even more important, despite active attempts to diversify sources of supply, including through LNG supply from the US. Supplies of gas and oil from Russia today remain the most convenient from the point of view of available infrastructure and the potential for its development. As for Russian imports, according to Eurostat data, cars and transport equipment (45 percent of the total volume), chemical products (18 percent), and medicines and agricultural products traditionally predominate. This significantly reduces Russia's economic security and creates crucial dependence on one market in terms of technological goods supply (Table 7.2).

Table 7.1 Russian exports to EU by SITC section, 2013–2018, € million

SITC06/TIME	*2013*	*2014*	*2015*	*2016*	*2017*	*2018*
Total – all products	206 972,0	182 389,2	136 394,2	118 870,1	144 978,8	168 279,9
Food and live animals	1 176,0	1 409,8	1 428,5	1 488,1	1 440,2	1 799,8
Beverages and tobacco	82,5	104,7	120,3	121,5	117,2	139,4
Crude materials, inedible, except fuels	3 671,5	3 567,8	3 275,8	3 440,6	4 268,5	4 818,5
Mineral fuels, lubricants, and related materials	160 648,3	136 755,6	92 386,7	78 135,7	97 370,0	114 796,4
Animal and vegetable oils, fats, and waxes	440,9	144,3	119,7	95,1	90,4	97,8
Chemicals and related products, n.e.s.	6 297,7	6 324,1	5 434,8	4 451,0	4 881,6	5 780,8
Manufactured goods classified chiefly by material	12 387,3	13 600,6	13 972,2	14 729,0	17 186,8	19 506,4
Machinery and transport equipment	1 937,5	1 985,3	2 357,2	2 253,6	2 233,9	2 182,0
Miscellaneous manufactured articles	431,0	375,2	396,8	476,8	534,3	537,1
Commodities and transactions not classified elsewhere in the SITC	19 899,0	18 121,9	16 902,5	13 678,9	16 856,0	18 621,8

Source: Eurostat 2019.

Table 7.2 Russian imports from EU by SITC section, 2013–2018, € million

SITC06/TIME	*2013*	*2014*	*2015*	*2016*	*2017*	*2018*
Total – all products	119 447,5	103 281,8	73 787,3	72 425,2	86 034,1	85 262,5
Food and live animals	8 756,1	6 372,4	3 302,6	3 186,8	3 659,9	3 700,5
Beverages and tobacco	1 681,2	1 574,9	1 184,6	1 270,4	1 517,4	1 628,7
Crude materials, inedible, except fuels	1 741,3	1 366,[illegible]	1 187,9	1 282,6	1 505,3	1 549,9
Mineral fuels, lubricants, and related materials	1 104,5	791,7	613,3	590,5	650,4	722,2
Animal and vegetable oils, fats, and waxes	442,9	249,9	149,4	183,4	196,8	150,5
Chemicals and related products, n.e.s.	20 116,3	19 132,9	15 746,3	15 734,9	17 938,3	17 709,4
Manufactured goods classified chiefly by material	12 561,1	11 236,3	8 370,3	8 011,1	9 555,8	9 105,4
Machinery and transport equipment	56 555,1	47 428,2	32 106,2	31 183,3	39 012,9	38 694,5
Miscellaneous manufactured articles	14 875,1	13 427,4	9 505,7	9 424,2	10 809,3	11 018,6
Commodities and transactions not classified elsewhere in the SITC	1 613,7	1 701,8	1 620,5	1 558,5	1 188,1	983,1

The above-mentioned data lead to the logical conclusion that the creation of a rational, modern trade structure for foreign trade, through the development of an appropriate industrial base within the country, remains a strategic task for Russian industrial and trade policy and, apparently, from the perspective of the national economy.

The European Union as a whole and its members are also the largest investors in the Russian economy: up to 75 percent of foreign direct investment in Russia comes from EU member states, including Cyprus, through which (as well as through other offshore jurisdictions) reinvestment into the national economy of funds previously withdrawn from the country come back as FDI (Table 7.3). In the modern economy, there is a logical relationship between the openness of international trade, foreign direct investment, and economic growth. This interconnection and interdependence is especially evident under conditions of the functioning of global production chains, which is one of the weakest aspects of Russian-European cooperation. FDI can promote export promotion, expand import substitution, or increase trade in the share of intermediate production costs between the headquarters and their subsidiaries. Besides, an open trade regime is generally accompanied by a favourable investment climate. Investment cooperation with the EU and its members is therefore no less important than trade operations, and any restrictions in this area are extremely sensitive for the Russian economy.

According to these data, the FDI inflow from Europe is several times bigger than from any other country (Table 7.3). That is why a three-fold reduction in the inflow of European investments could not but negatively affect industrial

Table 7.3 FDI inflow to Russia, 2008–2018, US$ million

Partner	*2008*	*2010*	*2013*	*2014*	*2015*	*2016*	*2017*	*Q1–Q3 2018*
TOTAL	74 783	43 168	69 219	22 031	6 853	32 539	28 557	5 704
CIS states	265	154	882	476	602	522	114	93
EU member states	37 016	23 297	35 582	7 077	−3 307	2 681	15 071	−1 755
incl:								
Cyprus	20 428	12 287	8 266	3 158	−7 069	−436	8 674	−4 815
Finland	1 415	347	216	124	−272	253	50	−118
France	604	2 592	2 121	2 224	1 686	1 997	854	842
Germany	3 379	3 196	335	349	1 483	224	470	517
Netherlands	10 184	3 733	5 716	1 102	−246	165	−1 427	1 807
UK	1 007	1 142	18 927	120	1 112	478	2 076	3 015
China	−49	336	597	1 271	645	345	140	112
Japan	195	473	369	295	447	140	83	325
Republic of Korea	313	318	71	130	116	83	59	104
USA	2 161	435	485	708	209	402	495	370
Rest of world	34 883	18 155	31 234	12 075	8 140	28 366	13 373	7 365

Source: Central Bank of Russia 2019.

cooperation and business activities. Of course, the capital imported from these countries in many cases is of Russian origin and does not always entail the attraction of new technologies and knowledge. However, the investment brings many projects in the fields of wholesale and retail trade, logistics, and manufacturing, which contribute to the creation of jobs and the expansion of a wide range of goods and services. Capital withdrawal by many European companies from the Russian market would be more difficult to compensate for than restoring or diversifying trade flows.

Legal base for bilateral relations

The complex of bilateral relations between Russia and the EU is not limited to economic issues. The strategic partnership based on common interests and development goals is provided through continuous communication both in bilateral format and within the framework of key international venues – the UN, the Council of Europe, the OSCE, the WTO, as well as negotiations with EU member states. In the context of the challenges and threats to the world economy, both parties are interested in strengthening cooperation in countering terrorism, organized crime, illegal migration, slave trade, the proliferation of drugs and weapons of mass destruction, as well as in resolving conflicts in the Middle East, the Balkans, Afghanistan, and other regions. One substantial area of cooperation is the elimination of the negative effects of climate change. Meanwhile, negotiations in almost all areas are suspended. Progressive development of bilateral foreign economic cooperation is impossible without the creation of an appropriate broad contractual and legal framework.

The regulatory issue traditionally represents the main problem for intensive and extensive development of bilateral relations. That is why we decided to concentrate on the legal base – e.g. trade policy – to discover whether there is a lack of effective regulation. Since 1997, the Partnership and Cooperation Agreement (PCA) for bilateral relations between Russia and the European Union has created a fundamental legal framework for the comprehensive development of Russia–EU dialogue in various fields. The document was signed in 1994 and entered into force only in 1997; de facto relations, however, were established and entered a new stage of development in 1991. The PCA has become the basic treaty for Russia and the EU, which laid the foundation for large-scale cooperation in the economic sphere, as well as on a wide range of bilateral relations issues. This agreement became a comprehensive document in Russian trade policy practice since it covered all spheres of economic and financial cooperation, extending the principles and norms of the GATT/WTO to them. According to Article 15, all quantitative restrictions on imports were abolished, except for certain goods (textiles, steel, fissile materials), with an exemption for so called "sensitive industries", such as trade in textiles (Article 20) and coal and steel (Article 21). Quantitative restrictions under the agreement were allowed as special safeguard measures in compliance with WTO rules (Article 17). Parties also scheduled additional negotiations on space launches and deliveries of Russian nuclear fuel cycle materials and nuclear fuel to the EU, and also started consultations for settlement of mutual disputes.

Alongside trade in goods, the PCA covered trade in services, becoming a new area of cooperation for Russia. Section IV of the "Regulations on Business and Investment" included provisions related to the movement of persons and services, and Article 23 contained a provision on the right to recruit citizens in the territory of another contracting party on the basis of the principle of non-discrimination and with regard for working conditions, remuneration, and dismissal. Russia and the EU also reached an agreement on granting MFN treatment in respect to the establishment of companies, the activities of companies' subsidiaries and branches (with the exemption of certain sectors – in particular, banking and insurance services, maritime transport, and some other sectors that later became the subject of specific Russian commitments under the GATS).

In the author's opinion, despite all the advantages of the PCA, certain difficulties arose in the development of trade and economic cooperation between Russia and the European Union in the late 1990s. In a wide range of cases, the parties did not follow the commitments they made when signing the PCA. In particular, Russia failed to adopt national legislation pursuant to the requirements of the Agreement (e.g. a number of Customs Code provisions, the law on state regulation of foreign trade in terms of definition clarification and trade in services, and in some specific regulations, like the alcohol import regime, etc., that were in contradiction to the provisions of the PCA). The EU also committed similar violations[3] of agreement provisions.

To eliminate some problems and to ensure the realization of the PCA, beginning in 1999, both Russia and the EU adopted several strategic documents that highlighted the most urgent areas and problems of cooperation.[4] Significant changes occurred after the unprecedented EU enlargement in 2004. Given the fact that the enlargement process had been in preparation for ten years, the problems that arose after the actual entry of new members into the integration group were not as critical as in previous cases. In April 2004, during the summit in Luxembourg, a protocol and a joint statement on the expansion of the EU were signed, practically settling all the controversial issues of bilateral relations between the Russian Federation and the EU regarding enlargement. The main Russian concerns were addressed and both parties tried to mitigate significant injury; some of these concerns, however, still affect bilateral trade policy.

One of the most important regulatory issues occurred in the context of the "market status" of the Russian economy – an issue that was decisive in terms of normal price and dumping margin calculation in the course of anti-dumping investigation. Even the recognition of Russia as a country with a market economy didn't settle this complication that became one of the arguments in the current trade dispute between Russia and the EU on cost adjustment methodologies (WTO DS 2018).

Besides, the settlement of some other issues was crucial – for example, issues related to ensuring the energy independence of the European economy, which does not encourage expanding the export of Russian energy resources to the

European market that would entail increased revenues from exports for the Russian budget. In accordance with the rules of European competition policy, the EU's dependence on energy imports from one source cannot exceed one-third of total imports, with a total dependence on energy imports of about 50 percent.

Under these circumstances, the Energy Dialogue (a dialogue that was supposed to eliminate existing problems and define new strategy towards energy cooperation and market regulation) became a special dimension of bilateral cooperation. The main contradictions appeared to be on the application of the European Energy charter provisions to Russia's energy policy. This issue is still considered to be under dispute by both sides, leading to the initiation of a trade dispute in the WTO. However, as mentioned by many experts in this particular field, this area of cooperation is very politicized. The different approach to the content of energy security and its economic and political dimension was emphasized by N. Kaveshnikov (Kaveshnikov 2010). The current state of negotiations and different approaches of EU members to the North Stream pipeline project are the best demonstrations of the differences in political views.

Cooperation in transport and logistics required a special approach, as Russia and the EU share a common geographical border. The EU–Russia Transport Dialogue was launched in October 2005 in connection with the signing of the document "General Principles, Objectives and Structure of the Russia-EU Dialogue in Transport and Infrastructure".

Given the length of the common borders, special attention was paid to cross-border cooperation and liberalization in this area based on WTO principles. It should be emphasized that all the most recent programmes of cross-border cooperation were approved after the cooling of relations, which began in 2014: in December 2015 the European Commission approved the Joint Action Program Kolarctic Cross-Border Cooperation 2014–2020.[5] Some other initiatives, like the Karelia Program (Karelia CBC 2018) or the South East Finland-Russia Programme (South East Finland-Russia CBC 2018), were also updated and deferred until 2020.

To clarify, and even deepen, the provisions of PCA – four road maps for common spaces were adopted in 2005: the common economic space; the common space of freedom, security, and justice; the common space for external security; and the common space of science and education, including cultural aspects. These documents served as the basis for the further intensification of trade and cooperation and the elaboration of the Partnership for modernization as a part of long-term bilateral strategy. A part of the Partnership was devoted to the approximation and possible unification of technical regulation and standardization and certification systems, as well as the strengthening of the rule of law with regard of the creation of the Customs Union of Russia, Belarus, and Kazakhstan, and the replacement of national technical regulations by EAEU norms.

At that time, it also became obvious that the PCA had become outdated as the existing legal base and should be replaced by a new type of agreement – the New Basic Agreement. The approach of Russia was that it should be either a Free Trade

Agreement (FTA) or a document that would lead to the creation of FTA. During 12 negotiation rounds, parties failed to reach consensus on the future format. The first suspension of the negotiations took place in 2009 due to the military conflict in Georgia, and in 2014 the negotiations were terminated due to the political confrontation in Ukraine.

The creation of the Customs Union of Russia, Belarus, and Kazakhstan, and later the Eurasian Economic Union, made it even more difficult to balance Russia and EU interests in terms of potential future agreement. The transfer of trade policy competence to the EAEU level assumes that an arrangement must be concluded between the EU and the EAEU, while the European approach to the Eurasian integration was quite sceptical, if not negative, and the recognition of the EAEU is still in question. Industrial and sectoral dialogue between the EU and Russia also became "a victim" and "a hostage" of political confrontation, so the current situation could certainly be described as the worst in the history of bilateral trade and economic cooperation regulation.

Analysis of the trade policy legal framework provokes the question: how much trade policy really affects the formation of partners' trade flows? Empirical analysis allows the assertion that a favourable trade regime contributes significantly to the expansion of trade and allows resolving existing controversial problems. At the same time, modern trade policy cannot be effective without a close linkage with industrial policy. This means that when forming a strategy for external relations and their purposeful regulation, a country should proceed from what its profile in world markets will be, what products will saturate the domestic market through imports, and what goods and services will form the export profile. Foreign economic and trade strategies play an important role not only as an integral part of macroeconomic policy, but also as critical determinants of the strategy of national firms. At the same time, the interests of the business sector significantly influence decision-making in the sphere of trade policy at the state level. Taking into consideration the fact that prospects for the development of the world economy will be determined by the acceleration of innovation activity and scientific and technological progress, as well as the emergence of a post-industrial mode of production and the knowledge-based economy, the priorities of Russia–EU trade and investment will focus on increasing the share of science-intensive products, technologies, and intellectual property. That's why an important factor for the formation of an effective strategy is the strengthening of interaction between the state and business sectors in the development of competitive industries, as in the development of the human factor. Based on this, we could argue that the application of trade policy measures in Russia–EU relations should be inspired and designed by national companies and their mutual strategic interests in compliance with generally accepted multilateral and bilateral arrangements.

The author believes that Russian trade policy towards the EU in the pre-crisis period had its own specific character since the European market was the key for both Russian trade and investment, as well as for scientific and technological collaboration. Certainly, the EU also approached, and still approaches, Russia in a special way that makes current economic and trade-targeted sanctions so sensitive for both parties. This, however, excludes the possibility of discrimination, since the individual approach did not envisage special benefits for European companies in the Russian market; but it did mean special attention to individual areas of cooperation and regulation of the most sensitive sectors on the basis of separate sectoral agreements of mutual interest. The main argument for such specificity and scope for the legal base of cooperation, which includes many documents and agreements belonging to different plans, is the need to use trade policy to address specific goals and objectives of developing mutually beneficial bilateral cooperation.

The influence of sanctions on bilateral trade, investment, and trade policy

The political crisis of 2014, provoked by local, as it initially seemed, conflict in Ukraine, has grown into an all-European and even global crisis, and has provoked both discussion of the problem of political diplomacy as a tool of promotion of a stronger partner's interests and its intervention in the economy and politics of a weaker partner, as well as the use of economic instruments to achieve political goals. As mentioned by Averre and Wolczuk (2016), fast-changing events in Ukrainian and thus Russian policy there is the longer-term perspective for bilateral relations and Russia's relations with the EU. The latest development has contributed to significant changes in light of Russia's economic and political development and its place in the modern world as well as trade policy towards different partners. The lessons of modern political and economic crisis must become grounds for deep analysis of the destructive actions of all actors involved in the conflict (Isachenko 2015, p. 46).

Both European trade policy towards Russia, as well as Russian trade strategy towards the EU, have never been free from certain concerns. For Russia, these concerns were mainly economic, while for Europe they went beyond mere economics (Dettke 2008). As mentioned above, for Russia, the EU as a whole, and some of its member states, were and remain the main potential partners for modernization, energy cooperation, and service sector development, as well as scientific and cultural cooperation. A dramatic change in the political situation in Europe and the world, a new round of confrontation between Russia and its partners, and the introduction of restrictive measures in trade and investment cooperation had a very serious negative impact on bilateral contacts in all spheres and made serious changes in the priorities of the trade policies of both partners. It is worth mentioning that as far as the EU is concerned, it commonly tended to use sanctions as an instrument of economic diplomacy less frequently, and to do so most often under pressure from the USA as their largest economic and political partner (Kozhanov and Sutyrin 2012).

That is why the use of such a tool by the most important trade and investment partner created substantial difficulties for the Russian economy in general and forced the country to reconsider its foreign economic strategy. Besides, the sanctions policy revealed the problem of excessive dependence on one partner and the lack of initiatives outside the European continent. Sanctions could not but affect the bilateral economic cooperation between Russia and European countries, as well as the whole of Russian national economic development. In addition, the sanctions coincided with or, to some extent, provoked a worsening of the general economic situation in the world, which in turn had a negative impact on the country's economy. The contemporary sanctions war between Russia and its main partners, including the EU, goes significantly beyond all possible prognoses and expectations. Beginning in 2014, the EU and the US imposed the most severe economic sanctions against Russia since the end of the Cold War. The stagnation of the Russian economy, the fall in oil prices, the weakening of the rouble (exacerbated by sanctions), the decline of mutual trade in goods, services, and investments, and the limited access of Russian companies to financial resources and technologies – all these consequences led in turn to the decrease of the Russian share of world markets. The introductions of sanctions has significantly changed the trade policy practice and led both countries to the revision of some trade policy tools, such as the use of import substitution subsidies, trade preferences, export and import ban.

Despite the fact that, unlike US sanctions, the European ban extended only to new contracts, and already signed contracts were not terminated, all measures turned out to be extremely sensitive for Russia. The initial package of sanctions measures has affected the important areas of cooperation; its extension has questioned the implementation of some bilateral projects, mainly in gas and oil industry. Even after four years of sanctions, the Russian Federation is certainly still feeling serious negative effects. Russia appeared to be more sensitive to European sanctions due to the position of the EU as Russia's main trade, technology, and investment partner. Nevertheless, the sharpest and most severe impacts of sanctions appeared during the 18 months to two years after the introduction of sanctions; they first had a shock effect, though the impact has gradually weakened (Gurvich and Prilepsky 2016). In a certain sense, the Russian economy has adjusted to the current situation, but that doesn't mean that it managed to regain the dynamics of previous years. The effects of the sanctions were subject to quantitative analysis by many economists, however the results differ significantly (from 0.5 percent to 9 percent of GDP decline). Certain calculations were made by the IMF (IMF 2015), as well as by Russian experts – Gurvich and Prilepsky (Gurvich and Prilepsky 2016), and by Shirov, Yantovskiy and Potapenko (Shirov et al. 2015). In all the above cases, the sanctions impact is estimated as a percentage decrease of GDP (approximately one percentage point per year), yet the long-term effect is not studied.

Some foreign economists also made calculations. For example, Chang from the American Foreign Policy Research Institute claims that, "In financial terms, Russia felt the most damaging impact of the West's economic sanctions within the first year of their imposition" (Chang 2017). At the same time, he points out that the sanctions have not broken the Russian economy – rather, they have merely caused structural vulnerability. A certain stabilization of global commodity prices made Russia's economy more resilient and prevented an even deeper recession. Of course, if the sanctions are not lifted in the immediate future,[6] but are maintained for a long time, they will function as serious constraints on the development of the Russian economy, above all in terms of technological development and in terms of access to financial resources that are crucial for many Russian industries, even beyond the high technology markets.

Assessments of the impact of sanctions on the European economy were also presented in the official report of the Policy Department of the EU Directorate-General for External Policies (Fritz et al. 2017). The report presented a summary of several studies attempting to estimate the costs of the sanctions considering economy-wide multiplier effects. Some of the cited papers (Moret et al. 2016) provided a first assessment of potential costs and impacts of the sanctions. According to the estimations of the European Parliamentary Research Service study (Szczepański 2015), the damage to Europe's economy and the overall costs of the sanctions and counter-sanctions at €40 billion (−0.3 percent for EU GDP) in 2014 and €50 billion (−0.4 percent) in 2015. According to the report, the overall side effect of sanctions and counter-sanctions was to cause a loss to EU GDP of 0.3 percent in 2014 and 0.4 percent in 2015 (€40 and 50 billion respectively).

Besides the economic impact, the severe political confrontation almost led to complete disruption of economic and political contacts and the cancellation of some contracts, as well as limitations on scientific and humanitarian contacts and joint research. In our view, these complications make assessing the total impact of sanctions extremely difficult, if not impossible.

Subsequently, the influence of sanctions and counter-sanctions, introduced by Russia, could not but have a negative impact on the interests of the European producers, primarily farmers. In the European Parliament's Employment and Social Affairs briefing, Russia was the second most important destination for EU agricultural products (after the USA). That's why the EU was the most affected region, since 73 percent of imports appeared to be banned. Those EU countries most concerned are the Baltic States (above all Lithuania), Finland and Poland (by share of GDP in 2013), Germany and the Netherlands (absolute values) (European Parliament 2014). The impact of these retaliation measures also doesn't elicit uniform official and scientific evaluation. The most relevant study by a group of European economists provided a modelling of resource reallocation based on the GTAP multi-region CGE model (Boulanger et al. 2015). The study focused on Russia's key trade partners most affected by the ban (i.e. EU, Canada, USA, Norway, and Australia) and a 12-sector aggregation of banned commodities. The results demonstrate that the impact on all fruit and vegetables exporters was the same; while for the suppliers of other products the effect was very different. At the same time, it should be noted that the counter-subsidies influenced the Russian consumer market, primarily in terms of prices.

One could argue that the sanctions even had a positive impact on Russian industry, since the country has gotten the chance to develop import substitution (mainly in agriculture). In the author's opinion, that statement can be justified from a quantitative, but not qualitative, point of view. Russian agricultural producers have actually gained a unique opportunity that might not be provided under normal conditions, to get unlimited agricultural subsidies in the absence of strong European competitors. From the qualitative point of view, however, substitution couldn't be achieved swiftly or comprehensively since many products originating in European countries are not produced in Russia, the EAEU, or other partner countries.

The quantitative assessment of sanctions becomes even more problematic if we consider trade flows via EAEU countries. In some cases, the agricultural products banned in the Russian market get access via the Belarus market, which mitigates all effects.

The uncertain effect of sanctions becomes much more obvious if we analyse the results of the four-year break in negotiations on the bilateral relations format. It should be emphasized that the sanctions imposed by the EU and the US against Russia did not have the expected effect and did not change the political course of Russia towards Ukraine. Besides, as mentioned by an expert from the Eurasian Bank of Reconstruction and Development (Pereboyev 2017), the EU began to slowly lose the "Eurasian" markets after the establishment of the Eurasian Union (EAEU). The turn of the EAEU to the East was picking up pace: in 2016, the EU accounted for 40.8 percent of the EAEU total import, while the APEC countries comprised 42.3 percent (Vinkurov and Pereboyev 2016). In 2017, the situation continued: for the period January through June, imports from the EU amounted to US$44.5 billion, and from APEC – US$46.4 billion. Some countries therefore proposed the cancellation of sanctions or expressed doubt about the extension of sanctions. Some countries proposed restoration of the negotiations process between Russia and European countries.

Further developments didn't provide any significant improvement of the political climate, and the interaction between policy and economics deepened. However, if a restrictive economic policy continues to be pursued towards Russia by many foreign states and blocks, it will become necessary for Russia to develop retaliation measures aimed at the protection of the national economy. The last sanctions package introduced by the US in August 2017 created a situation of uncertainty in Russia–EU bilateral trade regulation. Progress significantly depends on the EU approach to the use of sanctions as a policy tool, as well as on the ability of Russia to create and maintain mutually beneficial contacts with other countries and regions.

European context: lessons for future and alternatives

Future development of relations between Russia and the EU could be analysed from several points of view. Firstly, the necessity to negotiate the New Basic Agreement is still real. It is difficult to assume under current conditions that the goal of this agreement will be the formation of a freetrade area; rather, in this agreement, the goal may be cooperation on many issues of bilateral importance (e.g. customs cooperation, combating counterfeit products, transport cooperation, technical regulation, other regulation, and sanitary and veterinary control, etc.). Besides, with regard to trade policy and trade regulation, all issues in this area can and should be addressed exclusively at the level of the EAEU, since competence in this area is elevated to the level of the bloc. A few years ago, the EU expressed its unwillingness to negotiate with the Customs Union, justifying its position by the argument that Kazakhstan and Belarus were not WTO members. Under conditions where the majority of EAEU countries are WTO members, this argument is not justified.

It is also worth mentioning that by 2010 all other existing modes and areas of negotiations lost their legitimacy. The concept of four Common Spaces did not achieve full-scale realization, and neither the Common Space of freedom, security, and justice, nor the Common Space of cooperation in external security, were created. Certain progress occurred only in research, education, and culture, as well as in forming a common economic space, with trade as the prevailing form of economic cooperation. Despite the fact that the EU was one of the main negotiators and provided active support to Russian accession into the WTO, developments in the 2000s raised more questions than answers about the future of Russia–EU trade dialogue. We believe that currently it would be more effective to negotiate firstly with different EU members in the context of their competence, then adjust "best practises" and solutions to the EAEU-EU level.

With the beginning of the Eastern Partnership (EP), the EU reassured Russia that everything done within the EP wouldn't affect bilateral relations, but the EU rejected any possibility of a tripartite format for trade negotiations with Russia. The formation of the Deep and Comprehensive Free Trade Area between the EU and Ukraine (DCFTA) has complicated mutual trade policy, making it even more unclear and restrictive. Taking into consideration the above effects of sanctions introduced due to political developments, as well as the accumulated tension in the European region and collapse of the Europe from Lisbon to Vladivostok project, both parties came to the conclusion that there was a need to search for new ways to restore dialogue. The current situation provides evidence of a deficit of effective and systematic negotiation platforms for pursuing cooperation between the EU and Russia, as well as an absolute lack of EU understanding of the role of the EAEU, whether at the level of governments, supranational bodies, business communities, or expert communities. Nevertheless, now the EAEC is the third largest trading partner of the European Union, which underscores the necessity and importance of continuing cooperation.

Negotiations in a new format and under new conditions will certainly be less ambitious and should be restarted almost from the very beginning, since under conditions of dynamic development previous experience is not relevant – however it remains of great importance for determining opportunities. Nowadays, neither Russia nor the EAEU are interested in a FTA format with the EU, since as WTO members (Belarus excepted), they have already opened their markets; the further reduction of tariffs and liberalization of trade in services, of interest to the EU, could injure some industries. With regard to EAEU export structures, led by commodities, the asymmetry of trade operations will only deepen. Evidently, trade would not and should not continue to be the main area of cooperation. As mentioned by Skvarya (2017), even in the conditions of deterioration and sanctions the Russian Federation remains an attractive market for European investors due to the importance of the fuel and energy complex for the EU countries, the need to ensure the energy security of the European Union and the effective implementation of the Energy Dialogue with Russia.

Given the domination of political factors and the so called "invisible American presence"[7] in Russia–EU relations, it is hardly possible to expect a significant increase in investment and technological cooperation across a wide range of industries and in the short-term perspective. The successful settlement of trade disputes, initiated by both Russia and the EU, could serve as a positive experience; certain "training" of Russian companies would not, however, contribute to the improvement of bilateral economic and political relations. Such developments raise the question of future relations that depend solely on the ability and readiness of both parties to conduct a progressive and ongoing dialogue, on a search for compromise, and on a pragmatic approach free of political prejudice and confrontation. There exists an analytical, expert, and academic community of interest that could provide significant support for such work; the optimal format would be industrial dialogue and scientific cooperation in fields of mutual interest. The path to progress will clearly not be easy, but it must be pursued to the end.

Notes

1 In terms of industrial structure and specialization profile countries in transition are more comparable with developing economies.
2 COMECON – The Council for Mutual Economic Assistance was an economic block of socialist countries that existed from 1949 to 1991.
3 In 2000 without completing consultations with the Russian side, as per the PCA, the EU imposed restrictions on the import of Russian steel. Because of the unilateral violation by the European side of the Russia–EU agreement on steel, contracts over €50 million were canceled, which caused damage to both Russian exporters and EU consumers (Ministry of Foreign Affairs of the Russian Federation 2000).
4 In 1999 the European Council approved the "Collective Strategy of the European Union towards Russia" and in the same year, Russia presented the "Strategy for the Development of Relations of the Russian Federation with the European Union for the Medium-Term Perspective (2000–2010)". In particular, both strategies acknowledged the importance of FDI as a guarantee for the stable development of trade and economic growth, and most new economic trends, and areas and instruments of mutual trade policy, were defined. At the same time, in the beginning of 2000, some new contradictions appeared in bilateral relations. The issue of transit through the territory of Lithuania of Russian residents of the Kaliningrad region also required special settlement and persistent negotiations. The solution of the problem was achieved in the Joint Statement of the Russian Federation and the European Union on transit between the Kaliningrad region and the rest of the Russian Federation, pursuant to which regulations were adopted establishing a simplified transit document for multiple crossings of Lithuanian territory by all types of land transport, hence requiring a lot of formalities and special rules to be observed.
5 Kolarctic CBC 2014–2020 is a financing programme for supporting cooperation between the countries in the North Calotte (Finland, Sweden, Norway) and northwest Russia. It is one of several EU programmes supporting cross-border cooperation across EU external

borders. The Programme offers EU funding and National financing to projects that are in line with the Programme's strategy (Kolarctic 2018).

6 The latest developments, including the serious conflict between Russia and Great Britain, supported by almost all EU countries, resulting in diplomatic measures and the expulsion of diplomats by all parties involved in the conflict, provide no optimistic arguments for the improvement of the political environment, preserving the domination of political factors over economic interests.

7 The invisible American presence means the extraterritorial application of US law and trade regulation that allows US administrations to apply restrictive measures towards companies that work in the US market, but even some states do not follow US policy in sanctioned markets.

Bibliography

Averre, D and Wolczuk, K 2016, 'The Ukraine Crisis and Post-Cold-War Europe', *Europe-Asia Studies*, vol. 68, no. 4, pp. 551–555.

Bhagwati, J, Panagariya, A and Srinivasan, TN 1998, *Lectures on International Trade*, 2nd edition, The MIT Press, Cambridge.

Borko, Y 2010, 'Poiski Rossiej svoego mesta v mire XXI veka I yeyo imperskoje proshloye', *Mir XXI veka: scenario budushego dlya Rossiji*, Research paper no. 274, The Institute of Europe of the Russian Academy of Sciences, Moscow.

Boulanger, P, Dudu, H, Ferrari, E and Philippidis, G 2015, *The Cost of Import Prohibition for Political Reason: CGE Analysis of the Russian Ban on Agri-Food Products*, Paper prepared for the 18th Annual Conference on Global Economic Analysis 'Information for the Policy Maker: Practical Economic Modelling for Tomorrow', June 17–19, Melbourne, Australia, viewed 14 May 2018, http://citeseerx.ist.psu.edu/viewdoc/download?doi=10.1.1.851.4656&rep=rep1&type=pdf

Butorina, OV and Borko, YA (eds.) 2006, *Raschirenie Evropejskogo Soyuza I Rossia*, Delovaya Literatura, Moscow.

Cameron, F 2009, 'The Politics of EU-Russia Energy Relations', *Oil, Gas & Energy Law*, no. 2, viewed 14 May 2018, www.ogel.org/article.asp?key=2874

Central Bank of Russia 2018, viewed 24 March 2019, www.cbr.ru

Chang, FK 2017, *Effectiveness of Economic Sanctions on Russia's Economy*, Geopolitics: FPRI Blog, viewed 14 May 2018, www.fpri.org/2017/06/effectiveness-economic-sanctions-russias-economy/

Dettke, D 2008, 'Russia and the EU: The Difficult Path to a New Partnership', *European Affairs*, vol. 9, no. 3, viewed 14 May 2018, www.europeaninstitute.org/index.php/9-european-affairs/european-affairs/47-russia-and-the-eu-the-difficult-path-to-a-new-partnership

Emerson, M (ed.) 2006, *The Elephant and the Bear Try Again: Options for a New Agreement Between EU and Russia*, Centre for European Policy Studies, Brussels.

Entin, ML and Entina, EG 2015, *Rossija i Evropejskij Sojuz v 2011–2014 godah: v poiskah partnerskih otnoshenij*, Izdatel'stvo Je, Moscow.

European Commission 2018, *European Union, Trade in Goods with Russia*, viewed 14 May 2018, http://trade.ec.europa.eu/doclib/docs/2006/september/tradoc_113440.pdf

European Parliament 2014, *The Russian Embargo: Impact on the Economic and Employment Situation in the EU*, Employment and Social Affairs Briefing, viewed 14 May 2018, www.europarl.europa.eu/RegData/etudes/BRIE/2014/536291/IPOL_BRI(2014)536291_EN.pdf

Eurostat 2019, viewed 24 March, 2019, www. ec.europa.eu/eurostat

Federal Customs Service of the Russian Federation 2018, viewed 14 May 2018, www.customs.ru/index.php?option=com_content&view=article&id=13858&Itemid=2095

Fritz, O, Christen, E, Sinabell, F and Hinz, J 2017, *Russia and the EU Sanctions: Economic and Trade Effects, Compliance and Way Forward*, EU Policy Department, Directorate-General for External Policies, October, viewed 14 May 2018, www.europarl.europa.eu/RegData/etudes/STUD/2017/603847/EXPO_STU(2017)603847_EN.pdf

Gurvich, E and Prilepskiy, I 2016, 'The Impact of Financial Sanctions on the Russian Economy', *Russian Journal of Economics*, vol. 1, no. 4, pp. 359–385.

IMF 2015. Russian Federation staff report for the 2015 article IV consultation, October, viewed 14 May 2018, http://www.imf.org/en/News/Articles/2015/09/28/04/53/socar080315b

Isachenko, T 2013, 'The Trade Policy of Russia: Latest Developments and Main Priorities', *Rivista di Studi Politici Internazionali*, no. 2, pp. 347–360.

Isachenko, T 2015, 'Ekonomicheskaja diplomatija v uslovijah politicheskogo krizisa', *Vestnik Sankt-Peterburgskogo universiteta. Seriya 5: Ekonomika*, no. 3, pp. 46–65.

Karelia CBC 2018, viewed 14 May 2018, www.kareliacbc.fi

Kaveshnikov, N 2010, 'The Issue of Energy Security in Relations Between Russia and the European Union', *European Security*, vol. 19, no. 4, pp. 585–605.

Kolarctic 2018, *Kolarctic CBC 2014–2020 Vision & Strategy*, viewed 14 May 2018, http://kolarctic.info/kolartic-2014-2020/

Kozhanov, NA and Sutyrin, SF 2012, 'Mezhdunarodnye jekonomicheskie sankcii kak instrument 'prinuzhdenija k vypolneniju kontrakta' (na primere Islamskoj Respubliki Iran)', *Vestnik Sankt-Peterburgskogo universiteta. Seriya 5: Ekonomika*, no. 1, pp. 108–118. (in Russian).

Krugman, PR, Obstfeld, M and Melitz, M 2014, *International Economics: Theory and Policy*, 10th edition, Pearson Series in Economics, Pearson, London.

Ministry of Foreign Affairs of the Russian Federation 2000, *Ob obespechenii nediskriminacionnyh uslovij dostupa rossijskih jeksporterov na vneshnie rynki (na primere metallurgicheskogo kompleksa)*, April 28, viewed 14 May 2018, www.mid.ru/materialy-po-voprosam-ekonomiceskogo-razvitia-rossii/-/asset_publisher/oSUNZRJVOK4D/content/id/604832

Moret, E, Biersteker, T, Giumelli, F, Poretla, C, Veber, M, Jarosz, D and Bobocea, C 2016, *The New Deterrent? International Sanctions Against Russia Over the Ukraine Crisis; Impacts, Costs and Further Action*, PSIG, Geneva.

Myrdal, G 1956, *An International Economy*, Harper & Brothers, New York.

Pereboyev, V 2017, 'Evrosoyuz nachinaet teryat rynki stran Evraziiskogo soyuza', *Evrazija Jekspert*, September 26, viewed 14 May 2018, http://eurasia.expert/evrosoyuz-nachinaet-teryat-rynki-stran-evraziyskogo-soyuza/

Porter, ME 1990, *The Competitive Advantage of Nations*, Free Press, New York.

Shirov, A, Yantovskiy, A and Potapenko, V 2015, 'Ocenka potencial'nogo vlijanija sankcij na jekonomicheskoe razvitie Rossii i ES', *Problemy Prognozirovaniya*, no. 4, pp. 3–16 (in Russian).

Skvarya, LV 2017, 'Rossijsko-evropejskie investicii: dinamika i struktura v uslovijah sankcij', *Vestnik Rossijskogo universiteta druzhby narodov. Serija: Jekonomika*, vol. 25, no. 2, pp. 189–198.

South East Finland-Russia CBC 2018, viewed 14 May 2018, www.scfrcbc.fi/

Sutyrin, S and Trofimenko, O 2017, 'Do Formal Institutions Really Matter for Foreign Direct Investments to the Russian Federation? Case of FDI Flows From the European Union to Russia', in: K Liuhto, SF Sutyrin and JF Blanchard (eds.) *The Russian Economy and Foreign Direct Investment*, Routledge, London and New York.

Szczepański, M 2015, *Economic Impact on the EU of Sanctions Over Ukraine Conflict*, European Parliamentary Research Service Briefing, October, PE 569.020, viewed 14 May 2018, www.europarl.europa.eu/RegData/etudes/BRIE/2015/569020/EPRS_BRI(2015)569020_EN.pdf

Vinokurov, E and Pereboyev, V 2016, *Mapping the Potential EU-EAEU Cooperation Agenda: Readmission Agreements, Visa-Free Regime, Labour Migration, Mobility of Pensions, Large-Scale Educational Exchanges, Recognition of Professional Diplomas and Certificates*, Working Paper of the International Institute for Applied Systems Analysis, no. 16–013, viewed 14 May 2018, https://eabr.org/upload/iblock/042/wp_vinokurov_pereboev_mapping_the_potential_eu_eaeu_cooperation_agenda.pdf

WTO DS 2018, *DS474: European Union – Cost Adjustment Methodologies and Certain Anti-Dumping Measures on Imports from Russia*, viewed 14 May 2018, //www.wto.org/english/tratop_e/dispu_e/cases_e/ds474_e.htm

8 Adaptation of Finnish food exporters to Russia's food import restrictions

Kari Liuhto and Teemu Itälinna

Introduction

Finnish food exports to Russia had already experienced major historical transformations before the current sanctions. Thus, it will be enlightening to look at the historical development before addressing the main objective of the chapter, i.e. before analysing the impact of Russia's contemporary food-related sanctions on Finnish food exporters to Russia.

As a side story to the Napoleonic Wars, the remaining part of Finland, which previously belonged to Sweden, was annexed to the Russian Empire in 1809.[1] At the end of Swedish rule, Finland's external sales, comprising mainly tar, agricultural products, and metals, were predominantly directed towards the West, or more precisely, to Stockholm (Sweden), Lybeck (Germany) and the Netherlands (Mäntylä 1987a, 1987b).

After Finland was annexed to Russia, its external trade began to shift from the West towards the East. In 1827, Russia accounted for 20 percent of Finland's outbound deliveries, whereas by 1860 the share was already 40 percent (Alho et al. 1986). In 1860, agricultural products accounted for 40 percent of Finland's exports to Russia. Due to the industrialization of Finland and the development of the Finnish export structure, by 1913 the share of agricultural goods in the Finnish exports to Russia had dropped to 20 percent (Pihkala 1969).

During the First World War and the mayhem of the October Revolution, Finland gained its independence from a disintegrating Russian Empire in December 1917. As the war paralysed the Western markets, as much as 97 percent of Finland's exports went to Russia in 1917, and agricultural products covered a bit over one tenth of Finland's exports to the Russian mainland (Pihkala 1969; Liuhto 2018a).

In the aftermath of the civil war in Russia, exports from an independent Finland to Russia stopped. After the Russian Revolution (1917–21), Finnish sales to Russia gradually started to recover (Gregory and Stuart 2001; Ollus and Simola 2006). During the New Economic Policy, NEP (1921–28), 4 percent of Finland's total exports ended up in the Soviet Union, while paper dominated Finnish exports to the USSR at the time (Hirvensalo and Sutela 2017). In 1928, the USSR abandoned the NEP and began to implement its centrally planned economy which, according to Dohan (1976), pursued economic autarky; a policy intended to reduce the dependency of the Soviet Union on foreign trade. Consequently,

Finnish sales to the USSR halted again in the mid-1930s. It is important to note that Finnish trade with the Soviet Union had already stalled before the Second World War. From 1939 to 1944, Finland did not trade with the USSR, as Finland and the Soviet Union were part of rival camps (Ollus and Simola 2006).

The Soviet share in Finland's exports jumped from zero to 30 percent right after the war in 1945, as Finland was forced to pay war reparations to the Soviet Union. At the beginning of the 1950s, a bilateral clearing trade was introduced to Finnish-Soviet trade (Laurila 1995). With the help of the clearing trade, Finland managed to avoid a chronic shortage of convertible currencies in the USSR. Thus, Finland succeeded in increasing its exports to the Soviet Union. Since the mid-1950s until the *Perestroika* era in the second half of the 1980s, the Soviet share of Finland's exports fluctuated between approximately 10 and 25 percent (Ollus and Simola 2006). From 1945 to 1960, the proportion of foodstuffs in Finnish exports to the USSR was negligible. Thereafter, the proportion began to increase (Ollus and Simola 2006). From 1970 to 1985, the average annual share of foodstuffs in Finnish exports to the USSR was 5 percent (Alho et al. 1986).

As the *Perestroika* era caused disorder in the USSR,[2] the Soviet share in Finland's exports dropped from 20 percent in 1986 to 5 percent five years later, when the Soviet Union collapsed (Liuhto 2018a). Despite a major slump in overall exports from Finland to the Soviet Union, the share of foodstuffs remained fairly unchanged, i.e. 4 percent of Finland's total exports to the USSR from 1987 to 1991 (Customs Finland 2019).

Finland's Eastern sales recovered relatively fast following the disintegration of the centrally planned Soviet economy. As a sign of the recovery, more than 10 percent of Finland's exports went to Russia as early as 2007. The global crisis of 2008 halved Finnish exports to Russia one year later. After the crisis, Finnish exports to Russia increased until the spring of 2013, when the decline in Finnish exports to Russia started, i.e. the decline in Finnish exports to Russia began before the Western sanctions and Russia's counter-sanctions of 2014.[3] However, the sanctions have deepened the decline. As Russia's food-related ban was introduced in the autumn of 2014, the full impact of Russia's counter-sanctions became evident for the first time in 2015.

Because of Russia's ban on meats imports, Finnish meat exports to Russia stopped.[4] In addition to a stop in meat exports, Finnish dairy exports to Russia have suffered the most from Russia's sanctions. In 2013, Finland's dairy and egg exports were valued at over €250 million, whereas five years later these exports were worth less than €2 million. Furthermore, Finnish fish exports to Russia have declined considerably (Customs Finland 2019).[5]

In 2013, Russia represented 29.1 percent of Finland's total food exports and foodstuffs constituted 7.5 percent of Finland's exports to Russia. In 2018, these shares were 6.5 percent and 2.5 percent, respectively. Despite the considerable decrease of the Finnish food exports to Russia, Finland's total food exports have already survived from Russia's sanctions, i.e. the value of Finland's food exports nearly reached the pre-sanction level already in 2018 (Table 8.1).

Table 8.1 The development of Finnish food exports to Russia, 2002–2018

	2002	*2007*	*2012*	*2013*	*2014*	*2015*	*2016*	*2017*	*2018*
Annual change in Finland's total exports to Russia (percent)	11	8	7	−6	−13	−32	−6	15	−3
Finland's total food exports (€ million)	808.3	1,133.6	1,366.2	1,376.7	1,344.3	1,235.7	1,208.7	1,350.5	1,294.3
Food exports from Finland to Russia (€ million)	182.0	267.0	389.5	401.3	301.4	103.1	103.6	112.3	83.5
Share of Russia in Finland's total food exports (percent)	22.5	23.5	28.5	29.1	22.4	8.3	8.6	8.3	6.5
Share of foodstuffs in Finland's exports to Russia (percent)	5.8	4.0	6.9	7.5	6.5	3.3	3.5	3.3	2.5
Meat [1] (€ million)	12.5	35.4	16.0	20.1	6.2	0.2	0.1	0.0	0.0
Dairy and eggs [2] (€ million)	84.2	123.0	240.7	253.1	164.4	0.9	0.2	0.6	1.6
Fish [3] (€ million)	3.4	15.1	11.5	9.0	5.3	1.7	3.0	2.3	1.8
Total [1–3] (€ million)	100.2	173.5	268.2	282.2	175.9	2.8	3.2	2.9	3.4
Share [1–3] of Finland's total exports to Russia (percent)	3.2	2.6	4.7	5.3	3.8	0.1	0.1	0.1	0.1

Source: Customs Finland (2019).

To summarize, agricultural products dominated Finnish outbound sales to the Russian mainland in the nineteenth century (in 1860, it was over 40 percent), but, due to industrialization, its share decreased considerably up to the independence of Finland. In 1917, agricultural goods constituted just a bit over one tenth of Finland's exports to Russia (Pihkala 1969). After the separation of Finland from the disintegrating Russian Empire and the emergence of socialism in Russia, Finland's foodstuff exports to the East disappeared. Food exports remained marginal until the beginning of the 1960s. Thereafter, foodstuffs started to constitute 3–5 percent of Finland's exports to the Soviet Union (Ollus and Simola 2006), and remained at this level until the disintegration of the USSR, when their proportion began to grow. From 1992 to 1997, the annual average share of foodstuffs in Finnish exports to Russia exceeded 10 percent. Even if the share dropped as a result of the Asian crisis in 1998–99, it picked up again and, in 2013, stood at over 7 percent (Customs Finland 2019). However, Russia's counter-sanctions of 2014 halted Finnish food exports to Russia, and it could be argued that Finnish food exporters received a major shock in the Russian business environment in 2014.

The main objective of this study is to analyse the impact of this shock and the adaptation of Finnish food exporters to Russia's food import restrictions, which were introduced in August 2014. In the following section, the accomplishment of the research is described.

The accomplishment of the research

From January–February 2018, the authors began to collect background information, i.e. statistics, company analyses, and media reports on Finnish food exports to Russia and food export companies. The researchers decided to focus their study on three sectors that have been most severely affected by Russia's food import ban. Thus, research emphasis was placed on exporters of meat, dairy, and fish products to Russia.

The researchers selected case companies using the ideology of purposeful sampling (Merriam 2009). To put it another way, the authors chose the largest corporations among Finnish meat, dairy, and fish exporters to Russia, as the macroeconomic impact of Russia's food import ban is the most significant in these corporations. Hence, Atria Plc, Valio Ltd, and Kalaneuvos Ltd were selected as case companies.

Qualitative research and case studies as a methodological approach were seen as the most suitable research approach since they provide the researchers with in-depth insights into the phenomenon within its real-world context (Dul and Hak 2008; Yin 2014). Furthermore, as Saunders and Lewis (2012) point out, case studies are applicable in exploratory and explanatory types of studies in which the goal is to find out why companies make certain decisions.

In March 2018, interviews with a company representative about the Russian operations of each company were conducted via telephone. The interviewees represented the executive management of the case companies. The interviews were recorded and then transcribed. This was followed by an analysis in order to establish how the answers fit the theoretical framework (Farquhar 2012). An interview guide method was used (Dul and Hak 2008; Yin 2014) and the themes of the interviews followed the structure of the theoretical model developed by Ferreira et al. (2011).

The interviews were divided into four main parts: (1) the ability of the studied companies to adapt to the business environmental change; (2) the companies' adaptation strategies to the changed business environment; (3) the performance of the studied companies in the Russian market before and after the shock to the business environment; and (4) changes in the competitive position of the studied companies.

Each interview lasted around 30 minutes. Interviews were considered the best technique for collecting information that is not publicly available. The main downsides of interviews are as follows: the small number of cases does not allow generalization of the findings; close exposure to the case companies may bias the findings; the respondents' answers may be subject to poor recall or bias. Moreover, conducting interviews by telephone may be challenging in several ways. Firstly, it may be difficult to gain the interviewee's trust and elicit sincere answers if the meeting is not face to face. Secondly, the lack of visual interaction does not permit the interviewer to observe the respondent's body language. It may therefore be difficult to interpret the responses (Saunders and Lewis 2012; Yin 2014). These challenges were carefully taken into account. To overcome potential trust issues, researchers strived to achieve transparency. To eliminate the possibility of misinterpretation, the interviewers made sure that the questions were as clear as possible.

The adaptation of a firm to a shock in its international business environment

Nearly half a century ago, Nehrt et al. (1970, p. 109) acknowledged the significance of the interrelationship between a firm's operations and its international business environment (IBE) when they wrote that research is "*concerned with the interrelationship between the operations of the business firm and international or foreign environments in which the firm operates*". One of the few early attempts to disaggregate the IBE was made by Farmer and Richman (1970), who identified several business environmental variables, such as economic, educational-cultural, political and legal, and sociological-cultural variables. In turn, Andrews (1971) defined a firm's business environment as the pattern of all the external conditions that influence a firm's development. He identified five main dimensions in a business environment, namely (1) economic; (2) physical; (3) political; (4) social; and (5) technological.

Three decades later, Guisinger (2001) attempted to identify elements constituting the international business environment. His taxonomy is based on eight elements that form the IBE. In alphabetical order, these are as follows: (1) culture; (2) econography, i.e. a combination of economic geography and demography;

(3) exchange rates; (4) income levels; (5) legal systems; (6) political risks; (7) restrictions; and (8) tax regimes.

Ferreira et al. (2009) analysed approximately 1,000 relevant studies on the international business environment. However, despite their extensive literature review, they failed to offer a clear definition of the international business environment. Ferreira et al. (2009, p. 291) concluded as follows: "*although many scholars agree that the IBE is the context and should be examined holistically, we found that the IBE has been, at best, a rather peripheral issue. Although omnipresent, the IBE is not operational, and remains a vague 'everything out there'*".

Suarez and Oliva (2005) produced an adequate typology of business environmental change on the basis of four attributes of change, namely frequency, amplitude, speed, and scope. Variations in these four attributes offer five main types of business environmental change: (1) regular change; (2) hyperturbulence; (3) specific shock; (4) disruptive change; and (5) avalanche.

As this study deals with the third type of business environmental change, a few words about its characteristics are appropriate. The third type of business environmental change, i.e. specific shock, corresponds to business environmental changes that are rapid and high in intensity, occur rarely and are relatively narrow in scope. Suarez and Oliva describe industry regulation as a typical example of such a type of change (Table 8.2).

According to Ferreira et al. (2011, p. 641), "*environmental changes, and specifically how firms respond to these changes, cause variation. Firms are selected in or out, depending (at least partly) on their pool of capabilities and resources that permits them to perform, given the environment. Only those best-fitted should survive, being retained – albeit it is likely that the best performers develop a set of new resources and capabilities that renders them an idiosyncratic competitive position*" (Figure 8.1).

In their model, Ferreira et al. (2011) suggest that firms operate in a multi-level environment. The first level comprises firm-specific capabilities, such as tactics and strategies, organizational structure, staff, and experience, which all interact to develop the skills and optional strategies of the company. The second level contains the industry environment and the third level comprises the wider national environment. Finally, the respective dimensions, which determine how companies are able to operate within the IBE, are found beyond the three levels.

Table 8.2 A typology of business environmental change

Type of Business Environmental Change	*Frequency*	*Amplitude*	*Speed*	*Scope*
Regular change	Low	Low	Low	Low
Hyperturbulence	High	Low	High	Low
Specific shock	Low	High	High	Low
Disruptive change	Low	High	Low	Low
Avalanche	Low	High	High	High

Source: Modified from Suarez and Oliva (2005, p. 1022).

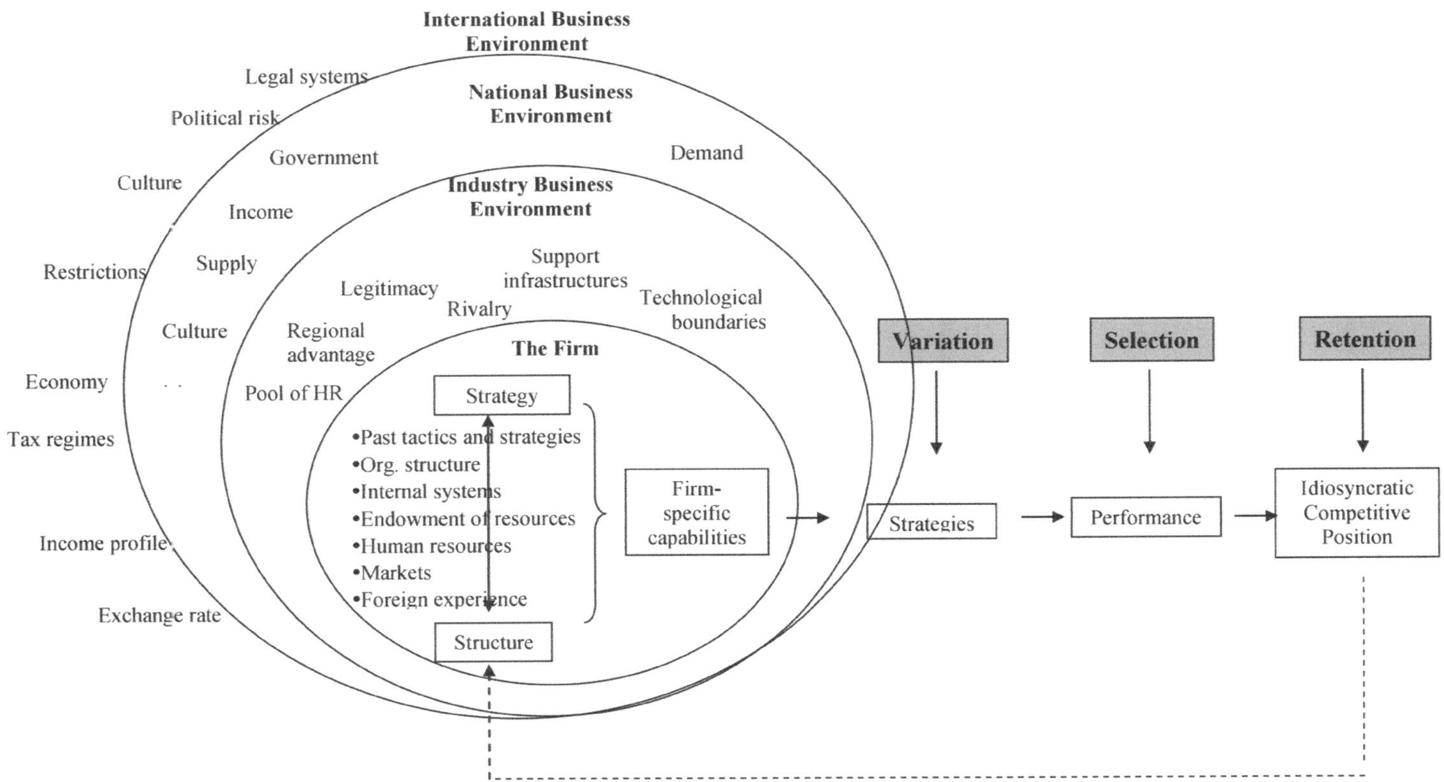

Figure 8.1 The adjustment of a firm to its international business environment

Source: Ferreira et al. (2011, p. 640).

The authors used the aforementioned theoretical framework to analyse the empirical data presented in the following section of the article.

Three case studies of Finnish food exporters to Russia

Case companies and the recent development of their operations in Russia

Atria, a company that can trace its history back to 1903, is one of the largest meat and food industry companies in the Nordic countries and Russia. Atria began its expansion into the Russian market in 1987, although a major step was taken in 2005 when Atria bought the St. Petersburg-based meat-processing company, Pit-Product. A further step was taken in 2008 when Atria acquired another meat-processing company, CampoMos. Again, in 2009, Atria opened a new factory in Gorelovo, St. Petersburg, doubling the company's production capacity in the region. In 2013, the firm decided to centralize its Russian operations to St. Petersburg, shut down the CampoMos factory and end its primary production of pork in Moscow (Atria 2018a). Consequently, St. Petersburg is Atria's main market in Russia, although the company still has a small market share in Moscow (Atria 2018b).

Atria's turnover ranged from over €1,300 million in 2010, some €1,400 million in 2013, to over €1,350 million in 2016. The Russian subsidiary's share in turnover halved in six years from almost 10 percent in 2010 to just over 5 percent in 2016. The total investments of the company almost doubled from over €46 million in 2010 to almost €83 million in 2016. The new plant in Finland that was completed in 2017 explains the exceptionally high figure for 2016. The share of Russia in Atria's investments dropped from 49 percent in 2010 to only 3 percent in 2016. Major investments in Russia in 2009 and 2010 explain these figures (Atria 2018a). Atria's total exports remained at €65–70 million but the share of Russia in exports dropped from approximately 15 percent in 2010 and 2013 to zero in 2016 (Table 8.3).

After Russia imposed the counter-sanctions, Atria's Annual Report (2014, 3) noted that "*[t]he most difficult situation was in Russia. The initial optimism for being able to achieve a positive performance was shuttered already in January [2014], when Russia imposed an import ban on pork. As a consequence, the price of meat increased by dozens of per cent in the blink of an eye. In August, Russia's import ban was extended to all European meat, and raw material prices increased again. In December, the value of the rouble collapsed*". In light of this statement, it is clear that the restrictions significantly impacted Atria's businesses in Russia. However, investments in production facilities in Russia, such as the Gorelovo factory, have mitigated the impact. Overall, the restrictions did not severely impact Atria's overall performance – at least not in the long term. The disadvantages were mostly indirect, as the weakened purchasing power and volatile Russian rouble weakened profits. The strategic decisions of product differentiation by local producers, product development and improvements in supply chain efficiency appear to have dampened the economic blows resulting from global politics (Atria 2015, 2017; Lindholm 2017).

Table 8.3 Development of the case companies, 2010–2016

ATRIA PLC	*2010*	*2013*	*2016*
Total turnover (€ million)	1,301	1,411	1,352
Total exports (€ million)	65–70	65–70	65–70
Total investments (€ million)	46	41	83
Share of Russia in turnover (percent)	9.9	8.6	5.3
Share of Russia in exports (percent)	approx. 15	approx. 15	0
Share of Russia in investments (percent)	49.0	8.7	3.0
VALIO LTD	*2010*	*2013*	*2016*
Total turnover (€ million)	1,822	2,029	1,638
Total exports (€ million)	433	503	353
Total investments (€ million)	68	118	127
Share of Russia in turnover (percent)	15.5	18.6	4.0
Share of Russia in exports (percent)	56.4	49.2	0.9
Share of Russia in investments (percent)	n/a	n/a	n/a
KALANEUVOS LTD	*2010*	*2013*	*2016*
Total turnover (€ million)	39	44	60
Total exports (€ million)	0.7	1.1	9.0
Total investments (€ million)	0.9	0.9	0.9
Share of Russia in turnover (percent)	1	2	0
Share of Russia in exports (percent)	49	64	0
Share of Russia in investments (percent)	n/a	n/a	n/a

Valio, founded in 1905 as a dairy farmers' cooperative, is a dairy market leader in Finland. The company has a long history of trading with Russia, but the opening of the branch office in St. Petersburg in 1994 marked the beginning of modern operations in the neighbouring country. Russia was Valio's main export destination until the restrictions came into force in 2014. The nature of business has changed and now the bulk of products sold in Russia are produced locally, although the subsidiary, OOO Valio, has been operating in Russia since as early as 2002. In addition to local production, certain products, notably baby foods, berry soups, juices, and lactose-free milk are still being exported from Finland, since they are not covered by the restrictions (Valio 2017, 2018).

Valio's turnover increased from approximately €1,800 million in 2010 to over €2,000 million in 2013 and then decreased to over €1,600 million in 2016. Russia's share in turnover was 19 percent in 2013 but only 4 percent in 2016. Valio's total exports dropped from over €500 million in 2013 to over €350 million in 2016. Russia's share in exports was particularly high, almost 50 percent before the restrictions, but only 1 percent in 2016. The total investment of the company varied from around €70 million in 2010 to €130 million in 2016. The company has not invested much in Russia in recent years, mainly because of its surplus capacity in existing premises, and its collaboration with subcontractors.

As Sutyrin and Trofimenko (2017) have noted, the food ban altered Valio's business model. To maintain its market share in Russia, Valio expanded production in Russia. In 2014, Valio started milk and cream production using the facilities of its partner company Galaktika. In 2015, the company started yoghurt and cheese production in the Moscow region in cooperation with German company Ehrman. Furthermore, Valio started contract butter production by the company Kochmeister Rus and increased production at Valio's own factory near Moscow. Hence, the use of partners' facilities enabled Valio to increase its local production and adapt to the business disruption caused by the restrictions. Despite these adjustments, the restrictions have caused some problems. As the Finnish broadcasting company YLE reported, Valio terminated almost 130 fixed-term contracts and temporarily laid off 50 employees in Finland as a result of the anticipated reduction in revenue ('Valio to . . .' 2014). Subsequently, as reported by the Russian newspaper the *Moscow Times*, Valio closed a production plant in Tampere due to the food ban ('Finnish Dairy . . .' 2016).

Kalaneuvos, formerly known as V. Hukkanen Oy, was founded in 1975. This family-run company is the largest operator in the fishing industry in Finland. The group currently comprises three companies: (1) Kalaneuvos, (2) Nordic Trout, and (3) Martin Kala. The company processes fish in Finland and exports to more than ten countries (Kalaneuvos 2018). The company has grown in recent years. For instance, in 2016, export operations and sales increased fivefold (V. Hukkanen Oy 2010, 2013, 2016). In 2017, exports amounted to almost €14 million and the main export countries were the Baltic States, Belarus, Spain, Sweden, and Ukraine (Heinonen 2017).

Kalaneuvos' turnover has steadily increased from nearly €40 million in 2010 to almost €60 million in 2016. Another record year was 2017, with a turnover of almost €70 million. Russia's share in turnover was minimal before the restrictions, only 1–2 percent, and zero percent after the restrictions. The total investments of the company amounted to almost €1 million in 2010, 2013, and 2016, although the company made major investments between these years. Total exports have increased from €0.7 million in 2010 to €9.0 million in 2016 and amounted to €13.5 million in 2017. Russia's share in exports was exceptionally high before the restrictions: 49 percent in 2010 and 64 percent in 2013.

The adaptation of the case companies to Russia's food import restrictions

Firm-specific ability to change

According to Ferreira et al. (2011), interacting components and company routines develop the company's distinctive skills and pool of alternative strategies, i.e. the ability to adapt to business environmental change. Foreign experience was one of the key skills that helped the case companies adapt to the changed environment. Atria, for example, faced a comparable situation a few years earlier with the pork ban.[6] In addition, Atria's Russian subsidiary was used to dealing with fluctuating meat prices and the poor availability of raw materials. As pointed out by the representative of executive management, Atria had experienced complex situations and huge losses in Russia before, and the experience had helped to identify the right kind of solutions. The experience in Russia also helped Kalaneuvos adapt to the shock to the business environment. The executive manager stated that the company had faced similar problems in the late 1990s when the devaluation of the Russian rouble forced it to end the exports that had been initiated six months previously. Valio has extensive experience of Russia, although the representative of the executive management team critically highlighted the fact that even the long history of trading in Russia could not help predict the developments.

None of the firms had any special mechanisms in place for observing the Russian business environment. Atria and Valio had their subsidiaries operating inside the Russian border but Kalaneuvos, as a smaller operator, did not. The corporate executive of Atria mentioned that the East Office of Finnish Industries, the Ministry for Foreign Trade and Development, and European trade associations were the main sources of information. The director of Valio commented that the company primarily observed the development of currency and purchasing power, which was not sufficient. None of the companies had changed their monitoring mechanisms since 2014.

The companies approached the situation differently, but none of the firms were adequately prepared. The business executive of Kalaneuvos noted that the restrictions came unexpectedly. The company had just started a collaboration with the Finnish retail company S Group in Russia, but the restrictions halted its plans. Similarly, the recently started collaboration with the Finnish Kesko Corporation ended. Both Atria and Valio understood that restrictions could be introduced, but the scope, extent, and duration of the counter-sanctions came as a surprise. As pointed out by the director of Valio, even though the threat and opportunities had been evaluated, there was no other option but to keep their eggs in the same basket and continue business as usual for as long as possible.

Strategies to change

According to Ferreira et al. (2011), firms respond to environmental changes using different strategies. Naturally, the most crucial factor that helped overcome the negative effects of the restrictions was the existing local production in Russia. Valio had local production plants, unlike many foreign companies in the dairy industry that eventually had to terminate their Russian operations. Atria also had local production plants and, as the top manager noted, the company was regarded as a local company in Russia. For Kalaneuvos the situation was different since its Russian business depended entirely on exports. Thus, the only option for the company was to find alternative export channels. One effective solution used by fisheries was to sell, reprocess, and resell the fish to Russia via Belarus. The export volumes remained virtually constant, only the export destination changed.

The interviewees agreed that the strategic importance of Russia decreased as a result of the counter-restrictions. For Atria, Russia was seen as an engine of growth. Thus, the company's disappointment was huge when the restrictions came into effect. The company's representative noted that Atria now avoids taking risks in Russia and its investments are allocated to safer targets. Also, the director of Valio mentioned that the company now deals more cautiously with the Russian market. Valio considers Russia to be a completely different market, as noted by the top manager. However, as a local producer the company is safe, since it acquires raw materials from local producers. Nevertheless, the significance of the Russian market for the company has decreased dramatically and it has diversified its export channels to include EU countries and other countries within the Eurasian Economic Union. Kalaneuvos did not modify its strategy as a result of the restrictions *per se*, but invested heavily in order to take over the whole production chain from raw materials to refined products.

Performance

The pool of capabilities and resources determines how the firm is able to perform in the environment (Ferreira et al. 2011). The shock to the business environment forced the case companies to adjust their performance and the companies adjusted their organizational structure and internal systems accordingly. For instance, Atria relocated some of its employees and Valio increased production in Russia, while laying off employees and closing down factories in Finland. Kalaneuvos invested in production, although this was largely in spite of the sanctions.

A high-priority issue for Valio was resolving where to direct the daily milk flows. The short-term solution was to shift the production to powdered milk, cheese, and other long-lasting products, as well as seek other sales channels for its products. Moreover, Valio built on the partner network in Russia in order to maintain the production quotas. The first operational issue for Atria was acquiring raw materials for the Russian factories, since imported materials were no longer available. Furthermore, Atria increased its material flexibility, sought new sales channels and increased product prices. On a local level Atria was able to maintain adequate profit margins with product segmentation. Kalaneuvos lacked these options so it needed to approach the situation differently. The first issue was redirecting a lorry that had been returned from the border. Eventually, the only option was to discontinue manufacturing certain products. It took approximately six months to find alternative markets, namely Belarus, Ukraine, and Vietnam, before production started again.

The restrictions affected the decision-making of the companies in different ways. Kalaneuvos focused on identifying alternative export destinations. Atria increased its use of local production and local raw materials and increased cooperation with local processing plants. No changes were made to either distribution or product development, but some alterations were made to product recipes. In addition, Atria opened new export channels. Most recently, in 2017, the company was granted a licence to export pork to China. Valio already used local milk in Russia and the company therefore had no supply difficulties. Instead, it increased production close to Moscow and centralized sales in Moscow and St. Petersburg. Minor product development took place, including the introduction of new additive-free, low-fat and low-salt products. However, Valio had to find new markets for its export surplus from Finland. As the new markets were located further away, i.e. in China, Poland, Spain, and the United Kingdom, the company had to produce longer-lasting products.

Idiosyncratic competitive position

According to Ferreira et al. (2011), only adaptive companies survive, and those companies that remain will have procured resources and developed capabilities that provide them with a distinctive competitive position. Although this statement seems intuitively correct, the reality of the case companies was more complex. Both Atria and Valio were large corporations and were able to keep even unprofitable subsidiaries running for some time. The representative of Atria admitted that, as a stand-alone business, the company would probably not have lasted through the changed business environment. According to the top manager, the meat industry has experienced notable changes in Russia. A few foodstuff-agricultural conglomerates, such as Cherkizovo, Miratorg, Ostankino, and Rusagro, have emerged as strong competitors. These Russian competitors now control fields, primary production, processing plants and butchers, as well as the manufacturing industry. The situation favours local operators and the only foreign operator besides Atria is the Thai conglomerate Charoen Pokphand. The business environmental changes also favoured large corporations in the dairy industry. Companies, such as Danone and PepsiCo, have strengthened their position, while many smaller companies ended their operations in Russia entirely. The perspective of the fishing industry was different as Kalaneuvos had no local production. As a silver lining, as noted by the top manager, the restrictions encouraged the company to seek alternative export destinations, which has enabled it to grow. In fact, 2016 and 2017 marked consecutive record years for the company in terms of turnover and exports (Table 8.4).

To summarize, the adaptation of the case companies had elements of a planned strategy, as Ferreira et al. (2011) suggest, but also a significant volume of reactive responses. The case companies collected information on business environment levels in order to enhance knowledge, although their methods varied. The companies identified vulnerable internal resources and assessed the most optimal external opportunities that contributed to a better environmental fit. None of the case companies were able to predict the events. Thus, the nature of their actions was more reactive than proactive. To a certain extent, the adaptation process observed the classification of Ferreira et al. (2011). All the case companies had distinctive skills and strategies and their adaptive responses altered the strategies of the respective company. The case companies performed according to their pool of capabilities, which helped the companies adapt and left them in an idiosyncratic competitive position.

Table 8.4 Summary of the main empirical findings

	Meat Exporter (Atria)	*Dairy Product Exporter (Valio)*	*Fish Exporter (Kalaneuvos)*
Firm-Specific Ability to Change	– Foreign experience and the subsidiary in Russia played a significant role – Organizational structure and internal systems permitted change – No special mechanisms for monitoring the business environment – The firm was not adequately prepared for Russia's counter-sanctions	– Foreign experience and the subsidiary in Russia played a significant role – Organizational structure and internal systems permitted change – No special mechanisms for monitoring the business environment – The firm was not adequately prepared for Russia's counter-sanctions	– Foreign experience played a moderate role – Russian business depended entirely on exports – Change in organizational structure and internal systems was not possible – No special mechanisms for monitoring the business environment – The situation arose unexpectedly
Strategies to Change	– The firm increased local production, acquired raw materials from local producers and sought alternative markets – The strategic importance of Russia has decreased – As a result, the company avoids taking risks in Russia and only invests in safe targets	– The firm increased local production, acquired raw materials from local producers and sought alternative markets for its surplus exports from Finland – The strategic importance of Russia has decreased – As a result, the company avoids taking risks in Russia and only invests in safe targets	– The firm directed exports to (and via) alternative countries – The company did not modify its strategy because of the restrictions – The strategic importance of Russia has decreased

Performance	– The firm acquired local raw materials for its factories, increased material flexibility, sought new sales channels, undertook product segmentation and increased product prices – The company increased the use of local raw materials and increased cooperation with local production plants – The firm did not change distribution channels or product development	– The firm had to resolve where it should direct the daily milk flows – The company shifted production to long-lasting products, sought alternative sales channels and built on partner network – The firm used local materials in Russia and had no supply problems – The company increased production in Russia and engaged in minor product development	– The firm discontinued production of some products until alternative export destinations were found
Idiosyncratic Competitive Position	– The large corporation was a crucial support that permitted the running of an unprofitable Russian subsidiary – The situation favoured local conglomerates and major operators	– The large corporation was a crucial support – The situation favoured large operators	– The firm had no local production plants and only a limited number of foreign competitors

Conclusion

The impact of Russia's food-related restrictions on Western food exports to Russia was significant. A statistical illustration helps to comprehend the magnitude of the impact. In 2013, the EU's food and live animal exports amounted to €8,800 million. Four years later the respective value was €3,700 million. However, the EU's exports that were not sanctioned by Russia have declined even more in absolute terms, i.e. in terms of monetary value. From 2013 to 2017, EU exports to Russia, excluding food and live animals, have declined from approximately €110,000 million to around €90,000 million. In relative terms, the EU's food and live animal exports to Russia have declined by nearly 60 percent during 2013–17, whereas the drop of the non-food exports was only 20 percent (EU 2018a, 2018b).[7]

The Finnish food export industry has suffered more than EU countries on average (Appendix 8.1). On the other hand, Finland has nearly recovered from Russia's food import sanctions by finding export markets elsewhere (see Table 8.1). Finnish dairy product exports in particular have been most severely affected by Russia's food import restrictions. Finnish dairy product and eggs exports to Russia have fallen from €250 million in 2013 to less than €2 million. It became evident that Valio, the largest exporter of Finnish dairy products to Russia, was not adequately prepared for Russia's food-related restrictions. The situation was similar with Atria, Finland's largest exporter of meat products to Russia, and Kalaneuvos, Finland's leading exporter of fish to Russia. After the shock resulting from the cessation of exports to Russia, large companies, such as Valio and Atria, were able to increase their local production in Russia and acquire more raw materials from local producers. However, a smaller company, Kalaneuvos, did not start its operations in Russia. As a reaction to Russia's sanctions, this fish firm has increased its sales to alternative export destinations. On the whole, the strategic importance of Russia has decreased in the studied companies, and these companies have started to avoid taking risks linked to Russia. The empirical evidence suggests that the case companies will most probably prioritize their investments in more predictable business environments in the future.[8]

To end, Russia's food-related counter-sanctions have caused "a specific shock" to the case companies as classified by Suarez and Oliva (2005). These food-related restrictions came as a shock and a surprise to all the case companies, as they were not adequately prepared for Russia's countermeasures. However, the case companies' financial resources, managerial capabilities and organizational structures enabled them to recover from the shock, thus enabling them to continue their operations in Russia. Even if the studied companies are able to continue with their Russian operations, the EU-Russia sanctions have left a lasting impression in the organizational memory of these case companies, which may reduce their future investments in Russia.

Notes

1 Due to its defeat in the Great Northern War, Sweden had already lost the easternmost part of Finland (so called "Old Finland") to Russia in 1721 and another part of Finland until the Kymi river after its loss in the Russo–Swedish War of 1743. The remaining part

of Finland was annexed to Russia after Sweden lost the Finnish War in 1809 (Mäntylä 1987a, 1987b).

2 The clearing trade between Finland and the USSR continued until early 1991 (Laurila 1995).

3 Russia's food-related sanctions were introduced in August 2014 when Russia banned fruit, vegetables, meat, fish, milk, and dairy imports from the EU member states and the USA, plus Australia, Canada, and Norway (Rankin 2014; Russell 2016).

4 A major decline in Finnish meat exports to Russia took place in 2010, i.e. even before Russia's contemporary sanctions. In 2009, Finnish meat exports to Russia were valued at €31 million, whereas one year later they amounted to just €14 million. The collapse of 2010 was due to accusations by Russian authorities that some Finnish meat exporters had used antibiotics in their raw materials ('Russian import . . .' 2010).

5 Finnish fish exports to Belarus have significantly increased during the sanctions era. If Finnish fish exports in 2017 to Belarus and Russia were calculated together, it would be noted that the combined sum would exceed their export value of 2013. This means that Finnish fish has found its way into the Russian market via Belarus, which belongs to the Eurasian Economic Union. The same phenomenon has occurred on a much larger scale with Norwegian fish (Liuhto 2018b).

6 The Finnish broadcasting company YLE reported as follows: "*Beef and pork products from the meat packer Atria have been banned from Russia since February [2010], after Russian inspectors found traces of antibiotics in the company's meat. Atria insists that the antibiotics in question have never been used in Finland, and there has been speculation that the ban has more to do with political maneuvering in Russia than any real concern about the safety of Finnish food imports*" ('Russian import . . .' 2010).

7 China's food exports to Russia that were not sanctioned by the Russian government have also declined, which supports the conclusion that the sanctions or the counter-sanctions are not the only reason for the trade decline.

8 The data of the Central Bank of Russia supports the views of the respondents, since the average annual foreign direct investment flow from Finland to Russia was over US$500 million from 2007–13, whereas the corresponding figure was below US$40 million from 2014–17 (Bank of Russia 2018).

Bibliography

Alho, K, Forssell, O, Huttunen, J, Kotilainen, M, Luukkonen, I, Mattila, O-T, Moilanen, J and Vartia, P 1986, *Neuvostoliiton kauppa Suomen kansantaloudessa*, ETLA, B 50 Series, Helsinki.

Andrews, KR 1971, *The Concept of Corporate Strategy*, Dow Jones-Irwin, Homewood, IL.

Atria 2014, *Annual Report*, viewed 22 February 2018, www.atria.fi/en/group/investors/financial-information/annual-reports/

Atria 2015, *Annual Report*, viewed 22 February 2018, www.atria.fi/en/group/investors/financial-information/annual-reports/

Atria 2017, *Annual Report*, viewed 22 February 2018, www.atria.fi/en/group/investors/financial-information/annual-reports/

Atria 2018a, *The First 114 Years of Atria*, viewed 27 February 2018, www.atria.fi/en/group/company/history/#26957

Atria 2018b, *Market Position in Russia*, viewed 20 February 2018, www.atria.fi/en/group/investors/atria-as-an-investment/market-position/market-position-atria-russia2

Bank of Russia 2018, *Direct Investment*, viewed 4 June 2018, www.cbr.ru/Eng/statistics/?PrtId=svs

Customs Finland 2019, *Uljas – International Trade Statistics Search*, viewed 27 March 2019, http://tulli.fi/en/statistics

Dohan, MR 1976, 'The Economic Origins of Soviet Autarky 1927/28–1934', *Slavic Review*, vol. 35, no. 4, pp. 603–635.

Dul, J and Hak, T 2008, *Case Study Methodology in Business Research*, Elsevier, Amsterdam.

EU 2018a, *European Union, Trade in Goods with Russia*, viewed 28 March 2018, http://trade.ec.europa.eu/doclib/docs/2006/september/tradoc_113440.pdf

EU 2018b, *European Union, Trade in Goods with Russia*, viewed 5 June 2018, http://trade.ec.europa.eu/doclib/docs/2006/september/tradoc_113440.pdf

Farmer, RN and Richman, BM 1970, *Comparative Management and Economic Progress*, Cedarwood Publishing Co, Irwin Bloomington, IN.

Farquhar, JD 2012, *Case Study Research for Business*, SAGE Publications, London.

Ferreira, MP, Li, D, Guisinger, S and Ribeiro Serra, FA 2009, 'Is the International Business Environment the Actual Context for International Business Research?', *RAE*, vol. 49, no. 3, pp. 282–294.

Ferreira, MP, Ribeiro Serra, FA and Reis, NR 2011, 'On the Adaptation of the Firm's Strategies to the International Business Environment: A Knowledge-based and Evolutionary Perspective', *European Journal of International Management*, vol. 5, no. 6, pp. 633–655.

'Finnish Dairy Company Valio to Close Plant Due to Russian Food Embargo' 2016, *The Moscow Times*, 1 June, viewed 22 February 2018, https://themoscowtimes.com/articles/finnish-dairy-company-valio-to-close-plant-due-to-russian-food-embargo-53120

Gregory, PR and Stuart, RC 2001, *Russian and Soviet Economic Performance and Structure*, Addison Wesley, Boston.

Guisinger, S 2001, 'From OLI to OLMA: Incorporating Higher Levels of Environmental and Structural Complexity Into the Eclectic Paradigm', *International Journal of the Economics of Business*, vol. 8, no. 2, pp. 257–272.

Heinonen, J 2017, 'Ennen menestystä kalaneuvos joutui ulosottoon: "Kysyin virkailijalta, jätänkö vaatteenikin"', *Talouselämä*, 11 November, viewed 15 March 2018, www.talouselama.fi/uutiset/ennen-menestysta-kalaneuvos-joutui-ulosottoon-kysyin-virkailijalta-jatanko-vaatteenikin/1b644a56-0d39-3254-bab4-20d03b7389a7

Hirvensalo, I and Sutela, P 2017, *Rahat pois bolsevikeilta: Suomen kauppa Neuvostoliiton kanssa*, Siltala, Helsinki.

Kalaneuvos 2018, *Fish From Cold, Fresh and Clean Nordic Waters*, The Kalaneuvos Group, viewed 15 March 2018, https://kalaneuvos.fi/en/

Laurila, J 1995, *Finnish-Soviet Clearing Trade and Payment System: History and Lessons*, Bank of Finland Studies A:94, Helsinki.

Lindholm, J 2017, *Capital Markets Day Atria Russia*, Presentation, viewed 22 February 2018, www.atria.fi/en/group/investors/financial-information/ir-presentations/

Liuhto, K 2018a, *Finland's Economic Relations with Russia*, Presentation, viewed 5 February 2018, www.researchgate.net/publication/322342500_Finland%27s_economic_relations_with_Russia_-_2018_update

Liuhto, K 2018b, *The Economic Relations Between Norway and Russia*, Presentation, viewed 5 February 2018, www.researchgate.net/publication/322924934_The_economic_relations_between_Norway_and_Russia

Mäntylä, I 1987a, 'Suurvaltakausi', in: S Zetterberg (ed.) *Suomen historian pikkujättiläinen*, WSOY, Porvoo, pp. 181–271.

Mäntylä, I 1987b, 'Vapauden aika', in: S Zetterberg (ed.) *Suomen historian pikkujättiläinen*, WSOY, Porvoo, pp. 273–311.

Merriam, SB 2009, *Qualitative Research: A Guide to Design and Implementation (Revised and Expanded From 'Qualitative Research and Case Study Applications in Education')*, Jossey-Bass (Wiley), Hoboken, NJ.

Nehrt, LC, Truitt, JF and Wright, RW 1970, *International Business Research: Past, Present and Future*, Indiana University Graduate School of Business, Bloomington.

Ollus, S-E and Simola, H 2006, *Russia in the Finnish Economy*, SITRA Reports 66, viewed 5 June 2018, https://media.sitra.fi/2017/02/28142123/Raportti66.pdf

Pihkala, E 1969, *Suomen ulkomaankauppa 1860–1917*, Bank of Finland, viewed 4 June 2018, https://helda.helsinki.fi/bof/handle/123456789/14325

Rankin, J 2014, 'Russia Responds to Sanctions by Banning Western Food Imports', *The Guardian*, 4 August, viewed 5 February 2018, www.theguardian.com/world/2014/aug/07/russia-retaliates-western-sanctions-ban-food-imports

Russell, M 2016, *Sanctions Over Ukraine – Impact on Russia*, European Parliamentary Research Service, viewed 28 March 2018, www.europarl.europa.eu/EPRS/EPRS-Briefing-579084-Sanctions-over-Ukraine-impact-Russia-FINAL.pdf

'Russian Import Restrictions on Finnish Food Take Effect' 2010, *The Finnish Broadcasting Company YLE*, 23 July, viewed 1 March 2018, https://yle.fi/uutiset/osasto/news/russian_import_restrictions_on_finnish_food_take_effect/5602337

Saunders, M and Lewis, P 2012, *Doing Research in Business & Management: An Essential Guide to Planning Your Research*, Pearson Education Limited, Harlow.

Suarez, FF and Oliva, R 2005, 'Environmental Change and Organizational Transformation', *Industrial and Corporate Change*, vol. 14, no. 6, pp. 1017–1041.

Sutyrin, S and Trofimenko, O 2017, 'Do Formal Institutions Really Matter for Foreign Direct Investments to the Russian Federation? The Case of FDI Flows From the European Union to Russia', in: K Liuhto, S Sutyrin and J-MF Blanchard (eds.) *The Russian Economy and Foreign Direct Investment*, Routledge, New York.

Valio 2017, *A New Era for Valio in Russia*, viewed 22 February 2018, www.valio.com/articles/a-new-era-for-valio-in-russia/

Valio 2018, *History*, viewed 22 February 2018, www.valio.com/history/

'Valio to Lay Off 126 After Russian Dairy Sanctions' 2014, *The Finnish Broadcasting Company YLE*, 27 August, viewed 22 February 2018, https://yle.fi/uutiset/osasto/news/valio_to_lay_off_126_after_russian_dairy_sanctions/7436820

V Hukkanen Oy 2010, *Financial Statement*, Virre Information Service, Finnish Patent and Registration Office, viewed 15 March 2018, https://virre.prh.fi/novus/home?execution=e3s1

V Hukkanen Oy 2013, *Financial Statement*, Virre Information Service, Finnish Patent and Registration Office, viewed 15 March 2018, https://virre.prh.fi/novus/home?execution=e3s1

V Hukkanen Oy 2016, *Financial Statement*, Virre Information Service, Finnish Patent and Registration Office, viewed 15 March 2018, https://virre.prh.fi/novus/home?execution=e3s1

World Bank 2018, *World Integrated Trade Solution*, viewed 26 June 2018, https://wits.worldbank.org/

Yin, RK 2014, *Case Study Research: Design and Methods*, 5th edition, SAGE Publications, Los Angeles.

Appendix 8.1

Table 8A.1 EU member states' exports of food products, animals, and vegetables to Russia in 2013 and 2016

EU Member State	*Food product, animal, and vegetable exports to Russia in 2013 (US$ million)*	*Food product, animal, and vegetable exports to Russia in 2016 (US$ million)*	*Change 2013–16 (US$ million)*	*Change 2013–2016 (percent)*
Austria*	315	131	−184	−58
Belgium	790	341	−449	−57
Bulgaria	71	42	−29	−41
Croatia	21	28	7	33
Cyprus	18	1	−17	−94
Czech Republic	126	105	−21	−17
Denmark	856	167	−689	−80
Estonia	507	238	−269	−53
Finland	586	127	−459	−78
France	971	359	−612	−63
Germany	2,180	1,024	−1,156	−53
Greece	224	42	−182	−81
Hungary	356	213	−143	−40
Ireland	297	67	−230	−77
Italy	913	454	−459	−50
Latvia	660	310	−350	−53
Lithuania	1,829	467	−1,362	−74
Luxembourg	12	3	−9	−75
Malta	0	0	0	0
The Netherlands	1,991	883	−1,108	−56
Poland	1,684	420	−1,264	−75
Portugal	65	38	−27	−42
Romania	55	64	9	16
Slovakia	41	16	−25	−61
Slovenia*	39	24	−15	−38
Spain	777	267	−510	−66
Sweden	136	92	−44	−32
UK	227	140	−87	−38
TOTAL	15,747	6,063	−9,684	−50 (country average)
Comparison				
China	1,983	1,853	−130	−7
Norway	1,161	24	−1,137	−98
USA	1,319	249	−1,070	−81

* The 2016 data was not available so the 2015 data has been used.

Source: Authors' calculations of data from the World Bank (2018).

9 Russia's trade with China

In the face of sanctions a search for new market opportunities

Liudmila V. Popova and Zhou Weidi

Introduction

Between 2014 and 2016 Russia's foreign trade experienced a deep decline caused by a number of negative external shocks and an ensuing economic recession. Under the sanctions, Russia was forced to replace traditional import sources with new ones and find new markets for its own exports. To minimize the negative effect of sanctions, Russia announced a partial redirection of its trade flows from Europe to Asia and launched an import substitution policy along with export support programmes. Commodity diversification of exports away from hydrocarbons and integration into global value chains has become the main priority of its trade policy. Negotiations with trade partners from Asia and other regions to improve market access for Russian non-energy goods have significantly intensified.

China, a key economic and political partner of Russia in the Asia-Pacific region, is at the centre of this "Pivot to Asia" policy. Deteriorating relations with the West since 2014 have further strengthened Russia's economic ties with China as bilateral exchanges have become more comprehensive, encompassing deeper cooperation in strategic sectors, including energy, finance, transport, and telecommunications. The introduction of anti-Russian sanctions accelerated the conclusion of the agreement on the "Power of Siberia" international gas pipeline, helped revive arms sales, and intensified efforts on the de-dollarization of bilateral deals. China played a vitally important role by providing Russia with the necessary finance for key energy projects and increasing its investment in the Russian economy. The Eurasian Economic Union (EAEU) and China have initiated their own integration projects in Eurasia, and recently signed an Agreement on Trade and Economic Cooperation, which is the first step towards a bilateral FTA.

At the present stage, closer economic relations with China have not fundamentally changed the structure of Russian–Chinese bilateral trade. Fuel continues to dominate Russian exports to China, and even in the face of a sharp fall in oil prices in 2014–2015, Russia has significantly increased the volume of oil deliveries to its Asian neighbour. As anticipated, in the coming years, Russian energy exports to the Chinese market will continue to grow, given the implementation of contracts in the oil and gas sector. However, along with increased fuel supply, Russia's efforts to diversify exports away from hydrocarbons have produced notable results, as the country has improved the penetration of non-energy products into China, including high-tech and agricultural goods. Subsequently, China became one of the largest export markets for Russian non-defence industrial products and agricultural commodities. This advance is facilitated by depreciation of the Russian currency, an emerging system for export promotion, and gradual removal by China of trade barriers against Russian agricultural products as a result of bilateral trade negotiations. Two political factors contribute to the further expansion of Russian exports in China. Firstly, the Chinese government's proclamation of the policy of building a "moderately prosperous society", an aim matched by a significant reduction in import duties on a wide range of goods, including food, consumer products, and equipment. Another factor is the trade war unleashed by the United States against China, which forced the latter to restrict imports from the US as a retaliatory measure. All this opens up new niches for Russian exports in the Chinese market, primarily food products.

In this study, we aim to examine the effect of Russia's "Pivot to Asia" policy, which includes efforts to improve access to the Chinese market, on a bilateral trade pattern with primarily Russian exports to China. For this purpose, we applied such indicators as trade intensity and trade specialization indices. Secondly, the study puts particular focus on determinants and prospects of the growth of Russia's non-primary exports to the Chinese market. In this regard, we tried to reveal an impact of recent trade promotion measures on the extent of intra-industry trade between Russia and China in general, and agro-food trade, in particular.

The remainder of this chapter is organized as follows. The next section provides a literature review and discussion on Russia's "Pivot to Asia" policy followed by an account of the methodology used. The following section gives a brief overview of developments in Russian–Chinese trade between 2011 and 2017 and provides empirical estimations of trade intensity, trade specialization, and the trend in intra-industry trade between Russia and China during the period. The next section outlines the direction of Russian–Chinese agro-food trade and reveals the determinants of the growth of Russia's agricultural exports. It also stresses the extent of intra-industry trade in agricultural commodities. The final section offers concluding remarks and suggestions for further research.

Literature review

Russian–Chinese economic relations are often considered in the broader context of Russia's "Pivot to Asia", the cornerstone of which is further rapprochement with China. This strategy has received quite controversial assessments both in Russia and abroad. Some researchers perceive Russia's turn towards Asia as a response to deterioration of relations with the West, and often criticize the policy for its bias towards just one country – China. This, they argue, leads to Russia's increasing dependency on its eastern neighbour (Makocki and Popescu 2016; Suslov 2016). Despite closer political ties and recently created opportunities in new sectors, economic relations between the two countries are becoming increasingly asymmetric with the growing one-sided dependence of Russia on China (Simola 2016). The scholars argue that Russia's turn to Asia is essentially due to an increase of its hydrocarbon exports, mainly to the Chinese market. The countries' integration in mutual value chains is also highly asymmetrical (Sanghi et al. 2017).

China derives great advantages from anti-Russian sanctions, gaining more and better access to the Russian market, and at better prices (Chase et al. 2017). Russia eased barriers to Chinese investors in previously closed-off sectors and thus provided better opportunities in the market compared to companies from other countries. It even expanded the territorial scope of its "Pivot to Asia" to its arctic regions, though they had previously been restricted to foreigners (Saalman 2017). China captures the gains of diverted trade by displacing its Western competitors in the Russian market. The substitution effect is especially noticeable with respect to the supply of equipment and high-tech products (Herrero and Xu 2016). However, Afontsev (2015) and Obolenskiy (2016, 2017a) argue that China can only serve to compensate for the loss of Russia's middle-end technologies and consumer goods suppliers from Europe and the US, but it can hardly completely replace Europeans and Americans as suppliers of the high-tech equipment that is essential to Russia's modernization.

Some Russian scholars, while recognizing the growth of Asian countries in Russia's foreign trade, claim this shift to be a purely statistical phenomenon as the increase of Asia is due to the reduction of trade with other countries, primarily with the EU. They note that China, along with other Asian countries, has not become an alternative to Western capital markets and direct investment. Despite the increase in FDI from China, the main foreign investors in the Russian economy are still Western countries. The bulk of China's recent FDI is related to the acquisition of assets in Russian energy companies but not to the development of the Russian manufacturing sector (EAEU and Eurasia: Monitoring and Analysis of Direct Investments – 2017; Ivanov 2017). As for external loans, only individual Russian companies received valuable financial resources from Chinese state-owned policy banks. For most Russian enterprises, investors in China are virtually inaccessible (Obolenskiy 2017a; Makocki and Popescu 2016).

Another strand of literature contains empirical assessments of Russian–Chinese trade. A number of papers by Chinese researchers explore bilateral trade through its composition, intensity, and revealed comparative advantage (Yang and Wang 2005; Lu 2010; Dong 2010). They demonstrated the high complementarity between China and Russia in merchandise trade, and suggested that its growth potential is huge. However, trade has mainly developed according to a traditional pattern based on comparative advantage. Zhang (2012) studied the potential for bilateral trade between China and Russia through a gravity model. He concluded that further expansion of bilateral trade is feasible through strengthening regional cooperation and the establishment of an FTA, as well as by adjusting the structure of trade. Concerning commodity composition of bilateral trade, Lu (2010), Wan and Li (2011) revealed that, although in recent years it has undergone significant changes, trade is still largely driven by industries with low added value and thus remains more backward in its patterns as compared to China's trade with the US or Japan.

Zhang (2013) and Ding et al. (2010) analysed the level of intra-industry trade between China and Russia using the Grubel-Lloyd index. They revealed that the overall level of intra-industry trade between China and Russia is low. They explain this by the differing industrial structures of the two countries and resulting differences in the specialization of the international division of labour. In their view, to promote the development of intra-industry trade, the countries should increase the added value of exported goods and integrate more actively their mutual value chains.

A number of studies focus on trends in the development of the Russian–Chinese agro-food trade. Alexandrova (2017a, 2017b) believes that Russia has great advantages in exporting agricultural products to the Chinese market because of geographical proximity and competitive prices. Further growth in Russian exports is supported by continued increase in the incomes of the Chinese population and the gradual liberalization of food imports. She points out that, despite recent progress, most of Russia's food exports to the Chinese market are low-value-added products. Sun (2016) analysed the complementarity and determinants of agricultural trade between Russia and China between 2001 and 2013. He revealed that the growth of Russian exports to China is due to increased market demand and enhanced export competitiveness. Tong and Shi (2017) studied the marginal intra-industry agricultural trade between Russia and China. They concluded that this trade is mostly inter-industry, although the value and level of intra-industry trade are both growing. Gong and Liu (2015) used various measurement alternatives, such as the Grubel-Lloyd index, Brülhart index, and Thom and McDowell index, for assessing the level of intra-industry trade in agricultural products. They distinguish the horizontal and vertical product differentiation within intra-industry trade. Their findings also indicate that inter-industry trade dominates the agro-food trade between the countries, whereas within intra-industry exchanges, vertical product differentiation is becoming increasingly important.

There seem to be no empirical studies devoted to the impact of Russia's "Pivot to the East" policy on the evolving Russian–Chinese trade pattern. This study tries to fill this gap by making a modest contribution to the research on Russia-Chinese merchandise trade in general, and agricultural trade in particular, from the perspectives of Russian exports to China.

Methodology

Several statistical indices can be used to measure trade relations between two nations. This study uses a simple technique called the trade intensity index developed by K. Kojima (Kojima 1964). The trade intensity index (TII) is used to determine whether the value of trade between two countries is greater or smaller than would be expected on the basis of their importance in world trade. It is defined as the share of one country's exports going to a partner divided by the share of world exports going to the partner. It is calculated as:

$$T_{ji} = \frac{X_{ji} / X_{it}}{X_{wj} / X_{wt}}$$

Where x_{ji} and x_{wj} are the values of country i's exports and of world exports to country j and where X_{it} and X_{wt} are country i's total exports and total world exports respectively (WITS 2018). An index of more than one indicates that bilateral trade flow is larger than expected given the partner country's importance in world trade. If the index value is 1, the countries trade with each other with the same intensity as with the rest of the world. An index less than one means low trade intensity between the countries. This also indicates that expanding trade between the two countries has great potential.

To analyse the level of trade specialization in Russia's bilateral trade with China, we used a merchandise trade specialization index (TSI). The TSI index, also known as normalized trade balance by product, measures the degree of specialization in the production/consumption of goods through trade. Calculated for each product group it compares the net flow of goods (exports minus imports) to the total flow of goods (exports plus imports). The TSI measure can be interpreted as a measure of the potential competitiveness of the international trade sector of a specific country. TSI is mathematically represented as follows:

$$TSI_{ji} = \frac{X_{ji} - M_{it}}{X_{jt} + M_{ji}}$$

where j stands for the economy (nation or nation group), i denotes the product or product group, X_{ji} represents economy's j exports of goods i; and M_{ji} denotes economy's j imports of goods i. The range of values is between -1 and $+1$; the positive value signifies that an economy has net exports (thus, it specializes in the production of the particular product). Conversely, a negative value means that an economy imports more than it exports (net consumption). The higher the TSI index, the higher is the degree of specialization (Kellman and Shachmurove 2011).

Intra industry trade (IIT) refers to the exchange of commodities from the same industry. Alternatively said, it can be defined as the simultaneous exports and imports of commodities of similar factor intensity (Bhagwati and Davis 1994). Several alternative measures have been developed in the literature to estimate the degree of intra-industry trade (IIT) (Grubel-Lloyd index, The Aquino index, The Bergstrand method, and others (Grubel and Lloyd 1975; Aquino 1978; Bergstrand 1990). The most standard and widely preferred index to measure the extent of IIT is Grubel-Lloyd (G-L). This index measures intra-industry trade as a percentage of a country's total trade, which is assumed to be balanced, that is exports equal imports. For an individual product group or industry *i* the share of IIT is formulated as:

$$GL_i = \frac{(X_i + M_i) - |X_i - M_i|}{X_i + M_i} = 1 - \frac{|X_i - M_i|}{X_i + M_i}; 0 \le GL_i \le 1$$

where X_i and M_i stand, respectively, for the exports and imports of industry *i*. If all trade is balanced G-L index equals 1. On the other hand, if all trade is one-way, G-L index would equal zero. Thus, the closer G-L index is to 1 (that is, $X_i = M_i$), the more trade in industry *i* is intra-industry trade. The closer G-L index is to zero (that is, either $X_i = 0$ or $M_i = 0$), the more trade in industry *i* is inter-industry trade. Therefore, the index of intra-industry trade takes values from 0 to 1 as the extent of intra-industry trade increases, that is, $0 \le GL_i \le 1$. Higher values indicate a higher level of IIT between countries, showing that a country is more integrated in the world economy.

In this study, we used trade data collected from the UN COMTRADE statistics database for the period from 2012 to 2017. COMTRADE covers more than 90 percent of world trade, or around 160 countries. The choice of the period is due to a number of factors. Firstly, at the end of 2012 Russia joined the WTO and thus became a full member of the international trading system. After accession, Russia set about creating a system of state support for non-primary exports and shifted the focus of its trade policy to bilateral free-trade agreements. Secondly, this period covers the introduction of anti-Russian sanctions and the subsequent economic crisis that forced Russia to make further adjustments to its economic and trade policy. In 2017, the Russian economy and foreign trade showed signs of recovery, thus we can identify the changes that have occurred in its trade pattern during this cycle.

New priorities of Russian trade policy and major trends in Russian–Chinese trade during the sanctions period

Western sanctions and the deterioration of foreign policy relations accelerated the development of a national export support system in Russia, spurred geographic diversification of exports with an emphasis on Asian countries and other emerging markets, and prompted the formation of industries with export potential as part of an import substitution policy. The key priorities of trade policy have been the improvement in the export structure in favour of the non-primary sector and services, as well as the development of value chains with the country's main trading partners. The task is to almost double the value of non-primary non-energy goods in Russian exports from US$134 to 250 billion between 2018 and 2024 (TASS 2018).

In 2015, the government established the Russian Export Center (REC), which is to become a pillar of the national export support system. Currently, the support of

Russian exporters of non-primary non-energy goods is based on a project-oriented approach. Within the framework of priority projects, such as "System Measures for the Development of International Cooperation and Export", "International Cooperation and Export in Industry", and "Export of Agricultural Products", a comprehensive toolkit of export support measures has been developed, including for high-tech and innovative products, as well as agricultural goods (Pravitel'stvo Rossii 2018). Key industries with high export potential embrace aircraft construction, agriculture, railway machinery, the automotive industry, and some others. The package of support measures, among other things, consists of subsidization of interest rates on export credits, compensation of costs for transportation (up to 80 percent), certification of products, protection of intellectual property rights, and compensation for development of after-sales service programmes (Rossiiskii Eksportniy Tsentr 2018). Efforts are also being made to improve trade logistics, in particular, to develop new export rail corridors for Russian non-primary exports.

After 2014, Russia has significantly intensified bilateral negotiations with a number of partners to conclude free trade agreements and to improve market access for agricultural and other goods. As of 2018, the EAEU has a functioning FTA with Vietnam, a non-preferential agreement with China, a preliminary agreement on the establishment of a free trade zone with Iran, and an agreement on the establishment of a Russian industrial zone in Egypt (Spartak et al. 2018; RBK 2018). Currently the EAEU is negotiating an FTA with Singapore, Egypt, India, Israel, and Serbia and in the near future will most likely move to negotiations on the establishment of the FTA with other developing countries, such as Indonesia, Chile, Thailand, and Cambodia. Furthermore, during the Sochi 2016 summit, Russia came with an initiative to establish an EAEU–ASEAN freetrade area, which was supported by ASEAN member countries.

Since the period of application of export support measures in Russia is short and coincides with the sharp devaluation of the ruble at the end of 2014, subsequent economic downturn and a decline in foreign trade, we can only give a preliminary assessment of the effectiveness of these instruments. According to Russian experts, the average annual growth rate of physical supplies of non-primary non-energy goods over the past five years amounted to 4.8 percent, which exceeded the growth rate of total Russian exports (Spartak et al. 2018). The growth of export support contributed to the diversification of the Russian export basket, which now includes new export goods. The share of non-primary non-energy goods in the total value of Russian exports enlarged from 28 to 37 percent between 2014 and 2017, with the fastest growth demonstrated by agricultural products. However, if calculated at current prices, the value of non-energy exports in 2017 only returned to the level of 2014.

China is the largest export market for Russian non-energy goods with enormous potential for further export expansion. Therefore, the bulk of financial and non-financial support in Russia is directed towards companies supplying their products to China, and negotiations to improve access to the Chinese market for Russian non-energy goods are the most effective so far. Among the most significant projects to promote non-primary exports is the 2016–2018 launch of new export rail corridors from Vorsino (Kaluga region) and Krasnodar to China led by the Russian Export Center in partnership with RZD Logistic and other companies. These enjoy a 50 percent transport subsidy granted mostly to exporters of engineering and agricultural goods. To ensure the supply of grain to China, Russia currently is creating a land "grain corridor" that includes construction of a grain terminal in Eastern Siberia and other infrastructure. The Russian export centre also provides other assistance in promoting Russian products to the Chinese market, including through e-commerce channels. These efforts lead to an increase in the volume of Russian non-primary exports to China, observed since 2014. The main drivers of this growth are machinery and equipment, the chemical industry and the agro-industrial complex. Below, we consider the main trends in the development of Russian–Chinese trade.

Russia's trade with China has expanded considerably over the past two decades. From 2010, China has become Russia's largest trade partner with a turnover reaching US$88 billion in 2014 (in the early 2000s it equalled less than US$10 billion a year) (Figure 9.1). With the growth of trade, China's share in Russia's trade turnover has also increased, including recent years when Russia has been exposed to Western sanctions. Overall, China's share in Russian trade enlarged from 10.5 to 15 percent from 2013 to 2017; and although China became the main source of imports for Russia several years ago, in 2017 it became its largest export market for the first time. At present, China accounts for almost 21 percent of Russian imports and 10.9 percent of its exports significantly exceeding the share of Germany (Federal Customs Service of the Russian Federation 2018).

Over the past ten years, Russian–Chinese trade has sharply reduced twice under the influence of a decline in world oil prices and fluctuations in the value of the Russian ruble. During the global financial crisis, commodity turnover fell by almost a third, although in the following year, trade recovered and even exceeded the pre-crisis level. In 2015, under the impact of a number of unfavourable external shocks for the Russian economy, bilateral trade fell by 28 percent to US$62 billion, and China's exports declined even more due to a reduced demand and a steep depreciation of the ruble. In late 2016, the Russian economy returned to modest growth amid rising oil prices and macroeconomic stability. Commodity turnover between Russia and China jumped by 30 percent year-on-year, reaching US$86.9 billion in 2017, returning to the level prior the sanctions. The countries have recently set a goal to boost trade to US$100 billion by 2018 and US$200 billion by 2020 (Spanger 2016).

Over time, bilateral trade became more inter-industry in terms of its composition as Russian raw materials increasingly flowed to China in exchange for manufactured goods. Russia's export basket in trade with China has become more concentrated than it was in the early 2000s while imports from China are now more diverse and sophisticated (Spanger 2016). Mineral fuels account for 67 percent of Russia's exports to China, up from 19.8 percent in 2003. Other natural resources such as wood constitute about 12 percent of Russia's exports to China (Sanghi et al. 2017). Supplies of equipment and hi-tech products decreased from 12.2 percent in 2003 to just 2.2 percent by 2011, although later their share recovered to 5 percent in 2017. Whereas exports from Russia to China consist generally of primary resources, China's exports to Russia are comprised mostly of finished goods (capital goods account for 37.3 percent, and consumer goods constitute another 45.3 percent of total exports) (Table 9.1). Since 2007, Russia has been running a trade deficit with China, which reached a height of US$17.5 billion in 2013.

From 2011 to 2017, the composition of the basket comprising the top ten items of Russia's export to China has seen certain changes (Figure 9.2). "Fuels" (HS27) and "wood" (HS44) remained the largest export groups with their value increased. The positions of machinery and electronics (HS84, HS85) improved substantially; consequently, this group of goods now ranks third in Russian exports to China.

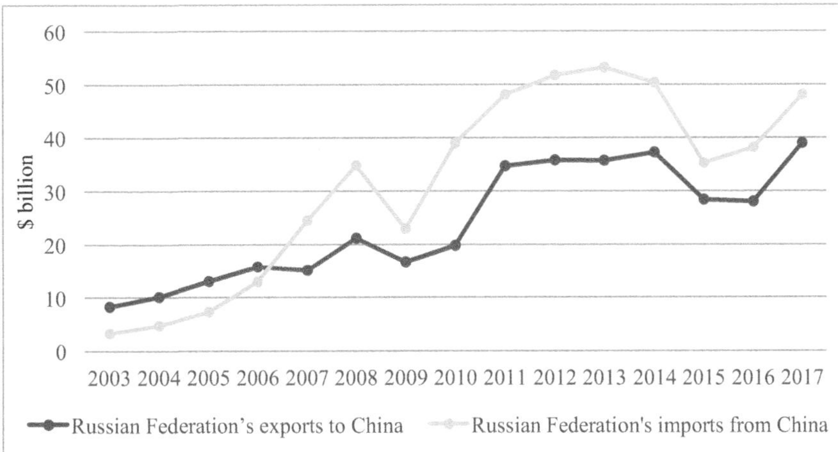

Figure 9.1 Russia-China's trade turnover, 2003–2017

Source: UN Comtrade (2018).

Table 9.1 Composition of bilateral trade by stage of processing, 2003–2016

	2003	*2007*	*2016*
Russian exports to China, percent			
Raw materials	20.92	56.46	66.9
Intermediate goods	36.93	26.86	15.45
Consumer goods	11.07	8.36	9.01
Capital goods	15.14	7.06	6.27
Chinese exports to Russia, percent			
Raw materials	5.66	1.63	2.95
Intermediate goods	8.51	14.75	14.30
Consumer goods	72.3	61.09	45.27
Capital goods	13.44	22.53	37.32

Source: WITS (2018).

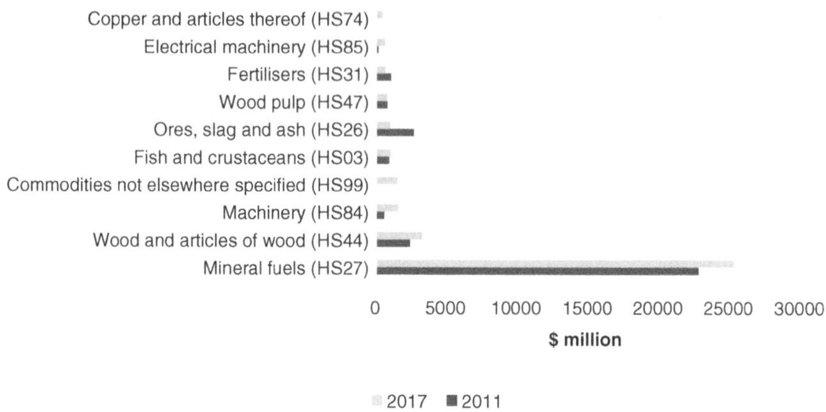

Figure 9.2 Top ten Russia's export commodities to China in 2007 and 2011

Source: UN Comtrade (2018).

Two new product groups entered the basket, namely "copper" (HS74) and a special category of goods (HS99), which significantly expanded in Russia's overall exports in 2015–2016.[1] The shares of "fish and crustaceans" (HS03), as well as "wood pulp" (HS47) in Russian exports to China remained virtually unchanged. Because of a slowdown of the economy and overproduction, China significantly reduced purchases of metals and chemical products from Russia. Therefore, the corresponding groups (HS28, 29, 39) left the basket of top ten goods.

In recent years, the main article of Russian exports to China has been oil. Expansion of oil exports leads to greater volatility in bilateral trade, as world oil prices are subject to frequent fluctuations. As oil prices fell in late 2014, Russia continued to increase its exports in volume terms. Since 2016, Russia has become China's biggest crude oil supplier ahead of Angola and Saudi Arabia. In turn, China is now purchasing over one-fifth of the total value of Russian oil exports. The expansion of oil supplies to the Chinese market occurs simultaneously with a decrease in exports to the EU countries, a fact which has prompted concern in Europe over the future price of Russian oil (Figure 9.3) (Cheong 2018).

Russian oil is sent to China by both pipeline and sea. At the end of 2017, the construction of the second section of the Skovorodino–Daqing pipeline was completed, which will double the supply of oil to the Chinese market to 30 million tons (mt) from 2019. In addition, Russian oil is exported via a pipeline through Kazakhstan (about 10 mt per year) and through the port of Kozmino, the final terminal of the Eastern Siberia-Pacific Ocean (ESPO) pipeline. Between 2014 and 2017, China's seaborne oil imports from Kozmino increased almost threefold, leading to Russia becoming China's sixth-largest seaborne crude oil supplier

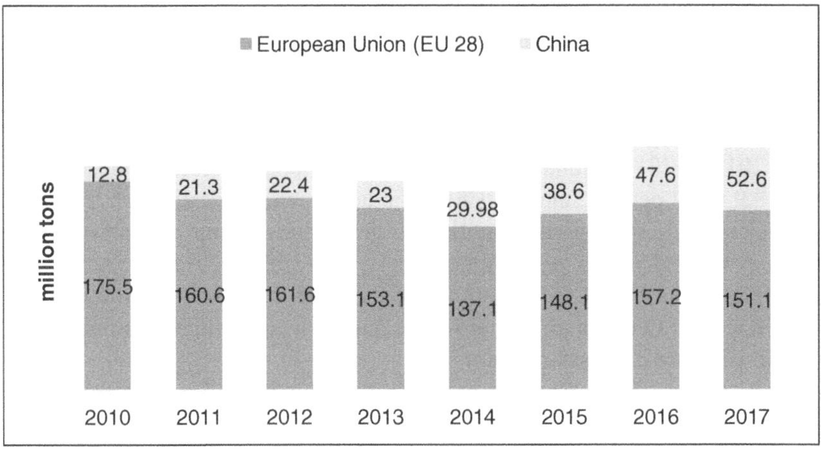

Figure 9.3 Russia's oil export to the EU and China compared, 2010–2017

Source: Authors' calculations of data from UN Comtrade (2018).

(Starinskaya 2018; Dezan Shira and Associates 2017). This rapid growth largely reflects the increase in demand from independent Chinese refineries after the Chinese government allowed them to process imported oil in the second half of 2015.

In the short term, Russia is to become a major supplier of natural gas to China. At the end of 2017, the construction of the first stage of the LNG plant in Yamal was completed, and the LNG shipments have already gone on line. According to an agreement, more than half of LNG will be supplied to Asian markets, including 3 mt (4.1 bcm) to China annually. The construction of The Power of Siberia gas pipeline with a capacity to transport 38 bcm per year is underway (Ivanov 2017). The contract was signed in 2014 with first deliveries currently planned to begin between 2019 and 2021. Two other gas pipeline projects connecting Russia with China are under consideration.

Along with further expansion of Russian fuel resources to China, in recent years Russia has been making efforts to promote non-primary products to China, including high-tech goods, as well as agricultural commodities and consumables. Non-energy goods now account for more than a quarter of the total Russian exports to China. This growth largely resulted from their increased competitiveness due to the devaluation of the ruble and attempts by Russia to expand its trade with Asia to minimize the negative impact of sanctions. To stimulate non-primary exports, vehicles, engineering products, and agricultural goods in particular, Russia has been increasing financial and non-financial support to companies, and creating new export corridors to improve trade logistics (Chertkov 2017; Ivanov 2018; Zubkov 2017). Significant efforts have also been made to reduce non-tariff barriers to trade.

In particular, the Russian exports of equipment and electronics (HS84–85) to China between 2011 and 2017 increased by 28.6 percent, consequently the share of machinery and equipment in Russia's total exports in China reached almost 5 percent, against 2.2 percent in 2011. Exports of machinery and equipment, as well as vehicles and other high-tech products to China grew faster than the corresponding goods in the Russian exports with the rest of the world. Accordingly, from 2011 to 2017, China's share in the corresponding sector almost doubled, from 8.9 to 17 percent, making China the largest export destination for Russian machinery and equipment. Remarkably, the export of high technologies grew more dynamically than agricultural supplies; and if, in 2011, the value of the former was lower than the export of food, now it exceeds it (Figure 9.4). Nevertheless, the value of high-tech goods is quite low, only slightly influencing the overall structure of Russian exports.

At its current stage, Russia's exports of machinery and equipment to China (excluding chapter HS99) have also seen a certain diversification. This is made up of dual-use items: primarily turbojets, nuclear reactors, electrical machinery. Other dynamically growing high-tech articles include lasers, radar equipment, liquid crystal devices, and measuring instruments. Export of motor vehicles, particularly passenger cars and agricultural machinery, has also expanded. Specifically, the supply of agricultural machinery to China in 2017 increased tenfold, from a base that was recently nonexistent (Kulikov 2018). As for the arms trade, it has not seen much of a breakthrough despite the revival of military ties and the mitigation of Russia's opposition to the transition of some of its most advanced

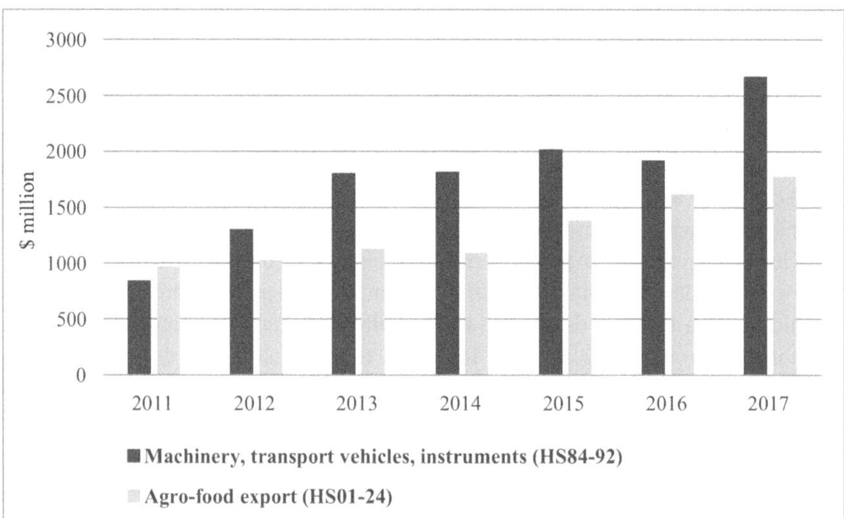

Figure 9.4 Russia's export growth to China by category, 2011–2017

Source: UN Comtrade (2018).

systems to China after 2014. Currently, arms sales account for just 5 percent of total trade, although China remains one of the most important export markets for Russia (Gabuev and Kashin 2017).

Russia imports a wide range of industrial goods from China – machinery and electronics (HS84, HS85) specifically (Figure 9.5). These goods constitute a significant share in Chinese exports in general, but for Russia, their recent growth is also associated with the continued replacement of Western sources of imports with Chinese ones. For food trade, once Russia had imposed a food embargo against the EU and Turkey, Chinese companies quickly occupied a free niche in the market and became the largest suppliers of food products to Russia, fruits and vegetables in particular (Byrkova 2018). These developments confirm the general pattern observed in other countries once being under sanctions – a withdrawal of businesses from a sanctioning country opens opportunities for firms from other countries, which either do not support the sanctions or are more lenient toward them (Shin et al. 2016).

Machinery and electronics (HS84, 85) account for over a half in Russia's import from China, which is the largest supplier of these articles to Russia. The introduction of anti-Russian sanctions contributed to the further strengthening of China's position in the Russian market for high technology goods, as their exports from Western economies declined. Most noticeable was the reduction of the supply of machinery and equipment from the EU countries, mainly due to falling exports from Germany (Herrero and Xu 2016). Whereas in 2011 the EU-28 countries accounted for 51.1 percent of the total exports of machinery and equipment (HS84) to Russia, by 2017 their market share has diminished to 44.2 percent, while the China's stake at the same time enlarged from 22.6 to 30.1 percent. In particular, China became the main supplier of liquefying equipment for Russia in the Yamal LNG project. It also took a significant market share from the EU in exports of electrical machinery (HS85) and motor vehicles (HS87) in the Russian market.

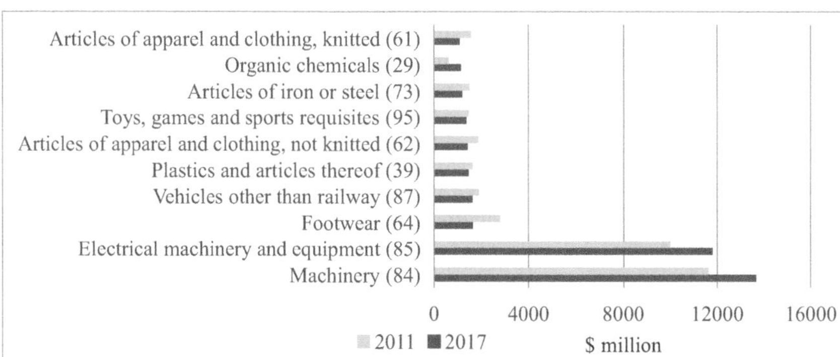

Figure 9.5 The top 10 commodity groups in Russia's import from China in 2011 and 2017

Source: UN Comtrade (2018).

In recent years, China and Russia have accelerated their steps to promote national currencies in bilateral transactions. This share is steadily growing and currently makes up 17 percent of bilateral trade, whereas a few years ago, it was just 4.5 percent (Central Bank of Russia 2018). In April 2017, when the Russian Central bank opened its first overseas office in Beijing, China responded with the establishment of a clearing bank in Moscow for handling transactions in Chinese yuan.[2] To mitigate the exchange rate risk, the Peoples' Bank of China established a payment-versus-payment (PVP) system for yuan-ruble transactions. Payments through the PVP system are carried out directly, without passing through SWIFT. The establishment of the clearing center and the launch of PVP system allow countries to diminish their dependence on the US dollar (Katasonov 2018). Extension of the use of national currencies for cross-border transactions could also potentially reduce the volatility of yuan and ruble exchange rates. Russia is currently considering the use of the cross-border Chinese payment system (CIPS) as an alternative to SWIFT for international bank transfers (Lousianin 2017).

In May 2018, the EAEU signed a non-preferential agreement on trade and economic cooperation with China that does not provide for the reduction or abolition of customs duties in mutual trade, but aims at trade facilitation ("China, EAEU sign agreement" 2018). It covers sectoral and customs cooperation, sanitary, veterinary, and phytosanitary measures, and technical barriers. It also pays much attention to intellectual property protection and greater transparency in trade remedy actions and subsidies (Karaganov et al. 2017). The agreement should facilitate implementation of joint projects and the formation of the pan-Eurasian value chains within the EAEU and the Chinese "One Belt, One Road" megaproject, and is seen as the first step towards the creation of a freetrade zone.

Recent developments in bilateral trade are perceived differently in Russia. On the one hand, there are concerns about asymmetry in trade growing along with Russia's dependence on the Chinese market, including the supply of crude oil (Saalman 2017). Although China's share in Russia's trade turnover continued to expand, Russia's stake in China's foreign trade remains small. Thus, China is still a much more important partner for Russia than Russia is for China. At the same time, there are signs of diversification in Russia's exports towards non-primary goods (Spartak et al. 2018). It is difficult to predict whether the observed changes in the structure of bilateral trade are a long-term trend; but given that this trend continues along with an increase in state support for exports, Russia stands to enjoy an important opportunity to seize most of the higher end of the value chain.

We estimated the effect of Russia's Pivot to Asia policy since 2014 on its trade with China by applying three indicators, i.e. the Trade Intensity Index (TII), the merchandise Trade Specialization Index (TSI), and Grubel-Lloyd Index for intra-industry trade. The time range under consideration covers the period from 2012 to 2017. The results of estimating the TII are presented in Table 9.2. We can see that, before the Western sanctions, TII in Russian–Chinese trade was less than 1, suggesting a low degree of interdependence between the countries in terms of trade. However, after 2014, TII in Russian–Chinese trade began to increase. In 2016–2017, it reached 1, signifying the countries are currently trading with each

Table 9.2 Trade Intensity Index in Russian–Chinese merchandise trade, 2012–2017

Year	*Russia's exports to China, US$ billion*	*Russia's total export, US$ billion*	*China's total import, US$ billion*	*Total world import, US$ billion*	*TII*
2012	357.7	5237.7	18182.0	186150.0	0.699
2013	356.3	5272.7	19499.9	189040.0	0.655
2014	374.2	4978.3	19592.3	191040.0	0.733
2015	283.4	3439.1	16795.6	167640.0	0.822
2016	280.2	2854.9	15876.2	162120.0	1.002
2017	389.2	3570.8	18390.0	168800.0	1.000

Source: Authors' calculations of data from UN Comtrade (2018).

other with the same intensity as with the rest of the world compared to the period before 2014. Russia was exposed in 2015–2016 to external negative shocks and these developments could be explained by the smaller impact of such shocks on its trade with China, the partial reorientation of trade flows from the European region towards its Asian partner, and increased focus by the Russian state on export promotion towards the Chinese market. After the fall in 2015–2016, Russian exports to China are recovering more rapidly than overall Russian exports.

To determine the impact of Russia's new trade policy on its exports to China by certain categories of goods, we use the merchandise Trade Specialization Index (TSI). An analysis of changes in the value of exports of the six categories between 2012 and 2017 is presented in Table 9.3. It can be seen that the export of mineral and chemical products after reaching its peak in 2014 subsequently decreased, although it still exceeds significantly the export of other goods. Export of the third and the fourth categories has also improved, although it is subject to fluctuations in demand in the Chinese market. The most remarkable is the increase in the value of exports of agricultural products and machinery. The growth of the sixth group reflects the expansion of the group HS99 from 2015 onwards.

Below is an overview of the change in the merchandise TSI for individual commodity groups. For various industries, the index of trade specialization of Russian exports to China is different (Table 9.4). In horizontal comparisons, it can be found that, with the exception of the second category "mineral products and chemicals", which has always had a relatively large competitive advantage, other categories of goods have different degrees of disadvantages. Through vertical comparison, we see an improvement in trade specialization of five groups of the Russian exports to China. The indices of trade specialization of the fourth category "metals, jewelry, and ceramics" and the fifth category "machinery" are basically at −0.8, which indicates that Russia has a large disadvantage in trade of these goods. Both indices did not change much during the 2012–2017 period, although after 2014 they improved slightly. Russia's trade disadvantage also decreased for the sixth category "miscellaneous goods" due to the inclusion of products under the secret code. The most obvious improvement in the specialization index occurred

Table 9.3 The structure of Russian exports to China, 2011–2017

Year	Agricultural products, US$ billion	Mineral and chemical products, US$ billion	Textile, leather, and wood products, US$ billion	Metals, jewellery, and ceramics, US$ billion	Machinery, instruments, US billion	Miscellaneous, US$ billion
2012	10.27	301.61	28.86	3.86	13.02	0.05
2013	11.33	292.32	30.11	4.24	18.03	0.22
2014	10.95	307.62	33.37	3.97	18.15	0.09
2015	13.81	214.26	30.79	4.27	20.16	0.05
2016	16.21	200.63	34.28	3.15	19.21	0.67
2017	17.74	279.80	41.84	7.90	26.68	1.53

Source: Authors' calculations of data from UN Comtrade (2018).

Table 9.4 The merchandise Trade Specialization Index in Russia's trade with China by category of commodities, 2012–2017

Year	Agricultural products	Mineral and chemical products	Textile, leather, and wood products	Metal, jewellery, and ceramics	Machinery, instruments	Miscellaneous
2012	−0.223	0.746	−0.534	−0.878	−0.912	−0.997
2013	−0.196	0.732	−0.534	−0.867	−0.893	−0.987
2014	−0.273	0.738	−0.443	−0.860	−0.874	−0.995
2015	−0.060	0.719	−0.273	−0.774	−0.811	−0.995
2016	0.000	0.689	−0.196	−0.823	−0.824	−0.501
2017	0.000	0.725	−0.202	−0.670	−0.828	−0.298

Source: Authors' calculations of data from UN Comtrade (2018).

for the first category "agricultural goods" and the third category "textile leather and wood products". Specifically, Russia's position in food trade with China has changed from −0.22 to zero. All these developments largely reflect the reduction in Russia's trade deficit with China due to the increased competitiveness of Russian products because of the ruble devaluation and efforts to promote exports of non-energy goods.

Using the Grubel-Lloyd index, we have estimated the intra-industry trade index for the top Russian exports to China for the years 2012–2017 at a two-digit level of the Harmonized System (HS). The data is limited to products of the top chapters in Russia's exports to China. We excluded from the analysis products under the secret code (HS99), but added "plastics" (chapter HS39) and "vehicles" (chapter HS87) (Table 9.5). In aggregate, these 12 chapters account for over 90 percent of Russian exports to China. Results presented in Table 9.4 reveal that, in general, inter-industry trade dominates Russian–Chinese trade within the selected products. There is almost zero intra-industry trade for the chapters: mineral fuels; ores, slag, and ash; wood pulp; and fertilizers. A rather high magnitude of intra-industry trade exists in the following sections: organic chemicals; copper and copper products; fish and crustaceans, and plastics, though for the former two the

Table 9.5 An index of intra-industry trade between Russia and China, 2012–2017 (Russia's top export commodities)

HS code	*Product*	*2012*	*2013*	*2014*	*2015*	*2016*	*2017*
27	Mineral fuels, mineral oils	0.013	0.009	0.001	0.008	0.005	0.007
44	Wood and articles of wood	0.249	0.252	0.231	0.118	0.089	0.075
84	Machinery, mechanical appliances	0.145	0.182	0.223	0.307	0.196	0.205
03	Fish and crustaceans, mollusks	0.392	0.413	0.503	0.292	0.346	0.360
26	Ores, slag, and ash	0.027	0.014	0.020	0.019	0.014	0.009
47	Wood pulp	0.001	0.000	0.000	0.001	0.000	0.000
31	Fertilizers	0.001	0.003	0.005	0.007	0.017	0.008
85	Electrical machinery, equipment, and parts	0.021	0.017	0.013	0.014	0.040	0.100
74	Copper and copper products	0.723	0.653	0.422	0.754	0.211	0.327
29	Organic chemicals	0.622	0.846	0.640	0.533	0.343	0.415
39	Plastics and plastic products	0.225	0.291	0.268	0.340	0.239	0.319
87	Vehicles, non-railway	0.002	0.006	0.014	0.147	0.259	0.251

Source: Authors' calculations of data from UN Comtrade (2018).

G-L index of intra-industry trade decreased. The trade pattern for wood and wood products has also shifted towards inter-industry trade. The downward trend is largely determined by declining imports or exports of corresponding commodities to China during the period examined. At the same time, the G-L indices indicate a slightly upward trend in intra-industry trade for plastics and plastic particles, machinery, and electronics (HS84, HS85), and, in particular, motor vehicles, which can be associated with increased export support for these articles in Russia in recent years.

Recent trends in agro-food trade: can Russia feed China?

A fundamentally new trend in bilateral trade is the growth of Russian agro-food exports to China. This expansion is associated with a change in Russia's status in the global agricultural market and its transformation into a new food exporter. Russian agriculture has significantly increased its importance for the country's economy and has become the fourth largest industry after the oil, gas, metallurgical, and chemical industries in terms of export revenues (Shagaida and Uzun 2017). Since 2010, the share of agricultural products in overall Russian exports has increased almost threefold, reaching 6 percent in 2017 (Figure 9.6). In 2016, agro-food exports exceeded that of machinery and arms and almost equalled the export of fertilizers and those from the chemical industry (Sinelnikov-Murylev 2017). In the long term, Russia can become a net exporter of agricultural products.

Over the last 15 years, Russia has increased its capacity to export grain ninefold, overtaking the United States as the world's biggest wheat exporter in 2017. In grain exports, it became the second largest exporter behind the US (Devitt 2017; Koroleva 2018). With the growth of exports, Russia diversifies its exports of agricultural goods, entering new markets outside the CIS, including China,

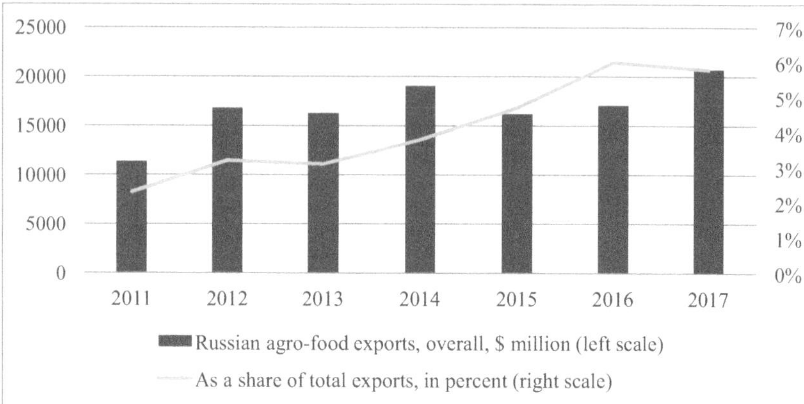

Figure 9.6 Russian agro-food exports, 2011–2017

Source: Authors' calculations of data from Rosstat (2017).

Asia, and Europe. Thus, besides Turkey and Egypt, Russia has expanded its grain supply to Asian countries such as Bangladesh, Vietnam, and the United Arab Emirates. In addition to grain, Russian exports of goods with higher added value, such as meat and meat products, vegetable oil, and dairy products, is also growing. In the export of meat, Russia is penetrating markets in the Middle East, Hong Kong, Vietnam, and Iran (Byrkova 2017).

The main factor contributing to Russian agricultural exports is the growth of domestic production. Over the past ten years, agricultural output has increased at the level of the growth of the entire economy; and in the past five years, its growth has further accelerated and exceeded that of GDP. In 2015–2016, falling incomes lead to narrowing of domestic demand and forced agricultural producers to switch to foreign markets, while the devaluation of the ruble boosted the competitiveness of Russian products abroad (Sinelnikov-Murylev 2017; Obolenskiy 2017b). Along with this, Russia began to introduce a system for promoting agricultural exports and significantly intensified negotiations with its main trade partners on expanding access of Russian food products to their markets (Spartak 2017). An advancement in Russian agro-food exports have led to a change in priorities in domestic agricultural policy and a paradigm-shift from self-sufficiency in food towards greater exploitation of Russia's competitive advantages in world markets. In 2016, the Ministry of Agriculture of Russia developed a priority project "Export of agricultural commodities". The purpose of this project is to increase agro-food exports by at least 12.5 percent by the end of 2018, and no less than 26.7 percent by the end of 2020 (Shagaida and Uzun 2017).

In the context of Russia's new policy of promoting agrarian exports, the Chinese food market is gaining in importance. This market is highly attractive for foreign producers, as it is growing by 15–20 percent annually (OECD/FAO

2017). Since the mid-2000s, China has become a net importer of food including wheat, rice, and maize (Yu 2017). The main articles of Chinese food imports are oil seeds and fats, as well as oils of animal or vegetable origin. Import of meat, dairy products, and cereals is also growing. Consequently, agricultural imports have become an important element in China's contemporary food security policy (Alexandrova 2017b). The OECD-FAO Agricultural Outlook foresees that in the coming decades consumption growth in China will exceed that of production. The highest growth in demand is expected for wheat[3] and meat (OECD/FAO 2017).

Rapid growth of food imports is due to a number of factors. Firstly, it is associated with a general rise in the welfare of Chinese people and a change in their consumption pattern. The growth in living standards stimulated the consumption of pork, poultry meat, and other food, which until recently were not accessible to the majority of the population. The consumption of dairy products, foreign wines, other alcoholic beverages, and chocolate is also expanding. Secondly, the Chinese middle class is becoming more concerned about food safety and nutrition quality (Baan et al. 2017). Thirdly, the growth of agricultural imports stems from increased domestic support for agriculture and border protection policies. Recent rises in domestic outputs have been associated with higher domestic market costs and prices as compared to the corresponding world market prices, a fact which has led to rising imports and high domestic stocks of major agricultural products (Yu 2017).

Despite its attractiveness, the Chinese food market is characterized by a high level of protectivism, though one still lower than that of many other Asian countries (Karaganov et al. 2017). Though they experienced a significant reduction following China's accession to the WTO, the level of simple average MFN duties on food imports has remained virtually unchanged since the middle of the past decade. In 2018, a new economic policy aimed at stimulating consumption led to the Chinese government announcing an almost two-fold reduction in import tariffs on almost 1,500 products, including food and beverages. Currently, the highest duty rates of 65 percent are applied to certain types of wheat and rice, natural grape wines, as well as for imports outside of quotas. The duty of 54 percent applies to maize or corn, 57 percent for certain types of tobacco, and 50 percent for certain types of sugar. In addition, the tariff quota applies to wheat, maize, rice, sugar, wool, and cotton. Within quotas, the tariff rate ranges from 0 to 15 percent, the over duty quota reaches 65 percent (Eurasian Economic Commission Department of Agro-Industrial Policy 2017). According to the terms of China's accession to the WTO, state trading enterprises (STE) have the right to import most of the volume within the quota for such commodities, as wheat, corn, and sugar, and private companies import the remaining amount. For example, 90 percent of wheat and 60 percent of maize are imported by state-owned trading enterprises.

After the collapse of the Soviet Union, Russia became a net importer of food from China, mainly fruits and vegetables. Prior to 2006, China also was the largest supplier of rice to Russia. Though the share of food has never been high in overall bilateral trade, food imports from China were vital even in early 2000s for the Russian Far East (Hsu and Soong 2014; Alexandrova 2017a). With the growth of domestic production, food imports – including those to the Russian Far East – declined. The turning point of Russian–Chinese trade in agricultural products was 2014–2015, after which growth in food exports from Russia became a trend. According to the Russian Export Center China, along with Turkey, became the largest importer of Russian food in 2016 accounting for almost 10 percent of total Russian agro-food exports (Alexandrova 2017a). In value terms, Russia's agro-food exports to China in 2017 reached US$1.75 billion (Figure 9.7). The status of the countries involved in agricultural trade has also changed. Since Russia as a former food importer from China became a supplier, in 2017 its negative balance in bilateral agro-food trade turned into a small surplus. Along with depreciation of the currency, an important factor for these developments has been the sanctions imposed on Russia, which accelerated intergovernmental negotiations on access to the Chinese market that have continued for many years. Until recently, China almost completely prohibited imports of Russian grain, vegetables, meat, and dairy products (Eurasian Economic Commission Department of Agro-Industrial Policy 2017).

The composition of Russian agrarian exports to China is becoming more diverse. Until recently, the dominant article was fish and crustaceans (chapter HS03). Thus, in 2011 this article accounted for more than 97 percent of Russian food exports to this country. However, in 2017, Russian food exports consisted of four large commodity groups, which included products with high added value, while the share of fish decreased to 61 percent (Figure 9.8). As of 2017, the main commodities of Russian agrarian exports to China in addition to fish (HS03) were animal or vegetable fats and oils (14 percent in agro-food exports), oil seeds and oleaginous fruits (11 percent), cocoa and cocoa preparations (4 percent), and products of the milling industry (2 percent).

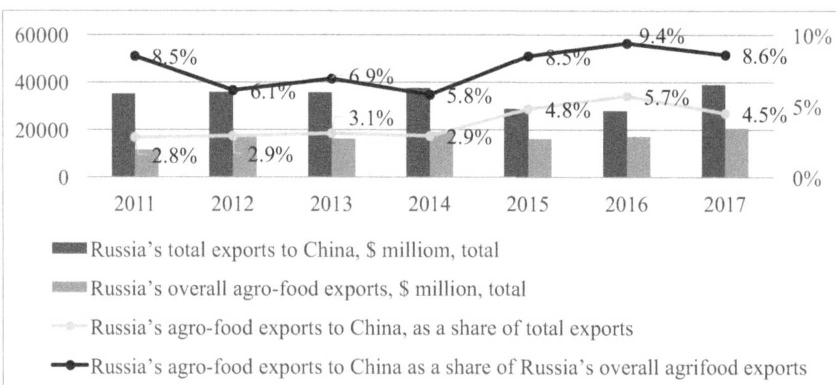

Figure 9.7 The development of Russian–Chinese agro-food trade, 2011–2017

Source: UN Comtrade (2018).

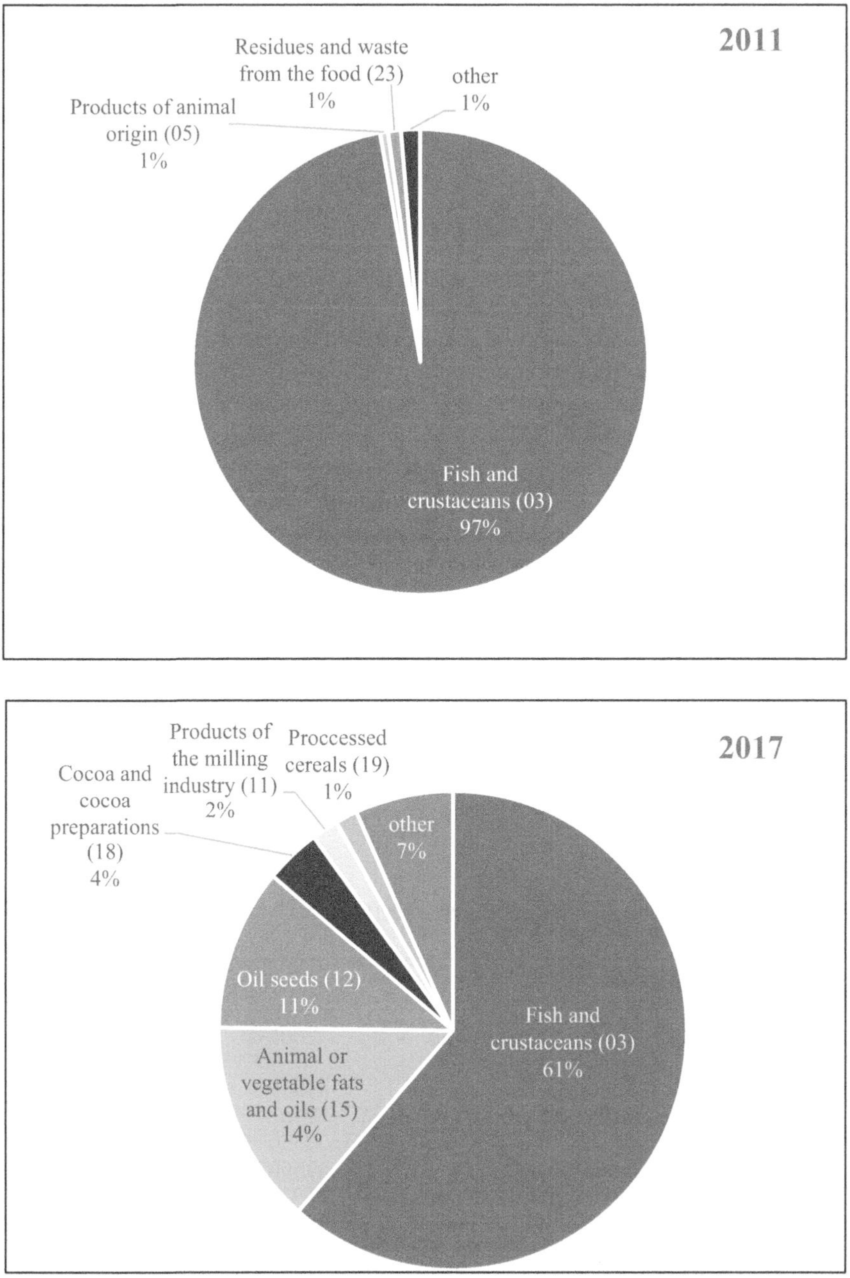

Figure 9.8 Russia's agro-food exports to China by commodity in 2011 and 2017

The highest growth in Russian agrarian exports was for processed cereals (chapter HS19), sugars and sugar confectionery (chapter HS17), cocoa and cocoa preparations (chapter HS18), cereals (chapter HS10), dairy products (chapter HS04), and oil seeds (chapter HS12). Growth of these commodities between 2011 and 2017 exceeded 10,000 percent, although exports increased from a very low base (Table 9.6). China also became one of the most important destinations for Russian sunflower and soybean oil, chocolate, honey, soybeans, and confectionery. Russia sends to China one-third of fish exports and more than 80 percent of soybeans.

Russian food products are rapidly gaining popularity among Chinese consumers, especially the inhabitants of Xinjiang and Northeast provinces of China. Against the deteriorating environmental conditions in China, Russian products are associated with a healthy diet, and gaining a reputation for high quality and environmental responsibility. The governments of a number of Chinese border regions, primarily Heilongjiang province, actively promote food imports from Russia through the internet or by establishing duty-free zones and Russian trade districts in border cities.

At present, Russia's share of Chinese food imports is relatively small. While the US sells about US$20 billion of food products to China annually, Russian exports to this country account for less than US$2 billion. Nevertheless, for a number of commodities, including soybeans, sunflower, and soybean oil, Russia is becoming an important supplier for China and has good prospects for further expansion in the market. The trade war against China recently unleashed by the US has prompted reciprocal restrictions on American goods. In response, China has raised import duties on a wide range of American food products; i.e. soybeans, cotton, dairy products, pork, most cheeses, and seafood (State Council of

Table 9.6 Articles of Russian agro-food exports to China with the highest growth, 2011–2017

HS2 code	*Product*	*Growth by value, 2017/2011, percent*
19	Preparations of cereals, flour, pastrycooks' products	422005
17	Sugars and sugar confectionery	91839
18	Cocoa and cocoa preparations	62162
10	Cereals	37550
04	Dairy products	17500
12	Oil seeds and oleaginous fruits	10979
11	Products of the milling industry	6778
22	Beverages, spirits, and vinegar	1112
16	Preparations of meat, of fish or of crustaceans, mollusks or other aquatic invertebrates	1015
33	Food industry residues and waste; prepared animal fodder	375

Source: Authors' calculations of data from UN Comtrade (2018).

the Peoples' Republic of China 2018). Rising trade tensions between China and the US open up new niches for Russian agricultural exports to China.

Russia has good prospects for the supply of cereals, which it began to export to China only recently. Over the years, imports of Russian grain have been banned, in particular, wheat imports have been restricted since 1976 as China pursued a policy of self-sufficiency in these crops. China formally opened a grain market for Russia, including wheat only on December 17, 2015, after ten years of negotiations. Import of other grains (maize, rice, and rapeseed) and soya beans has been liberalizing slowly (Trade Representative of the Russian Federation in China 2018). Grain supplies are allowed from a limited list of regions, mainly from the regions of the Far East and Siberia. In addition, Russian farmers are obliged to supply maize, rice, soybean, and rapeseed not in bulk, but in bags or special vehicles, which is considered a kind of restriction (Eurasian Economic Commission Department of Agro-Industrial Policy 2017).

So far, China is not even among the top 50 destinations for Russian grain suppliers, but has a chance to become one of its key importers in the short term. However, even with insignificant grain deliveries (24,000 tons in 2017), Russia has already entered the top ten sources of imports for this commodity to China, significantly lagging behind Australia, the US and Kazakhstan. To ensure the supply, Russia currently is creating a land "grain corridor", which includes construction of a grain terminal in Eastern Siberia, as well as 29 grain elevators in different parts of Russia.[4] It is expected that the planned terminals near China will add about 11 million tons to the Russian export capacities by 2020, which will surpass today's volumes of Russia's supplies to Turkey and Egypt. In addition to grain, other commodities, in particular soybeans, barley, rape, flax seeds, and sunflower oil are to be transported along this corridor. According to forecasts, by 2028 the total volume of exports will reach 52 million tons (Bolgova 2017).

For a long time, China has banned the import of Russian meat ostensibly to reduce the risk of disease exposure and has gradually begun to open its market only in the last couple of years. In July 2016, China allowed the import of poultry from Russia. In September 2017, the ban on the import of pork and beef from 49 Russian regions was also lifted. In early 2017, Russia began to export pork, whereas export of poultry meat and beef supplies should begin from 2019. At present, China still restricts the import of milk and dairy products from Russia, except for ice cream. The ban also applies to the import of eggs and their products (Eurasian Economic Commission Department of Agro-Industrial Policy 2017).

New export opportunities are attracting China's direct investment in Russian agriculture. The Chinese have long invested in this sector in Russia at an individual level, both legally and illegally, but in recent years there has been an increase of investments by large Chinese companies with the aim of growing crops for subsequent exports to China. For example, in the Omsk region, Chinese investors have created an agro-industrial cluster whose products are to be sent to China. In 2016, COFCO opened a branch in the Russian Far East for the cultivation and processing of soybeans, as well as for the export of meat and water to China (Novoselova 2017).

In comparison with the overall Russian–Chinese trade, agricultural trade with China in general is mostly composed of intra-industry exchanges, especially so after the imposition of anti-Russian sanctions. In 2016–2017, the G-L index reached 1, which means a situation where all trade is intra-industry (Table 9.7). The upward trend in intra-industry trade in agricultural products positively correlates with the growth in the Russian–Chinese TII and improvement in Russia's advantages in the bilateral TSI for agro-food products. We further calculated the G-L index for the top ten export commodity sections for 2012–2017 in order to reveal the growing specialization of Russia for specific product groups. The results of calculations are presented in the Table 9.7.

According to results presented in the table, the revealed pattern for most of the Sino-Russian food trade during the period under investigation is inter-industry, as the G-L index for the ten major commodity groups remained below 0.4 including for the "fish and crustaceans", which is the largest article of Russia's food exports to China. Food industries (chapter HS23), oil seeds and oleaginous fruits (chapter HS12), and animal or vegetable fats and oils (chapter HS15) showed a high degree of IIT index, where IIT levels in these products were 0.879, 0.783, 0.644 in 2012,

Table 9.7 An index of intra-industry trade of agricultural products between China and Russia, 2012–2017

HS code	*Product*	*2012*	*2013*	*2014*	*2015*	*2016*	*2017*
1–24	*Agricultural products*	*0.782*	*0.803*	*0.727*	*0.940*	*1.000*	*0.999*
03	Fish, crustaceans, mollusks, and other aquatic invertebrates	0.392	0.413	0.503	0.292	0.346	0.360
11	Products of the milling industry	0.285	0.922	0.516	0.148	0.110	0.040
12	Oil seeds and oleaginous fruits	0.783	0.669	0.881	0.347	0.383	0.373
15	Animal or vegetable fats and oils and their cleavage products	0.644	0.807	0.528	0.668	0.058	0.042
18	Cocoa and cocoa preparations	0.016	0.149	0.395	0.724	0.444	0.258
19	Flour, starch or milk; pastrycooks' products	0.009	0.033	0.085	0.871	0.506	0.824
21	Miscellaneous edible preparations	0.029	0.023	0.061	0.105	0.301	0.284
22	Beverages, spirits, and vinegar	0.478	0.689	0.940	0.496	0.371	0.449
23	Food industries, prepared animal fodder	0.879	0.997	0.886	0.726	0.940	0.781
24	Tobacco and manufactured tobacco substitutes	–	0.548	0.581	0.401	0.478	0.503

Source: Authors' calculations of data from UN Comtrade (2018).

respectively. However, with Russia's food export expansion, the extent of intra-industry trade decreased to a different extent for most chapters. It declined more precipitously for animal and vegetable oils and fats (chapter HS15) from 0.644 to 0.042, for oil seeds and oleaginous fruits (chapter HS12) from 0.783 to 0.373, and for products of the milling industry (chapter HS11) from 0.285 to 0.040. This can be explained by the sharp transition of Russia from the category of net importer to the category of exporter for these commodities. Trade has become more intra-industry for cereals and starches (HS19), as the G-L index for this commodity group increased from almost zero to over 0.8 during the period along with the rise of Russian exports. The G-L index for beverages and tobacco remained above 0.4 during 2012–2017, so we may assume these commodity groups have a high potential for developing intra-industry trade.

Thus, the Russian–Chinese trade in agricultural products, as well as bilateral trade in general, continues to develop along an inter-industry pattern. With few exceptions, the transition of Russia from the category of importers to the exporters of agricultural products to China was not accompanied by an increase in intra-industry trade. On the contrary, after 2014, the extent of intra-industry trade decreased for most of the agricultural commodity groups surveyed.

Conclusion

This chapter studies the changes in the structure of Russian exports to China in the context of growing support for non-primary exports and the current policy of Russia's "Pivot to Asia". Analysis shows that, despite the general trend of further fuel expansion in Russian exports to China, recently new trends in bilateral trade have been emerging. Russia has significantly improved the penetration of non-primary commodities into its neighbour's market, including non-military industrial goods. Though as a whole, exports of these goods are still less than the value of fuel exports, their growth has been dramatic. Particularly impressive is the expansion of agricultural and food products, which Russia has not previously exported to China. Accordingly, Russia's status in bilateral trade has changed from a net food importer to an exporter. The determinants of growing agro-food exports are the rise of agricultural production and an emerging system for export promotion in Russia, enhanced competitiveness due to a ruble devaluation from the end of 2014, as well as the growth of incomes of the Chinese population along with changes in consumer patterns. The geographical proximity and gradual removal of China's trade barriers also add to export expansion. Further prospects of Russian non-energy exports in China are associated with changes in the economic course toward building a "moderately prosperous society", accompanied by a significant reduction in import duties on a wide range of goods, as well as growing trade frictions between the US and China.

To empirically estimate the effect of Russia's new foreign policy since 2014 on its trade with China, we used the Trade Intensity Index (TII) and the merchandise Trade Specialization Index (TSI). The results show that, before Western sanctions, the countries traded with low intensity, as TII remained far below 1. After

2014, however, the intensity of trade between Russia and China began to grow, and the corresponding index reached 1 in 2016–2017. This implies that the countries currently trade with each other with the same intensity as with the rest of the world compared to the period before 2014. The improvement of the TII is due to the partial reorientation of trade flows from European partners and other countries to China after a souring in Russia's relations with the former since 2014. Our analysis reveals an improvement in trade specialization of Russian exports to China for five commodity groups out of six. An advantage to Russia has improved most noticeably in agricultural trade with China. This change reflects a reduced trade imbalance and increased competitiveness of Russia in bilateral agro-food trade.

The analyses of the extent of intra-industry index over 2012–2017 proved that the Russian–Chinese trade of top commodities is significantly composed of inter-industry trade, which was expected considering China and Russia have comparative advantages in different sectors of the economy. However, the G-L index indicates an increasing degree of ITT for commodities sectors, including machinery and agricultural goods, which are receiving increased export support in Russia after the imposition of sanctions. The study also shows, that unlike the overall Russian–Chinese trade, agricultural trade with China in general is significantly composed of intra-industry trade, especially after the imposition of anti-Russian sanctions. The upward trend in intra-industry trade in agricultural products positively correlates with an increasing TII in Russian–Chinese trade and improvement in Russia's TSI in bilateral trade in agro-food products. However, with few exceptions, for the ten largest goods of Russian agricultural exports to China, their export expansion and the transition of Russia from the category of importer to agricultural exporter were not accompanied by an increase in intra-industry trade.

Our estimates of intra-industry trade in agricultural products between Russia and China provides an idea of the evolving pattern of trade. However, results should be interpreted with caution, since the value of the IIT index depends on the value of aggregation chosen. A more accurate calculation of the IIT index can be obtained by means of a disaggregated analysis of intra-industry trade at the level of four or six digits. In order to more accurately determine the pattern of intra-industry trade between Russia and China, whether through vertical or horizontal specialization, one must use other methods of IIT measurement. Finally, a comparative analysis of the development of Russia's intra-industry trade with the world as a whole, with trends in bilateral intra-industry trade with China, can give us a deeper insight of Russia's emerging specialization in the world economy under the new trade policy.

Notes

1 The HS99 commodity group includes dual-use goods, defence and aviation industry products, as well as natural gas.
2 The Industrial and Commercial Bank of China (ICBC) officially started operating as a Chinese renminbi clearing bank in Russia.
3 Imports of wheat to China in the end of 2017 increased by 27.3 percent compared to 2016, up to 4.3 million tons.
4 In 2017, the countries signed an agreement on the development of this corridor.

Bibliography

Afontsev, S 2015, 'Vykhod iz krizisa v uslovyakh sanktsii: missiya ne vypolnima', *Voprosy economiki*, no. 4, pp. 20–36.

Alexandrova, M 2017a, *Export rossiiskoi selhozproduktsii v KNR: sostoyaniye prodovol' stvennyh rynkov i vosmozhnye perspektivy sotrudnichestva*, Reports of the RAS IFES – 2016, Institute of the Far East of the Russian Academy of Sciences, Moscow, pp. 79–118.

Alexandrova, M 2017b, 'Prodovol'stvennaya bezopasnost' KNR i export sel'hozproduktsii na kitaiskii rynok', *Problemy Dal'nego Vostoka*, no. 6, pp. 27–38.

Alexandrova, M 2017c, 'Prigranichnoye i mezhregional'noye sotrudnichestvo Rossii i KNR', in: S Lousianin (ed.) *Modern Russian-Chinese relations*, DeLi plus, Moscow.

Aquino, A 1978, 'Intra-industry Trade and Inter-industry Specialization as Concurrent Sources of International Trade in Manufactures', *Weltwirtschaftliches Archiv*, no. 114, pp. 275–295.

Baan, W, Luan, L, Poh, F and Zipser, D 2017, *Double-Clicking on the Chinese Consumer. The New Health Craze, the Rise of the Post-90s Generation, and Other Trends Worth Watching*, McKinsey and Company, viewed 3 October 2018, www.mckinsey.com/~/media/mckinsey/global%20themes/china/double%20clicking%20on%20the%20chinese%20consumer/double-clicking-on-the-chinese-consumer.ashx

Bergstrand, JH 1990, 'The Heckscher-Ohlin-Samuelson Model, the Linder Hypothesis and the Determinants of Bilateral Intra-Industry Trade', *Economic Journal*, vol. 100, no. 403, pp. 1216–1229.

Bhagwati, J and Davis, DR 1994, 'Intra-industry Trade Issues and Theory', *Harvard Institute of Economic Research Discussion Paper*, no. 1695, viewed 10 December 2017, www.columbia.edu/cu/libraries/inside/working/Econ/ldpd_econ_9394_697.pdf

Bolgova, E 2017, 'Rossiya sostavit v Kitai 52 mln tonn sel'khozproduktsii do 2028 goda', *Komsomol'skaya pravda*, 29 March, viewed 10 October 2017, www.dag.kp.ru/online/news/2698845/

Byrkova, E 2017, *Rossiiskoe myaso budet osvaivat' rynki arabskih i afrikanskih stran*, 7 November, viewed 14 January 2018, http://xn-b1ae2adf4f.xn-p1ai/article/44945-possiyskoe-myaso-budet-osvaivaty-pynki-apabskih-i-afpikanskih-stpan.html (in Russian).

Byrkova, E 2018, *Kak Kitai zahvatyvaet nash rynok produktov*, 22 February, viewed 19 March 2018, https://xn-b1ae2adf4f.xn-p1ai/article/46406-kak-kitay-zakhvatyvaet-nash-rynok-produktov.html

Central Bank of Russia, viewed 14 October 2018, www.cbr.ru

Chase, M, Medeiros, E, Roy, J, Rumer, E, Sutter, R and Weitz, R 2017, *Russia-China Relations: Assessing Common Ground and Strategic Fault Lines*, NBR special report, no. 66, viewed 12 March 2018, www.nbr.org/wp-content/uploads/pdfs/publications/special_report_66_russia-chinarelations_July2017.pdf

Cheong, S 2018, *Russia-China Oil Friendship Makes Crude Costlier for Europe*, Bloomberg, 02 January, viewed 12 March 2018, www.bloomberg.com/news/articles/2018-01-02/russia-s-oil-friendship-with-china-makes-crude-costly-for-europe

Chertkov, A 2017, 'Stavka na export', *Expert Severo-Zapad*, no. 12–13, viewed 25 January 2018, http://expert.ru/northwest/2017/12/stavka-na-eksport/

China, EAEU Sign Agreement on Trade, Economic Cooperation 2018, Xinhuanet, 18 May, viewed 20 May 2018, www.xinhuanet.com/english/2018-05/18/c_137187295.htm

Devitt, P 2017, 'Worried About Russia's March on Grain Markets? It Could be Worse', *Reuters*, 3 November, viewed 10 December 2017, www.reuters.com/article/us-russia-grains-analysis/worried-about-russias-march-on-grain-markets-it-could-be-worse-idUSKBN1D30GK

Dezan Shira and Associates 2017, *China-Russia Bilateral Trade is World's Fastest Growing Opportunity Corridor*, China Briefing, 30 August, viewed 20 February 2018, www.china-briefing.com/news/2017/08/30/china-russia-bilateral-trade-is-worlds-fastest-growing-opportunity-corridor.html

Ding, Z, Meng, S and Wang, Z 2010, 'Zhong e chanye nei maoyi shizheng yanjiu', *Northern Economy and Trade*, no. 9, pp. 6–7.

Dong, R 2010, 'Zhong e maoyi hubuxing shizheng fenxi', *Northeast Asia Forum*, vol. 19, no. 3, pp. 51–57.

EAEU and Eurasia: Monitoring and Analysis of Direct Investments 2017, EDB Centre for Integration Studies, Saint Petersburg, viewed 25 January 2018, https://eabr.org/upload/iblock/3f8/EDB-Centre_2017_Report-47_FDI-Eurasia_ENG_1.pdf

Eurasian Economic Commission Department of Agro-Industrial Policy 2017, *Analiz bar'erov dostupa sel'skohozyaistvennyh tovarov na rynok Kitaya*, viewed 3 October 2018, www.eurasiancommission.org/ru/act/prom_i_agroprom/dep_agroprom/monitoring/Documents/%D0%91%D0%B0%D1%80%D1%8C%D0%B5%D1%80%D1%8B%20%D0%B2%20%D0%9A%D0%B8%D1%82%D0%B0%D0%B5.pdf

Federal Customs Service of the Russian Federation 2018, viewed 3 October 2018, http://customs.ru/index.php?option=com_content&view=article&id=13858&Itemid=2095

Gabuev, A and Kashin, V 2017, *Vooruzhennaya druzhba: kak Rossiya i Kitai torguyut oruzhiem*, Moscow Center Carnegie Foundation, viewed 15 November 2017, http://carnegie.ru/2017/11/02/ru-pub-74601

Gong, X and Liu, N 2015, 'Zhong e nongchanpin chanye nei maoyi shuiping yu jiegou fenxi – jiyu sichou zhilu jingjidai zhanlue beijing', *Asia Pacific Economic Review*, no. 2, pp. 50–54.

Grubel, HG and Lloyd, PJ 1975, *Intra-industry Trade: The Theory and Measurement of International Trade in Differentiated Products*, Macmillan, London.

Herrero, A and Xu, J 2016, *The China-Russia Trade Relationship and Its Impact on Europe*, Breugel Working Paper, no. 4, viewed 3 October 2018, http://bruegel.org/wp-content/uploads/2016/07/WP-04_2016.pdf

Hsu, J and Soong, J 2014, 'Development of China-Russia Relations (1949–2011)', *The Chinese Economy*, vol. 47, no. 3, pp. 70–87.

Ivanov, I (ed.) 2017, *Russian-Chinese Dialogue: The 2017 Model. Report N 33*, The Russian Council on Foreign Affairs, viewed 17 June 2017, http://russiancouncil.ru/en/activity/publications/russian-chinese-dialogue-the-2017-model/

Ivanov, I (ed.) 2018, *Russian-Chinese Dialogue: The 2018 Model. Report N 39*, The Russian Council on Foreign Affairs, viewed 02 June 2018, http://russiancouncil.ru/papers/Russia-China-Report39-Ru.pdf

Karaganov, S, Bordachev, T, Bezborodov, A, Kashin, V, Korolev, A, Likhacheva, A, Makarov, I, Shumkova, V, Sokolova, A and Stepanov, I 2017, *Toward the Great Ocean 5: From the Turn to the East to Greater Eurasia*, Valdai Discussion Club, Moscow, viewed 29 September 2017, valdaiclub.com/files/15300/

Katasonov, V 2018, 'PVP, ili tikhaya voina protiv dollara', *Fond Strategicheskoi Kultury*, 24 February, viewed 26 February 2018, www.fondsk.ru/news/2018/02/24/pvp-ili-tihaya-vojna-protiv-dollara-45662.html

Kellman, M and Shachmurove, Y 2011, 'Diversification and Specialization Paradox in Developing Country Trade', *Review of Development Economics*, vol. 15, no. 2, pp. 212–222.

Kojima, K 1964, 'The Pattern of International Trade Among Advanced Countries', *Hitotsubashi Journal of Economics*, vol. 5, no. 1, pp. 16–36.

Koroleva, A 2018, 'Rossiiskoe zerno zavoevyvaet mir, imeya problemy v tylu', *Expert Online*, 23 January, http://expert.ru/2018/01/23/rossiya-vzyala-vtoroe-mesto-v-mirovom-zernovom-eksporte/

Kulikov, S 2018, 'Eksport rossiiskoi sel'khoztekhniki v Kitai vyros v 10 raz', *Rossiiskaya Gazeta*, 1 February, viewed 18 February 2018, https://rg.ru/2018/02/01/eksport-rossijskoj-selhoztehniki-v-kitaj-vyros-v-10-raz.html

Lousianin, S 2017, 'Rossiya i Kitai: mezhdunarodno-politicheskiye, ekonomicheskiye i gumanitarnye sviazi (2016 – nachalo 2017 goda)', in: S Lousianin (ed.) *Modern Russian-Chinese relations*, DeLi plus, Moscow.

Lu, R 2010, 'Zhong e maoyi hubuxing shizheng fenxi', *Darong shangwu*, no. 6, pp. 89–91.

Makocki, M and Popescu, N 2016, 'China and Russia: An Eastern Partnership in the Making?', *Chailot Paper*, no. 140, viewed 18 February 2018, www.iss.europa.eu/sites/default/files/EUISSFiles/CP_140_Russia_China.pdf

Novoselova, L 2017, 'Rossiisko-kitaiskoye investitsionnoye sotrudnichestvo v kontekste "Povorota Rossii na vostok"', *Russia and the Modern World*, no. 3, pp. 149–163.

Obolenskiy, V 2016, 'Vneshnyaya torgovlya Rossii: barometr predskazyvaet buryu', *Mirovaya ekonomika i mezhdunarodnye otnosheniya*, vol. 60, no. 2, pp. 15–25.

Obolenskiy, V 2017a, 'Vneshneekonomicheskaya povestka: preodoleniye spada', *Rossiiskii vneshneekonomicheskii vestnik*, no. 5, pp. 19–26.

Obolenskiy, V 2017b, 'Vneshniaya torgovlya Rossii v usloviyah snizheniya mirovyh tsen i sanktsionnoi voiny', *Rossiiskii vneshneekonomicheskii vestnik*, no. 9, pp. 33–44.

OECD/FAO 2017, *OECD-FAO Agricultural Outlook 2017–2026*, OECD Publishing, Paris.

Pravitel'stvo Rossii 2018, *Podderzhka nesyr'evogo jeksporta: nekotorye fakty za 6 let*, 11 April, viewed 23 April 2018, http://government.ru/info/32209/

RBK 2018, *EAES i Iran podpisali soglashenie o zone svobodnoi torgovli*, 17 May, viewed 11 June 2018, www.rbc.ru/rbcfreenews/5afcf4ca9a79473f6081ad95

Rossiiskii Eksportniy Tsentr 2018, *Spetsial'nye programmy po podderzhke eksporta*, viewed 15 May 2018, www.exportcenter.ru/services/subsidirovanie/

Rosstat 2017, *Rossiiskii statisticheskii ezhegodnik*, viewed 3 October 2018, www.gks.ru/free_doc/doc_2017/year/year17.pdf

Saalman, L (ed.) 2017, *China-Russia Relations and Regional Dynamics: From Pivots to Peripheral Diplomacy*, Stockholm International Peace Research Institute (SIPRI), Stockholm, viewed 3 October 2018, www.sipri.org/sites/default/files/China-Russia-relations-regional-dynamics.pdf

Sanghi, A, Burns, A, Djiofack, C, Prihardini, D, Dissanayake, J and Hollweg, C 2017, *A Rebalancing China and Resurging India: How Will the Pendulum Swing for Russia*? The World Bank, Washington, DC.

Shagaida, N and Uzun, V 2017, *Tendentsii razvitiya i osnovnye vyzovy agrarnogo sektora*, Tsentr Strategicheskikh Razrabotok, visited 3 October 2018, www.csr.ru/wp-content/uploads/2017/11/Doklad_selskoe_hozyai-stvo_veb.pdf

Shin, G, Choi, S and Lou, S 2016, 'Do Economic Sanctions Impair Target Economies?', *International Political Science Review*, vol. 37, no. 4, pp. 485–499.

Simola, H 2016, 'Economic Relations Between Russia and China – Increasing Interdependency?', *BOFIT Policy Brief 6*, Bank of Finland Institute for Economies in Transition (BOFIT), viewed 3 October 2018, www.bofit.fi/en/publications/policy-brief/

Sinelnikov-Murylev, S (ed.) 2017, *Rossiiskaya ekonomika v 2016 gody: tendentsii i perspektivy*, Izdatel'stvo Instituta Gajdara, Moscow.

Spanger, H 2016, *Russia's Turn Eastward, China's Turn Westward: Cooperation and Conflict on the New Silk Road*, Valdai paper no. 47, viewed 17 April 2018, http://valdaiclub.com/files/11422

Spartak, A 2017, 'Vosmozhnosti rossiiskoi ekspansii i ee gosudarstvennaya podderzhka', *Rossiiskii vneshneekonomicheskii vestnik*, no. 5, pp. 3–18.

Spartak, A, Knobel, A, Flegontova, T, Ismagilova, O, Koval, A, Levashenko, A, Pyzhikov, N, Sneg, M, Hohlov, A and Yakubovskiy, I 2018, *Perspektivy narashchivaniya Rossiiskogo nesyre'evogo eksporta*, Tsentr Strategicheskikh Razrabotok, viewed 17 April 2018, www.csr.ru/wp-content/uploads/2018/04/Report-Non-energy-Export.pdf

Starinskaya, G 2018, 'Rossiya uvelichit eksport nefti v Kitai', *Vedomosti*, 12 January, viewed 27 January 2018, www.vedomosti.ru/business/articles/2018/01/12/747646-rossiya-uvelichit-eksport-nefti-kitai

State Council of the Peoples' Republic of China 2018, *China and the World Trade Organization*, White Paper, 28 June, viewed 25 August 2018, http://english.gov.cn/archive/white_paper/2018/06/28/content_281476201898696.htm

Sun, Y 2016, 'An Analysis of the Growth Potential of Intra-industry Agricultural Trade Between China and Russia in the Context of "One Belt and One Road" (Based on UN Comtrade Data for the Period From 2001 to 2013)', *Chinese Agricultural Science Bulletin*, vol. 32, no. 26, pp. 181–187.

Suslov, D 2016, 'A Pivot Towards Asia, Integration and Mega-regions. Balancing Russia's APR Policy', *Valdai Discussion Club*, viewed 17 September 2017, http://valdaiclub.com/a/highlights/a-pivot-towards-asia-integration-and-mega-regions-balancing-russia-s-apr-policy/

TASS 2018, *Rossiiskii eksportnyi tsentr na PMEHF provedet diskussiyu o razvitii nesyr'evogo ekhksporta*, 07 May, viewed 11 June 2018, http://tass.ru/pmef-2018/articles/5181695

Tong, G and Shi, L 2017, 'Jiyu chanye nei de zhong e nongchanpin maoyi shizheng fenxi', *Issues in Agricultural Economy*, vol. 6, pp. 89–100.

Trade Representative of the Russian Federation in China 2018, *Torgovye ogranicheniya dlya rossiiskih tovarov na kitaiskom rynke*, viewed 23 March 2018, www.russchinatrade.ru/ru/ru-cn-cooperation/torg_ogran

UN Comtrade 2018, viewed 12 February 2018, https://comtrade.un.org/

Wan, H and Li, L 2011, 'Zhong e maoyi shangpin jiegou jiqi yingxiang yinsu yanjiu', *International Business*, no. 5, pp. 25–34.

WITS 2018, *World Integrated Trade Solution*, The World Bank, viewed 12 February 2018, https://wits.worldbank.org/wits/wits/witshelp/Content/Utilities/e1.trade_indicators.htm

Yang, X and Wang, D 2005, 'Zhong e maoyi hubuxing fenxi', *Quyu yu guobie yanjiu*, no. 7, pp. 71–77.

Yu, W 2017, *How China's Farm Policy Reforms Could Affect Trade and Markets: A Focus on Grains and Cotton*, International Center for Trade and Sustainable Development, viewed 12 February 2018, www.ictsd.org/sites/default/files/research/wusheng_yu_paper_final.pdf

Zhang, M 2013, 'Zhong e maoyi jizhongdu ji chanye nei maoyi fazhan zhuangkuang', *Social Sciences in Heilongjiang*, no. 1, pp. 78–81.

Zhang, Y 2012, 'Jiyu yinli moxing de zhong e shuangbian maoyi liuliang yu qianli yanjiu', *International Economics and Trade Research*, vol. 28, no. 6, pp. 25–35.

Zubkov, I 2017, 'Subsidii na eksport edy v Kitai dostignut 3 mlrd rublei', *Rossiiskaya Gazeta*, 19 September, viewed 10 December 2017, https://rg.ru/2017/09/19/petr-fradkov-subsidii-na-eksport-edy-v-kitaj-dostignut-3-mlrd-rublej.html

10 Trade cooperation between Russia and Korea during the period of sanctions 2014–2017

Implications for trade policy

Irina A. Korgun

Introduction

A discussion about the impact of Western sanctions on the Russian economy and on Russia's trade with its partners is ongoing (Veebel and Markus 2015; Crozet and Hinz 2016, 2017; Dolidze 2015; Korhonen et al. 2018). Studies agree that trade with Russia's main economic partner the European Union had contracted sharply following restrictive measures adopted by both the EU and Russia (Crozet and Hinz 2016, 2017; Dreger et al. 2016). An impact of Western sanctions on Russia's trade with non-sanctioning countries has not received much attention so far and requires academic investigation in order to understand the broader impact of sanctions. Trade with Republic Korea can be a good object of study because the country is an important economic partner for Russia in East Asia and takes an active part in state projects for the development of the Russian Far East. Republic of Korea (further Korea) did not support the sanctions although there was a pressure on the government to do so ('US demands Korea's participation' 2014). Moreover, in the course of its New Norther Politics, Korea continued to view Russia as an important economic partner. So, the question that is asked in this research is whether Russian-Korean trade suffered as a result of sanctions and what it can mean for the future trade policy regarding mutual cooperation.

To find an answer, several major points are discussed in the chapter, amongst them the dynamics of bilateral trade flows between Russia and Korea and of their structure during 2014–2017; reaction of Korean businesses that invest in Russia towards sanctions. Connection between trade and investment is straightforward as investment projects generate trade flows; coherence between trade, investment, and trade policy is a key to development in general. Moreover, trade plays a crucial role in investment decisions, according to an OECD exploratory survey (Duval 2008). Therefore, actions of Korean companies, who are major investors in bilateral relations, can provide additional information about the effect of restrictive measures imposed by the West.

The chapter proceeds as follows. After this introduction comes a section that briefly reviews previous studies about the potential effect of sanctions on non-sanctioning country and with a representation of the methodological approach used in this research. Then Korea's reaction to Western sanctions is discussed and bilateral trade flows and their structure during 2014–2017 are analysed. "Korean business in Russia during the sanction period" section examines the business strategy of Hyundai company during the sanctions, focusing on what measures the company management took to stay in the market. Lastly, "Concluding remarks" offer some considerations about how trade policy can be used to foster trade cooperation between Russia and Korea.

Previous studies and methodology

Previous studies

A number of studies, policy briefings, and reports on the effect of Western sanctions on the Russian economy has been published among them Gurvich and Prilepskiy (2015), Fritz et al. (2017), and Crozet and Hinz (2016, 2017). Authors differ in their assessment of the economic impact of sanctions and sometimes these differences are substantial. An important thing here is the lack of evidence supporting the idea that sanctions really hit Russia; on the contrary "despite Western efforts, the country is playing an increasingly prominent role on the global stage" (Russell 2018). It also remains unclear what causes the contraction in the Russian economy: the sanctions or the fall in the international oil prices (Korhonen et al. 2018; Dreger et al. 2016). Average crude oil prices fell from $98.89 per barrel in 2014 to $52.32 in 2015 and further to $43.74 in 2016 (Statista 2018), and for the Russian economy dependent on earning from export of oil it was a serious blow.

Literature on the problem of sanction has focused predominantly on those parties directly involved, that is, Russia and EU or Russia and the US, and a question of the potential effect of sanctions on Russia's relations with non-sanctioning countries, like Korea, did not get much attention. One of the relevant studies that it was possible to find had focused on Israel and Switzerland, which did not support sanctions. Authors (Sanandaji and Avorin 2018) started with an assumption that a possible substitution effect might be expected, but arrived at a conclusion that against expectation "from April 2014 to December 2016 export levels of the two countries have in fact fallen. The reduction in trade flows was similar, if not quite as high, as for the four largest sanctioning economies". More precisely, the level of reductions was 74 percent for Switzerland and 75 percent for Israel (Sanandaji and Avorin 2018). Authors think that value chains are responsible for such a big deterioration in trade: in their opinion because Russia is integrated in global value chains (although views about the degree of integration can vary, the mere fact of participation is more important) even goods that are not part of the sanction measures become affected resulting in losses for non-sanctioning countries.

Korea like Israel and Switzerland did not support sanctions, and at the same time it is deeply integrated into global value chains. In this regard it would be interesting to see an impact of sanctions on Korea's trade with Russia.

Methodology

This chapter is exploratory, based on analysis of statistical data on trade, derived from various sources like Korea International Trade Association (KITA), WTO,

Central Bank of Russia. The second part represents a case study that uses certain features of game theory. The case study is an adaptation of Hyundai Motors Manufacturing Rus to the new economic realities in Russia during the period of sanctions. The company is one of the biggest Korean conglomerates and its activity is significant for economic cooperation between the two countries in question. It is also an important stakeholder in Korea's trade policy and has demonstrated the ability to influence policy decision, for example by lobbying for preferential trade agreements with other countries. So, Hyundai's actions in the period of sanctions can give information on problematic areas and possibilities for the improvement of trade policy.

In more detail, the case study focuses on a strategy that the company's management had chosen in order to overcome difficulties that it faced during 2014–2017. The strategy here is understood as a set of strategic decisions taken in four important areas – price, production, distribution, and promotion. For the purposes of structuring and presentation of information about Hyundai's choices, the game theory logic has been applied.

The game theory has not been much used to explain corporate strategy as it is thought to suit more theoretical rather than practical purposes. However, as Lindstädt and Müller (2009) in their article for McKinsey point out the theory deserves to come to "the forefront as a strategic tool, for it offers perspectives on how players might act under various circumstances". They also suggest that under "higher uncertainty of today's global economy corporate decision-making can be paralyzed while 'game theory can revitalize and contribute clear information' for a strategic long-term vision" (Lindstädt and Müller 2009).

To propose an original view of looking on the company action in the Russian market during sanctions, we relied on a simplified framework of game theory ('Game theory' 2018) to structuralize Hyundai's strategic choices. Materials for this part of the chapter were derived from various news reports by Russian media, particularly from "Autostat" – an online resource that monitors major developments in the Russian auto manufacturing industry.

Korea's reaction towards sanctions and Russian-Korean trade in goods in 2014–2017

Korea's reaction towards sanctions

When sanctions were announced by the US in 2014, Korea found itself stuck between two different directions of its foreign economic policy. In one direction lay its strategic military alliance with US and in the other was the New Northern Policy, an initiative by the Korean government to foster economic cooperation with countries located to the North of Korea in an attempt to stimulate growth of the national economy. Adopted by the former president Park Geun Hye, the New Northern Policy sought closer economic ties with Russia. In 2014 the US administration tried to put pressure on Seoul demanding to clarify Korea's position on sanctions and to support them in a direct way ('US demands Korea's participation' 2014). Korea hesitated, as it wanted to give a "proportionate" response. On the one hand, historic, strategic, and economic significance of US-Korea alliance did not allow demands of the US to be ignored, but on the other hand, the situation surrounding Crimea that preceded sanctions did not fall into the direct sphere of Korea's national interests, which are centered more on North Korea and China. So, Korea decided not to take any direct restrictive measures. In other words, trade policy has not been changed to target trade in any way.

Here it is necessary to mention that Korea's attention was distracted from the sanctions by two other events of a more urgent nature. In 2016 and 2017 Korea struggled with a domestic political crisis surrounding its former president Park, caught at the centre of a corruption scandal.[1] Another issue was a growing military presence of the US in the region. Seoul's consent to deploy the controversial Terminal High-Altitude Area Defense (THAAD) anti-missile system by US was not well received in Russia and China ('"Destabilizing factor": Russia' 2017). Beijing had even taken economic measures to reduce import from Korea in response to Seoul's action ('China, Russia share' 2017; 'South Korea export growth' 2016). As a consequence, exports to China, Seoul's main trade partner, shrank, causing decline in manufacturing activity (Ho 2017).

Due to these challenges that coincided with the sanctions, Russian-Korean political dialogue was not quite active during the period under review. Moon Jae-in, a Korean president who came into office on May 10, 2017, endorsed the New Northern Policy of his predecessor and took a more proactive approach towards economic cooperation with Russia. In September of the same year he visited the Far Eastern Economic Forum and proposed a wide economic cooperation programme "9 bridges" ('Optimistic Korean accent' 2017).

Summing up, Korea did not join the sanctions and was more interested in further cooperation. The next section takes a closer look at how non-participation reflected on trade.

Bilateral trade during the period of sanctions

This section starts with Korea's export to Russia and then proceeds to Russia's export to Korea. It could be assumed that as Russia cut imports from sanctioning countries Korean products could become a substitute for them leading to an increase in Korean shipments to Russia. However, this did not happen, and Korea too had to face falling export to Russia. Export started to show signs of contractions the same year as the first package of sanction measures was adopted, i.e. in 2014. From its historic maximum of over $11 billion achieved in 2013 (Figure 10.1), export fell by 9.1 percent to $10.1 billion and continued to decline as Western sanctions were being widened. In 2015 export contracted 53.7 percent year-on-year basis reaching the lowest point of $4,686 million in six years. In total, Korea has lost almost 70 percent of its pre-sanction exports. In 2016, shipments to Russia started to increase slowly with a more robust growth of 44 percent in 2017 (Figure 10.1).

The downsizing of Korean export in Russia was reflected not only in value but also in physical volumes. Volumes shipped by Korea started to decrease already

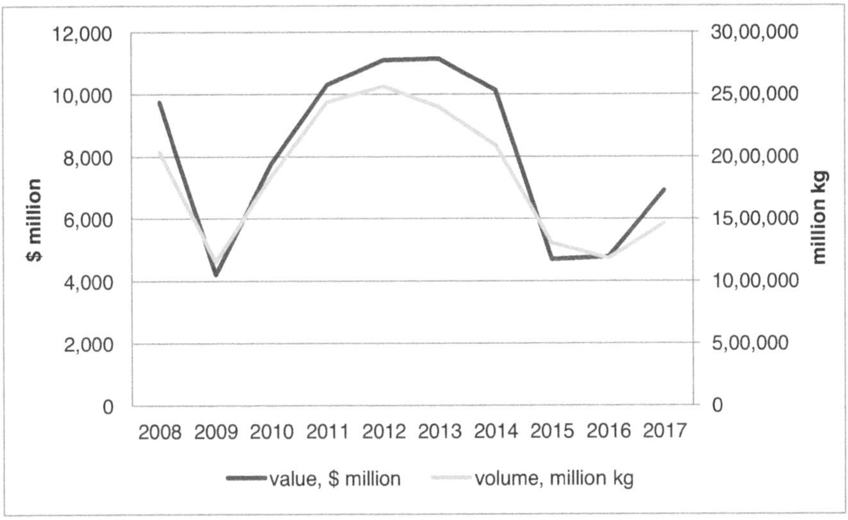

Figure 10.1 Korea's export to Russia, 2008–2017

Source: KITA (2018).

in 2013, or a year before the sanction, and continued its fall till 2016. In total, over the four years of contraction in 2013–2016 Korea suffered a loss of 53 percent of exported physical volumes. So, when volumes are taken into consideration, the contraction was longer than contraction in value. One possible explanation for this could be a slowdown in Russia's GDP growth that reduced demand from manufacturing industries for Korean products.

There are certain similarities in a pattern of export contraction during the period of sanctions and during the Great Recession of 2008–2009 – another important landmark in bilateral trade. In 2009 Korea lost 75 percent of its export value and 43.4 percent of physical volumes in just one year (Figure 10.1). But in 2010 Korean export returned to growth regaining pre-crisis level and even surpassing it. (Figure 10.1). A factor that brings these two situations close despite different backgrounds of contraction is exchange rate volatility, and more precisely changes in the value of the Russian ruble against the US dollar.

In the first quarter of 2009 price of the ruble jumped to ₽34 from ₽25 at the end of 2008 and then stabilized at around ₽30 per $1 (Figure 10.2). Korean exports reflected these changes: it fell following the weakening of the Russian currency and returned to growth when the exchange rate stabilized, and uncertainty reduced. A similar behaviour can be seen during the period of sanctions: Korean export was declining as the ruble was falling, and returned to growth after the Russian currency showed a strengthening trend. So, it is obvious that Korean export is highly responsive to currency behaviour and unpredictability in

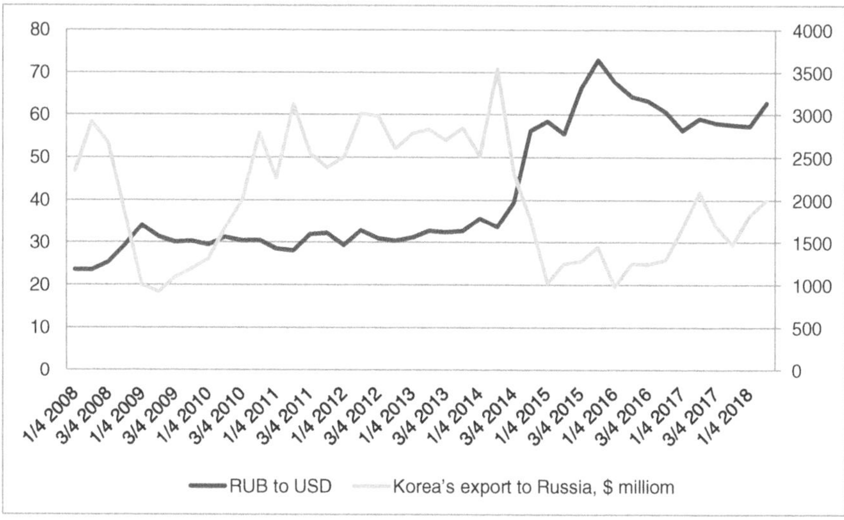

Figure 10.2 Korea's export to Russia and fluctuations of RUB/USD exchange rate; 1st quarter 2008–1st quarter 2018

Source: Central Bank of Russia (2018) and KITA (2018).

the international markets. This point is not unique to trade with Russia, but rather represents a fundamental characteristic and vulnerable point of Korean trade in general.

It should also be taken into account that sanctions coincided with a period of low prices for oil, another important factor in Korean trade. As price for oil fell sharply in July 2014 and by December of the same year lost more than 40 percent of its value, Korean export was negatively affected. According to the *Financial Times* persistence of low prices in 2014–2015 contributed to negative performance of Korean export ('South Korea economy pays' 2016). Thus, in 2015–2016 a combination of factors not directly associated with sanctions was influencing Korean trade with Russia rather than the sanctions themselves.

Now we take a look at how export contraction influenced its product structure, if at all. As a matter of fact, the decrease was felt across all major exported product categories. Industrial products like electrical machinery, plastics, rubber, and general machinery faced a bigger contraction, reflecting a lower demand from Russia. But this did not result in any noticeable changes in the overall composition of exports. The top-10 product categories by the HSK two-digit classification remained almost the same as in previous years: automobiles and auto parts together with industrial machinery made up more than 80 percent of Korean export to Russia (Figure 10.3).

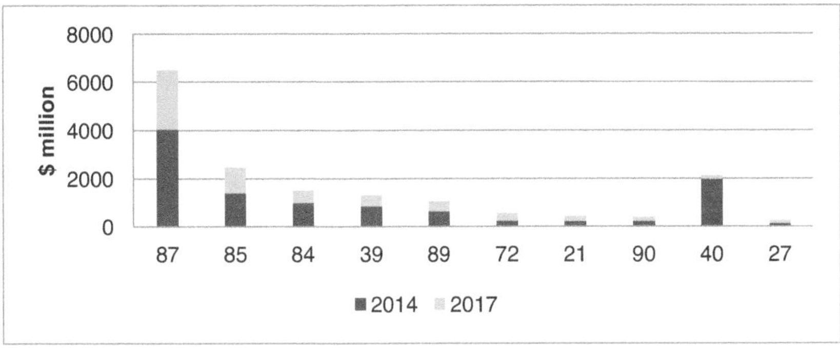

Figure 10.3 Korea's top-10 exports to Russia in 2014 and 2017

Note: Classification used is HSK two-digit classification. Codes' descriptions below:

87 – vehicles; 85 – electrical machinery and equipment; 84 – machinery, boilers; 39 – plastics; 89 – vessels; 72 – iron and steel; 21 – miscellaneous food ingredients; 90 – optical, measuring and other precision equipment; 40 – rubber and its articles; 27 – mineral fuels, mineral oils and waxes

Source: KITA (2018).

Russian export to Korea during the period of sanctions followed a very different pattern. This becomes obvious when comparing graph 4 with graph 1: while graph 1 for Korea takes an inverted "U" shape both for value and volume, graph 4 for Russian export shows two dissimilar trends for value and volume. For value, one can observe a zig-zag pattern for the dollar-denominated export and a steady increase for the physical volume. Russian export in value terms declined by 27.8 percent in 2015 and by 23.6 percent in 2016 on a year-on-year basis. In total, over two years, Russia's export to Korea shrank in almost the same proportion as after the Great Recession when in 2009 Russia lost 30.6 percent of its export to Korea in a single year. On the contrary, the volume shipped to Korea during the same period increased by 17.7 percent in 2015, 1 percent in 2016 and 7.4 percent in 2017 on a year-on-year basis (Figure 10.4). So, the question arises why Russian export had grown in volume but had contracted in value.

The answer to this question will be very much the same as an explanation for a negative performance of Korean export, i.e. currency fluctuations and low oil prices combined with a structure of Russian export to Korea. Russia's shipments are concentrated on a handful of product categories that influence the whole picture. Predominance of mineral fuels in shipments to Seoul (more than 80 percent) makes export performance dependent on international oil prices. As international prices for oil fell in 2014 and remained low for two consecutive years, Russia's exports to Korea in US dollars have fallen as well. But for Korea, which is a net energy importer and one of the largest world consumers of oil and gas, lower energy prices were beneficial. Korea was stimulated to buy Russian supplies at lower prices. This observation is further supported by statistics about export to Korea. In 2017,

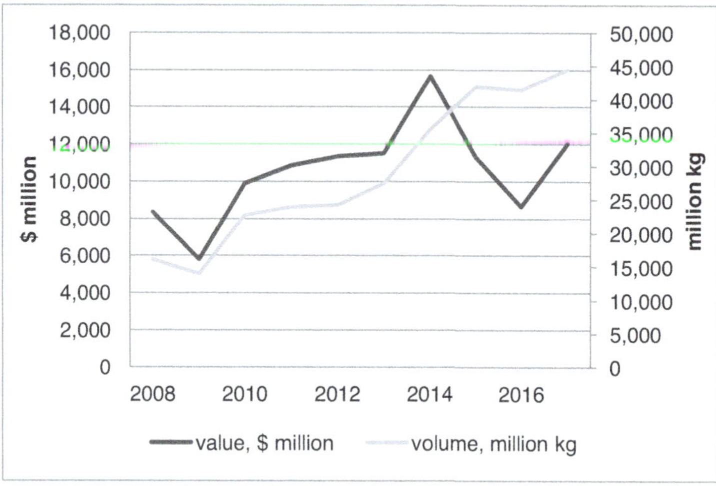

Figure 10.4 Russia's export to Korea, 2008–2017

Source: KITA (2018).

Russia has sent 40,878 kilograms to Seoul under HSK article 27 – mineral fuels, or 30 percent more than in 2014.

Increase in actual shipments helped Russia to cushion drop in oil prices. Without this, the blow to export and bilateral trade in general would have been much more substantial. Another important thing worth mentioning is that none of the parties was restricted by any measure in selling to or buying goods from each other.

Except for mineral fuels, other positions in the top-10 Russian exports to Korea in 2014 and 2017 were fish, iron and steel, aluminium, chemical, and wood (Figure 10.5). This structure of export has prevailed for more than a decade and has not changed during the sanctions period. A new addition during these years that can be positively regarded as a small step towards diversification was export of grains (mainly wheat, code 10 by HSK two-digit classification). Korean import of Russian wheat has seen a steady increase since 2013 and by 2017 has reached 207 million USD. An opportunity to start export was given through WTO membership, because the Korean agricultural market including wheat one remains strongly protected *vis-à-vis* non-member states. Applied MFN duty for wheat is 4 percent, the binding level stands at 8.7 percent while non-MFN rate can reach as high as 13 percent (WTO 2018). The Korean wheat market is quite promising as wheat is one of the top imported agricultural products for Korea (in 2017 Korea imported $958 million worth of wheat in total according to WTO) (WTO 2018), and trade in this product may open a way for a wider cooperation between Russia and Korea in the agricultural sector.

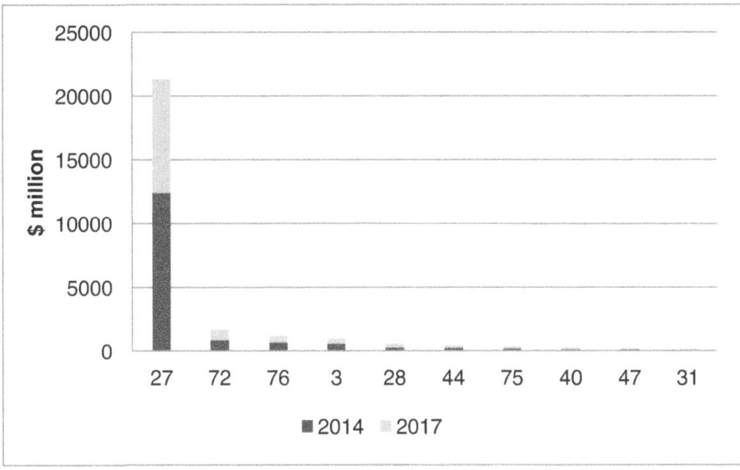

Figure 10.5 Russia's top-10 export to Korea in 2014 and 2017

Note: Classification used is HSK two-digit classification. Codes' descriptions below:

27 – mineral fuels; 72 – iron and steel; 76 – aluminium; 3 – fish and fish products; 28 – inorganic chemicals; 44 – wood and articles of wood; 75 – nickel; 40 – rubber and its articles; 47 – pulp of wood; 31 – fertilizers.

Source: KITA (2018).

Higher volumes of export of energy resources by Russia to Korea during the period of sanction can be regarded as a sign of its deeper integration into Korea's supply networks. Over the years Korea has managed to create long and agile supply chains that are key to Korean competitiveness in the international product markets. These supply chains are supported by various structures that include preferential trade agreements like FTA (free trade agreement), regional cooperation in various formats like ASEAN+3, and international organization membership like WTO membership. By effectively operating these structures at different levels Korea manages to find the best conditions either for market access or for resource supplies. And the fact that Russia's increased presence in Korean supply network in the future can lead Korea to intensify efforts and create similar agreements with Russia. There is some evidence for this. In private communications during the Russia-Korea Dialogue Summit in Moscow in June 2018 representatives of the academic community and policy-makers have admitted that FTA with the Eurasian Economic Union[2] is discussed at the highest level in Korea.

Growing deficit in trade with Russia also increases the desirability of FTA for Korea. As a matter of fact, Russia's vibrant exports, on the one hand, and falling Korean exports, on the other hand, helped Russia to achieve a positive balance of trade (Figure 10.6). For the first five months of 2018 only, the positive balance was 50 percent larger than for the whole of 2017 and almost equal for the total result of 2016. In the past, when Korea was in the situation of accruing negative

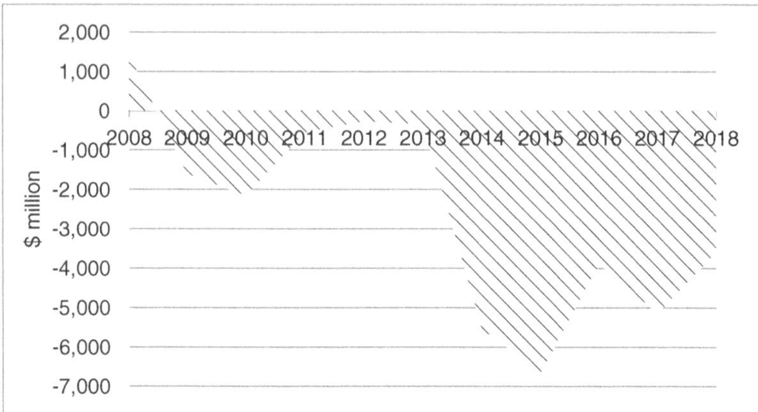

Figure 10.6 Korea's balance in trade with Russia, 2008–2018
Source: KITA (2018).

trade balances with other countries, the government was looking for opportunities to increase its export of goods and/or services either through participation in the large projects or through more favourable terms of market assess. A good example from the past could be construction projects in the Middle East at the end of the 1980s that helped the Korean government offset a mounting trade deficit resulting from import of mineral fuel. A more recent example is a merge between resource diplomacy and FTA policies in the 2000s when Korea started to seek FTAs with South East Asian, Latin American, and some other countries with the purpose of realizing a combined effect of access to resources and to domestic markets in order to balance its trade. FTA with the Eurasian Economic Union could potentially become an important milestone for bilateral cooperation. But, on the other hand, its feasibility is not so certain due to Russia's own integration strategy in post-Soviet space. In any case, such discussion could bring positive results by directing attention to other areas of the trade policy and seeking new possibilities to facilitate trade.

Summing up the discussion in this section, several observations regarding Russian-Korean bilateral trade during 2014–2017 could be made. Neither of the countries has introduced a trade policy measure that could restrict their trade, however, the sanctions did influence it in an indirect way. The effect came mainly through the ruble depreciation and uncertainty about the national economy. Because the Korean products became more expensive for the Russian consumers on the one hand, and because of the low demand from domestic manufacturing industries on the other hand, Russia's import decreased significantly. So, there are no clear signs of a substitution by Korean products for goods from the sanctioning countries. Russian export to Korea, on the contrary, has seen an increase as a result of growing energy supplies to Korea. However, these results can hardly be regarded as a consequence of the sanctions only, a combination of international factors interfered and among them low prices for energy resources. From the viewpoint of trade policy, the developments of trade during the period of sanctions has brought to light several issues. First of all, it showed that the WTO membership is stimulating trade as Russian has got access to Korea's agricultural market. Secondly, is a necessity for some preferential agreement already felt by one party. This is a sign that more discussion on the trade policy issues between the partners will most probably take place. Thirdly, as a comparison with the Great Recession of 2018 has shown, Russian-Korean trade is highly susceptible to uncertainties in international markets, so one of the areas to work on could be the trade policy measures to balance this uncertainty. It could be, in particular, a consultation mechanism to reduce the negative impact of instability.

Korean business in Russia during the sanction period

A strategic ability of business to manage risks has important implications for economic cooperation between the countries. In the periods of high unpredictability, like sanctions, firm-level decisions ultimately determine whether the bilateral relations can adapt to a difficult situation or not. But this, of course, is possible if two governments do not take any restrictive measures with regard to each other. Since the Korean government did not introduce this type of measure, the Korean firms with a business in Russia could choose between staying or exiting the Russian market.

In 2014 after the sanctions were introduced, Korean Trade and Promotion Agency (KOTRA) surveyed Korean firms in Russia and asked whether they anticipated any direct threat from the sanctions to their business and what actions they had planned under these circumstances (Chae 2014). Results showed that overall Korean companies did not expect that they would suffer from the sanctions directly; their worries mainly concerned an indirect impact. All respondents pointed out that the economic fundamentals in Russia – like the weakening of the Russian ruble against the US dollar, inflation and overall resilience of the Russian economy – looked worrisome. Another dangerous area in the eyes of the companies was the real income of the population that in dollar-denominated terms had fallen considerably and this had negatively affected the purchasing ability of the consumers. The Korean firms clearly saw that their products were becoming expensive for the majority of Russian citizens. At the same time their view about the potential of the Russian market remained strong and they had no plans to withdraw their investments.

According to the same survey (Chae 2014), depending on the sector of their activity, Korean companies thought of different strategies. Those involved in purely trading activities were going to halt their operations and wait to see how the adaptation process continued. Firms in the food processing sector that depended on a procurement of raw materials from Europe were seeking the new local suppliers, while companies in electronics (like Samsung) experimented with new and cheaper logistic routes through China to secure their cost-efficiency ('Samsung and Russian Railways' 2016). Firms in the manufacturing sector were designing more elaborate cost-saving strategies, and auto giant Hyundai even dared a more aggressive approach with the aim of increasing its market share.

Examples of the individual firms and how they adapted to a new business environment characterized by depreciation of the Russian ruble and falling consumer spending would provide more information on the effect of sanctions and bring to light policy issues that Russia and Korea could work on to create a better environment for their business. The strategy of Hyundai during the period of sanctions represents a particularly interesting case for a number of reasons. Hyundai Motors Manufacturing Rus (HMMR or Hyundai), as an entity registered in Russia, is one of the largest Korean investment projects and one of the largest foreign auto firms operating in the Russian market. Also, being a big Korean corporation, Hyundai in its activities is closely watched by other Korean companies. And the latter would assess their market opportunities by Hyundai successes and failures.

HMMR was launched nearby St. Petersburg in 2011.[3] The plant operation capacity is 230,000 cars per year, and it reached this figure in 2013, which means that in 2014 when sanctions started to affect the national economy, Hyundai injected a large number of cars. When the sanction measures had been adopted and the market dwindled Hyundai found itself in a very difficult situation. Management took a decision to "tie the belt" and to go through the difficult times with as few losses as possible ('Head of Hyundai Manufacturing' 2016). Such determination resulted in an aggressive strategy aimed at improving Hyundai's market positioning in Russia.

The game theory can help to structure HMMR's strategy. The game theory suggests a number of strategic choices regarding price, output, product offer, and the promotion and payoffs they bring ('Game theory' 2018). The options regarding price and output are to raise, to lower or to hold; regarding product offer they are to keep existing or develop new models; and finally, regarding promotion – to spend more, to spend less or to keep spending at the same level (Figure 10.7). Each individual combination of these decisions can help to achieve one of the following payoffs: more profits for shareholders; larger market share, higher chances of survival or getting rid of the rivals. As Figure 10.7 shows, Hyundai's choice for a strategy included: holding prices, decreasing output and gradually introducing new models and spending more on advertising. The final goal was to maximize the company's market share as much as possible even if it incurred losses for shareholders. And HMMR did have to absorb the losses, which were estimated at approximately 15 million USD ('Hyundai losses are estimated' 2016).

Below are some more specific details of Hyundai's actions in each of the outlined areas.

Price

Price-wise Hyundai operates in a segment between low-cost and mass-market brands ('Hyundai increased prices' 2017), meaning that the brand's consumers are highly price-sensitive. Immediately after the ruble started to depreciate, HMMR

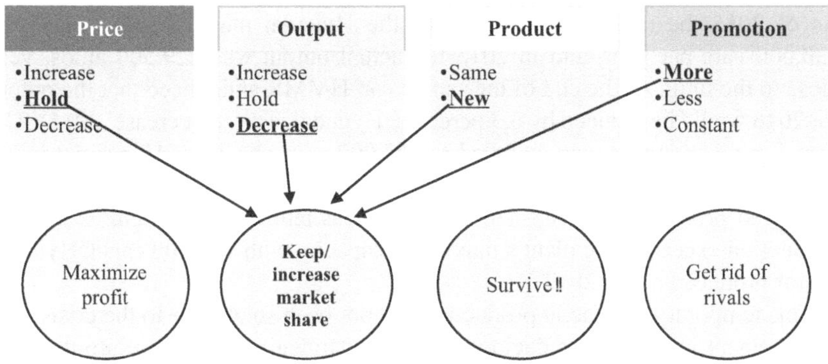

Figure 10.7 Hyundai's strategy choices in Russia according to the game theory

Source: Created by the author.

decided that it was crucial to let the consumers know that the company was well aware of their difficulties and ready to keep prices in rubles unchanged for some of its basic models. For the additional options prices were increased in the range of 10 percent. Of course, later, as the economy stabilized, the price strategy became more sophisticated and included a mix of price increases and discounts. Here are the examples.

In mid-2015 prices for the Model Elantra jumped by ₽20,000 but the discount given by the company amounted to ₽40,000, so the price corrected to an even lower level than before the increase. Crossover ix35 in all versions increased in price by ₽100,000 but a discount in ₽150,000 actually lowered the prices for consumers. Solaris was discounted by ₽40,000 and later the discount period was extended further in order to attract new customers ('Hyundai in Russia increased prices' 2015).

At the end of 2016 – and the beginning of 2017, another discount programme was introduced. It focused on auto parts and components: a discount in the range between 7 and 23 percent was offered to those customers who purchased Hyundai cars during 2014–2015 and it was time to do a technical maintenance for them ('Hyundai lowers prices' 2017). The management acted thoughtfully as it tried to minimize the effect of ruble depreciation on the cost of a car and simultaneously lower exploitation expenses associated with the renewal of expendable materials.

These aggressive policies did not bring profits for the company, but neither were they intended to. The task was to raise the popularity of the Hyundai brand and firmly establish the car manufacturer in the Russian market. And this plan worked well as the models Hyundai Solaris and Huyndai Creta became among the top selling models in the country ('Hyundai Creta kept its leading' 2017; 'Hyundai Creta rose to lead' 2018; 'Hyundai Solaris in 2017 kept' 2018; 'Hyundai Solaris became' 2017).

Output

As of 2015 the maximum capacity of the Hyundai manufacturing plan was 230,000 cars per year, and in 2015 the actual output was 229,500 autos, very close to the limit. At the end of the same year, HMMR announced that the output for 2016 would be reduced by 6.3 percent ('Hyundai is set to decrease' 2015). The actual production that year equalled to 207,000 cars, or almost 10 percent lower than in the previous year, and lower than initially announced ('Hyundai in Russia decreased production' 2016). This decrease was temporary, though, as in 2017 production exceeded the plant's maximum capacity with 233,000 cars ('Hyundai Motor produced more' 2017).

This temporary decline in production has not been solely due to the crisis. The management in Russia has decided to make a strategic investment into the optimization of the production process for the future ('Hyundai in Russia modernized' 2016). Hyundai allocated $100 million for bringing in the latest technologies in artificial intelligence (AI) to equip the plan. An additional 53 advanced robots in an assembly lime were installed, bringing the total number of robots to 230 ('Hyundai will invest 100 million' 2016). With this decision the management was catching two birds at the same time: reducing future costs of production and adapting to new technological trends.

Product

Korean car producer released two new models Hyundai Solaris and Hyundai Creta ('Hyundai in Russia modernized' 2016), which were welcomed by the market and, as already mentioned, became among the most popular models ('Hyundai launched mass production' 2017). In addition, Hyundai decided to diversify its presence into a premium segment and introduce its executive four-door luxury sedan Genesis. Before bringing Genesis to Russia the model was distributed mainly in the US and Canada, even at the current time the official website for this car offers localization for Korea, the US, Canada, and Russia only, reflecting the major distribution network. Genesis is 100 percent produced in Korea and is imported to Russia as a finished product. During the first year when the model was launched in Russia, 48 cars were shipped from Korea to Russia mostly to Moscow and Saint Petersburg, which looked pretty modest. Even during the period of sanctions the upper segment of the Russian car market remained highly competitive with a strong presence of German and other European automakers. In order to expand its presence HMMR will need more time and more intensive efforts to promote its luxury model and increase market share. Yet, a decision by management to introduce a new model in a segment different from its prime one demonstrates an intention to work further in Russia.

Promotion

The advertising campaign by Hyundai was built on two pillars: Firstly, attractive financing offers linked to the Russian government programmes to support purchases of the new cars for those who had never had a car before (this programme was called "First car program") and secondly, increasing the number of dealers. Under the conditions of the "First car" the Russian government financed two-thirds of the base interest rate of the Bank of Russia for customers who were using auto financing programmes. For example, in late 2016 the Bank of Russia lowered the rate to 10 percent, therefore under the programme the government had to cover 6.67 percent and the customer 3.33 percent. Also, a prospective car owner had to bear the rate of the commercial bank that financed the purchase. So, if the final percentage for an auto credit was 15 percent, the Russian government financed 6.67 percent and the customer 8.33 percent. ('Right of the first purchase' 2017).

In addition to loan subsidies, the government financed a 10 percent discount from the car price for families with two and more children and for those customers who were buying their first auto. These measures helped to support the auto industry in general, and Hyundai was among the brands that benefited from the scheme. According to the estimates by industry insiders, more than 50 percent of Hyundai car sales in 2016–2017 happened under these financial programmes ('Hyundai losses are estimated' 2016).

Hyundai brand recognition was successfully improved through partnership with various rent and lease services as well. In St. Petersburg, the second largest city in Russia, Hyundai started to provide such conditions for a car leasing that allowed the renting companies to offer better rates for their daily rents for Hyundai models. According to one of the largest renting companies with services in Moscow, St. Petersburg and other major cities in Russia, Rentexpress – the cost of Hyundai Solaris for one day averages ₽1900 and this price can fall by 20–30 percent if a car is rented for a period exceeding 10 days, which makes it a very competitive offer (personal communication June 30, 2018). For comparison, the price of a Smart, compact city car engineered with Mercedes-Benz, averaged ₽2300, or almost 20 percent higher than Hyundai (personal communication June 30, 2018).

Investments into the dealing network have brought HMMR positive returns through a higher customer satisfaction. Survey of 3,000 new car users showed a high satisfaction index for Hyundai cars – 78.3 points out of 100, with only Japanese manufacturers being in the front ('Rating of autobrands' 2018).

The choice of strategy made by Hyundai in the face of economic difficulties might seem risky taking into account that it did not have a long history of manufacturing in Russia and had to establish its place. This strategy did not bring profit for Hyundai in the short-term, but it was a big investment into the brand name. Choosing an aggressive line was akin to saying that "we came here to stay". This attitude reflects the general mindset of the corporation and fits with its generally assertive price-focused strategy-mix, which has always defined Hyundai's activities on a global scale. As Carney (2008) observes "Korean firms have typically followed a strategy of late market entry by investing heavily in large scale plants . . .". Big manufacturing facilities gave Korean firms benefits from the economies of scale. A similar pattern is observed in Russia where the Hyundai manufacturing plant is by far one of the largest among other foreign auto firms like Toyota or Nissan. HMMR has one of the highest localization indexes as it not only assembles the car but also manufactures necessary parts and components in St. Petersburg. Carney further continues that "they [Korean firms] typically seek to occupy aggressive cost-leadership strategies". Substantial corporate resources accumulated in the Korean headquarter stand behind each project in individual countries and made it possible for the Korean automaker to engage in intensive price competition. In Russia, corporate resources assisted Hyundai to go through the tumultuous period that sanctions triggered.

Another essential feature of Hyundai's global strategy is to enter uncontested, unexplored, and thus often more difficult to operate in markets. The reason for this was described by Chung (n.d.) with regard to the early years of the company's internationalization in the 1990s but is still relevant today: "Hyundai could simply not afford to build up a viable presence in the heart of the developed country. Globalization strategy was the build up of manufacturing capacities on the periphery of the world regions". It was one of the first car manufacturers to establish production in Eastern Europe and Latin America during times of transition in the 1990s and early 2000s, and this experience taught Hyundai how to adjust to an unpredictable environment. So, operations under difficult economic conditions in Russia in 2014–2017 were not something completely new for the company. The Hyundai management tested its accumulated knowledge and became one of the most important carmakers in Russia.

The sheer size of the project also makes it one of the major stakeholders in Russian-Korean trade and relations. Russian authorities are interested in the presence of companies like Hyundai and further extended its support. In July 2018, the Minister of Industry and Trade Dmitriy Manturov mentioned that the government is ready to extend a special investment contract with Hyundai that grants tax benefits in exchange for participation in government programmes ('Minpromtorg plans' 2018).

So, apart from lessons of adaptability to the changing economic realities, what can Hyundai Manufacturing Rus. tell us about trade and how can this be used for the purposes of trade policy? Broadly speaking, trade flows present a sum of operations of multiple actors like Hyundai. Therefore, the situation of every actor and the actions that this actor takes has a deep impact on the state of trade flows. From the Hyundai example we can see that Korean exporters to Russia had to fight for the consumers who became highly price-sensitive in the wake of the weakening ruble. Their active price strategies helped to keep a substantial stream of consumer goods. However, such results are not possible without a certain amount of state support. The intentions of both governments continue to play a big role in shaping the climate for cooperation and reducing uncertainty. Better operating conditions and clear communication of the policies is the key to sustainable trade.

As trade develops further it will become more diverse in goods that are exchanged and the ways they are traded. The Hyundai example showed that even whole cars could be imported. This fact raises questions of customs and rules compliance. Despite WTO-unified standards, differences are possible, and two countries could work on this to create a better framework for the business. Also, not all forms of trade are equally developed, for example e-commerce remains a weak spot although it has good potential for growth, allowing more firms to become involved in the bilateral trade.

Risk mitigation is another issue to consider. Hyundai is a big international company with a substantial amount of its own resources, but not all participants of Russian-Korean trade have access to such vast financial resources. Many find it challenging to obtain access to finance during periods of economic uncertainty. An appropriate finance related trade measure could make it possible to address weaker, but important sectors and companies for the sake of diversifying trade flows. A good initiative could be special trade financing and risk insurance for small and medium-sized businesses. This can help to facilitate cross-border transactions and hedge risks attached to the exchange rate movements.

Concluding remarks

Concluding the discussion on the effect of sanctions on Russian-Korean trade, a few remarks could be made. Broadly speaking the sanctions have not influenced Russian-Korean relations as both countries remained interested in developing their mutual ties further. Neither side introduced restrictive measures thereby targeting the other side into their trade policies. Moreover, despite a certain amount of pressure Korea did not join the sanctions because this conflict lies outside the sphere of direct national interests of the country and because it had to solve more urgent domestic and regional issues.

At the same time, this research illustrates the substantial effect of factors associated with the sanctions on Russia's trade with the non-participating country. This effect is indirect and produced by a weakening of the national currency and a worsening of domestic economic conditions like the contraction of consumers' purchasing power, inflationary pressures, and rising uncertainty. These reasons are not the only ones, as psychological perceptions regarding the economic situation of trade participants (like firms) seem to matter as well. When business lacks information about the future they prefer to wait especially when they do not have sizeable resources to rely upon. Some of the Korean firms preferred to wait until the situation stabilizes. In contrast to that, big companies like Hyundai were taking a set of measures aiming not just to stay active, but rather to expand their market share.

In any case, sanctions have shown that instability remains one of the major challenges for trade and trade policy can be a useful tool to minimize its negative impact. Russia and Korea can work together to stimulate participation of the companies from the different sectors through simplification of customs and other bureaucratic procedures. Special provisions could be designed to support trade by the SMEs, like the temporary measure to minimize negative impact of currency fluctuations. This is a difficult task and perhaps cannot be managed within a trade policy framework only, however trade policy can set an agenda that will be further developed by competent institutions within the relevant countries. Thus, better alignment in the work of various institutions with the objectives of trade policy can also contribute to a more sustainable mid- and long-term growth in trade between Russia and Korea.

Obviously, during the period of sanctions, Russian-Korean relations were put to the test. So far, both sides have demonstrated a willingness to find ways to keep cooperation and extend it despite economic uncertainties. Further work to deepen trade ties through better trade policy could become an agenda for the 30th anniversary of bilateral relations in 2020.

Notes

1 Following the trial and conviction process of the former president to 22 years in jail, BBC has produced a detail analysis of how the scandal unfolded ('South Korea's presidential scandal' 2018).

2 Being a member of this alliance with a single external import tariff Russia is unable to establish any free trade agreements of its own.

3 In one of our previous works we have looked into more details of Hyundai investment project in St. Petersburg (2017).

Bibliography

Carney, M 2008, *Asian Business Groups: Context, Governance and Performance*, 1st edition, Chandos Publishing, Cambridge.

Central Bank of Russia 2018, viewed 27 June 2018, www.cbr.ru

Chae, SW 2014, 'Survey of Korean Business Regarding US and EU Sanctions Against Russia', *KOTRA*, 22 September, viewed 26 June 2018, https://news.kotra.or.kr/user/globalBbs/kotranews/6/globalBbsDataView.do?setIdx=322&dataIdx=135942

'China, Russia Share Opposition to U.S. THAAD in South Korea: Xi' 2017, *Reuters*, 3 July, viewed 25 July 2018, www.reuters.com/article/us-china-thaad-russia-idUSKBN19O0N8

Chung, MK n.d., 'Internationalization Strategies of Korean Motor Vehicle Industries', *GERPISA*, viewed 29 June 2018, http://gerpisa.org/ancien-gerpisa/actes/18/article4.html

Crozet, M and Hinz, J 2016, *Collateral Damage: The Impact of the Russia Sanctions on Sanctioning Countries Exports*, CEPII Working Paper, no. 2016-16, June, CEPII, PARIS.

Crozet, M and Hinz, J 2017, 'Friendly Fire: The Trade Impact of the Russia Sanctions and Counter-Sanctions', *Kiel Working Paper*, viewed 17 June 2018, www.ifw-members.ifw-kiel.de/publications/friendly-fire-the-trade-impact-of-the-russia-sanctions-andcounter-sanctions/kwp_2059-updated-version-july-2017

'"Destabilizing Factor": Russia Urges US, S. Korea to Reconsider THAAD Anti-missiles Deployment' 2017, *Russia Today*, 29 April, viewed 2 August 2018, www.rt.com/news/386536-korea-thaad-destabilizing-factor/

Dolidze, T 2015, 'EU Sanctions Policy Towards Russia: The Sanctioner-Sanctionee's Game of Thrones', *CEPS Working Document*, viewed 12 June 2018, www.ceps.eu/system/files/WD%20402%20TD%20Sanctions.pdf

Dreger, Ch, Fidrmuc, J, Kholodilin, K and Ulbricht, D 2016, 'Between the Hammer and the Anvil: The Impact of Economic Sanctions and Oil Prices on Russia's Ruble', *Journal of Comparative Economics*, vol. 44, no. 2, pp. 295–308.

Duval, Y 2008, 'Trade and Investment Linkages and Policy Coordination: Lessons From Case Studies in Asian Developing Countries', *OECD VII Global Forum on International Investment*, March 27–28, OECD, viewed 16 October 2018, www.oecd.org/investment/globalforum/40300944.pdf

Fritz, O, Christen, E, Sinabell, F and Hinz, J 2017, 'Russia's and the EU's Sanctions: Economic and Trade Effects, Compliance and the Way Forward', *European Parliament's Committee on International Trade*, EP/EXPO/B/INTA/2017/11, PE 603.847.

'Game Theory', *Economics Online*, viewed 30 June 2018, www.economicsonline.co.uk/Business_economics/Prisoner's_dilemma.html

Gurvich, E and Prilepskiy, I 2015, 'The Impact of Financial Sanctions on the Russian Economy', *Russian Journal of Economics*, vol. 1, no. 4, pp. 359–385.

'Head of Hyundai Manufacturing Rus: I Do Not Know How We Can Survive' 2016, *RBC*, 25 February, viewed 13 July 2018, www.rbc.ru/spb_sz/25/02/2016/56ceed359a7947774ad0edc3

Ho, J 2017, 'South Korea's Export Recovery Is on Thin Ice', *Nikkei*, 13 April, viewed 3 July 2018, https://asia.nikkei.com/Economy/South-Korea-s-export-recovery-is-on-thin-ice2

'Hyundai Creta Kept Its Leading Position in SUV Segment in June' 2017, *Sena Auto*, 7 July, viewed 15 July, 2018, https://cena-auto.ru/all_news/hyundai/creta/496/

'Hyundai Creta Rose to Lead Auto Market in St. Petersburg in January' 2018, *Autostat*, 16 February, viewed 15 July 2018, www.autostat.ru/news/33174/

'Hyundai Increased Prices for Solaris' 2017, *Autostat*, 4 September, viewed 10 July 2018, www.autostat.ru/news/31243/

'Hyundai in Russia Decreased Production by 10% in 2016' 2016, *Two Auto*, 23 December, viewed 14 July 2018, https://two-auto.ru/bez-rubriki/rossijskij-zavod-hyundai-v-2016-godu-snizil-proizvodstvo-na-10.html

'Hyundai in Russia Increased Prices for a Range of Models' 2015, *Autostat*, 7 September, viewed 10 July 2018, www.autostat.ru/news/22767/

'Hyundai in Russia Modernized Its Production Site to Launch New Creta' 2016, Hyundai Official Web-site, 06 June, viewed 16 July 2018, www.hyundai.ru/news/rossijskij_zavod_hyundai_moderniziroval_proizvodstvennye_moshhnosti_dlja_zapuska_creta

'Hyundai Is Set to Decrease Production Volume in Russia in 2016 by 6.3% Until 215 Thousand Autos' 2015, *Auto Newsru*, 30 December, viewed 18 July 2018, https://auto.newsru.com/article/30dec2015/hyundai_plans

'Hyundai Launched Mass Production of New Solaris' 2017, *Auto Dealer*, 15 February, viewed 17 July 2018, http://auto-dealer.ru/news/2017-02-15-hyundai-zapustil-massovoe-proizvodstvo-novogo-solaris/

'Hyundai Losses Are Estimated to Exceed One Billion in 2015' 2016, *Lenta*, 23 March, viewed 15 July 2018, https://m.lenta.ru/news/2016/03/23/automarket/amp/

'Hyundai Lowers Prices for Auto Parts' 2017, *Autostat*, 23 June, viewed 11 July 2018, www.autostat.ru/news/30457/

'Hyundai Motor Produced More Than 233 000 Autos in Russia in 2017' 2017, *Kolesa*, 28 December, viewed 15 July 2018, www.kolesa.ru/news/hyundai-motor-vypustil-v-rf-bolee-233-000-avtomobilej-v-2017-godu

'Hyundai Solaris Became the Most Sold Model in Russia in 2016', *Autostat*, *12 January 2017*, viewed *18* July 2018, www.autostat.ru/news/28651/

'Hyundai Solaris in 2017 Kept Its Leading Position in St Petersburg Market' 2018, *Autostat*, 18 January, viewed, 15 July 2018, www.autostat.ru/news/32804/

'Hyundai Will Invest 100 Million USD to Develop Its Manufacturing Plant in Russia' 2016, *Autostat*, 25 February, viewed 15 July 2018, www.autostat.ru/news/25050/

KITA 2018, *Korea International Trade Association Official Web-site*, viewed June–July 2018, www.kita.net

Korgun, I 2017, 'Investment Cooperation Between Russia and the Republic of Korea During 1999–2009: Major Trends and Main Lessons', in: K Liuhto, S Sutyrin and JM

Blanchard (eds.) *The Russian Economy and Foreign Direct Investment*, Routledge, Oxon and New York, pp. 192–212.

Korhonen, I, Simola, H and Solanko, L 2018, *Sanctions, Counter-sanctions and Russia: Effects on Economy, Trade and Finance*, Bank of Finland BOFIT Policy Brief, no. 4, viewed 3 July 2018, https://helda.helsinki.fi/bof/bitstream/handle/123456789/15510/bpb0418.pdf?sequence=1

Lindstädt, H and Müller, J 2009, 'Making Game Theory Work for Managers', *McKinsey and Company*, December, viewed 26 July 2018, ttps://www.mckinsey.com/business-functions/strategy-and-corporate-finance/our-insights/making-game-theory-work-for-managers

'Minpromtorg Plans to Extend Support for Auto Industry Until 2019' 2018, *Delovoi Peterburg*, 9 July, viewed 1 August 2018, www.dp.ru/a/2018/07/09/Minpromtorg_prodlit_podde

'Optimistic Korean Accent at the Eastern Economic Forum' 2017, *RIA*, 7 September, viewed 2 August 2018, https://ria.ru/analytics/20170907/1501993793.html

'Rating of Autobrands by Customer Satisfaction Regarding Service (Based on Auto Owners Survey)' *2018, Autostat, 26 February,* viewed *17* June 2018, www.autostat.ru/infographics/33282/

'Right of the First Purchase' 2017, *Rossiiskaya gazeta*, 11 July, viewed 1 August 2018, https://rg.ru/2017/07/11/v-rossii-vveli-novye-lgoty-na-avtokredity.html

Russell, M 2018, *Sanctions Over Ukraine Impact on Russia*, Briefing for the European Parliament, European Parliamentary Research Service PE 614.665, January, viewed 3 July 2018, www.europarl.europa.eu/RegData/etudes/BRIE/2018/614665/EPRS_BRI(2018)614665_EN.pdf

'Samsung and Russian Railways Announced Cooperation to Develop "The New Silkroad"' 2016, *Samsung*, 8 October, viewed 12 July 2018, https://news.samsung.com/ru/samsung-%D0%B8-%D1%80%D0%B6%D0%B4-%D0%BE%D0%B1%D1%8A%D1%8F%D0%B2%D0%B8%D0%BB%D0%B8-%D0%BE-%D1%81%D0%BE%D1%82%D1%80%D1%83%D0%B4%D0%BD%D0%B8%D1%87%D0%B5%D1%81%D1%82%D0%B2%D0%B5-%D0%B4%D0%BB%D1%8F-%D0%B4

Sanandaji, N and Avorin, D 2018, 'Disrupting Global Value Chains: "Friendly Fire" and Unintentional Consequences of the Sanctions on the Russian Federation', *ECEPR*, viewed 12 June 2018, www.ecepr.org/wp-content/uploads/2018/02/ECEPR-Disrupting-Global-Value-Chains.pdf

'South Korea Economy Pays Price for China Slowdown and Cheap Oil' 2016, *The Financial Times*, 22 May, viewed 25 July 2018, www.ft.com/content/129efeac-1745-11e6-b8d5-4c1fcdbe169f

'South Korea Export Growth Slows to Trickle as China Demand Wanes' 2016, *The Financial Times*, 26 January, viewed 25 July 2018, www.ft.com/content/6c097e58-c3f4-11e5-b3b1-7b2481276e45

'South Korea's Presidential Scandal' 2018, *BBC*, 6 April, viewed 1 August 2018, www.bbc.com/news/world-asia-37971085

Statista 2018, Annual Average WTI and Brent Crude Oil Spot Prices From 1990 to 2017 (U.S. Dollars Per Barrel), The Statistics Portal, New York, USA, viewed 17 July 2018, www.statista.com

'US Demands Korea's Participation in Sanctions Against Russia' 2014, *Hankyorye*, 29 July, viewed 5 July 2018, www.hani.co.kr/arti/politics/diplomacy/649022.html#cb#csidxf3a2df26ad562e9923b62fcdb69b143

Veebel, V and Markus, R 2015, 'Lessons From the EU-Russia Sanctions 2014–2015', *Baltic Journal of Law & Politics*, vol. 8, no. 1, pp. 165–194.

WTO 2018, *Tariff Profiles*, viewed 1 August 2018, http://stat.wto.org

11 Contemporary Russian–Brazilian trade relations

Alexandra G. Koval and Alexis Dantas

Introduction

The Russian Federation has significantly changed its foreign economic policy from the beginning of the twenty-first century onwards. Russia, as a re-emerging power, has expanded its economic ties across the world, primarily intensifying trade cooperation and promoting further business networking. The country has reinforced its links with the most remote regions, including Latin America.

In 2014, after the visit of the Russian president, Vladimir Putin, to the Latin American states of Cuba, Nicaragua, Argentina, and Brazil, many scholars in Russia and abroad emphasized Russia's re-engagement in Latin America (Ellis 2016; Jeifets 2015). Western economic sanctions and retaliatory contra-sanctions have encouraged the Kremlin to review its foreign strategy in order to remedy the decline in trade and investment flows with traditional partners. This has triggered the Russian Federation's growing interest in Latin America.

Contemporary discussions on Russian–Latin American relations tend to include geopolitical rhetoric (Astrada and Martín 2013; Garay Vera 2010; Martynov 2015). However, Russia's current approach to Latin America is based much more on the consideration of national interests than on ideological blinkers (Sizonenko 2016). There is certainly potential for the development of commercial ties with the region (Yakovlev 2017). The main channel for Russian cooperation with Latin America remains through trade: its share in Russian turnover has been slowly increasing, achieving about 2.5 percent in 2017. The investment flows between Russia and Latin America are much less significant, and trade is seen as a driving force for economic cooperation between countries (Koval 2017).

The development of contemporary Russian–Latin American trade relations largely runs through Brazil. Firstly, the country is Russia's main trading partner in the region, accounting for the lion's share of Russian trade with Latin America – 36.5 percent in 2017. Secondly, Brazil has been perceived as a leader of the significant regional integration bloc MERCOSUR (the Southern Common Market), which also includes Argentina, Paraguay, and Uruguay, and as an initiator of economic cooperation under UNASUR (the Union of South American Nations), comprising 12 South American countries. Through MERCOSUR and UNASUR, Brazil has expanded its bargaining power in the global trade network and represents a "sub-core" in South America (Pérez-Oviedo et al. 2018). For Russia, as a driving member of the Eurasian Economic Union (EAEU), cooperation with MERCOSUR presents certain opportunities and challenges.

Finally, Brazil, as a BRICS (Brazil, Russia, India, China, and South Africa) member, represents a major partner for the Russian Federation in Latin America (Davydov 2016). This political dialogue primarily focuses on the strengthening of the bargaining power of emerging economies in the global governance. However, annual BRICS summits and discussions on deeper cooperation between states in support of the multilateral trading system affects their trade policies and intensifies inter-BRICS trade (Koval and Pioch 2017).

The aim of this chapter is to underline trends and challenges in Russian–Brazilian trade relations. The period under analysis will be 2000–2018, with greater focus on recent developments. The investigation relies on a state-centric approach and institutional analysis of bilateral trade cooperation, with the proper use of relevant statistical data. The main idea behind the analysis is that the significant distance between the two countries prevents the development of their commercial relations due to the shortage and asymmetry of market information. In this sense, presidential visits and other institutional frameworks of state-to-state cooperation could give incentives for economic cooperation while providing an information exchange. Testing this hypothesis, the authors identify the main stages and key factors for contemporary Russian–Brazilian trade relations.

This chapter is based on explanatory analysis, with an indication of focal points and determinants in the development of commercial ties between the countries. The next section presents a review of the literature relevant to the topic. The research continues with analysis of trends in the development of Russian–Brazilian trade relations, providing explanations of their nature. The findings focus on the question of whether state visits, EAEU–MERCOSUR relations and BRICS development encourage Russian–Brazilian trade. In the conclusion, the authors indicate the prospects for Russian–Brazilian cooperation and give recommendations for future studies.

Theoretical foundation

Russia's newfound focus on Latin America could primarily refer to the recovery of economic relations with the region after the collapse of almost all business ties during the period of Russia's transformation in the 1990s (Koval 2009). However, economic improvements in both Russia and Latin America were not as strong an incentive for their cooperation as the changes in the political discourse at the turn of century. From one side, Russia, as a re-emerging power, has increased its role on the global scene and accordingly aimed to broaden its relations with Latin America. From the other side, left-driven politicians taking the lead in many Latin American states have tried to escape US influence and have expanded their relations with other partners (Astahov 2009). The most recent developments in global politics, such as the Western sanctions against Russia and revision of US policy under Trump's presidency, as well as political crises in Brazil and Venezuela, have strengthened geopolitical discussions about Russian–Latin American relations.

Therefore, a geopolitical perspective prevails in most recent studies on Russian cooperation with the region, while relatively modest attention has been paid to trade and economic links between states. Some scholars examine Russia as a threat to US predominance in the region (Patiño Villa 2014; Sánchez Ramírez 2010). The country has expanded its military power and increased arms supplies to Latin America (Cruz 2015). Other experts assess Russian energy interests in the region and consider political effects of projects in the oil and gas sector (Blank and Kim 2015). Davydov (2016) and Pavlova (2017) argue that Russia has moved closer to Latin America in sharing similar attitudes to establishing and maintaining the multipolar order.

Political factors could play their role in Russia's economic cooperation with Latin America and, to a certain extent, encourage its development through building strategic partnerships and signing agreements or memoranda of cooperation in different fields (Yakovlev 2016). Nevertheless, the political focus often narrows Russia–Latin America analysis down to Russia's cooperation with Venezuela, Cuba, Nicaragua or other left-driven states (Davidov 2010), and gives very limited focus on ties with countries in the region where major business developments are present. Taking into account that Russian policy on Latin America tends to be pragmatic (Jeifets et al. 2018), there is a need for studies on the understanding of trends in economic relations, and the main challenges and prospects for trade cooperation with major prospective partners. In this sense, Brazil, being a core business partner for Russia in the region, has attracted our attention.

The majority of studies on Russian–Latin American trade relations primarily include a general analysis of trade dynamics and structure, with an overview of commercial ties with main partners, including Brazil (Massarova 2013; Shkolyar 2013). The relevant investigations highlight that trade turnover between Russia and Latin America remains insignificant, with a large share of exports from Russia comprising non-manufactured goods (fertilizers, metals, oil), and its import consisting mainly of agricultural products (meet, sugar, fruits, etc.). According to the goals, concepts, and forecasts of the Russian government (Government of the Russian Federation 2008; Ministry of Economic Development of Russia 2013), the country aims to increase and diversify trade relations with Latin America through manufactured and highly technological export. Some scholars indicate a certain potential in this field, and there is a corresponding need for development of an institutional framework for better exchange of business information and product promotion (Paniev 2013; SELA 2011; Yakovlev 2017). The most recent study by Lopez Areval (2018) seems to be more sceptical, but also highlights a special role for Brazil in enhancing Russian–Latin American relations.

Analysis of Russian–Brazilian trade is usually conducted under the above-mentioned general investigations or, more recently, within the framework of BRICS studies. The development of Russia's relations with Brazil in BRICS is often seen as a significant channel for strengthening Russian–Latin American ties (Dabagyan 2011). However, empirical studies of BRICS trade patterns show that Russian trade intensity is relatively low in BRICS countries and its main comparative advantages remain in traditional export products (Maryam et al. 2018;

Rasoulinezhad and Jabalameli 2018). Moreover, both states maintain a high level of protectionism, representing a significant barrier to development of their bilateral trade (Koval and Trofimenko 2017; Pioch 2017).

Very few studies focus on Russian–Brazilian trade *per se*. Jubran (2012) analysed Russian–Brazilian relations during 1992–2010 from a perspective of international relations theories and found that both countries paid little attention to the development of economic cooperation. He mentions two main reasons for this: distance and third countries' influence. With regards to the first point, research by Disdier and Head (2008) confirmed that transportation costs matter and distance negatively affects bilateral trade. Moreover, a long geographical distance means remoteness between markets, which causes a lack of business information and higher transaction costs. General analysis of Russian–Latin American relations proves that an asymmetry of information represents a stumbling block for the development of Russia's trade with the region (Koval 2009; Volpe et al. 2010) and, most likely, with Brazil as well. Nevertheless, Jeifets et al. (2018), by comparing Russian and Chinese activities in Latin America, have questioned whether distance plays such a crucial role. In addition, Brazil could be pursuing trade with BRICS and cooperation with Russia in order to balance its relations with the USA and China, thus avoiding bandwagoning (Dantas and Koval 2016).

Examining trends in Russian–Brazilian trade, some scholars have highlighted the importance of cooperation between states as leaders of regional blocs – customs unions (Koval and Dantas 2013; Tuktarov and Fedorenko 2015). However, the focus of these studies relies more heavily on comparative analysis of MERCOSUR and the Customs Union of Russia, Belarus, and Kazakhstan/EAEU rather on the development of Russian–Brazilian relations under these institutions.

Finally, some recent investigations of Russian–Brazilian trade concentrate on analysis of specific case studies – in particular, the trade of beef. The food embargo established by Russia as a contra-sanction against the West led to an increase in beef exports from Brazil to the country by 10 percent in 2014; however, there was a subsequent fall in deliveries due to the slowdown of the Russian economy. Analysis of the beef trade case demonstrates the importance of institutional and geopolitical environment as well as market conditions, *per se*, in the development of Russian–Brazilian cooperation (Schierhorn et al. 2016). Another study, by Thomé et al. (2012), reveals that the main challenges to increased Russia–Brazil beef trade are institutional barriers and uncertainty due to market volatility. These two specific case studies have proved that an institutional framework of bilateral cooperation is a substantial determinant for its development.

Thus, the literature review indicates the following gaps. Firstly, there has been no detailed investigation of modern trade relations between Russia and Brazil, as the majority of studies refer to Russian–Latin American economic cooperation in general. Secondly, previous studies focused either on the political dimensions of cooperation or on analysis of trade statistics. Thirdly, some researchers revealed institutional barriers and a shortage of information on Russian–Brazilian relations that all lead to higher transaction costs. However, no studies examined how the institutional framework of Russian–Brazilian cooperation affects bilateral trade.

This research attempts to fill the above-mentioned gaps and considers the most recent evolution of Russian–Brazilian trade relations and its institutional basis. To accomplish this research task, the authors rely on a state-centric approach of neoliberal institutionalism.

According to this approach, states tend to cooperate precisely in order to deal with asymmetrical information and to limit the degree of uncertainty (Keohane 2005). The further the distance between countries, the more state interactions are needed in order to decrease trade uncertainty (van Bergeijk 2009). Proper economic diplomacy could encourage trade links between states (Moons and van Bergeijk 2016), and this includes state visits and other forms of governmental interaction.

There is an evident lack of studies on the role of state visits and governmental cooperation for Russian–Brazilian trade development. It is worth mentioning that state visits and other meetings at the higher level are usually associated with the number of bilateral agreements signed. However, they have an even greater impact through their information exchange decreasing uncertainty. An empirical study by Nitsch (2007) proved that state visits could increase exports by about 8 to 10 percent, and these results are sensitive to the type of visit. In the case of Russian–Brazilian relations, the following types of visits took place: official state visits, meetings of presidents during BRICS summits, and meetings of higher officials in the framework of cooperation between MERCOSUR and the EAEU. They will represent the key focus of this research.

This chapter will not discuss the issue of Russian and Brazilian interactions in the framework of the multilateral trading system. Since Russia has only recently acceded to the WTO, the country is not yet intensively involved in WTO trade negotiations. In contrast, Brazil has already been very active (Koval and Sutyrin 2012). The research will not investigate the activities of the National Committee for the Promotion of Economic Cooperation with Latin America (NC SESLA), established by the Russian Chamber of Industry and Commerce and Ministry of Foreign Affairs of the Russian Federation, or other similar organizations, since they assume state-to-business interactions, but not state-to-state interactions.

The next section will be structured as follows. The authors reveal the key stages in the contemporary development of Russian–Brazilian trade relations. Detailed analysis of these stages provides an opportunity to test three hypotheses:

1. The increase in Russian–Brazilian trade has been largely assisted by state visits;
2. BRICS, as a certain institutional framework for state-to-state cooperation, has encouraged Russian–Brazilian trade;
3. Cooperation between regional trade agreements (RTAs), with the leadership of Brazil in MERCOSUR and Russia in the EAEU, has intensified trade between the countries.

This comprehensive study of the contemporary political and economic environment for cooperation will indicate the challenges and prospects for further development of Russian–Brazilian trade.

Research findings

Russian–Brazilian trade has risen significantly over the last 15 years. Intensification of Russian–Brazilian relations began in 2002, when the Brazilian president, F. H. Cardoso, visited Moscow. It was the first in a series of Russian–Brazilian meetings at the highest diplomatic level (Figure 11.1).

The visit represented the starting point for the renewal of bilateral trade cooperation. In the 1990s after the Soviet collapse, Russia substantially destroyed its economic ties with Latin America (Koval 2009), but the presidential meeting demonstrated Brazil's growing interest in the Russian market and encouraged intensification of governmental and business contacts between the countries. However, this visit did not have any immediate significant effect in terms of increased bilateral trade. Figure 11.2 shows that Russian–Brazilian trade started to grow from 2004 onwards, when the countries began building a strategic partnership.

Building a strategic partnership between Russia and Brazil during 2004–2008

The changes in Russian–Brazilian trade during 2004–2008 could be associated with, among other factors: (a) new directions of Russian foreign policy due to re-engagement in Latin America after Russia's first high-level visit to the region; (b) changes in Brazilian foreign policy under the government of President Lula da Silva (Workers' Party); and (c) developments in the BRIC negotiations of this period.

Russia's first presidential visit in the history of Russia/USSR–Brazil relations in 2004 strongly intensified trade contacts among states. Russia identified Brazil as a primary partner in the Latin American region; notably, President Putin highlighted this in his statement for the media (Kremlin 2004):

> Russia and Brazil are confidently moving along the path of forming relations of a special kind, a partnership of special content.

The state visit led to an explosion of articles in newspapers, media reviews, and business workshops on Russian relations with Latin America in general and Brazil in particular. The Russian government initiated the development of a strategic partnership with Brazil that intensified business contacts between the countries. Russian export to Brazil grew by 44 percent during 2003–2004 (Table 11.1).

The Brazilian president made a reciprocal visit to Moscow in 2005. At this meeting, Lula da Silva and Putin signed the bilateral Russia–Brazil Strategic Alliance agreement. These steps towards state-to-state cooperation increased bilateral trade: during 2004–2005, the annual rises in Russian exports/imports to/from Brazil were 64 and 71 percent, respectively (Table 11.1).

Then, in 2006, the Brazilian president again visited Russia during the G8 summit in St Petersburg. At that time, Brazilian foreign policy relied on the following aspects. Firstly, a central role was played by MERCOSUR in defining the directions

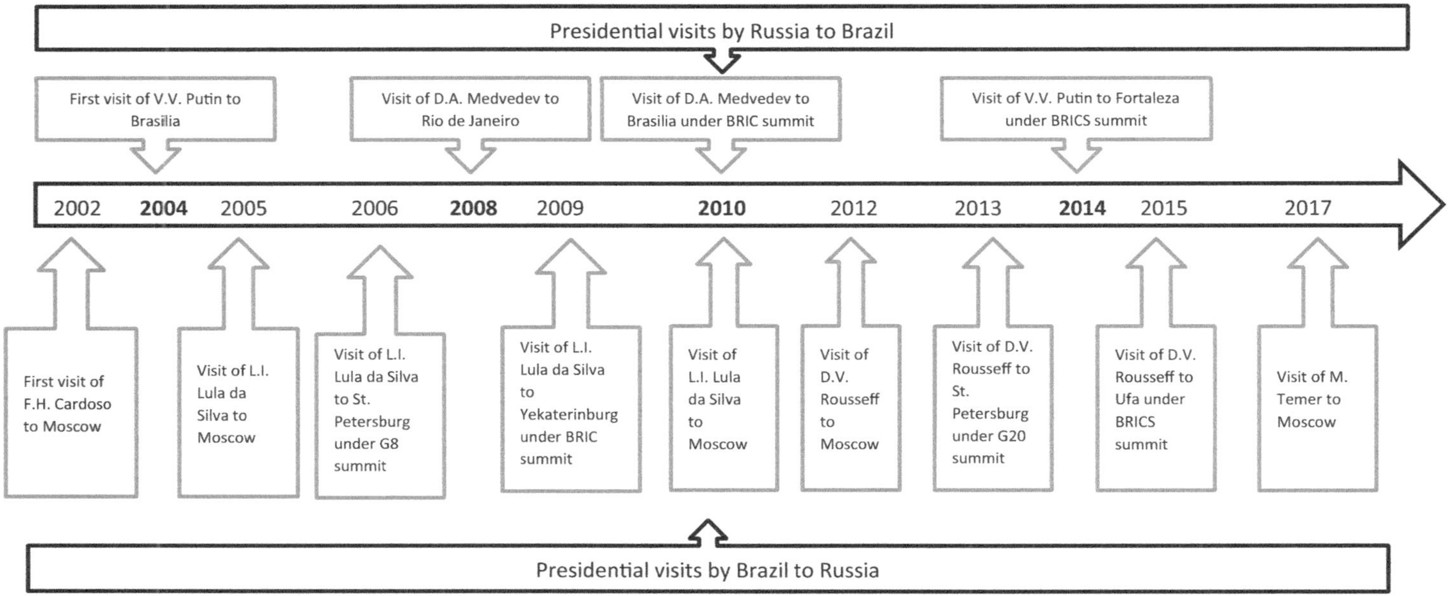

Figure 11.1 Presidential visits in Russian–Brazilian relations, 2002–2017

Source: Compiled by the authors on the basis of the Ministry of Foreign Affairs of Russia (2018).

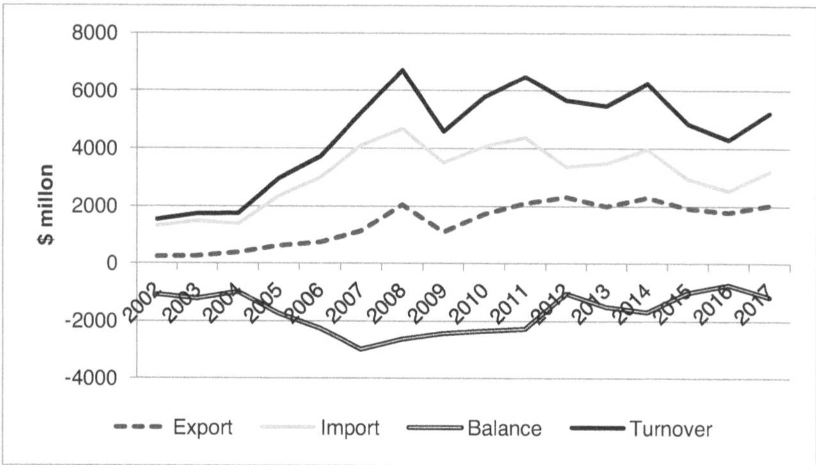

Figure 11.2 Russian Trade with Brazil, 2002–2017

Source: ITC Trade Map (2018).

of the foreign policies of the countries it comprised. Russia had already increased its contact with MERCOSUR as an institution since 2003, when the Russian Minister of Foreign Affairs, I. S. Ivanov, participated in the MERCOSUR summit and signed a joint statement on the establishment of a mechanism for a multilateral political dialogue between Russia and MERCOSUR. Russia's relations with MERCOSUR subsequently increased. Secondly, and most importantly, Brazil searched for broader international integration, favouring a strengthening of cooperation with developing countries and emerging economies. The BRIC initiative, first announced in 2006, was seen as a great achievement in South–South cooperation, and it additionally introduced Russia as a "new" partner for Brazil. In an interview with DW Brasil (França 2015), the Foreign Minister of the Lula government, Celso Amorim, pointed out that Brazil totally supported BRICS activities:

> I would say that what led us to an approximation initially was a movement between three countries that had many affinities, namely the so-called IBSA: India, Brazil and South Africa. And Russia and China – countries that do not fit in the logic of the G7 [group formed by the United States, Germany, Canada, France, Italy, Japan and the United Kingdom], but at the same time cannot be considered mere developing countries – have made several indirect actions to approach IBSA. In 2006, the Russian [Foreign Minister], [Sergei] Lavrov, proposed that we had to try to make some conversations involving the BRIC group, which at the time did not include South Africa. Finally, after a long history, we have the BRICS as they are today since 2011, a group of countries that have the affinity, perhaps, of not sharing some of the affinities of the G7.

Table 11.1 Annual change in Russian–Brazilian trade, 2002–2017

	2002–2003	*2003–2004*	*2004–2005*	*2005–2006*	*2006–2007*	*2007–2008*	*2008–2009*	*2009–2010*	*2010–2011*	*2011–2012*	*2012–2013*	*2013–2014*	*2014–2015*	*2015–2016*	*2016–2017*
Russian export to Brazil, annual change, percent	12	44	64	20	56	81	−47	59	22	10	−14	15	−16	−7	14
Brazilian export to Russia, annual change, percent	13	−7	71	27	38	14	−25	16	8	−23	4	14	−26	−14	27

Source: Authors' calculations of data from ITC Trade Map (2018).

In 2008, President Medvedev embarked on a four-nation Latin American tour, which was characterized by a majority of experts as Russia's return to Latin America (Koval 2009). During this trip, the Russian president visited Brazil, where he stipulated the aim to double bilateral trade and expand high-technological cooperation (Shchedrov 2008). In Russia's Concept of the Foreign Policy 2008 (Kremlin 2008), Brazil was represented as the most important strategic partner in Latin America.

Therefore, state visits demonstrated that both Russia and Brazil highlighted the certain potential and mutual interests in cooperation. Under these circumstances, bilateral trade continued to increase and reached its peak in 2008 with a trade turnover of more than US$6.7 billion (Figure 11.2). Moreover, Russian exports to Brazil increased by 81 percent during 2007–2008 (Table 11.1). The intensification of state visits reflected the transformation of foreign economic policy in both countries aimed at rapprochement. State visits seemed to establish the proper institutional framework for the development of trade cooperation. There is no doubt that the growth of bilateral trade was also linked to the substantial economic development of both Russia and Brazil during the analysed period of 2004–2008, but state visits provided a significant institutional basis for strengthening commercial cooperation.

Russian–Brazilian cooperation under BRICS during 2009–2013

The year 2009 opened a new stage for Russian–Brazilian trade relations. The international financial crisis greatly influenced both Russia and Brazil, but to different degrees, and in 2009, the first BRIC summit was organized, enhancing cooperation between its members in various fields, including trade.

The international financial crisis and the turbulence of the world economy demonstrated the difficulties that Western states had in maintaining stable economic development. This enhanced the role of emerging economies in global governance and played a part in the establishment of BRICS. As Figure 11.1 shows, Russia and Brazil steadily increased bilateral contact during these annual meetings (as well as during summits of other international forums). Moreover, Figure 11.1 only presents meetings within the territories of investigated countries, and it should be noted that Russian and Brazilian leaders, as well as representatives of their business societies, also met during BRICS summits in other states. In addition, each summit would inevitably be followed by meetings of various ministries as well as business and academia representatives.

Remarkably, during 2009–2013, Brazilian leaders visited Russia four times, while the Russian President visited Brazil only once. This intensification of state visits from Brazil to Russia might demonstrate that, of the two parties, Brazil was more strategically interested in cooperation. This might be due to stronger established dimensions of Brazilian foreign policy towards cooperation with Russia explained by both geopolitical and economic perspectives. Brazil has always had a positive trade balance with Russia; however, during 2009–2013, the gap between Brazilian exports/imports to/from Russia steadily decreased. Therefore, despite state visits made by the Brazilian side every year, their effects on trade dynamics were not obvious. Brazil also tried to enhance relations with Russia through the development of cooperation between MERCOSUR and the Customs Union of Russia, Belarus, and Kazakhstan. However, negotiations under this framework did not come to any valuable agreements.

Russia seemed to focus more on the BRICS initiative rather than encouraging a Russian–Brazilian alliance. Thus, according to the Foreign Policy Concept of 2013, Russia continued "the development of strategic cooperation with Brazil, including within the framework of BRICS" (Ministry of Foreign Affairs of Russia 2013). The only visit made by the Russian leader to Brazil during 2009–2013 was organized under the BRIC summit in 2010. In comparison, the Brazilians visited Moscow twice under the framework of international forums in 2009 and 2013, and twice more with the explicit aim of building bilateral cooperation with Russia in 2010 and 2012. All meetings promoted the dissemination of information on business opportunities; however, bilateral trade did not increase respectively.

State visits seemed incapable of outweighing unfavourable market conditions. The drastic fall in Russian–Brazilian trade in 2009 reflected the heavy effects of the international financial crisis on Russia. In Brazil, the consequences of this crisis were much less prevalent. This is why Russian exports to Brazil during 2008–2009 dropped by 47 percent, while imports decreased by only 25 percent. However, the crisis directly had only short-term effects, as the recovery had already started during 2010–2011 (Figure 11.2, Table 11.1). Nevertheless, during 2012–2013, Russian–Brazilian trade turnover slightly decreased due to the emerging political crisis and economic disorganization in Brazil.

Meanwhile, as Table 11.2 shows, there was no significant rise in the Brazilian share of Russian exports or in the Russian share of Brazilian imports. During 2009–2013, they annually accounted for about 0.4 and 0.8 percent, respectively.

Table 11.2 Russian and Brazilian shares in bilateral trade, 2002–2017

	Brazilian share in Russian trade, percent		*Russian share in Brazilian trade, percent*	
	Export	*Import*	*Export*	*Import*
2017	0.6	1.4	1.5	1.3
2015	0.6	1.6	1.5	1.1
2014	0.5	1.4	1.8	1.0
2013	0.4	1.1	1.4	0.8
2011	0.4	1.4	1.7	0.9
2009	0.4	2.1	2.3	0.8
2008	0.4	1.7	2.4	1.2
2006	0.2	2.2	2.2	0.8
2004	0.2	1.8	1.4	0.6
2002	0.2	2.8	2.2	0.5

Source: Author's calculations of data from ITC Trade Map (2018).

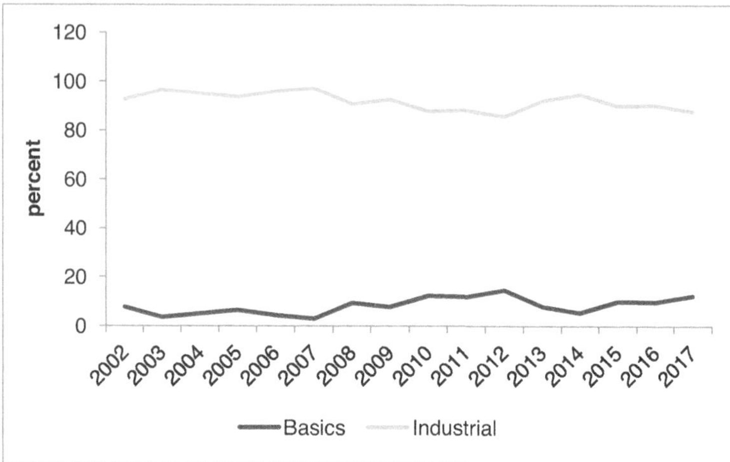

Figure 11.3 Basics and industrialized products in Russia's export to Brazil, 2002–2017

Source: MDIC Brazil 2018.

At the same time, Brazilian exports to Russia reached 2.3 percent of the total Brazilian exports in 2009, but fell by a significant amount in 2013 (to 1.4 percent). The Brazilian share of Russian imports also decreased from 2.1 percent in 2009 to 1.1 percent in 2013.

The unstable trade dynamics during 2009–2013 reflected the turbulence of the economic situation in Russia after the international financial crisis, as well as the beginning of a political and economic crisis in Brazil. As for the composition of trade between these countries, some points must be highlighted. Firstly, the structure of Russian exports to Brazil has actually remained the same from the beginning of the twenty-first century. It has been characterized by a large share of manufactured goods (Figure 11.3). The most important items – fertilizers and petrochemical derivatives – together accounted for more than 50 percent of the total Russian deliveries to the Brazilian market (for instance, in 2017, their combined share comprised 52.28 percent). Thus, despite being manufactured products, they are characterized by low technological content.

Secondly, Brazil's foreign sales to Russia show two distinct periods throughout 2002–2017. Initially, between 2002 and 2012, exports of basic products and manufactured goods showed a balance, despite a prevalence of basic products (about 60 percent of the volume exported, compared to approximately 40 percent for manufactured goods). This trend changed in 2012, when sales of basic products occupied about 65 percent of the total, increasing to 78 percent during 2012–2014 and maintaining 71–73 percent in 2015–2017 (Figure 11.4). The reduction of exports of processed meat from 2012 onwards, when they represented almost 25 percent of total Brazilian exports to Russia, explains the change in the basic/manufactured composition thereafter. The top five exported products were soy,

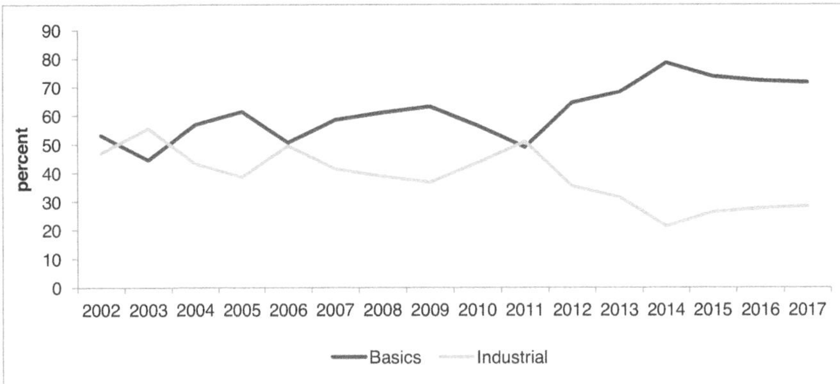

Figure 11.4 Basics and industrialized products in Russia's import from Brazil, 2002–2017

Source: MDIC Brazil 2018.

sugar, chicken, coffee, and coffee beans in 2017. All in all, agricultural products comprised a large share of Brazilian exports to the Russian market.

Russian–Brazilian trade during 2014–2018, and present challenges

In 2014, Russian–Brazilian trade exceeded US$6 billion, and Russian–Brazilian relations improved greatly. The Russian president visited Brazil and discussed a roadmap for bilateral economic cooperation. The results of negotiations were incorporated in the Action Plan for Russia–Brazil Trade and Economic Cooperation 2014–2015 (Ministry of Economic Development of Russia 2014). One of its main goals was to reach a turnover of US$10 billion in the medium term – an ambitious goal, which had already been declared in 2008.

The Ukrainian crisis started in 2014 and led to Western economic sanctions against Russia and, subsequently, Russian contra-sanctions in the form of a food embargo. The geopolitical situation forced Russia to diversify trade relations and focus on strengthening cooperation with emerging and developing economies, including the BRICS states. For instance, the food embargo provided more opportunities for Brazilian exports of agricultural products to Russia. Moreover, the creation of the Contingent Arrangement of Reserves and the New Development Bank (NDB) under BRICS clearly demonstrated the intensification of cooperation among its members. In 2015, the Brazilian president, D.V. Rousseff, visited Moscow under the framework of the BRICS summit.

Despite the favourable institutional conditions, for 2014–2016, a drop in exports from Russia to Brazil, and vice versa, can be observed (Table 11.1). This reflected the reduction of international commodity prices and, internally, the disorganization of the Brazilian economy as a result of the country's political crisis that led to the impeachment of President Rousseff in 2016 – with devastating effects on domestic production. Simultaneously, the decrease in oil prices challenged Russia's economic development and trade, with sanctions leading Russia to focus more on the import substitution strategy.

After 2014, exports dropped, but not as significantly as the reduction of imports from Brazil. The Western sanctions provided an opportunity for an increase of Brazilian exports to Russia due to the food embargo against the EU and the USA. However, economic decline in Russia, combined with the political and economic crisis in Brazil, diminished the potential positive effect of sanctions for the development of Russian–Brazilian trade. Brazilian exports fell dramatically between 2015 and 2017 as a direct consequence of the political crisis. Russia's share of Brazilian exports decreased in 2015 to an estimated 1.5 percent, while in 2014–2017, Russia's share of Brazilian imports increased from 1.0 to 1.3 percent (Table 11.2). In general, the Brazilian share of Russia's turnover in 2008–2017 remained about 0.9 percent. The common point to observe is that trade relations between Brazil and Russia still only account for a very small percentage of their total trade.

The years 2015–2016 provided new adjustments to Russian–Brazilian trade cooperation. Firstly, after the establishment of the EAEU in 2015, the Russian Federation has increasingly focused on its regionalist perspective and transformed its foreign economic strategy accordingly. Secondly, radical changes in Brazilian politics have affected foreign relations.

Since 2015–2016, Russian strategy has increased its focus on cooperation with regional blocs. According to the current Foreign Policy Concept of the Russian Federation (Ministry of Foreign Affairs of Russia 2016):

> Russia will seek to consolidate ties with its Latin American partners by working within international and regional forums, expanding cooperation with multilateral associations and Latin American and Caribbean integration structures, including the Community of Latin American and Caribbean States, the Southern Common Market, the Union of South American Nations, the Central American Integration System, the Bolivarian Alliance for the Peoples of Our America, the Pacific Alliance and the Caribbean Community.

Thus, Russia has examined its relations with Brazil as an integral part of cooperation with MERCOSUR. The political and economic dialogue between the EAEU and MERCOSUR has clearly intensified. In May 2018, the Russian Minister of Foreign Affairs, S. V. Lavrov, pointed out that the memorandum of cooperation between the EAEU and MERCOSUR was at the final stage of negotiations, with the member countries aiming to form a free trade agreement between the two customs unions (RIA Novosti 2018). It should be stressed that Russia's discussion of cooperation in this framework involves not only Brazil, but also Argentina. Nevertheless, Russia has also expanded its cooperation with the BRICS members, with Brazil continuing to represent the Latin American region. To some extent, Russia–Brazil relations have moved away from a strategic partnership concept towards cooperation under the umbrella of certain forums and organizations.

Regarding the current Brazilian political and economic crisis, it is necessary to emphasize the effects of the highly contractionary fiscal policy from 2015 onwards – in an environment of cyclical reversal and the onset of economic stagnation that began in 2014. The inability to overcome the political crisis, which led to the 2016 impeachment mentioned above, has exacerbated the economic situation in the country (Dantas and Jabbour 2017). In 2014, there was still a clear idea of the increase in Brazilian trade relations with the BRICS, but this situation has changed considerably since 2016. In this context, two aspects converge to create unfavourable expectations regarding Brazilian trade with Russia.

Firstly, the adoption of ultra-liberal measures in the economic policy of Brazil has transformed the pattern of growth and development options in the country. With a model based on the logic of the financial market, priorities are strictly related to monetary stability and a fiscal policy that guarantees "confidence" for financial agents. This is at the expense of concern for economic growth, job creation, and improvement of public services. This model is entirely associated with the principles of the "Washington Consensus", which was outlined in the 1980s and subsequently failed in the 1990s.

A policy of extreme austerity (symbolized by a new law capping public spending for 20 years) was adopted, which, in a scenario of cyclical inflationary reversal, has led to an unprecedented crisis in the Brazilian economy. Moreover, possible changes for a new cycle of growth do not seem feasible under current economic policy conditions, and if a new cycle of growth does emerge, it will be extremely slow. Thus, with reduced capacity to generate income and employment, it is impossible to imagine the resumption of industrial investment and the return of a sustainable cycle of growth. Brazilian trade has been negatively affected by this situation.

Secondly, the new government also radically altered the orientation of foreign policy adopted since President Lula da Silva's first term in January 2003. As mentioned previously, the Brazilian focus under the leadership of the Workers' Party was on re-strengthening of MERCOSUR, South–South cooperation, and BRICS. After the impeachment of 2016, this focus was structurally altered, highlighting three lines of thinking in Brazilian foreign policy: (a) reduced importance of MERCOSUR; (b) a search for rapprochement with the United States and the EU; (c) non-active participation in the BRICS.

MERCOSUR, the centre of foreign policy actions for the governments of the Workers' Party, ceased to be a target of commercial and strategic preference for the new government, especially following the declaration of a diplomatic war with Venezuela, which was a MERCOSUR member at that time. It is important to note that this country represented an important source of resources for the Brazilian economy, from a large trade surplus to an important set of joint investment plans, especially in the oil and gas sector. As the new government plans were to promote a broad denationalization of the sector, with the sale of assets of PETROBRAS and a strengthening of domestic production and supply, Venezuela and the previously implemented agreements would be an obvious obstacle. Despite the opposition of the Uruguayan government, Brazil, and Argentina (also led by an ultra-liberal government under Mauricio Macri) began a sequence of sanctions against the permanence of Venezuela in the economic bloc – which led to the country's suspension. In addition to relegating MERCOSUR to second place in foreign policy concerns, the Brazilian government attacked UNASUR's foundations.

Immediately after the impeachment, explicit attempts for rapprochement with the United States began – shortly after the impeachment vote in the Senate, the deputies and senators who would be indicated *a posteriori* for the country's Foreign Ministry attended a meeting with the US Department of Commerce to define the directions of Brazilian foreign policy. The election of President Trump, however, complicated this rapprochement, especially following the adoption of protectionist measures by the US government.

Another target of attack for the new government was the BRICS agreement, especially the new institutions created under the agreement, the Contingency Arrangement of Reserves and the New BRICS Development Bank. That is why, in prospective terms, the Brazil–Russia relationship might be weakened, especially if we look at the promising cooperation agreement for national defence, and its positive externalities for trade, industry, and technology policies. Nevertheless, the leader of the government, M. Temer, made an official visit to Moscow in 2017 and confirmed the intention to build a strategic partnership, most probably with the intention of increasing meat exports to Russia in order to receive a support from national meat producers (Sputnik 2017).

Meanwhile, Brazilian and Russian exports in bilateral trade increased during 2016–2017 by 27 and 14 percent, respectively (Table 11.1). There was a slight recovery in trade in 2017, but the turnover, estimated at only US$5,230 million, fell far short of the declared US$10 billion target (Figure 11.2). The recent state visit seemed not to have any great effect. It did not deal with a strategic partnership *per se*, but referred to a very broad political dialogue between the countries.

In July 2018, Russian and Brazilian leaders met at the 10th BRICS summit in Johannesburg, South Africa; however, they did not have a bilateral meeting, while President Putin had bilateral talks with the Chinese, Indian, South African and Argentinian leaders. In December 2018, Putin met BRICS leaders during the G20 summit in Buenos Aires, Argentina, and, moreover, participated in a special Russia–India–China (RIC) meeting. Some scholars argue that the Asian dimension has become much more important for Russia within the BRICS framework (REGNUM 2018).

Brazil's newly elected president, J. M. Bolsonaro, will most probably follow the above-mentioned direction of Brazilian policy. His support for President Trump will likely divert attention away from BRICS. However, many experts state that Brazil will not withdraw from BRICS, as it gives an opportunity for balancing relations with the USA (TASS 2018). Moreover, the current government will most probably continue to pay less attention to MERCOSUR integration, focusing more on regional trade agreements.

It is difficult to propose any forecasts for future development. According to the Federal Customs Office of Russia (2018), during January–October 2018, Russian–Brazilian trade decreased by 4.6 percent, while Russian exports to Brazil increased by 26.7 percent, and imports declined by 23.5 percent. It seems that Brazil still has some challenges in terms of economic recovery or could simply be entering a new stage in bilateral cooperation, which will be characterized by divergence in the dimensions of foreign economic policy in both countries.

Russia will probably concentrate its efforts on cooperation development with Asia through bilateral talks as well as in the framework of BRICS. BRICS, as a forum, nowadays faces certain challenges in the search for a future development path. Firstly, there are no signs of further institutionalization of BRICS. Secondly, recent summits were conducted in the format of BRICS+, with more participating countries, so it seems that BRICS is developing more in width than in depth.

Brazil will enhance its relations with Western states and pay less attention to BRICS cooperation. Moreover, given the above-mentioned circumstances, it is unclear whether Russia and Brazil will encourage dialogue within the EAEU–MERCOSUR framework. In our opinion, it is very unlikely, as MERCOSUR has lost its value for Brazil, and establishing RTAs between two customs unions is a very difficult task.

Conclusion

Russian–Brazilian trade relations have been enhanced under certain conditions including institutional ones. The process of this development from the beginning of the twenty-first century can be divided into five stages, as presented in Table 11.3. Each stage can be characterized by different trade dynamics and specific dimensions of Russian and Brazilian foreign policy, as well as the state-to-state institutional framework.

Prior to 2003, Russian–Brazilian trade relations were insignificant. Weak bilateral cooperation reflected the lack of an institutional framework and economic incentives from both countries. During 2004–2008, Russian–Brazilian trade demonstrated continuous growth. This can be explained by the economic development of both countries and an increase of their market attractiveness, but it was also due to changes in the focus of their foreign economic policies. The institutional framework, such as reciprocal state visits and an initiation of the BRICS forum, established the development of state-to-state cooperation, provided the dissemination of business information and encouraged trade growth.

During 2009–2013, BRICS represented an institutional incentive for Russian–Brazilian trade relations. Moreover, state visits frequently conducted by Brazil intensified commercial ties. However, despite favourable institutional conditions, trade volumes did not increase. The main reasons were the impact of the global financial crisis of 2008–2009 on both countries, especially Russia, and the beginning of a political crisis in Brazil. During 2014–2018, the institutional framework was further transformed, not only through BRICS, but also due to the EAEU–MERCOSUR cooperation development. However, bilateral trade decreased due to the Brazilian political and economic crisis and partly because of the Russian economic slowdown. Meanwhile, Russia remained interested in Brazil in order to potentially diversify its trade after the introduction of Western sanctions.

Table 11.3 Development stages of Russian–Brazilian trade relations, 2000 onwards

Years	*Stage characteristics*	*Trade dynamics*	*Russian dimension towards Brazil*	*Brazilian dimension towards Russia*	*Number of state visits (from Russia to Brazil/ from Brazil to Russia)*	*BRICS development*	*RTAs cooperation*
2000–2003	Pre-rapprochement	Steadily low trade	No focus on Latin America	Increase of interests in the Russian market	0 / 1	no	no
2004–2008	Building strategic partnership	Significant trade growth	Re-engagement in Latin America and Brazil as a priority partner	Russia as a new partner due to diversification strategy with more focus on "South–South cooperation"	2 / 2	Establishment of BRICS	Development of dialogue between MERCOSUR and Russia
2009–2013	Cooperation under BRICS	Fluctuating trade	Brazil mainly as a BRICS partner	Russia as a strategic and BRICS partner	1 / 4	Intensification of BRICS cooperation	Slow dialogue between MERCOSUR and Russia/ Customs Union of Russia, Belarus, Kazakhstan
2014–2018	Cooperation with regional focus	Slight trade decrease	Brazil as a MERCOSUR leader and an increased focus due to sanctions	Decreasing interests due to the internal political and economic crisis	1 / 2	Institutionalization of BRICS in New Development Bank	Intensification of EAEU–MERCOSUR cooperation
2019 onwards	Divergence of interests?	Unstable trade development	Turn towards Asia?	Turn towards the West?	–/–	BRICS at the crossroads	EAEU–MERCOSUR RTA?

In general, analysis of trends in Russian–Brazilian trade relations indicates that a better institutional framework of state-to-state cooperation, such as presidential visits and international forums, could be an incentive for broader commercial interactions, but it is only one of the determinants, and not a crucial one. Thus, reciprocal state visits during 2004–2008 supported bilateral trade growth; however, meetings at the higher level during 2009–2013 and 2014–2018 did not provide similar effects. The BRICS initiative was an important driver for the development of cooperation during 2009–2013, but it could not ensure its stable growth. EAEU–MERCOSUR dialogue played a very minor role in the development of commercial ties. The key finding is that economic conditions prevail over politically formed institutional dimensions.

Further research on the non-governmental institutional framework and business networking could present a deeper understanding of the value of institutions in Russian–Brazilian trade. Further studies could focus on the domestic dimensions of Russian–Brazilian trade relations based on analysis of the institutional framework for non-governmental cooperation, as trade policy and diplomacy have complicated links between institutions at different levels.

The current stage of bilateral cooperation seems not to be very optimistic. We assume that even institutional conditions have no strong incentives. Firstly, Russia is likely to focus more on its cooperation with Asian states, while Brazil will probably reconsider its relations and move closer to the West. The BRICS forum, which was an important driver, has faced certain challenges. The EAEU–MERCOSUR agreement could be an institutional impetus; however, taking into account the most probable changes in the Brazilian policy towards MERCOSUR, and the lack of EAEU experience in RTA development, many doubt that it will be signed in the near future. All in all, Brazil will remain an important partner for Russia in Latin America due to comparatively high Brazilian share of Russia's trade with the region, but their bilateral trade will not significantly increase and will remain relatively minor in terms of overall trade for both countries.

Bibliography

Astahov, EM 2009, 'Perspektivy razvitija Latinskoj Ameriki i ee mesto v budushhem miroustrojstve', *Latinskaya Amerika*, no. 7, pp. 32–37.

Astrada, ML and Martín, FM 2013, *Russia and Latin America: From Nation-State to Society of States*, Palgrave Macmillan, New York.

Blank, S and Kim, Y 2015, 'Russia and Latin America: The New Frontier for Geopolitics, Arms Sales and Energy', *Problems of Post-Communism*, vol. 62, no. 3, pp. 159–173.

Cruz, JA 2015, 'Strategic Insights: From Ideology to Geopolitics: Russian Interests in Latin America', *Current Politics and Economics of Russia, Eastern and Central Europe*, vol. 30, no. 1–2, pp. 175–185.

Dabagyan, E 2011, 'Rossijsko-latinoamerikanskie otnoshenija na sovremennom jetape', *Mirovaja jekonomika i mezhdunarodnye otnoshenija*, no. 12, pp. 89–97.

Dantas, AT and Jabbour, EMK 2017, 'Political Economy of the Coup d'État in Brazil', *Problemy Zarzadzania*, vol. 15, pp. 105–114.

Dantas, AT and Koval, AG 2016, 'Brazilian Foreign Economic Policy: Prospects for BRICS', in: *BRICS and Global Governance*, Shanghai People's Publishing House, Shanghai.

Davidov, VM 2010, 'Rusia en América Latina (y viceversa)', *Nueva Sociedad*, no. 226, pp. 4–12.
Davydov, VM 2016, 'Strategic Partnership in the Context of Russian–Latin American Relations', *Herald of the Russian Academy of Sciences*, vol. 86, no. 2, pp. 86–93.
Disdier, AC and Head, K 2008, 'The Puzzling Persistence of the Distance Effect on Bilateral Trade', *The Review of Economics and Statistics*, vol. 90, no. 1, pp. 37–48.
Ellis, E 2016, 'The New Russian Engagement With Latin America: Strategic Position, Commerce, and Dreams of the Past', in: S Santiago (ed.) *Russia in Latin America: Engagement and Its Implications for the United States*, Nova Science Publishers, New York.
Federal Customs Office of Russia 2018, viewed 30 December 2018, http://customs.ru/index2.php?option=com_content&view=article&id=25865&Itemid=1977
França, F 2015, *Brics deixam o mundo menos dependente de uma única fonte de poder*, DW Brasil, viewed 30 November 2018, www.dw.com/pt-br/brics-deixam-o-mundo-menos-dependente-de-uma-%C3%BAnica-fonte-de-poder/a-18567022
Garay Vera, C 2010, 'La Reemergencia de Rusia en el Mundo y América Latina', *Revista Política y Estrategia*, no. 116, pp. 143–168.
Government of the Russian Federation 2008, *Koncepcii dolgosrochnogo social'no-jekonomi cheskogo razvitija Rossijskoj Federacii na period do 2020 goda*, viewed 30 November 2018, http://static.government.ru/media/files/aaooFKSheDLiM99HEcyrygytfmGzrnAX.pdf
ITC Trade Map 2018, viewed 30 December 2018, https://trademap.org/Index.aspx
Jeifets, V 2015, 'Russia Is Coming Back to Latin America: Perspectives and Obstacles', *Anuario de la Integración Regional de América Latina y el Caribe*, no. 11, pp. 90–112.
Jeifets, V, Khadorich, L and Leksyutina, Y 2018, 'Russia and Latin America: Renewal Versus Continuity', *Portuguese Journal of Social Science*, vol. 17, no. 2, pp. 213–228.
Jubran, BM 2012, *Brasil e Rússia: política, comércio, ciência e tecnologia entre 1992 e 2010*, Universidade Federal do Rio Grande do Sul, Porto Alegre.
Keohane, RO 2005, *After Hegemony: Cooperation and Discord in the World Political Economy*, Princeton University Press, Princeton and Oxford.
Koval, AG 2009, 'Perspektivi razvitiya torgovo-ekonomicheskih otnosheniy Rossii so stranami Latinskoy Ameriki v usloviyah finansovogo krizisa', *Vestnik Sankt-Peterburgskogo universiteta. Seriya 5: Ekonomika*, no. 3, pp. 94–104.
Koval, AG 2017, 'Russian Outward Foreign Direct Investments in Latin America: Contemporary Challenges and Prospects', in: K Liuhto, SF Sutyrin and JF Blanchard (eds.) *The Russian Economy and Foreign Direct Investment*, Routledge, London and New York.
Koval, AG and Dantas, A 2013, 'Rússia e Brasil: Evolução Comercial Recente', *Revista del CESLA*, no. 16, pp. 245–256.
Koval, AG and Pioch, M 2017, 'Strany BRIKS v global'nom jekonomicheskom upravlenii na primere ih uchastija v VTO', *Science Journal of Volgograd State University: Global Economic System*, vol. 38, no. 1, pp. 111–121.
Koval, AG and Sutyrin, S 2012, 'Rusia en la OMC: Perspectivas Para América Latina', *Iberoamérica*, no. 4 (67), pp. 5–26.
Koval, AG and Trofimenko, OY 2017, 'Rol' BRIKS vo vneshnetorgovoj politike Rossii', *Mezhdunarodnaja jekonomika*, no. 10, pp. 20–29.
Kremlin 2004, *Zajavlenie dlja pressy po itogam rossijsko-brazil'skih peregovorov*, viewed 30 November 2018, http://kremlin.ru/events/president/transcripts/22703
Kremlin 2008, *Koncepcija vneshnej politiki Rossijskoj Federacii*, viewed 30 November 2018, http://kremlin.ru/acts/news/785

Lopez Arevalo, JA 2018, 'Las relaciones comerciales (intra e interindustriales) de Rusia con América Latina y el Caribe, 2000–2015', *Iberoamérica*, no. 2, pp. 68–97.

Martynov, BF 2015, 'El mundo, Rusia y América Latina: ¿Dónde buscar afinidade?', in: JG Paz and R Román (eds.) *Inteligencia estratégica latinoamericana: Perspectivas y ejes predominantes para la toma de decisiones estratégicas ante un mundo en cambio, antología*, Ministerio de Defensa, Ciudad Autónoma de Buenos Aires.

Maryam, J, Banday, UJ and Mittal, A 2018, 'Trade Intensity and Revealed Comparative Advantage: An Analysis of Intra-BRICS Trade', *International Journal of Emerging Markets*, vol. 13, no. 5, pp. 1182–1195.

Massarova, AR 2013, 'Latinskaja Amerika i Rossija: jevoljucija vzaimnyh vneshnejekonomicheskih interesov (1995–2011 gg.)', *Vestnik RUDN, serija Jekonomika*, no. 1, pp. 51–59.

MDIC 2018, viewed 30 December 2018, www.mdic.gov.br/

Ministry of Economic Development of Russia 2013, *Prognoz dolgosrochnogo social'no-jeko nomicheskogo razvitija Rossijskoj Federacii na period do 2030 goda*, viewed 30 November 2018, http://economy.gov.ru/wps/wcm/connect/9cb190804f0500cd8e6fee008a11733f/%D0%9F%D1%80%D0%BE%D0%B3%D0%BD%D0%BE%D0%B7+2030_%D0%B8%D1%82%D0%BE%D0%B3-21032013.doc?MOD=AJPERES&CACHEID=9cb190804f0500cd8e6fee008a11733f

Ministry of Economic Development of Russia 2014, *Rossija i Brazilija sformirovali Plan dejstvij po torgovo-jekonomicheskomu sotrudnichestvu*, July 15, viewed 30 November 2018, http://economy.gov.ru/minec/press/news/201407155

Ministry of Foreign Affairs of Russia 2013, *Concept of the Foreign Policy of the Russian Federation*, viewed 30 November 2018, www.mid.ru/foreign_policy/official_documents/-/asset_publisher/CptICkB6BZ29/content/id/122186?p_p_id=101_INSTANCE_CptICkB6BZ29&_101_INSTANCE_CptICkB6BZ29_languageId=en_GB

Ministry of Foreign Affairs of Russia 2016, *Foreign Policy Concept of the Russian Federation*, viewed 30 November 2018, www.mid.ru/foreign_policy/news/-/asset_publisher/cKNonkJE02Bw/content/id/2542248?p_p_id=101_INSTANCE_cKNonkJE02Bw&_101_INSTANCE_cKNonkJE02Bw_languageId=en_GB

Ministry of Foreign Affairs of Russia 2018, viewed 30 December 2018, www.mid.ru/ru/home

Moons, SJV and van Bergeijk, PAG 2016, 'Does Economic Diplomacy Work? A Meta-analysis of Its Impact on Trade and Investment', *The World Economy*, vol. 40, no. 2, pp. 336–368.

Nitsch, V 2007, 'State Visits and International Trade', *The World Economy*, vol. 30, no. 12, pp. 1797–1816.

Paniev, Y 2013, 'Cooperacion Economico-Comercial Ruso-Latinoamericana: Adelantos y Deficiencias', *Iberoamérica*, no. 3, pp. 111–127.

Patiño Villa, CA 2014, 'EE.UU.-Rusia: ¿Hacia una reconfiguración geopolítica de América Latina y el Gran Caribe?', *Análisis Político*, vol. 27, no. 82, pp. 196–211.

Pavlova, E 2017, 'A Russian Challenge to Multipolarity? The Prospects for Political Cooperation Between Russia and Latin America', *Problems of Post-Communism*, vol. 64, pp. 1–15.

Pérez-Oviedo, W, Cajas-Guijarro, J and Vallejo, MC 2018, 'South America: Trade and Integration in the New Global Trade Network', in: E Vivares (ed.) *Regionalism, Development and the Post-Commodities Boom in South America*, International Political Economy Series, Palgrave Macmillan, Cham.

Pioch, M 2017, 'BRICS in Trade Clusters: The Prospects of Convergent Trade Policies of Large Emerging Economies', *St Petersburg University Journal of Economic Studies*, vol. 33, no. 2, pp. 282–302.

Rasoulinezhad, E and Jabalameli, F 2018, 'Do BRICS Countries Have Similar Trade Integration Patterns?', *Journal of Economic Integration*, vol. 33, no. 1, pp. 1011–1045.

REGNUM 2018, *Ot amorfnogo BRIKS k perspektive "Bol'shogo" kontinental'nogo al'jansa*, viewed 12 December 2018, https://regnum.ru/news/polit/2529989.html

RIA Novosti 2018, *Memorandum EAJeS i MERKOSUR nahoditsja na zavershajushhej stadii podgotovki*, May 18, viewed 30 December 2018, https://ria.ru/20180518/1520896971.html

Sánchez Ramírez, PT 2010, 'Is a New Climate of Confrontation Between Russia and the United States Possible in Latin America?', *Latin American Policy*, vol. 1, no. 2, pp. 230–243.

Schierhorn, F, Meyfroidt, P, Kastner, Th, Kuemmerle, T, Prishchepov, AV and Müller, D 2016, 'The Dynamics of Beef Trade Between Brazil and Russia and Their Environmental Implications', *Global Food Security*, no. 11, pp. 84–92.

SELA 2011, *La evolución reciente de las relaciones económicas entre la Federación de Rusia y América Latina y el Caribe. Mecanismos institucionales y de cooperación para su fortalecimiento*, SELA, Caracas.

Shchedrov, O 2008, 'Russia's Medvedev in Brazil, Aims to Double Trade', *Reuters*, November 25, viewed 30 November 2018, www.reuters.com/article/brazil-medvedev-idUSN2525831520081125

Shkolyar, NA (ed.) 2013, *Rossija – Latinskaja Amerika: modernizacija jekonomicheskih otnoshenij*, VAVT, Moscow.

Sizonenko, A 2016, 'The Continuity Factor in Relations between Russia and Latin America', *International Affairs*, vol. 62, no. 4, pp. 106–115.

Sputnik 2017, *O que Temer foi fazer na Rússia*? viewed 30 November 2018, https://br.sputniknews.com/sputnik_explica/201706228702461-temer-visita-russia-crise-jbs/

TASS 2018, *Jeksperty: novyj prezident Brazilii ostanetsja v BRIKS, nesmotrja na orientaciju na SShA*, viewed 30 November 2018, https://tass.ru/politika/5734450

Thomé, KM, Vieira, LM and dos Santos, AC 2012, 'International Marketing Channels for Brazilian Beef: Comparison Between Russia and the United Kingdom', *Journal of East-West Business*, vol. 18, no. 4, pp. 301–320.

Tuktarov, RY and Fedorenko, KP 2015, 'Sovremennoe sostojanie i osnovnye napravlenija razvitija torgovo-jekonomicheskih otnoshenij mezhdu Rossiej i Braziliej', *Rossijskij vneshnejekonomicheskij vestnik*, no. 10, pp. 47–57.

van Bergeijk, PAG 2009, *Economic Diplomacy and the Geography of International Trade*, Edward Elgar Publishing, Cheltenham and Northampton.

Volpe, MC, Estevadeordal, A, Gallo, A and Luna, J 2010, 'Information Barriers, Export Promotion Institutions, and the Extensive Margin of Trade', *Review of World Economics*, vol. 146, no. 1, pp. 91–111.

Yakovlev, PP 2016, 'Rossija i Latinskaja Amerika: Parametry Strategicheskogo Partnerstva', *Latinskaya Amerika*, no. 1, pp. 5–14.

Yakovlev, PP 2017, 'Rossija – Latinskaja Amerika: strategija proryva na rynki nesyr'evoj produkcii', *Latinskaya Amerika*, no. 12, pp. 15–28.

12 Russian automotive industry

Beyond import substitution and export-led industrialization

Dmitry I. Tonkov[1]

Introduction

The decline of industrial production in Russia in the 1990s exacerbated the need for active industrial policy in a number of strategically important sectors – the automotive industry was one of them. Early in the 2000s, the Russian Government introduced a complex of stimulus so that the industry could increase their competitiveness and keep up with the increasing local demand for vehicles. Import substitution, as a tool to attract investment and foster technological development, became the flagship concept of the strategy.

Russia's accession to the WTO in 2012 commemorated a major shift in Russia's trade policy. On the one hand, it limited the policy space in terms of availability of classical import substitution tools – high import barriers for ready-made goods and administrative requirements for sourcing components and raw materials in the local market. On the other hand, Russia obtained serious opportunities for multilateral trade law enforcement within the organization when foreign partners do not honour their obligations. In principle, this could ensure better market access for exported products.

Unlike export-oriented steel and chemical production frequently listed by experts and officials among the main "beneficiaries" of accession, the balance of costs and benefits of the WTO membership for the automotive industry in Russia was perceived far less optimistically (Kukol 2012; Faskhiev 2013). At the final stage of accession negotiations, those who feared losing access to beneficial instruments of active industrial policy became especially vocal. At the same time, the most active "demandeurs" – the European Union, the United States, Japan, and Korea, which represented the major foreign investors in the industry – pushed for a liberal trade and investment regime. As a result, Russia's WTO obligations in this area were discussed virtually until the last day of negotiations, and the Russian delegation managed to preserve the support system until July 1, 2018.

Despite significant progress over the last 15 years – attraction of investments of all major producers, self-sufficiency in ready-made vehicles, and an increase of localization – the strategy has hardly led to the creation of full-fledged automobile industry. It remains dependent on foreign owners, suppliers, technologies, and markets. Given this, policy priorities are gradually changing. Nowadays, the

Russian automotive industry needs to shift to qualitative development, open up foreign markets, and expand its exports.

This chapter will consider the evolution of the Russian support policy in the automotive sector through the prism of trade policy theory. The first section provides an overview of the theoretical concepts of import substitution and export-led industrialization and elaborates on the methodology and information sources used in this study. The second section discusses the development of Russian trade-related industrial policies in the automotive industry, where the results and the outlook for the future are provided in the last section. The conclusion summarizes the main deliverables of the study.

Theoretical and methodological background

Theoretical basis

It is useful to analyse Russian trade and industrial policy in the automotive industry within the theoretical framework of import substitution and export-led industrialization strategies. In the context of trade liberalization under the WTO and expansion of preferential trade agreements nowadays, any of the strategies are seldom employed in pure form. Generally, they originate from the long-lasting dispute from the era of Adam Smith and David Ricardo, between advocates of free trade on the one hand, and proponents of protectionism on the other. Modern studies are mostly retrospective and based on the consideration of the Latin American and Asian experiences in the period between the 1930s and 1980s. By the end of this period, import substitution policies in many countries led to macroeconomic failures and debt crises. Consequently, governments shifted to export orientation, which generated several "success stories", especially among the "Newly Industrialized Countries" of East Asia.

Import substitution is generally characterized as a policy of limiting imports of consumer goods and stimulating domestic production of such products. For example, in the automotive sector, these goals are normally achieved through import barriers for finished products with a simultaneous reduction in tariffs for components and equipment, as well as other forms of incentives for domestic production.

Following the classical trade theory, certain elements of import substitution may be justified only if an "infant industry" needs protection. Classical scholars perceive this argument with substantial reservations. For example, Baldwin (1969) strongly criticizes "infant industry" protection through tariffs. He suggests that if costs incurred at the initial phase are later compensated by profits, the investment may be economically sound and, in principle, the industry must obtain financing in the capital market. To get protection, the industry must generate positive externalities for the society that are not remunerated (public goods). However, a tariff-induced move of productive factors into new industries cannot guarantee knowledge acquisition and a socially efficient allocation of resources. Instead of horizontal tariff protection, as the scholar concludes, policy-makers should rather use more targeted measures such as subsidies stimulating desired activities. A similar conclusion is drawn by Vousden (1990, p. 31), asserting that the best means of achieving a target level of output is an output subsidy, while a tariff on imports is the best means of restricting imports. With respect to local content requirements, Vousden suggests that content protection schemes achieve target levels of output of the intermediate goods at a lower welfare cost than a tariff (Vousden 1990, p. 43).

Despite recommendations of the classical scholars, an "infant industry" and other protectionist arguments are widely spread in policy-making. Many of them are based on a value judgement as to the right mode of welfare distribution. As Haberler (1961, p. 237) notes, "some arguments which are scientifically quite untenable and which can be refuted in a few sentences, have the greatest influence in practice, in Parliament, and in the discussion of the subject by interested parties and by the Press". The inclination to protectionism may also be reinforced by "market failures", such as capital market imperfections (high interest rates, risk-averse policies of banks, etc.), inability of markets to compensate new industry "pioneers" for the costs incurred when developing new products (poor enforcement of intellectual property rights), or market dominance of established market players (insufficient anti-monopoly laws, regulation, and/or enforcement). In addition, the choice of support instruments depends on the level of financial and bureaucratic infrastructure. Given specific circumstances of under-developed countries, their decision-makers may consider import duties as a more transparent and effective tool compared to direct subsidies (Linnemann et al. 1987, pp. 72–73).

The afore-mentioned publications established a classical approach to the issue of import substitution. Subsequent studies complement the theoretical structures with sector-specific empirical research, which shows that import substitution has several drawbacks, especially if applied in the automotive industry (for example, Chen 2016; Nidhiprabha 2016; Smitka 2016). Firstly, it may be inexpedient to support the creation of industries for which the country has no comparative advantages. Continuous sheltering of production without efforts towards the formation of long-term advantages can hardly allow the building up of an independent, mature industry. Secondly, import substitution systems are usually complex and include both tariff and non-tariff barriers, which seriously distort market incentives and establish imbalanced industry structures. Thirdly, the increase of domestic prices raises incentives for entry into the market, stimulating excessive investment in production capacities. As a result, individual firms do not benefit from economies of scale and do not invest in the development of new products or costs reduction. Consequently, the addition of local value and positive effects on employment are limited, as the focus on localization of the final stage of production leaves the component industry underdeveloped.

While import barriers may stimulate industrialization, their side effects, as illustrated above, eventually necessitate seeking to find alternatives. The classical solution, advocated by such institutions as the IMF and World Bank as a part of balance-of-payments assistance, is export-oriented industrialization (Linnemann et al. 1987, p. 85). This approach is characterized by the desire to use demand in foreign markets to increase the scale of domestic production. Accordingly, an emphasis is placed on the promotion of exports, including seeking liberalization of foreign trade regimes abroad, reduction of import duties for inputs and subsidies (for example, support directly linked to export performance or preferences for export-oriented special economic zones). An important element of this strategy is the stimulation of foreign investment inflow through the creation of favourable conditions for the transfer of production to the territory of the recipient country. A downside of this measure is an increased dependence of production on external demand shocks and decisions of foreign multinational corporations (Nidhiprabha 2016, pp. 129–132).

A comprehensive textbook analysis of the effects of these two policies carried out by Hout (1996, pp. 617–619) based on a data set for 84 developing countries reveals that overall import substitution has a negative impact on economic growth, especially if policies are implemented over a long period. At the same time, the study does not substantiate the positive economic effects of export promotion. However, from the structural point of view, orientation on export in contrast to import substitution largely stimulates the accumulation of capital and the shifting of developing countries from raw materials and agricultural specialization towards higher degrees of processing. Another finding suggests that, despite deeply entrenched views of theorists that these two strategies are mutually exclusive, countries, in practice, can apply elements of both industrialization strategies simultaneously.

Many developing countries carried out the structural transition from import substitution to export orientation in the 1970s and 1980s with a view to overcome the negative effects of the former strategy and expand demand through external markets. Experience in this regard is diverse. For example, Turkey followed the recommendations of the IMF and the World Bank but failed to effectively convert the growth of the export-oriented industries' profits into growth in employment and investment (Onanaran and Stockhammer 2005, pp. 66–67). The path of Korea, on the contrary, was more successful due to active state policy, especially in the financial and investment spheres. The Korean experience has shown that the structural transition should be gradual, and opening-up should be dictated by the ability of local industries to sustain international competition. In particular, Korgun and Sutyrin (2016, p. 34) concluded that throughout the GATT multilateral tariff negotiations, Korea's position was protectionist with respect to vulnerable sectors (agriculture and "infant industries") and gradually transitioned more to a free-trade model when strengthening new industries required increased access to foreign markets and cheaper inputs.

An interesting view on import substitution *versus* export orientation pertains to institutionalists (Reinert 2009; Cimoli et al. 2009a). They put forward the idea that "emulation" (as a synonym of "imitation") rather than a focus on "static" comparative advantage is a natural response to underdevelopment of an industry if policy-makers perceived it as significant for the economy. Following the institutional approach, if countries remained within existing comparative advantages, there would be little hope for them to create new industries. Consequently, the key factors of successful "emulation" are the ability of economic institutions to improve technological training and generate new comparative advantages. A retrospective look at successful examples of industrialized countries prompts that they adhered to the concept of "first imitation, then comparative advantage" and necessarily practiced "infant industry" protection at the initial stage. In other words, they adopted an "emulation" approach in the catching-up stage of development. Then they chose the moment for the market-opening phase when domestic producers were sufficiently independent so as not to suffer from external competition and afterwards, tried to impose a "static" concept of comparative advantage on trade policies of other countries when negotiating terms of trade. This process evolves naturally, as a strengthened industry "outgrows" the domestic market and seeks to expand sales through external demand to obtain positive effects of production scale. The authors estimated that Great Britain exercised tariff protection for 250 years, the United States – 100 years, and Korea – 40 years.

The theoretical debate around import substitution and export-led industrialization policies, especially if national contexts are considered, can hardly be compressed into several pages of this chapter. However, in order to provide a theoretical framework for this study, the views of different scholars may be summarized as follows.

At the initial phase, where a domestic industry is immature, despite all warnings from classical theorists, governments are seriously incentivized to limit imports. Conventional wisdom suggests that imported products should be eliminated from the marketplace in order to make the domestic industry flourish. Administrative limitations might complement this choice. If implemented effectively, this policy leads to the sought-after quantitative production expansion, but at the same time, entails overcapacity and limits qualitative development based on comparative advantages.

After that, when imports are squeezed and the industry "outgrows" the domestic market, its further prospects of scale expansion are directly linked to exports. Accumulated overcapacity is another argument for firms to seek new markets. Activist governments in such situations take up the promotion of exports. Here again, classical theorists' preoccupations about the harmful effects of such support in terms of social welfare are hardly taken into account.

However, in view of the author, both of these policies are shooting past the main target. While this study acknowledges a significant role of trade-related measures, the backbone idea is that the fundamental task of effective trade and industrial policy should be the shift from quantitative to qualitative growth and creation of new comparative advantages required for effective participation in international trade of the new industries. This approach goes along the same lines of the mentioned institutionalists' views and requires government action beyond pure trade policy.

Methodological basis

The study attempts to consider the impact of the trade-related support policies on the automotive industry of Russia since 2000. Their effectiveness is assessed by looking at the appropriate economic characteristics such as production, trade, and others. Based on this, the study will discuss possible ways forward.

The time span selected for the study covers nearly 20 years. Given its focus on trade policy measures, it heavily relies on publicly available official strategic and regulatory documents of the Russian Government, which provide an important source of hands-on data, realistic assessments, and strategic vision of the industry's prospects. For trade data, we rely on the United Nations [UN] "Comtrade Database", since the Federal Customs Service of the Russian Federation publishes trade data only for three preceding years. Federal support volumes may be approximately computed based on the legislation on implementation of the federal budget. Regional subsidies are normally marginal and are outside of the scope of this study. Some aggregate figures on local production and markets are drawn from industrial consulting companies.

The study intentionally aggregates data for all segments of the automotive market – cars, light commercial vehicles, trucks, and buses. Regional market differences are not considered. Such aggregation relies on the fact that, as the next section reveals, the Russian Government tends to apply "horizontal" incentives and the same general principles of industrial policy for the entire industry. Of course, there are differences, especially when it comes to specific subsidy programmes and the Government's ownership of some producers' shares, but these particularities seem to be minimal and do not change the overall picture.

It is worth noting that in terms of localization, the chapter relies on official estimations of the Russian Government. Independent calculations of this parameter would require some confidential business data. Also, we avoided making an interesting, though technically sophisticated and laborious estimation of the budget revenue forgone due to the "Industrial Assembly" regime of taxation of imported components. It would require 10-digit level import data and tracing nomenclature changes throughout the period of analysis. Instead, a rough estimation of such benefits is provided.

The last, but not the least, trade policy analysis must pay due attention to the international legal framework. Given a relatively narrow range of preferential trade agreements that Russia is a party to, we primarily keep in mind the multilateral rules. Probably, the most important among them are the binding of import duties (article II of the GATT), prohibition of subsidies contingent upon import substitution and export performance (article 3 of the SCM Agreement), and prohibition of requirements to use domestic products instead of imported ones (article 2 of the TRIMs Agreement). This framework limits governments' freedom in terms of a direct influence on the procurement or marketing decisions of private actors.

Evolution of trade and industrial policy in the automotive industry of Russia

Prerequisites for state support and the "Old Industrial Assembly" (2000–2010)

Before the financial crisis of 2008, the Russian automotive market was growing rapidly. This happened mainly because, during these years, purchasing power together with consumer lending increased and the national currency was strengthening. Despite this, the share of Russian manufacturers in the local automotive market was constantly decreasing because of their technological backwardness combined with a notably liberal import regime for imported vehicles, especially used ones. Previous dominance of the Russian carmakers in domestic market was nearly over.

In order to create conditions for foreign investment inflow into the Russian automotive industry, and to ensure its technological development and to create new jobs, in 2005, the Russian Government adopted a set of measures aimed at import substitution. This investment regime, heavily relying on trade policy measures, was called "Industrial Assembly". The main reasons for its introduction included expectations of growth in the Russian automotive market, shifting consumer preferences in favour of imported brands and desire to reverse stagnation in the domestic production.

Firstly, the Government increased import customs duties on ready-made cars. For new vehicles, rates were set close to prohibitive levels but allowed penetration into niches with low price elasticity (high-price segment). For cars and buses, the duty amounted to 30 percent, for light commercial vehicles and trucks – 25 percent.[2] For used vehicles, combined rates with almost prohibitive specific parts rates depending on the engine volume were introduced. Then, over time, the Government gradually increased these rates.

Secondly, the Government introduced separate tariff lines into the customs tariff for the declaration of imported components for "Industrial Assembly" purposes to ensure that they are used exclusively in the manufacturing of finished products – vehicles and auto components – in Russia (Government of the Russian Federation [GRF] 2005, 2006).[3] Duties on such components were set at the levels from 0 to 5 percent with a prevalence of the duty-free regime.

Through these two tariff measures, the Russian Government managed to effectively create advantages for methods of investment penetration into the Russian car market, i.e. for transfer of the final stage of production of vehicles to the territory of Russia. The total benefit for the "Industrial Assembly" participants may be roughly estimated as the difference between the value of imported cars after customs clearance at rates of 25–30 percent and the value of auto components after customs clearance at rates of 0–5 percent plus the cost of their assembly in Russia. In the same vein, for component producers, the regime ensured benefits through the difference between the value of the imported final components and the value of sub-components taxed at preferential rates plus assembly costs. In accordance with the principle of tariff escalation, Russian duties on components were kept at a low level but were still, on average, 5–10 percent higher than for "Industrial Assembly". Such a relatively low margin of preference was compensated by localization requirements for carmakers, ensuring stable demand for domestic components, as discussed below.

Thirdly, the Government established a system of requirements for investors wishing to obtain customs benefits. At the first stage of the so-called "Old Industrial Assembly" (Minjekonomrazvitija Rossii [MED] 2005), which was in force from 2005 to 2010, the investors were offered to undertake rather soft commitments.

They had to create production capacities only in the amount of 25,000 cars per year and were allowed during the first 1.5–2.5 years to produce using imported semi-knocked down (SKD) kits.[4] Only afterwards did the regime prescribe to organize welding, painting, and assembly at the assembly premises, i.e. to shift to the production using complete knocked down (CKD) kits.[5] After another two years, the company had to reduce the value of imported components by 10 percent. After 3.5 years, this figure had to reach 20 percent, and after 4.5 years – 30 percent. The contracts between the Government and the investors were signed for the term of eight years.

Overall, the "Old Industrial Assembly" sought to attract investments in car assembly, though small-scale and quite atomized. In addition, foreign manufacturers had to shift their production from SKD to CKD mode.

Launch of the "New Industrial Assembly" (2010–2012)

Given a limited success of the "Old Industrial Assembly",[6] in 2010, the investment regime was modified in order to make its requirements more conducive of the establishment of a full-fledged industry. The so-called "New Industrial Assembly" (MED 2010) provided for the same benefits with a significant revision of requirements and an extension of the agreement maximum until the end of 2020. The new conditions required an increase in the existing production capacities to 350,000 units per year or the establishment of new ones with a production capacity of at least 300,000 units per year. Local added value of 60 percent had to be achieved within six years, domestically produced engines and/or gearboxes had to be installed on at least 30 percent of the produced cars, stamping of body parts and R&D centres must have been organized within four years, and the use of SKD was limited to 5 percent of production. For manufacturers of automotive components, the agreements were extended until the end of 2020 under the condition of reaching 40 percent localization and performing certain technological operations at the assembly plant.

However, some requirements were eased. Firstly, aggregate capacity could be achieved in cooperation with other companies.[7] Accordingly, the companies focused on cooperation within production clusters, which did not necessarily lead to an increase of production concentration. Secondly, if the "Old Industrial Assembly" was about the final reduction of the list of imported components by 30 percent, the new formula of localization calculation, in fact, represented a ratio of all costs incurred by the enterprise locally to the ex-works prices of produced cars. Therefore, the actual level of "product localization" could have been much lower than the required 60 percent. Thirdly, the performance criteria of the R&D centres were not elaborated, leaving room for "nominal" compliance.

Accession to the WTO, recycling fee (2013), and cut-off date for "Industrial Assembly" (July 1, 2018)

The accession of Russia to the WTO brought two additional complexities for policy-makers. On the one hand, over time, import duties for the whole range of motor vehicles had to be reduced to bound levels. On the other hand, WTO-incompatible localization requirements and tariff preferences for importers of auto components had to be abolished by July 1, 2018 in accordance with delayed implementation conditions negotiated as part of Russia's accession package.

As we mentioned in the introductory part, the automotive industry anticipated negative consequences of Russia's accession to the WTO. Some Russian scholars also made gloomy assessments (for example, Faskhiev 2013). The main reason for such conclusions was the WTO commitment to reduce import duties on motor vehicles (HS 87), which had been agreed to with key trading partners before the introduction of active industrial policy in the early 2000s. In particular, the transition period for passenger cars had to be completed by 2019 with the final bound rate of 15 percent, for trucks – by 2015 (10 percent), and for light commercial vehicles – by 2017 (10 percent). An even larger concern was the reduction of the prohibitive specific part of duties on used vehicles that could again open the door for their imports.

It was considered that until the "infant industry"[8] moves to a sustainable development model (large-scale production based on a local component base and local R&D), import barriers were needed. According to official estimates, with the reduction of import duties in all segments of the market, the launch of new models could become unprofitable, and the share of imports of finished cars in the Russian market would grow significantly. Specifically, the following prospects were predicted (Minpromtorg Rossii 2010, chapter 3.3.2):

a sharp increase in the share of new and used imported vehicles in the segments of light commercial vehicles, trucks, and buses;
b overall decline of the share of domestic automotive products in Russia;
c significant slowdown in the development of the component industry and increased risk of failure to achieve the declared volumes of localization;
d negative reassessment of the Russian market attractiveness by investors, which could result in the loss of full-fledged automotive industry.

The stakes were high. A measure "designed to compensate for the sharp change in external factors influencing" the automotive industry (Minpromtorg Rossii 2010, chapter 3.3.2) was the so-called recycling fee (Federal Law of the Russian Federation No 128-FZ 2012). The measure was positioned as an ecological one: it was assumed that financial resources accumulated through the fee would create a recycling industry for decommissioned vehicles (at the time of introduction of this measure, the Russian car park accounted for 36 million units, which would have to be scrapped in 10–20 years).

It turned out that after the introduction of the measure, import growth predictions have never materialized. Such an effect could have been caused by two factors. Firstly, the fee rates were equal or in many cases, exceeded the reduction of the effective margin of tariff protection. Secondly, only imported cars were subject to the fee while domestic producers could provide a "guarantee of scrappage". It seemed to Russia's trading partners that as a result of the measure, they were deprived of certain long-awaited advantages of the car market liberalization following Russian accession to the WTO. Such "sentiments" were so high that Russia's "WTO honeymoon" (a period where more experienced WTO members refrain from challenging measures of a recently acceded country) ended during the first year of membership. In the summer of 2013, the EU and Japan filed requests for consultations on the issue of the recycling fee, claiming an alleged violation of the national treatment rule under Article III of the GATT (WTO 2013a, 2013b).[9]

Naturally, Russia had serious grounds to defend the fee under Article XX of the GATT as being a measure designed to protect the life and health of people and animals. However, eventually, it was decided to extend the application of the fee to all market participants. As a result, the EU and Japan's claims have never been developed at the panel stage.

Were Russia's trading partners satisfied? According to further discussions in the WTO, it was unlikely (WTO 2014a, 2014b). The United States, supported by the EU and Japan, accused Russia of introducing large-scale subsidies in parallel with the extension of the fee to domestic producers. Opponents in the WTO asserted that such actions could have been aimed at compensating for the fees paid and *de facto* maintaining the initial effects of the measure. It is not the aim of this chapter to consider these allegations. However, in order to complete the picture, it may be noted that the alleged "linkage" between fee payment and subsidies was not set out in any official documents, and the amounts of fees collected and subsidies granted have never been equal.

Now we turn to the second major Russian WTO accession obligation relevant to the purpose of this study. The period of temporary exemption of the "Industrial Assembly" from the application of the WTO rules ended on July 1, 2018. From that date, all WTO-inconsistent elements of the measure should have been abolished.

A serious challenge for policy-makers would be to find an alternative to the mechanism of preferential import duties. Taking into account article 1.1 of the Federal Law of the Russian Federation No 190-FZ (2013), the decision suggests: to compensate the duty payments by state subsidies. However, this path is quite risky in the context of an eventual dispute, where a WTO panel may find a *de facto* retention of customs privileges. At the same time, if the compensatory measures remain in place only until 2020, given the normal length of WTO disputes (normally at least two years), such a "temporary" *de facto* violation could become effective, but this is undesirable from the point of view of honouring Russia's WTO obligations.

Localization requirements, taking into account the development of the WTO dispute-settlement practices, could be transformed as follows. The requirement to create capacities for serial production of not less than 300,000 cars could be retained. The same applies to the establishment of R&D centres and the production of car bodies. The localization formula should undergo serious changes in order to abandon any linkage to import indicators. There is an option of focusing on the costs of a company within Russia, including expenses on manufacturing operations, investment, and other "trade neutral" costs. However, even these seemingly trade-neutral conditions should be carefully considered in light of the development of the WTO law interpretation.[10] As for the requirement for the installation of engines and gearboxes produced in Russia on at least 30 percent of cars, it would need a substantial review, regardless of the legal practice.

The above speculations are certainly without prejudice to the Russian Government's position on the issue. They only show that there are prospects for a careful transformation (not abolition) of the "Industrial Assembly" and related measures within the WTO.[11] In any case, further steps must rely on the assessment of the results of this policy.

Assessment of policy results and ways forward

Policy results

As the transitional period for the "Industrial Assembly" comes to an end and the Russian Government has to elaborate new measures in the automotive sector, there is a need to estimate the results of previous policies. A logical way to structure such an analysis is to single out parameters whose positive changes had probably been anticipated.[12] Based on the measures' structures, these may be the reduction in import dependence in motor vehicles; reduction in import dependence in auto components (localization); increase in international competitiveness. Table 12.1 provides the supporting data.

(i) Reduction of import dependence in motor vehicles

During the period under consideration, the increase of import tariffs combined with the stimulus for investment effectively reduced imports of both new and used vehicles.

Concerning used cars, a study based on official customs statistics ('Issledovanie Drom.ru' 2017) suggests that under the free trade regime, the quantity of imported used cars reached its peak in 2002, almost 500,000 units. After the first increase of import duties, imports in Russia dropped to 200–300,000. However, despite barriers, until 2008, the purchasing power growth outpaced internal output, and as a result, the quantity of imported used cars again reached 500,000 units. In 2009, after another round of tightening barriers, the import volumes finally fell to negligible levels, opening a large share of the Russian market for local manufacturers. Since then, the volume fluctuated near 20,000 units.

Import barriers for new vehicles were less stringent; therefore, imports of these products correlated with the purchasing power of Russian consumers. During the crisis and currency depreciation of 2009, imports of all vehicles dropped by four times, and imports of used vehicle almost disappeared due to additional tariff measures. After 2009, import dependence fluctuated between 35.7 percent and 41.5 percent. The situation changed again amid the crisis of 2014–2015: imports fell by double and import dependence decreased to 23.3 percent against the backdrop of a new wave of currency depreciation. By 2017, despite a slight recovery of the market, the share of imports continued to decline.

Table 12.1 Russian automotive industry data (aggregated figures for segments of cars, light commercial vehicles, trucks, and buses), 2005–2017

Index	*Unit*	*2005*	*2006*	*2007*	*2008*	*2009*	*2010*	*2011*	*2012*	*2013*	*2014*	*2015*	*2016*	*2017*
Domestic industry and market														
Domestic production	thd. units	1257	1501	1667	1799	722	1406	2001	2230	2176	1898	1383	1308	1552
Domestic sales	thd. units	n/a	1881	2367	2928	1466	1900	2651	2935	2777	2491	1602	1426	1596
Total capacities	mln. units	2.1	2.1	2.2	2.5	2.6	2.7	2.9	2.9	3.5	3.6	3.5	3.6	3.7
Capacity utilization	percent	59.8	71.5	75.8	72.0	27.8	52.1	69.0	76.9	62.2	52.7	39.5	37.4	44.3
Federal subsidies														
Total federal subsidies (direct grants or credit buy-backs)	₽ million	0	0	0	0	644	23985	31563	11173	10939	75340	9857	127278	164107
Federal subsidies per domestic vehicle	₽ thousand	0	0	0	0	0.9	17.1	15.8	5.0	5.0	39.7	71.3	97.3	105.8
Import (new and used)														
Import value	US$ million	8531	14026	24711	34863	9203	12776	21517	24526	20313	15464	7459	7179	8866
Import volume	thd. units	829	1120	1742	2144	548	748	1099	1214	991	770	374	289	301
Imported vehicle average price	US$ thousand	10.3	12.5	14.2	16.3	16.8	17.1	19.6	20.2	20.5	20.1	20.0	24.9	32.9
Import dependence	percent	n/a	59.5	73.6	73.2	37.4	39.4	41.5	41.4	35.7	30.9	23.3	20.3	18.9
Export (new and used)														
Export value	US$ million	1205	1415	1780	1817	659	520	857	1598	2193	2072	1595	1491	1738
Export volume	thd. units	182	179	187	177	57	52	78	136	169	155	119	84	101
Exported vehicle average price	US$ thousand	7	8	10	10	12	10	11	12	13	13	13,4	17,7	17,2
Share of vehicles produced for export	percent	14.5	11.9	11.2	9.9	7.9	3.7	3.9	6.1	7.8	8.2	8.6	6.4	6.5
Average price ratio between exported and imported vehicles		0.6	0.6	0.7	0.6	0.7	0.6	0.6	0.6	0.6	0.7	0.7	0.7	0.5

Sources: Author's calculations of data from Garant (2018), Minpromtorg Rossii (2010), PwC (2017), Shtanov (2016), United Nations (2018), and Vercity (2018).

It seems that purchasing power fluctuations affected imports more seriously than domestic production. Partially this may be explained by the fact that Russian producers focused on lower market niches while leaving more luxurious and less voluminous segments for imports (average price ratio between exported and imported vehicles fluctuated around 0.5–0.7). Another possible explanation – the effect of excess capacity that made local producers aggressively engage in price competition (in 2015–2017, only about 40 percent of capacities were used). And the third reason is the effect of subsidies that have constantly been growing since 2009 up to ₽105.8 thousand per vehicle in 2017. For the car segment, if a vehicle's price is near US$10,000, the benefit might equal 15–20 percent of the price. If benefits of "Industrial Assembly" are factored in (as roughly calculated above), the overall benefits of local producers might amount to 20–25 percent.

Overall, the system of import substitution measures combined with exogenous factors has successfully shifted the domestic market to locally produced vehicles. However, at what cost?

Corresponding to theoretical predictions, active import substitution entailed capacity expansion up to unsustainable levels. The volume of idle facilities was constantly growing: after 2009, less than 30 percent of the capacity was used, and by 2012, only the car segment succeeded in rebounding, reaching 81 percent while truck and bus manufacturers remained idle at near 50 percent (Minpromtorg Rossii 2010, chapter 3.2.1). Afterwards, this tendency only exacerbated.

Another important consequence of import substitution – the lack of production concentration measured as the average volume of output per vehicle platform (GRF 2018, chapter II.1, para. 11). Vehicle platform is a mechanical base used for the creation of various apparently dissimilar models. Platform sharing allows reduced development costs of the vehicle's mechanical parts and increased scales of production of components shared among different models. The current scale of production of cars per one platform in Russia is 1.5–3 times less than in developing countries (India, Thailand, Mexico) and 4–7 times less than in the leading producers.

Import substitution, therefore, comes at a price. Capacity expansion – the central target of the "Industrial Assembly" – showed its backside when the internal market reached its ceiling. Idle facilities put financial pressure on the industry and took away resources from qualitative development, while low production concentration discourages localization.

(ii) Reduction of import dependence in auto components (localization)

The goal to increase localization through various support measures became a tricky one. The official assessment of the Russian sectoral policy during the 2000s was far from optimistic. MIT (2010, "Introduction") stated: "The results of the state policy to attract foreign investment in the automotive industry were positive, first of all, for end users, while insufficient for the full-fledged development of the industry". The analysis leading to this conclusion revealed that the overall growth of the components market in the review period was followed by a constant excess of import growth rates over the growth of local production. This effect was attributed to the increase of the market share of international automakers with low localized assembly facilities in Russia and unchanged production volumes of national brands, which, in turn, were undergoing a process of delocalization and increased reliance on imported components. Besides, the production of the least sophisticated components developed most of all, as they did not require a developed technological base.

"New Industrial Assembly", of course, partially cured this situation by imposing more stringent localization criteria but did not change it dramatically. As the GRF (2018, chapter II.1, paras. 6–8) recognized, international companies had the ability to optimize indicators of localization, for example, through manipulations with imported components values. Furthermore, these producers had limited incentives to transfer their competencies to the Russian market. As a result, today the industry is more dependent on imported components than in 2008. In the segment of cars, the share of imported components is over 60 percent (in 2008 – less than 40 percent). For trucks, the figure is over 25 percent (in 2008 – near 10 percent). In parallel, the dependence on imports of components production has also increased. For example, for engines, in 2016, it amounted to 26 percent while in 2008 it was less than 2 percent.

Therefore, numerous localization requirements of "Industrial Assembly" have only partially ensured the desired result. The official assessments combined with the data in Table 12.1 suggest that an abrupt increase in self-reliance in 2009 in terms of ready-made vehicles was not followed by the same tendency in the components industry. This could be explained by at least three factors. Firstly, insufficient production concentration, as mentioned in sub-paragraph (i), did not induce bringing components production to the Russian territory. Secondly, as mentioned earlier, localization requirements were so structured that production of the most sophisticated parts and engineering competencies could be left abroad. Thirdly, there were no direct grants from the federal budget to this sub-industry, and the benefits from participation in the "Industrial Assembly" were not sufficient.

(iii) International competitiveness

Although sectoral policies in the automotive industry have been aimed at "catching up" with foreign competitors in the local market and "keeping up" with demand growth, the long-term underlying aim, as follows from the official documents, must have been the establishment of a full-fledged internationally competitive industry so that it could function without state support. In order to measure this parameter, it is useful to look at exports data.

During the two waves of domestic market growth (2005–2008 and 2009–2012), the Russian producers presumably tried to secure and expand their market shares, although capacity utilization figures showed their ability to expand production for export. However, the system of incentives has never put a serious emphasis on export performance. As a result, even the weakening Russian ruble in 2014–2015 and subsequent years did not ensure international competitiveness of the Russian vehicles. Overall, in the period between 2005 and 2017, the share of products destined for export decreased from 14.5 percent to 6.5 percent.

According to GRF (2018, Annex 2), by 2025, the domestic market may recover to the level of only 2.6 million units (including cars – 2.23 million). Butov (2017, p. 60) is even less optimistic, predicting that the car market will continue to decrease down to the level of 722,000 units by 2024. Both figures are significantly lower than the accumulated capacities of the Russian industry (near 3.7 million units per year as of 2017). Therefore, Russian automakers no longer can rely exclusively on the domestic market, and export expansion is a vital element of the industry's recovery.

Ways forward

The analysis in the previous sub-part shows that the Russian automotive industry has seemingly exhausted the potential of import substitution and should shift to export expansion. As theory suggests, this represents a natural way of development when the industry matures. Nevertheless, we are not there yet: negative consequences of import substitution have already emerged, while international competitiveness has not yet been reached.

Classical free-trade theory would suggest that the way chosen by the Government may be wrong, and the industry eventually needs market adjustment: lifting trade barriers, localization requirements, and support measures so that production and capacities could adjust to market demand. However, in such a scenario, it is highly likely that the emerging car industry would be quickly wiped out given that Russian comparative advantages in automotive production are still quite limited.

Is it affordable? Probably, not. The assembly of ready-made cars employed 170, 600 people in 2016 (Butov 2017, p. 11), and it ensured employment of 3.5 million people in related industries (GRF 2018, chapter 2, para. 3). In addition, the industry is in the middle of transformation and cessation of active industrial policy would probably reduce to zero past state investments (subsidies, forgone government revenue, acquisition of shares, etc.).

Then a tricky question of choice among future policies emerges. As outlined in the previous sub-part, three issues need to be resolved: overcapacity combined with low production concentration, insufficient localization, and international non-competitiveness.

The basic target would be to maintain self-sufficiency in motor vehicles (at least in lower market segments) to ensure demand for localized components and raise production concentration. For this reason, at least some elements of import substitution would be relevant.

The next logical element would be the expansion of production through exports. Building export promotion just on subsidies based on export quantities would be inefficient (even two-fold currency depreciation in 2014–2015 did not render Russian vehicles competitive in foreign markets) and most probably WTO-incompatible (article 3 of the SCM Agreement). The approach should combine permitted financial instruments (export finance and subsidies without a direct link to exports) and non-financial measures (such as market access and regulatory environment improvement). It is worth mentioning that at the current stage, import substitution and export promotion measures can come into conflict since the continuation of massive subsidization could encourage local producers in importing countries to initiate countervailing investigations in order to level price advantages of Russian vehicles.

However, none of these policies would really deal with the core issue – low competitiveness of the industry. As institutionalists suggest, government intervention should be directed towards technological "emulation" with the aim to build new national comparative advantages. In this respect, it is necessary to adjust support programmes so that benefits depend on R&D activities, the introduction of new products, and the inclusion of the industry in new technological trends. In parallel, it is vital to invest in "brains": support engineering education and improve national technological basis through, for example, acquisition of foreign intellectual property. Policies may focus not only on creation of new, but also on development of existing comparative advantages. In particular, there are prospects for further niche specialization on production of vehicles for price-sensitive markets (for example, "Niva" and "GAZelle"), creation of robust special purpose vehicles, such as "URAL" and "KAMAZ", and development of connected and autonomous products ("Yandex" has achieved certain progress in this area). Consideration of specific ways of fostering the industry's competitiveness may well constitute an object of a separate study.

It seems that this approach, naturally stemming from our previous analysis, is reflected, to a significant extent, in the recently published new strategy for the automotive industry (GRF 2018). Indeed, the Russian Government plans to move from subsidizing output (operating costs) to measures oriented at long-term competitiveness. In particular, by 2020, more subsidies will be focused on the creation of new products in the areas of electric and autonomous movement, connection through the "Internet of Things" and use of alternative fuels, as well as the stimulation of demand for such products and creation of the necessary infrastructure.[13] In parallel, a number of indirect support measures (human capacity development, government participation in R&D and, importantly, increased industrial coordination led by the government) are planned to increase the competitiveness of domestic products in terms of technical characteristics. The main administrative instrument would be "special investment contracts" with individual localization conditions for each producer that would exceed the "New Industrial Assembly" requirements and focus on concentration of production (Sivashenkov 2017).

In addition, a separate strategy has been adopted for the development of automotive exports (GRF 2017). It targets exports in value terms of at least US$4.41 billion and in volume terms of 250–300,000 cars by 2025.

Four directions of export support development are envisaged. Firstly, the creation of general conditions for the development of export-oriented production, including planning support measures in the long term, reduction of import duties in target markets (CIS, the Middle East, Eastern Europe, and selected countries of Western Europe, Asia, Africa, Latin America, and Southeast Asia) through preferential trade agreements, development of local input suppliers, reduction of logistical costs and harmonization of national technical regulation with international standards, and conclusion of agreements on mutual recognition of certificates of conformity. Secondly, support for the expansion of national producers with high localization of production to new foreign markets, including improvement of the technical level of products, support of the development of assembly plants, foreign sales and service networks abroad, export finance, and subsidies to foreign buyers of Russian vehicles. Thirdly, the localization of export-oriented models of international producers for increased supplies to the global markets. For this purpose, the mechanism of "special investment contracts" could be used. Fourth, the integration of Russian automotive component manufacturers into the production chains of international automotive manufacturers.

Overall, the new strategic vision of the Russian automotive industry strongly correlates with our assessment of the results of past policies and possible future steps, as elaborated in this study. Importantly, there is a clear new trend of moving from trade-related measures to more sophisticated tools, which would require "fine-tuning" the industry and building local technological capacities. The main risks for successful implementation of the strategy could include insufficient internal market recovery, the inability of the industry to concentrate its production on fewer platforms, lack of technological competences, and market access barriers for Russian vehicles destined for export. However, if the Russian Government succeeds, the new policies may lead to a "qualitative leap" for the industry so it could ultimately do without state support.

Conclusion

This study allows one to make certain conclusions.

1 Despite the warnings of classical trade theory, governments are inclined to engage in industrial policies based on trade-related import substitution measures (tariffs, local content requirements, etc.). However, such measures are only partially effective and mostly affect the quantitative parameters of domestic production. In the long run, they may become harmful. When an industry grown in such an environment, it usually suffers from overcapacity and small-scale production. Export promotion is a natural path towards achieving economies of scale; however, an effective trade and industrial policy should shift its focus from quantitative to qualitative growth and support the development of new long-term comparative advantages.
2 The Russian supports measures were timely and ensured preservation and expansion of the automotive industry. However, their emphasis on the quantitative increase of locally produced vehicles resulted in overcapacity and low production concentration, which was already obvious by 2009 and exacerbated subsequently. Against this background, components localization constantly lagged behind the production of ready-made vehicles due to lower incentives (financial and administrative) and low production volumes per

platform. Overall, focus on import substitution could hardly form new comparative advantages for an internationally competitive automotive industry.

3 After almost 15 years of consistent policies in the Russian automotive industry, there appeared to emerge both economic (overcapacity, low localization, international non-competitiveness) and legal (end of the WTO transition period) incentives to improve the support system and bring it in compliance with international obligations.

4 The adoption by the Russian Government in 2017 and 2018 of the new strategic vision of the automotive industry is an encouraging step. Notably, it can be highly beneficial to shift from operating costs support to subsidies and coordination aimed at building long-term comparative advantages in the areas of R&D and technological capacities, as well as stimulating exports through WTO-consistent measures.

Notes

1 This study is prepared in the author's personal capacity. Any views expressed here are those of the author and should not be attributed to the Government of the Russian Federation. The author expresses his gratitude to Maxim Medvedkov, Gennady Ovechko, Pavel Elizarov, Natalia Bayurova, and Ksenia Galitsyna for their invaluable and insightful advice in the preparation of this study.

2 Noteworthy, these rates roughly correspond to the recommendations for industries in the early stages of development put forward in an institutionalist's paper (Akyuz 2009, p. 160).

3 The use of "Industrial Assembly" components for resale in the secondary market was technically possible. However, if discovered, such action was penalized by the exclusion of the importing company from the regime.

4 SKD kits are usually classified for customs purposes as sets of large parts such as body, engine, and others. The aim is to bypass duties on finished vehicles.

5 CKD kits differ from SKD, as they require the performance of certain technological operations in the final assembly plant.

6 As the next section reveals, according to official estimates, the regime was mostly positive for end users but did not succeed in the creation of a full-fledged industry.

7 As of 1 April 2013, within the "New Industrial Assembly", four agreements with groups of companies were signed (Minpromtorg Rossii 2010, chapter 3.2.2, para. 8).

8 The Russian automotive industry was not an "infant industry" in the classical sense. However, due to low competitiveness (small domestic demand, expensive logistics, underdeveloped component base, etc.), the industry could not withstand international competition.

9 The requests were formally filed in relation to both new and used cars. It would have been interesting to see a WTO panel's assessment of claims under the national treatment rule regarding used products since there is still no unanimity of views on whether these GATT provisions apply to such products.

10 In "Brazil – Taxation" (WTO 2017), a WTO panel considered an ambiguity about measures requiring localization of production steps in the "Inovar-Auto" programme (similar to the "Industrial Assembly"). Brazil lost all claims under Article III:4 of the GATT, article 2.1 of the TRIMs Agreement, and article 3.1(b) of the SCM Agreement. The panel concluded in paragraph 7.746 that "the performance of certain . . . production-steps will result in the creation, in Brazil, of components or subassemblies that must be incorporated into at least 80 percent of finished motor vehicles". Mandatory production

steps and the limitation of the use of imported components were effectively equalized. The Appellate Body (WTO 2018) reversed the findings under article 3.1(b) of the SCM Agreement stating that this provision *per se* did not prohibit conditioning tax incentives on domestic performance of certain production steps. Nevertheless, the panel's conclusions regarding national treatment violation were unchanged.

11 It seems that negotiators of the WTO agreements deliberately envisaged throughout the texts certain elements of "vagueness" or "constructive ambiguity" allowing for a wide range of measures to achieve the objectives of industrial development (see, for example, Cimoli et al. 2009b; Koval et al. 2014).

12 As discussed in the previous section, the underlying aims of the "Industrial Assembly" programme were the attraction of investment, increase of technological development, and support of employment in the Russian automotive industry, which, as could have probably been anticipated, would enhance the industry's competitiveness and ultimately stimulate positive effects in terms of welfare, security, and social stability. However, in order to make a reliable assessment of the "Industrial Assembly" effects, this section focuses on the parameters directly targeted by the programme. Looking at the industry's evolution with the use of a larger array of socioeconomic parameters would be an interesting topic for a separate study.

13 Support of additive manufacturing (3D printing) would also be important, especially for components industry, but the strategy does not mention this aspect.

Bibliography

Akyuz, Y 2009, 'Industrial Tariffs, International Trade, and Development', in: M Cimoli, G Dosi and JE Stiglitz (eds.) *Industrial Policy and Development*, Oxford University Press, Oxford.

Baldwin, RE 1969, 'The Case Against Infant-Industry Tariff Protection', *Journal of Political Economy*, vol. 77, no. 3, pp. 295–305.

Butov, AM 2017, *Rynok novyh legkovyh avtomobilej*, Centr razvitija NIU-VShJe, viewed 11 June 2018, https://dcenter.hse.ru/data/2017/08/30/1173968062/Рынок%20новых%20легковых%20автомобилей%202017.pdf

Chen, T-J 2016, 'The Development of China's Solar Photovoltaic Industry: Why Industrial Policy Failed', *Cambridge Journal of Economics*, no. 40, pp. 755–774.

Cimoli, M, Dosi, G, Nelson, R and Stiglitz, JE 2009a, 'Institutions and Policies Shaping Industrial Development: An Introductory Note', in: M Cimoli, G Dosi and JE Stiglitz (eds.) *Industrial Policy and Development*, Oxford University Press, Oxford.

Cimoli, M, Dosi, G and Stiglitz, JE 2009b, 'The Future of Industrial Policies in the New Millenium: Toward a Knowledge-Centered Development Agenda', in: M Cimoli, G Dosi and JE Stiglitz (eds.) *Industrial Policy and Development*, Oxford University Press, Oxford.

Faskhiev, KA 2013, 'Will WTO Accession Affect Russia's Automotive Industry?', *Problems of Economic Transition*, vol. 56, no. 4, pp. 39–55.

Federal Law of the Russian Federation No 128-FZ 2012, *O vnesenii izmenenij v Federal'nyj zakon "Ob othodah proizvodstva i potreblenija" i stat'ju 51 Bjudzhetnogo Kodeksa Rossijskoj Federacii*, 28 July, viewed 15 June 2018, www.consultant.ru/document/cons_doc_LAW_133273/

Federal Law of the Russian Federation No 190-FZ 2013, *O nekotoryh merah gosudarstvennoj podderzhki otdel'nyh kategorij proizvoditelej motornyh transportnyh sredstv, ih uzlov i agregatov*, 27 July, viewed 21 June 2018, www.consultant.ru/document/cons_doc_LAW_149637/

Garant 2018, viewed 23 March 2018, http://base.garant.ru/

Government of the Russian Federation 2005, *Resolution No 166, O vnesenii izmenenij v Tamozhennyj tarif Rossijskoj Federacii v otnoshenii avtokomponentov, vvozimyh dlja promyshlennoj sborki*, 29 March, viewed 20 January 2018, www.consultant.ru/document/cons_doc_LAW_52683/

Government of the Russian Federation 2006, *Resolution No 566, O vnesenii izmenenij v Tamozhennyj tarif Rossijskoj Federacii v otnoshenii avtokomponentov, vvozimyh dlja promyshlennoj sborki*, 16 September, viewed 20 January 2018, www.consultant.ru/document/cons_doc_LAW_62916/

Government of the Russian Federation 2017, *Order No 1877-r*, *Ob* utverzhdenii Strategii razvitija jeksporta produkcii avtomobil'noj promyshlennosti v Rossijskoj Federacii na period do 2025 goda, 31 August, viewed 25 May 2018, www.consultant.ru/document/cons_doc_LAW_256219/

Government of the Russian Federation 2018, *Order No 831-r, Ob utverzhdenii Strategii razvitija avtomobil'noj promyshlennosti Rossijskoj Federacii na period do 2025 goda*, 28 April, viewed 23 May 2018, www.consultant.ru/document/cons_doc_LAW_297129/

Haberler, G 1961, *The Theory of International Trade With Its Applications to Commercial Policy*, William Hodge and Company, Ltd., London.

Hout, W 1996, 'Development Strategies and Economic Performance in Third World Countries, 1965–92', *Third World Quarterly*, vol. 17, no. 4, pp. 603–624.

'Issledovanie Drom.ru. Import b/u mashin: chto i otkuda vezut v Rossiju v 2017 godu' 2017, *Drom.ru*, 30 June, viewed 25 June 2018, www.drom.ru/info/misc/drom-ru-53343.html

Korgun, I and Sutyrin, S 2016, 'Korea's Trade Policy and Its Implications for the Russian-Korean Economic Cooperation', in: *Russia-Eurasia, Turkey-Eastern Europe*, Korean Institute for International Economic Policy, Seoul.

Koval, AG, Sutyrin, SF and Trofimenko OY 2014, 'Zashhita nacional'nyh proizvoditelej v ramkah WTO', *Vestnik Sankt-Peterburgskogo Universiteta, Serija 5*, no. 1, pp. 53–70.

Kukol, E 2012, 'Vot i WTO', *Rossijskaja gazeta*, 23 July, viewed 18 October 2018, https://rg.ru/2012/07/21/vto-site.html

Linnemann, H, Van Dijck, P and Verbruggen, H (eds.) 1987, *Export-Oriented Industrialization in Developing Countries*, Singapore University Press, Singapore.

Minjekonomrazvitija Rossii, Minpromjenergo Rossii, Minfin Rossii 2005, *Order No 73/81/58n, Ob utverzhdenii Porjadka, opredeljajushhego ponjatie "promyshlennaja sborka" i ustanavlivajushhego primenenie dannogo ponjatija pri vvoze na territoriju Rossijskoj Federacii avtokomponentov dlja proizvodstva motornyh transportnyh sredstv tovarnyh pozicij 8701–8705 TN VJeD, ih uzlov i agregatov*, 15 April, viewed 1 February 2018, www.consultant.ru/document/cons_doc_LAW_53087/

Minjekonomrazvitija Rossii, Minpromtorg Rossii, Minfin Rossii 2010, *Order No 678/1289/184n, O vnesenii izmenenij v porjadok, opredeljajushhij ponjatie "promyshlennaja sborka" motornyh transportnyh sredstv i ustanavlivajushhij primenenie dannogo ponjatija pri vvoze na territoriju Rossijskoj Federacii avtokomponentov dlja proizvodstva motornyh transportnyh sredstv tovarnyh pozicij 8701–8705 TN VJeD, ih uzlov i agregatov*, 24 December, viewed 1 February 2018, www.consultant.ru/document/cons_doc_LAW_110023/

Minpromtorg Rossii 2010, *Order No 319, Ob utverzhdenii Strategii razvitija avtomobil'noj promyshlennosti Rossijskoj Federacii na period do 2020 goda*, 23 April, viewed 8 June 2018, www.consultant.ru/document/cons_doc_LAW_104193/

Nidhiprabha, B 2016, 'The Rise and Fall of Thailand's Export-Oriented Industries', *Asian Economic Papers*, no. 3, pp. 128–150.

Onanaran, O and Stockhammer, E 2005, 'Two Different Export-Oriented Growth Strategies. Accumulation and Distribution in Turkey and South Korea', *Emerging Markets Finance and Trade*, vol. 41, no. 1, pp. 65–89.

PwC 2017, *Rynok legkovyh i kommercheskih avtomobilej v Rossii. Rezul'taty 2016 g. i perspektivy razvitija*, February, viewed 12 April 2018, www.pwc.ru/ru/automotive/publications/assets/automotive-market-of-russia-feb16/auto-report-rus.pdf

Reinert, ES 2009, 'Emulation Versus Comparative Advantage: Competing and Complementary Principles in the History of Economic Policy', in: M Cimoli, G Dosi and JE Stiglitz (eds.) *Industrial Policy and Development*, Oxford University Press, Oxford.

Shtanov, V 2016, 'Krizis v avtoprome budet dlit'sja dolgo', *Vedomosti*, 13 October, viewed 28 June 2018, www.vedomosti.ru/auto/articles/2016/10/13/660733-krizis-avtoprome#galleries%2F140737492966764%2Fnormal%2F1

Sivashenkov, A 2017, 'Spasti avtoprom. Kak budut rabotat' novye pravila gospodderzhki avtokoncernov', *Forbes*, 14 December, viewed 22 July 2018, www.forbes.ru/biznes/354351-spasti-avtoprom-kak-budut-rabotat-novye-pravila-gospodderzhki-avtokoncernov

Smitka, MJ 2016, 'China's Auto Industry: Success Despite Policy', *International Journal of Automotive Technology and Management*, vol. 16, no. 2, pp. 114–129.

United Nations 2018, *Comtrade Database*, viewed 17 January 2018, https://comtrade.un.org

Vercity 2018, *Mirovaja statistika avtomobil'nogo rynka*, viewed 1 June 2018, https://auto.vercity.ru/statistics/

Vousden, N 1990, *The Economics of Trade Protection*, Oxford University Press, Oxford.

WTO 2013a, *Russian Federation – Recycling Fee on Motor Vehicles*, Request for Consultations by the European Union, WT/DS462/1, G/L/1033, G/TRIMS/D/37, 11 July.

WTO 2013b, *Russian Federation – Recycling Fee on Motor Vehicles*, Request for Consultations by Japan, WT/DS463/1, G/L/1034, G/TRIMS/D/38, G/TBT/D/45, 23 July.

WTO 2014a, *Russia – Certain Measures Relating to Industrial Assembly*, Questions from the United States, G/TRIMS/W/134, 13 June.

WTO 2014b, *Russia – Certain Measures Relating to Industrial Assembly*, Replies to Questions from the United States, G/TRIMS/W/146, 21 October.

WTO 2017, *Brazil – Certain Measures Concerning Taxation and Charges*, Reports of the Panel, WT/DS472/R, WT/DS497/R, 30 August.

WTO 2018, *Brazil – Certain Measures Concerning Taxation and Charges*, Reports of the Appellate Body, WT/DS472/AB/R, WT/DS497/AB/R, 13 December.

13 GATS Mode 4 in Russia's migration policy

Liberalization and its limitation

Norio Horie and Olesya V. Veredyuk

Introduction

Liberalization of the temporary movement of natural persons (TMNP) is vital for enhancing international business and trade. Many World Trade Organization (WTO) member states are interested in doing business in Russia; however, Russian walls against TMNP are still viewed to be high. Russia's accession to the WTO was expected to provide an opportunity for liberalizing TMNP, but it resulted in only minor action. This chapter tackles the problem of why the movement of expatriates into Russia has been so restricted from an institutional point of view.

We analyse migration policy issues in their close interconnection with service-related trade policies. Indeed, greater trade intensity is often attributed to the increased mobility of professionals. We believe that these links are of particular importance for Russia, which is among the world's greatest net importers of services[1] and, at the same time, is one of the biggest host countries for international immigrants.[2] Research has revealed that liberalization in service trade has a positive impact on productivity in various industries of Russia (Knobel 2016), with business services assuming great importance[3] (Rodríguez and Melikhova 2015). We argue that the liberalization of skill- or knowledge-intensive labour service in trade may also be beneficial for the Russian economy.

In this chapter, we firstly discuss the ambiguity of the definition of TMNP because some types of TMNP in the framework of the General Agreement on Trade in Services (GATS) Mode 4 are not well addressed in migration studies and human resource management (HRM) studies. The weak criteria for classifying TMNP in the GATS framework should be examined in order to better understand barriers preventing the liberalization of TMNP. This chapter also develops a typology of migrants in the context of the liberalization of the service trade in the Russian migration regime. The divergent classifications of migrants in the context of migration studies and HRM studies have been discussed many times. However, practical understanding of these classifications in Russia has not been achieved. This chapter focuses on independent professionals in service-related trades. To elaborate a segment of service-related TMNP that has not been activated in Russia, we examine the typology of business expatriates in migration studies and

HRM studies and show the direction Russia can choose to further liberalize the TMNP.

Russia's policy approach to regulating TMNP is divided into two groups based on the countries of origin: "Far Abroad" and "Near Abroad" countries. The "Near Abroad" group includes Commonwealth of Independent States (CIS) countries. The "Far Abroad" group includes the rest of countries in the world. This division of immigrant labour is crucial, from Russia's perspective, for accomplishing a series of tasks, including fulfilling workforce shortages, easing demographic crises, and maintaining national or cultural identity. Therefore, Russia's migration policy measures are designed to fill the shortages of unskilled workers in domestic labour markets with CIS workers, who can adapt relatively easily to Russian society. Although the Russian government has made efforts to relax immigration requirements for highly qualified workers and expatriates in Russia, those groups are not well addressed in Russia's migration policies. Russia's WTO accession should have been a vital opportunity to address the status of highly qualified workers and expatriates in the migration regime. However, Russia still hesitates to liberalize TMNP for international business within its borders.

In the next section, we explain our theoretical and methodological approach to this research. In the third section, we examine different typologies and taxonomies in migration studies and HRM studies to reconsider the typology of TMNP in the framework of GATS Mode 4. In the fourth section, we follow the brief history of migration policy development in Russia and then examine the path-dependent features of Russian migration policy for expatriates. In order to do so, we focus on a category of expatriates missing in Russia. Finally, we suggest a possible direction of further liberalization of TMNP in Russia as a policy implication of this study.

Theoretical framework and approach to designing the research

The theoretical framework in this chapter relies on an institutional approach to TMNP in trade. Institutions are the foundation of social life; they consist of formal and informal rules, monitoring and enforcement mechanisms, and systems of meaning that define the context within which all actors operate and interact with each other (Campbell 2004, p. 1). Differences in national institutions are an important cause of variation across countries in political and economic performance (Campbell 2004, p. 7). Institutional changes are evolutionary, and the institutional legacies of the past limit the range of current possibilities and/or options in institutional innovations (Nielsen et al. 1995, p. 6). In this sense, institutional development is path-dependent. Russian migration policy options have been restricted by the experiences of the former Soviet Union and its collapse. People in CIS countries were once Soviet citizens but are now foreigners in Russian territory, and those who work in Russia are migrant workers. Expatriates from Western developed countries have been strangers to Russian citizens and are often considered to be advocates of new management and technologies. These events have affected the evolution of institutional settings in Russia's migration management. Even after its accession to the WTO, Russia's institutional evolution in migration management was restricted by these past experiences.

The approach used in this chapter relies on the analysis of key documents regarding migration policies in Russia, for example, Russia's migration laws and reports to the WTO and other documents relevant to liberalizing TMNP in service-related trade. This chapter also offers a critical review of the literature on the typology of expatriates in the framework of GATS Mode 4 in the scopes of service-related trade discussions, migration studies, and HRM studies. The divergent classifications of migrants and expatriates in the context of migration studies and HRM studies have been discussed in many reports. HRM studies have categorized expatriates in many ways, using different typologies and taxonomies (McNulty and Brewster 2017). Although institutional settings in which expatriates work are of common interest in international business studies, we have not found enough research on how these institutions of migration policies are relevant to the taxonomies in HRM studies. As we discuss in this chapter, Russia's legislative reactions to GATS Mode 4 ignore some categories of expatriates. Our examination of the typology of expatriates associated with the framework of GATS Mode 4 in Russian institutional settings can contribute to further understanding Russia's attitude toward GATS Mode 4.

Typology of TMNP in GATS, migration studies, and HRM studies

TMNP in HRM and migration studies

In HRM literature, TMNP is captured by the term of expatriation. In the context of the increasing internationalization of business through the establishment of international subsidiaries and representative offices, the intra-corporate transfer of managers, specialists, and trainees from one country to another is an important international HRM practice. These intra-corporate transferees are called expatriates in HRM literature, and recent discussions on the definition of expatriates pursue expanding the way this term is used. The traditional usage of expatriates refers to company-assigned expatriates, whose employers send them abroad for a temporary assignment (Suutari and Brewster 2000). They are assigned and transferred within one corporation, usually a multinational company. Their advantage in the migration process is that they do not need to move permanently across borders and are expected to return to their home country. Consequently, their temporary expatriation faces fewer restrictions than would popular labour migration (Lodefalk 2016).

Recent discussions in HRM studies have defined variations in expatriate groups. Bonache et al. (2001) developed five new categories of assignee movement across borders in descending order of time spent in the host countries: self-initiated expatriates, short-term assignees, commuter assignees, frequent travellers, and virtual workers. In addition to traditional assigned expatriates, Suutari and Brewster (2000) focused on self-initiated expatriates as a new category. They elaborated on and further developed the concept of self-initiated expatriates earlier propounded by Inkson et al. (1997) and further developed the concept. Inkson et al. (1997) originally examined the "overseas experience" of self-initiated expatriates, who are self-motivated and self-resourced for their own odyssey. Inkson et al. (1997) focused on young people traveling abroad to pursue cultural experience, who are more driven by curiosity than career development. Suutari and Brewster (2000) included not only such people in their early career phase but also more experienced people who have chosen international careers as "self-initiated expatriates". The new category includes various types of people engaging in expatriation, such as young opportunists, who are described by Inkson et al. (1997); job seekers, who lost opportunities or interest in seeking or keeping jobs in their homelands; officials who work within international organizations; localized professionals who show a preference for the local environment; and international professionals who are global specialists on the basis of their international experience. Therefore, self-initiated expatriates are defined by whether they are assigned, not by the duration of their expatriation or by their skills or occupations. Bozionelos (2009) translated these as "non-corporate-sponsored expatriates", focusing on expatriate nurses in Saudi Arabia. International business organizations employ self-initiated expatriates because they are an important human resource for organizations in the host countries with regard to understanding local and international markets, languages, and culture, and they often cost less than traditional assigned expatriates in terms of travel and living costs, salaries, and taxation (Al Ariss and Crowley-Henry 2013).

Berry and Bell (2012) raised the problem that international HRM literature had focused only on a specific minority of relatively privileged people as "expatriates" and claimed to shed light on people of diverse races, ethnicities, and economic and social means who are in less-privileged class positions and are labelled as "migrants". Haak-Saheem and Brewster (2017) surveyed variations of expatriate groups that HRM literature had defined. In the specific context of the host country, expatriates having "more menial jobs, manual jobs, and the lower-level office jobs" (Haak-Saheem and Brewster 2017, p. 426) can be categorized as "hidden expatriates". These people do not meet the criteria of "migrants" as defined in migration studies because they are expected to return home within a few years and because their management is an important component of the HRM of companies in the Gulf States. Therefore, recent HRM literature tends to capture the whole range of TMNP for work, some part of which has previously been discussed only in migration studies.

Contrary to these HRM studies, most literature in migration studies tends to capture the migration processes of unskilled or less-skilled migrant workers from developing countries to more developed countries. Of course, when the research target focuses on a specific type of professional, highly qualified workers can be a topic of research. Hedberg et al. (2014) analyzed highly skilled IT professionals from India to Sweden and illustrated institutional settings of their migration process that establish a transnational space "from above". They used the term "highly skilled labour migration", based on migration studies, but in fact described the migration processes of independent professionals or self-initiated expatriates from India to Sweden. The definition and usage of "expatriate" and "migrant" in migration studies and HRM studies vary and show how different understandings of the concept of TMNP for work are employed in these studies (Berry and Bell 2012).

Some literature crosses the boundaries between HRM studies and migration studies. HRM studies, especially, have tried to capture various types of migrants in the context of the effective management of international diversity at work, although this remains an under-theorized field of HRM studies (Al Ariss et al. 2012). In HRM studies, the term migrants is used when discussing the work experience of unskilled individuals (Al Ariss and Crowley-Henry 2013, p. 82), and this term is based on strong ethnic stereotypes (Al Ariss et al. 2012).

HRM literature has expanded the definition of expatriates to include not only highly skilled professionals but also low-skilled professionals, and migration studies have expanded their interests beyond low-skilled workers to highly skilled workers. The boundary between the two study fields rests on understanding self-initiated expatriates. TMNP in GATS Mode 4 is an essential part of international business; however, few studies address self-initiated expatriates in relation to GATS Mode 4.

Independent professionals in GATS Mode 4

GATS is structured to encompass four modes of service delivery. The first mode is the cross-border supply of services. In this mode, service suppliers and consumers remain in their own countries. The second mode is service consumption abroad; this mode represents the movement of consumers to the service provider's country. The third mode is the commercial presence of juridical persons to supply services in the host country. The fourth mode is the presence of natural persons in the host country. Modes 3 and 4 are often recognized as two sides of the same coin because most of the commitments by WTO member states in Mode 4 rely exclusively on intra-corporate transferees.

TMNP has become more important in service-related activities. Cross-border TMNP is often essential and inseparable from the contents of services (Ghosh 1997, p. 51). GATS defines a natural person as a national of a WTO member state or a natural person who has a right to permanent residence in that state. GATS Mode 4 is said to include two types of natural persons: self-employed service suppliers and employees of the service supplier (WTO 2009). The second type is strongly linked to intra-corporate transferees for the purpose of accomplishing activities in GATS Mode 3. Business visitors should also be included in this definition; however, many member states do not allow them to supply services and receive remuneration in the host country. They can conduct business negotiations for their service contracts and prepare for a commercial presence in the host country. Although the first type is said to be included in GATS Mode 4, ambiguity with regard to this type remains (Blouin et al. 2006).

According to Blouin et al. (2006), Mode 4 covers the following categories of mobility: self-employed or independent service suppliers (paid by the host country), employees of a foreign company who are sent to fulfil a contract with a host-country client, employees of a foreign company established in the host country, and business visitors (short-term stays, no remuneration received in the host country).

According to the Annex on the TMNP Supplying Services under the Agreement, GATS does not apply to measures affecting access to the employment market of the host country. In this sense, a foreign service supplier cannot be employed by a locally owned firm. Only when a person is employed by a subsidiary of a foreign-owned firm whose parent firm exports a service to the host country would that person's status be covered under GATS. Independent service suppliers should be based in their homeland and can enter WTO member states only when they have a specific assignment in a contractual relationship. In the framework of GATS Mode 4, the affiliates of service providers are the most important determinants.

When we examine the definitions of the TMNP in service-related trade, bilateral agreement on the TMNP in trade is useful for examining wider categories of natural persons in terms of mobility. The Comprehensive Economic and Trade Agreement (CETA) between Canada and the European Union provided definitions of each category of service providers that fall within the TMNP in service-related trade (CETA 2017). It defines three types of "key personnel": business visitors for investment purposes, investors, and intra-corporate transferees. Intra-corporate transferees include three sub-categories: senior personnel, specialists, and graduate trainees. In addition to these traditional assigned expatriates, CETA covers contractual service suppliers and independent professionals. Contractual service suppliers are natural persons employed by an enterprise of one party that has no establishment in the territory of the other party and that has concluded a bona fide contract to supply a service to a consumer of the other party that requires the temporary presence of its employees in the territory of the other party in order to fulfil a contract to supply a service. In this definition, contractual service suppliers should be "employed" by the service-exporting enterprises. Therefore, they are also a kind of traditional assigned expatriates. CETA also defines independent professionals as natural persons engaged in the supply of a service and established as self-employed in the territory of a party who have no establishment in the territory of the other party and who have concluded a bona fide contract to supply a service to a consumer of the other party that requires the temporary presence of the natural person in the territory of the other party in order to fulfil a contract to supply a service. Independent professionals should be self-employed in the service-exporting country. Both categories of natural persons pursue the realization of contracts they are offered, and their possible employment in the consumer country is not outside the scope of the definition.

The determination of independent professionals with self-initiated expatriates can be examined only in the phase that is related to "contingent labour". The concepts and definitions of self-initiated expatriates are developing and widening in HRM literature, as described above. When we equate the terms independent professionals and self-expatriates with the concept contingent labour, we can bridge the discussion of TMNP in GATS Mode 4 and HRM studies. The term contingent labour covers a wide range of job arrangements: part-time work, temporary employment, self-employment, contracting, outsourcing, and home-based work (Kunda et al. 2002, p. 235). These are free agents who can be found in highly skilled labour markets and who are often engineers, software developers, and information technology professionals. They can be called freelancers, and their roles in international management are also important in the changing nature of expatriation (Brewster and Scullion 1997). "Freelance expatriates" have just begun to garner academic attention and become a new category of self-initiated expatriates in international business (Chi and Levitt 2011). Independent professionals are self-initiated expatriates in the sense that they are not assigned and are not intra-corporate transferees. They are often freelance expatriates, conducting contractual work not requiring regular employment.

The flexible use of independent professionals in international business is important for service-related trade. Growing global operations in the field of information and communications technology (ICT) has led to a shortage of related skilled professionals and, at the same time, has created a large labour market for independent professionals. Technology allows people to work as freelancers.[4] This new state of the job market in developed countries encourages developing countries with respected systems of higher education to become major sources of highly skilled independent professionals for the developed countries. India is the country best known for sending independent ICT professionals to developed countries. Company-assigned expatriates from developed countries often change their status from traditional expatriates to independent professionals during their assignment. International assignments often encourage the development of individual competencies that are useful not only within but also across organizations (McNulty 2013). As their company-assigned expatriates accumulate "career capital" during their assignment, they can shift their job status from long-term regular employment to short-term organizational commitments as "free agents" to meet the demand of international business. These individuals are also called localized expatriates, global careerists, or independent international mobile professionals (McNulty 2013; Tharenou 2013; McNulty and Brewster 2017). These are self-initiated expatriates who can be referred to as "freelance expatriates" in international business.

Recent studies of the suggestion to increase human mobility in GATS Mode 4 tend to focus on labour migration. Poot and Strutt (2010) and Dawson (2013) examined the possibility of managing labour mobility under the WTO. Straubhaar (2003) argued in favour of global rules for international migration as a General Agreement on Movement of People (GAMP) under a multilateral regime. Raza (2018) tried to reframe temporary labour mobility as trade in service through the liberalization of temporary labour mobility via GATS Mode 4 but was disappointed that GATS Mode 4 is a weak and marginal institution for liberalizing labour mobility and only contributes to the mobility of highly qualified workers. Generally, the greater the labour intensity of the service to be traded, the more likely it is to be affected by restrictions to market access through regulations posed by migration policy, as suggested by Ghosh (1997, p. 51). Under the condition that GATS Mode 4 commitments made by WTO member states have been very limited and tend to have value only as "adjuncts to commitments allowing service providers to establish a commercial presence in a host country" (Dawson 2013), the commitment to liberalize the movement of independent professionals is a key breakthrough for further developing the international business mobility of people without requiring access to employment markets of the host countries or claiming citizenship, residence, or regular employment. It is an important step for WTO member states to liberalize the movement of independent professionals because it does not increase unskilled labour migrants but liberalizes skill- or knowledge-intensive labour service in trade, which may have advantages both for exporting and importing countries.

However, it is also true that the reluctance of WTO member states to make stronger commitments under Mode 4 comes from "the lack of incentive to proceed at the multilateral level" (Jacobsson 2013). The depth and coverage of GATS Mode 4 strongly depend on concessions given by WTO member states. Therefore, the historical, cultural, economic, political, and securitized contexts of WTO member states' institutional settings should be examined. In this sense, each WTO member state's initiatives to liberalize TMNP in service trade are contextual. We focus on Russia's commitments to GATS Mode 4 and analyse how their path-dependent contexts hamper the liberalization of the temporary movement of people in service.

Russian migration regime and service-related professional activities

Brief history of migration policy developments in Russia

Natural and juridical persons in Russia have the right to employ foreign citizens. Foreign workers must obtain two types of licences: a work patent and a work permit. A work patent can be issued to workers who come from visa-free countries without counting quotas or economic tests. This work patent was introduced in 2010. During the work patent launching period (from 2010 to 2015), foreign workers who obtained a work patent could provide labour service only to natural persons. The work patent for foreign workers employed by natural persons had its own Russian context. Personal service occupations, such as housekeeper, babysitter, care worker, etc., were rather new services in Russia, resulting from the rapid growth of personal income (Tyuryukanova 2007, p. 109). Guest workers from CIS countries who can speak Russian provide Russia with inexpensive labour. Such workers turned out to be the principal source of labour in this new service sector.

In 2015, a work patent became essentially a licence identifying foreign workers by their country of origin. Workers from CIS countries other than Turkmenistan (hereafter, CIS countries)[5] can obtain this licence no matter what type of entity employs them: natural or juridical persons. These workers enjoy more favourable consideration than others for a work permit and can easily access the bottom of the labour market in Russia, where local people scarcely work. They are known as "foreign labour force", "labour migrants", or "guest workers" in Russian official and academic documents and media reports.

A work permit was originally issued to those who worked for juridical persons, without specifying the country of origin. Since 2010, when the work patent was introduced, the work permit turned into a licence for those who work for juridical persons. Employment by juridical persons became an essential criterion for awarding a work permit to those required to obtain a visa. Expatriates in Russia often suffered through difficult procedures for obtaining work permits until Russia introduced a new category of work permit specialized for highly qualified workers.

The category of "work permit" specialized for highly qualified foreign workers was introduced in 2010. The new Article 13.2 of Federal Law No. 115-FZ, "On the Legal Status of Foreign Citizens in the Russian Federation", was supplemented and enacted on July 1, 2010. This article opened wide the door to the labour market in Russia for highly qualified foreign workers. These workers earning two million rubles or more per year are freed from the ceiling on annual work permit quotas and are allowed to work in Russia for a maximum of three years (this three-year permit is renewable). Furthermore, the family members of foreign workers can easily obtain visas to stay with them. Foreign workers in this category enjoy their status only when they are employed, with wages or remuneration from Russian commercial organizations or foreign business entities such as representative offices or subsidiaries in the territory of Russia.

Russia's entry into the WTO resulted in an additional amendment of its migration laws. Article 13.5 supplemented Federal Law No. 115-FZ in 2013 to adapt this law to the requirements of GATS Mode 4 and came into effect in 2014. It articulates the conditions of and procedure for obtaining work permits for foreigners who are employed by foreign business entities incorporated in WTO member countries. It can be understood as the Russian practical translation of GATS Mode 4, and it simplified procedures for expatriates from WTO member states to be employed in their representative offices, branches, and subsidiaries with parent companies in any WTO member state.

In 2014, soon after Article 13.5 was added to Federal Law No. 115-FZ, the number of highly qualified foreign specialists increased dramatically. China, Vietnam, Turkey, and CIS countries especially contributed to this expansion as WTO member states (see Figure 13.1). It reflects their active market access and the political situation around Russia. The EU has imposed economic sanctions against Russia and has decreased its volume of trade with Russia since 2014. China is Russia's biggest trade partner, and President Putin's initiative for Russia's pivot to the East encourages China and Vietnam to expand their economic ties with Russia. As compared to these countries, we find a relatively slow increase in the number of expatriates from the EU, USA, and other developed countries.

This relatively slow pace does not mean there is little demand for expatriates in Russia.[6] A question arises as to why Russia's accession to the WTO did not create an opportunity to encourage more expatriates from developed countries to work in Russia.

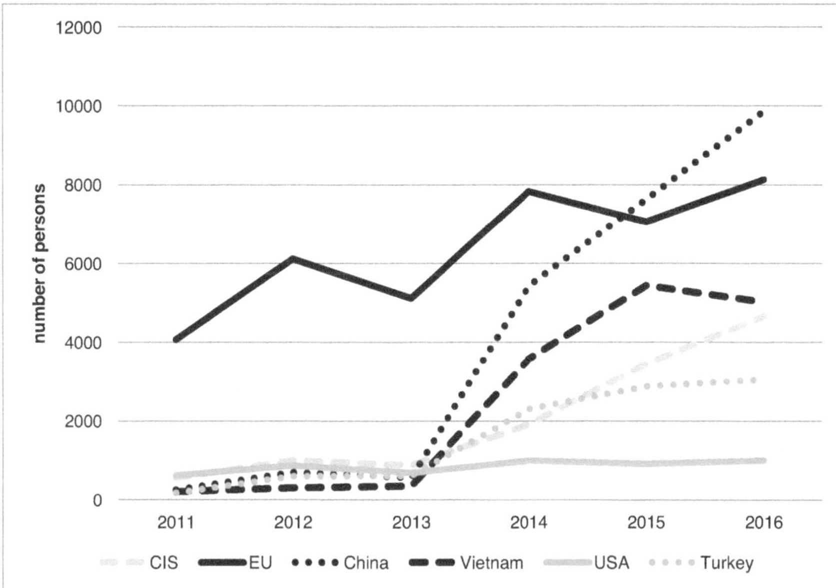

Figure 13.1 Foreign highly qualified specialists in Russia by country from 2011 to 2016

Source: The author's compiled data from the Federal State Statistics Service (2015, 2017).

Path-dependent migration policy development for expatriates in Russia

As we briefly examined the history of migration policy development in Russia, Russia has already opened wide the door to labour service providers from CIS countries. Based on strong demand for low-skilled and low-cost labour, Russia has stimulated the massive flow of labour from CIS countries. Russian migration policy has put greater stress on liberalizing the flow of workers to make up for a shortage in the Russian labour market. These workers are required to speak the Russian language and be familiar with Russian culture in order to reduce the cost of adaptation to Russian society. The study of Russian language, history, and laws became a requirement for migrant workers to obtain a work patent or work permit in 2015, and the policy that imposed this study strengthened this philosophy (Ryazantsev 2014). Those who obtain a work patent or normal work permit are, de facto, labour service providers from CIS countries.

Workers who obtain normal work permit can be recognized as labour service providers; however, their qualifications vary from low to high skill levels. Contrary to the liberalized attitude toward labour service providers from CIS countries, Russia's measures to manage the flow of labour service providers from non-CIS countries are strictly regulated via employment permits, work permits, and quantitative caps by work permit quotas. The procedures to obtain these permits force employers and employees to spend a lot of time and money. Although there are demands for foreign self-initiated expatriates to work in Russian companies and for Russian employers to employ expatriates, these procedures discourage employers from inviting foreign self-initiated expatriates to work in their companies (Sanzharovskaya 2014).

Russia's soft security agenda on migration concerns how to deal with illegal migrants, and its economic agenda concerns how to fulfil the nation's labour shortage. As a result, Russia's migration management mainly employs the quantitative regulation of labour service providers from non-CIS countries in accordance with its security agenda and encourages labour service providers to work in Russia in accordance with its economic agenda. This stance applies to the regulation even of highly qualified foreign specialists and does not encourage expatriates from developed countries to work in Russia. Most WTO member states are also reluctant to commit to the deregulation of labour service providers; however, they tend to widely accept highly qualified foreign professionals.

Russia's migration policy evolves within an environment of intense social intolerance toward the unexpected mass inflow of foreign professionals from non-CIS countries. For instance, the inflow of Chinese migrant workers into Russia likely influenced Russian migration policy. In the 1990s, xenophobia was often directed at Chinese migrants who had crossed the eastern border of Russia and engaged in trade and commerce in the Russian Far East. There is some evidence that Russia's government and local people have been cautious about accepting a massive inflow of expatriates from non-CIS countries. Before Russia's accession to the WTO, there was some discussion about the WTO potentially increasing the inflow of Chinese to Russia. Some local scholars mentioned a possible massive inflow of migrant workers from China as a result of Russia's negotiation with China for accession to the WTO (for example, Tkachenko 2010, p. 26). When Mikhail Kasyanov (then prime minister of Russia) visited Shanghai for a meeting with Zhu Rongji (then premier of the State Council of China), China, in fact, mentioned that if Russia joined the WTO, it should agree to open its borders to Chinese workers. China claimed to eliminate regulations for Chinese workers and open jobs that had been prohibited to foreigners, for example, chief accountant; however, the Russian government rejected Chinese negotiations to ease the difficult regulations for Chinese workers (Ryazantsev and Tkachenko 2010, p. 108). Russian local researchers also suggested that Russia's accession to the WTO would increase illegal Chinese migrants in Russia due to the facts that there are demographic and labour imbalances between Russia and China, and that China has enough motivation to export its domestic labour surplus to Russia (Solodilova and Khafizova 2012, p. 29). Although it has been said that Russians have overcome the widespread "China peril" complex of the 1990s (Korolev 2016, p. 66), the general caution toward migrants remains.[7] Ryazantsev (2017, p. 64) suggested that there is an ideological basis for Russian authorities to consider migration a potential risk to the country and migrants as potential violators of the rule of law.

Russian mass media also warned of an expatriate "invasion" of the Russian labour market. It claimed that Russia's accession to the WTO was required to guarantee conditions under which any foreign company could gain access to the Russian domestic market, and Russia's accession to the WTO would then facilitate the inflow of foreign uniquely highly qualified specialists or top managers, in other words, "elite guest workers", to threaten the employment of local specialists and managers ('Komu na Rusi zhit' khorosho' 2012). We call this the "expatriate threat" in Russia.

Formal institutional settings with regard to GATS Mode 4 can be examined in Russia's migration laws supplemented after its accession to the WTO and in the report of the working party on the accession of the Russian Federation to the WTO (WT/ACC/RUS/70). The supplemented migration law for GATS Mode 4 in Russia (Article 13.5) did not provide any additional liberalization measures for expatriates from WTO member states.[8] Rather, it added requirements to identify expatriates in the framework of GATS Mode 4. It listed three entities that can direct foreign workers to employment under the framework of the WTO in Russia: subsidiaries, branches, and representative offices of foreign commercial organizations. These juridical persons can apply for special work permits for their employees only when those employees have at least one year of paid employment in their companies prior to their entry to Russia.[9] This means that Russia's technical operation with regard to GATS Mode 4 is limited to company-assigned expatriates from their home countries. Worse, this new amendment placed quantitative restrictions on expatriates from WTO member states. The total number of expatriates per representative office is restricted to five persons (two persons for a representative office of a banking institution).

Independent professionals have little opportunity to work in Russia. In Russia's Schedule of Specific Commitments on Services on Mode 4, the representative of the Russian Federation clearly defined the coverage of TMNP in GATS Mode 4 (WT/ACC/RUS/70/Add.2). According to Article 13.5, Russia's coverage of TMNP in the framework of GATS Mode 4 has only two types: "key personnel" and business visitors. Key personnel are "persons working in senior positions within the commercial presence in the form of a subsidiary, representative office, or branch of a juridical person of another member, who primarily direct the management of such commercial presence, receiving general supervision or direction principally from the board of directors or stockholders or their equivalent, and persons working in the commercial presence in the form of a subsidiary, representative office, or branch of a juridical person of another member and possessing a high level of qualification and/or uncommon knowledge essential for the supply of services by such commercial presence". Therefore, independent professionals are not considered key personnel under GATS Mode 4 in Russia.

Contractual service providers, as defined in the third section of this chapter, are also not key personnel in the Russian migration regime. Therefore, they are not considered highly qualified specialists in Russian migration policy. However, it is possible for them to conduct their economic activities in Russia as foreign individual entrepreneurs even if they have no employment contract in Russia. Instead of the employment contract in Russia, they must have registered a temporary or permanent residence. The procedures for obtaining temporary or permanent residence are notoriously onerous for individuals (Maltby 2018). Furthermore, individual entrepreneurs must complete all of the procedures for defining the scope of their business, preparing the required registration documents, submitting the required documents at the tax registration office, and so on, which are written and conducted in the Russian language. These procedures are burdensome (Paragraph 222 of WT/ACC/RUS/70) and may attract only Russian-speaking foreign individual entrepreneurs (e.g. from Ukraine, Central Asia, and the Caucasus) and not attract other independent professionals to work in Russia.

Using the definitions of expatriates in HRM studies and the typology of service providers in trade, as described in the third section of this chapter, we examined the complex typology of TMNP in service-related trade in the Russian migration regime (Table 13.1). Intra-corporate expatriates working as senior personnel are allowed to work in Russia; however, the number of foreign senior managers in Russia is restricted. Intra-corporate expatriates working as specialists are conditionally allowed to work in Russia; they must prove a high level of qualification and/or uncommon knowledge essential for the supply of services by their organization's commercial presence in Russia. Consequently, graduate trainees are not allowed to work in Russia. Business visitors and investors are allowed to stay in Russia for 90 days. Non-key personnel are excluded from the Article 13.5 supplement to Federal Law No. 115-FZ, "On the Legal Status of Foreign Citizens in the Russian Federation", that is, the framework of GATS Mode 4. Therefore, practically speaking, independent professionals are not allowed to work in Russia. Contractual service providers are also not permitted to conduct service activities in Russia without registering their status as individual entrepreneurs.

As discussed in the previous section, the recent trend in international business is to employ or utilize a variety of expatriate workers. The growing importance of freelancers demonstrates that the flexible usage of independent professionals in international business is crucial. Yet, according to our typology, independent professionals have no space to demonstrate their ability in Russia. Russia's definitions of expatriates are still very traditional and narrowly defined.

The narrowly defined typology of expatriates from WTO member states does not contribute to the increase of highly qualified foreign workers in Russia. Its share of highly qualified workers is just 1.4 percent (26,531 persons) of the total number of foreign workers issued work permits and work patents (1,830,948 persons) in 2017, according to the official data of the Ministry of Internal Affairs of the Russian Federation. The door is open only for current exigent economic needs, not for supporting an environment conducive to international business in Russia.[10] Russia's accession to the WTO did not create an opportunity to liberalize TMNP in the framework of GATS Mode 4. Russia's migration policy for expatriates is rather restrictive and narrowly defines the scope for GATS Mode 4.

As we examined, there are two reasons Russia's accession to the WTO did not contribute to achieving a more liberalized migration policy for expatriates from developed countries. Firstly, the institutional settings for migration policy based on Russia's economic agenda are designed for Russia's demand for labour service providers from CIS countries. These institutional settings exclude labour service

Table 13.1 Typology of expatriates and their ability to work in Russia

*Typology of the TMNP in service-related trade**	*Sub-categories*	*Status in enterprise*	*Typology of expatriates in HRM studies*	*Employment status in their home country*	*Working in Russia*
Independent professionals		Non-key personnel	Self-initiated expatriates	Not employed	Not allowed
Contractual services suppliers			Traditional assigned expatriates		Possible on a case-by-case basis
Business visitors			Commuter assignees and frequent travelers	Employed	Allowed
Investors					Allowed
Intra-corporate transferees	Senior personnel	Key personnel	Traditional assigned expatriates		Allowed but limited
	Specialists				Allowed on a case-by-case basis but limited
	Graduate trainees		Short-term assignees		Not allowed

Note: The definition depends on the Comprehensive Economic and Trade Agreement (CETA) between Canada and the European Union.

providers from non-CIS countries. Therefore, Russian migration policy for expatriates plays a minor role in liberalizing labour mobility, and Russia's cautious position against expatriates remains tense. The pre-existing pool of labour in the territory of the former Soviet Union and the Russian dream of integrating the labour market there made institutional settings of labour migration more inclusive for CIS workers and more exclusive for non-CIS workers. Secondly, the institutional settings for migration policy based on Russia's security agenda narrowed the definition of TMNP in GATS Mode 4, reflecting the perceived "expatriate threat" in Russia. Therefore, Russia's accession to the WTO did not provide any additional liberalization measure to impact the flow of expatriates from developed WTO member states.

Conclusion

Russia's migration policy was expected to liberalize TMNP in the framework of GATS Mode 4, especially the movement of a wide range of expatriates. As we have discussed, Russia has already liberalized labour migration to meet their labour market demands and their cultural norms. Labour service providers from CIS countries enjoy quasi-internal migration in the territory of the former Soviet Union. The boundary between "Far Abroad" and "Near Abroad" inherited from the former Soviet Union remains and regulates the flow of expatriates into Russia. This historically contextual path-dependent feature of migration policy has been socially constructed and is embedded in the formal institutional settings. The "expatriate threat" is an example of the socially exaggerated caution regarding migrants from "Far Abroad". Therefore, Russia's accession to the WTO did not liberalize the movement of a wide range of expatriates from developed countries.

GATS Mode 4 is designed to liberalize TMNP only within the limited segment of service suppliers from other WTO members (Panizzon 2010; Poot and Strutt 2010). This regulatory framework can impact a regulatory regime only when it provides an opportunity to bring positive-sum economic benefits between WTO member states. Although there are potential synergies in efforts to expand TMNP under Mode 4 of GATS, it cannot be an incubator to set up a new regime of international labour migration that might provide more preferable conditions for migrant workers from developing and least-developed countries.

Since most WTO member states are reluctant to liberalize TMNP in the framework of GATS Mode 4, it is not fair to single out Russia for not making any effort to liberalize TMNP. However, we believe there is space to discuss further migration policy development in Russia within the framework of GATS Mode 4. Russian experts also claimed that the Russian migration policy has failed to introduce instruments that would structure the influx of professional and qualified workers; as a result, the unmet demand for workers remained high, and the current migrant qualification potential remained unrealized (Ivakhnyuk 2017). There may be many policy options for liberalizing TMNP into Russia; one should be to address the status of independent professionals or self-initiated expatriates in Russia's commitment to GATS Mode 4 and in the array of relevant migration laws. This option could enhance international business in Russia and facilitate trade.

Taking into consideration recent developments in Russian trade policy, further liberalization of its migration policy in respect to professional and qualified workers could stimulate the transfer of knowledge viewed as an alternative to the direct movement of technology and commodities.

Notes

1 Russia is ranked 17 (or 12 excluding intra-EU trade) (WTO 2017).
2 Russia is ranked fourth (after the United States of America with 49.8 million migrants, Saudi Arabia, and Germany with 12.2 million migrants each), hosting 11.7 million migrants (UN 2017).
3 Services are actively used by Russian industry as a factor of production and account for about a quarter of its output and costs (Knobel 2016, p. 96).
4 Freelancers made up 35 percent of the total US workforce in 2016, according to the survey "Freelancing in America: 2016". We must be careful about this figure. The definition of freelancers in the survey is "individuals who have engaged in supplemental, temporary, project- or contract-based work within the past 12 months". Thus the figure may include temporary workers ('New study finds freelance' 2016).
5 Workers from the member states of the Eurasian Economic Union (Armenia, Belarus, Kazakhstan, and the Kyrgyz Republic) can work without any special permissions.
6 According to Sanzharovskaya (2014), more than 60 percent of executives in a survey reported that the economic crisis had no effect on the number of foreigners in the organization, while 16 percent said that they had even more foreign colleagues. However, the recent devaluation of Russian rubles affects the demand for expatriates in Russia (Eremina 2017).
7 A recent survey conducted by the Levada Center reveals that Russian intolerance toward migrants from North Caucasus and Central Asian countries remains intense ('Attitudes towards migrants' 2017).
8 This amendment significantly affected the representative offices of foreign companies because, until the amendment was enacted, they had not been subject to the simplified procedure for engaging highly qualified foreign professionals.
9 Expatriates should also meet at least two of the following conditions: (1) not less than four years of experience in a relevant field of services, (2) a sufficient educational degree, (3) a letter of recommendation from the headquarters in their homeland or a relevant business association, and (4) proof of their achievements to support their qualifications, according to the Decree of the Government of the Russian Federation No. 424 of April 30, 2015, "On the requirements for the level of qualification of foreign citizens sent to work in the branches and subsidiaries of foreign commercial organizations registered in the territory of the member states of the WTO located in the territory of the Russian Federation".
10 In 2015, the Japan Business Federation, which is commonly referred to as the "Keidanren", raised issues related to immigration and employment procedures for expatriate staff (lengthy wait times for visas and work permits, frequent system changes, opaque procedures, etc.) as one of the seven problems that the Russian government needs to address for Japanese companies and workers doing business in Russia (Keidanren 2015).

Bibliography

Al Ariss, A and Crowley-Henry, M 2013, 'Self-initiated Expatriation and Migration in the Management Literature: Present Theorizations and Future Research Directions', *Career Development International*, vol. 18, no. 1, pp. 78–96.

Al Ariss, A, Koall, I, Ozbilgin, M and Suutari, V 2012, 'Careers of Skilled Migrants: Towards a Theoretical and Methodological Expansion', *Journal of Management Development*, vol. 31, no. 2, pp. 92–101.

'Attitudes Towards Migrants' 2017, *Levada Center*, viewed 4July 2018, www.levada.ru/en/2017/05/29/attitudes-toward-migrants/

Berry, D and Bell, M 2012, '"Expatriates": Gender, Race and Class Distinctions in International Management', *Gender, Work and Organization*, vol. 19, no. 1, pp. 10–28.

Blouin, C, Gobrecht, J, Lethbridge, J, Singh, D, Smith, R and Warner, D 2006, 'Trade in Health Services Under the Four Modes of Supply: Review of Current Trends and Policy Issues', in: C Blouin, N Drager and R Smith (eds.) *International Trade in Health Services and the GATS: Current Issues and Debates*, World Bank, Washington, DC.

Bonache, J, Brewster C and Suutari, V 2001, 'Expatriation: A Developing Research Agenda', *Thunderbird International Business Review*, vol. 43, no. 1, pp. 3–20.

Bozionelos, N 2009, 'Expatriation Outside the Boundaries of the Multinational Corporation: A Study With Expatriate Nurses in Saudi Arabia', *Human Resource Management*, vol. 48, no. 1, pp. 111–134.

Brewster, C and Scullion, H 1997, 'A Review and Agenda for Expatriate HRM', *Human Resource Management Journal*, vol. 7, no. 3, pp. 32–41.

Campbell, J 2004, *Institutional Change and Globalization*, Princeton University Press, Princeton.

CETA 2017, *Text of the Comprehensive Economic and Trade Agreement – Chapter Ten: Temporary Entry and Stay of Natural Persons for Business Purposes*, viewed 28 May 2018, 2018).www.international.gc.ca/trade-commerce/trade-agreements-accords-commerciaux/agr-acc/ceta-aecg/text-texte/10.aspx?lang=eng

Chi, C and Levitt, R 2011, 'Multinational Teams Incorporating Freelance Expatriates in the Construction Industry: Case Studies of High-speed Railways in China and Taiwan', *Engineering Project Organization Journal*, vol. 1, no. 3, pp. 169–181.

Dawson, L 2013, 'Labour Mobility and the WTO: The Limits of GATS Mode 4', *International Migration*, vol. 51, no. 1, pp. 1–23.

Eremina, N 2017, 'Dorogie Inostrancy: jekspaty bol'she ne nuzhny Rossii', *Gazeta.Ru*, 7 October, viewed 29 December 2018, www.gazeta.ru/business/2017/09/27/10909268.shtml?updated

Federal State Statistics Service 2015, *Trud i zaniatost' v Rossii: Statisticheskii sbornik*, the Federal State Statistics Service, Moscow.

Federal State Statistics Service 2017, *Trud i zaniatost' v Rossii: Statisticheskii sbornik*, Federal State Statistics Service, Moscow.

Ghosh, B 1997, *Gains From Global Linkages: Trade in Services and Movement of Persons*, Macmillan Press, Houndmills.

Haak-Saheem, W and Brewster, C 2017, '"Hidden" Expatriates: International Mobility in the United Arab Emirates as a Challenge to Current Understanding of Expatriation', *Human Resource Management Journal*, vol. 27, no. 3, pp. 423–439.

Hedberg, C, Hermelin, B and Westermark, K 2014, 'Transnational Spaces "From Above": The Role of Institutions in Promoting Highly Skilled Labour Migration From India to Sweden', *Tijdschrift voor Economische en Sociale Geographie*, vol. 105, no. 5, pp. 511–525.

Inkson, K, Michael, A, Pringle, J and Barry, S 1997, 'Expatriate Assignment Versus Overseas Experience: Contrasting Models of International Human Resource Development', *Journal of World Business*, vol. 32, no. 4, pp. 351–368.

Ivakhnyuk, I 2017, *Predlozheniya k migratsionnoy strategii Rossii do 2035 g*, Tsentr strategicheskikh razrabotok, Moskva.

Jacobsson, J 2013, 'Liberalisation of Service Mobility in the EU's International Trade Agreements: As External as It Gets', *European Journal of Migration and Law*, vol. 15, no. 3, pp. 245–261.

Keidanren 2015, *Fundamental Approach to Japan-Russia Economic Relations*, viewed 18 July 2018, www.keidanren.or.jp/en/policy/2015/113.html

Knobel, A 2016, 'The Influence of Services Trade Liberalization on Service Flows and Industry Productivity in CIS Countries and Russia', *Applied Econometrics*, no. 44, pp. 75–99.

'Komu na Rusi zhit' khorosho: Rossiyu zhdet nashestviye ekspatov' 2012, *RBK*, 2 February, viewed 28 May 2018, www.rbc.ru/economics/02/02/2012/5703f2a39a7947ac81a647a7

Korolev, A 2016, 'Russia's Reorientation to Asia: Causes and Strategic Implications', *Pacific Affairs*, vol. 89, no. 1, pp. 53–73.

Kunda, G, Barley, S and Evans, J 2002, 'Why Do Contractors Contract? The Experience of Highly Skilled Technical Professionals in a Contingent Labor Market', *Industrial and Labor Relations Review*, vol. 55, no. 2, pp. 234–261.

Lodefalk, M 2016, 'Temporary Expats for Exports: Micro-level Evidence', *Review of World Economics*, vol. 152, no. 4, pp. 733–772.

Maltby, D 2018, *Applying for Temporary (And Then Full) Residency . . . One Expat's Experience*, RussiaKnowledge, viewed 15 June 2018, www.russiaknowledge.com/2017/08/27/applying-for-temporary-and-then-full-residency-one-expats-experience/

McNulty, Y 2013, 'Are Self-initiated Expatriates Born or Made? Exploring the Relationship Between SIE Orientation and Individual ROI', in: V Vaiman and A Haslberger (eds.) *Talent Management of Self-Initiated Expatriates: A Neglected Source of Global Talent*, Palgrave Macmillan, Basingstoke.

McNulty, Y and Brewster, C 2017, 'The Concept of Business Expatriates', in: Y McNulty and J Selmer (eds.) *Research Handbook of Expatriates*, Edward Elgar, Cheltenham.

'New Study Finds Freelance Economy Grew to 55 Million Americans This Year, 35% of Total U.S. Workforce', 2016, Upwork, viewed 11 May 2018, www.upwork.com/press/2016/10/06/freelancing-in-america-2016/

Nielsen, K, Jessop, B and Hausner, J 1995, 'Institutional Change in Post-socialism', in: J Hausner et al. (eds.) *Strategic Choice and Path-Dependency in Post-Socialism: Institutional Dynamics in the Transformation Process*, Edward Elgar, Aldershot.

Panizzon, M 2010, 'International Law of Economic Migration: A Ménage à Trois? GATS Mode 4, EPAs and Bilateral Migration Agreements', *Journal of World Trade*, vol. 44, no. 6, pp. 1207–1252.

Poot, J and Strutt, A 2010, 'International Trade Agreements and International Migration', *The World Economy*, vol. 33, no. 12, pp. 1923–1954.

Raza, W 2018, 'Mode 4 Trade in Services: Promoting Temporary Labour Mobility Via the Trade Détour?', *Innovation: The European Journal of Social Science Research*, vol. 31, no. 3, pp. 227–250.

Rodríguez, M and Melikhova, Y 2015, 'Services in Russia: Past, Present, and Future', *Eurasian Geography and Economics*, vol. 56, no. 6, pp. 656–678.

Ryazantsev, S 2014, 'O yazykovoiy integratsii migrantov kak novom oriyentire migratsionnoiy politiki Rossii', *Sotsiologicheskiye Issledovaniya*, no. 9, pp. 25–29.

Ryazantsev, S 2017, 'Vneshnyaya migratsionnaya politika kak faktor demograficheskogo razvitiya Rossii', *Sotsiologicheskiy Al'manakh*, no. 8, pp. 63–71.

Ryazantsev, S and Tkachenko, M 2010, *Mirovoy rynok truda i mezhdunarodnaya migratsiya*, Ekonomika, Moskva.

Sanzharovskaya, Y 2014, 'Inostrannyy chelovecheskiy kapital: osobennosti privlecheniya vysokokvalifitsirovannykh inostrannykh spetsialistov', *Statistika i Ekonomika*, no. 6, pp. 142–146.

Solodilova, N and Khafizova, G 2012, 'Nekotoryye vozmozhnyye problemy i perspektivy Rossii v usloviyakh VTO', *Vestnik UGAES. Nauka. Obrazovaniye. Ekonomika. Seriya: Ekonomika*, vol. 1, no. 1, pp. 25–30.

Straubhaar, T 2003, 'Why Do We Need a General Agreement on Movement of People (GAMP)?', in: B Ghosh (ed.) *Managing Migration: Time for a New International Regime*? Oxford University Press, Oxford.

Suutari, V and Brewster, C 2000, 'Making Their Own Way: International Experience Through Self-initiated Foreign Assignments', *Journal of World Business*, vol. 35, no. 4, pp. 417–436.

Tharenou, P 2013, 'Self-initiated Expatriates: An Alternative to Company-assigned Expatriates?', *Journal of Global Mobility*, vol. 1, no. 3, pp. 336–356.

Tkachenko, M 2010, 'Effekty vneshnetorgovoy liberalizatsii dlya natsional'nogo rynka truda', *Natsional'nyye Interesy: Prioritety i Bezopasnost*, vol. 31, no. 88, pp. 21–26.

Tyuryukanova, E 2007, 'Sovremennyy migratsionnyy rezhim i ego osobennosti v Rossii', in: Z Zayonchkovskaya (ed.) *Metodologiya i Metody Izucheniya Migratsionnykh Protsessov*, Adamant, Moskva.

UN 2017, *International Migration Report*, viewed 28 May 2018, www.un.org/en/development/desa/population/migration/publications/migrationreport/docs/MigrationReport2017.pdf

WTO 2009, *Presence of Natural Persons*, Background Note by the Secretariat S/C/W/301, viewed 28 May 2018, https://docs.wto.org/dol2fe/Pages/FE_Search/FE_S_S009-DP.aspx?language=E&CatalogueIdList=108652

WTO 2017, *Trade Profiles*, World Trade Organization, Geneva.

14 Russian Federation in the WTO dispute settlement

First steps

Olga Y. Trofimenko

Introduction

The Russian Federation joined the World Trade Organization (WTO) on August 22, 2012 after an 18-year accession process. Many experts perceived the possibility of serving national trade interests through the WTO dispute settlement (DS) system as one of the key potential advantages of Russia's WTO membership. Indeed, in dozens of cases where Russian exporters claimed abuse of their rights, the country had a limited set of tools with which to influence the trade policy measures of its trading partners. The WTO membership could give Russia new opportunities, including access to the dispute settlement tools that WTO rules provide.

At the same time, the ability to participate in trade dispute settlement is not only an opportunity, but also a challenge. In addition to rights, the Russian Federation made a variety of commitments and acquired new obligations. Some trade policy measures of the Russian government raise questions among certain WTO members, who have challenged the most important issues using the WTO DS mechanism, and the country must respond.

The goal of the chapter is to assess the first Russian steps in using the WTO dispute settlement mechanism. The chapter is organized as follows. The literature overview is followed by a description of the methodology, in which the author discusses the applicability of game theory to the issue under investigation. It also contains general information about Russia's involvement in the WTO DS system. Then, it analyses Russia's behaviour as both a complainant and the respondent from the two-level game-theory point of view. Finally, the policy recommendation section and the conclusions contain general suggestions on the involvement of Russia in the WTO dispute settlement process.

Literature review

Many studies since 1995 have addressed the participation of countries in the WTO dispute settlement system. For example, Shaffer evaluates how private firms collaborate with government authorities in the United States (US) and the European Union (EU) to challenge foreign trade barriers "before the WTO legal system and within its shadow" (Shaffer 2003, p. 5). He defines "foreign trade barrier" as any measure that directly or indirectly results in an impediment to trade. He also talks about limitations US authorities face in bringing the WTO complaints and argues that they cannot challenge certain third-country measures as strongly as prejudiced US industries would like. He states that US trade litigation strategies also take into account domestic political movements (Shaffer 2003, p. 63). All in all, one must bear in mind that national authorities should represent national interests, but not companies' interest. Shaffer and Meléndez-Ortiz (2010) pay special attention to developing countries' involvement in the WTO DS. They discuss institutional challenges with regard to the issue and try to figure out when properly organized public-private partnerships generate successful outcomes.

Bown and Ruta (2010) look at the economic issues of WTO litigation and divide disputes into two categories: the first over WTO-inconsistent import-restricting and the second over export-promoting policies. Under the first category, arbitration should observe WTO-inconsistent trade-restrictive measures; the second one includes WTO-inconsistent government subsidies. This deviation is important in order to determine countermeasures in the first case and retaliation limits in the second. Magnus (2005) investigates challenges of compliance with the WTO dispute settlement decisions. Lau and Schropp (2017) argue that the choice of the proper litigation strategy might depend on economic analysis.

Perrelli and Grinols (2001) analyse the dispute game that the infringing and complainant countries subject to the WTO process play as a trade adjudication repeated game. They construct a theoretical model of international trade disputes as the rational outcome of a finite extensive form of noncooperative repeated game with one-sided incomplete information.

The literature thus far includes few studies devoted to Russia's participation in WTO dispute settlement. Knobel et al. (2016) and Bayeva (2015) describe the first attempts by Russia in the field. Bohanes and Markitanova (2015) analyse the prospects of the DS474 case, where the Russian Federation tries to challenge the EU's anti-dumping cost-replacement methodology.

Taşbaşı (2017) attempts to explore the possible outcomes of a trade dispute between Turkey and Russia, assuming that Turkey can lodge a complaint with the WTO Dispute Settlement Body (DSB) about a hypothetical Russian protectionist move. In general, his model is universal and applicable to cases initiated by both Russia and WTO members other than Turkey.

Despite the fact that the literature includes some estimations of Russia's participation in the WTO dispute settlement system, at the moment a comprehensive analysis of Russia's involvement does not exist. The author tries to fill some of the existing gaps.

Methodology

The basis for this chapter is the two-level game-theory approach introduced by Robert Putnam (1988), which regards international negotiations between states as simultaneous negotiations at both the intranational level (i.e. domestic) and the international level (i.e. between governments). Indeed, at the national level, governments must address various societal and business concerns and, at the same time, reach international deals. Central decision-makers cannot ignore either of the two games, so long as their countries remain interdependent, yet sovereign (Putnam 1988, p. 434). Putnam bases his idea on the concept that a legislator is simultaneously involved in two games: one in the legislative arena and the other in the electoral arena. In this model, a given action is simultaneously a move in two different games, and one player maximizes the sum of his payoffs from the two games (Putnam 1988, p. 434). The two-level approach recognizes the inevitability of domestic conflict about what the "national interest" requires. It also admits that central decision-makers strive to reconcile domestic and international imperatives simultaneously (Putnam 1988, p. 434).

A substantial number of later authors used this approach. Da Conceição-Heldt makes a comprehensive analysis of studies done in this field and provides their classification. She recognizes the possibility of applying this approach to WTO-related issues, in particular to show whether actor preferences at the international level or domestic political institutions or both explain the success of the Uruguay Round and the failure of the current Doha Round (Da Conceição-Heldt 2013).

The idea of looking at the issue from the two-level game point of view comes from the understanding of the nature of the WTO dispute settlement process. As Shaffer claims, WTO law, while formally a domain of *public* international law, profits, and prejudices *private* parties – particularly well-connected, wealthier, and well-organized ones – who attempt to use the WTO legal system to advance their commercial ambitions (Shaffer 2003, p. 3). Indeed, only properly organized domestic industries can push their government to participate in a long-lasting and rather expensive process.

The chosen approach has some limitations. Generally, interactions between private companies and governments take place behind closed doors. Media publications can partly reflect ongoing processes, but sometimes it is very difficult to judge which stakeholder started to lobby a certain measure and when exactly this happened.

The chapter investigates the institutional settings for Russia's participation in WTO-related disputes and, on the basis of a case-study approach, figures out key stakeholders and their interests, and distinguishes how these interests influence decisions on new dispute initiations (if Russia is a complainant) or maintaining/removing the existing measure that might violate WTO law.

Case studies use the following disputes: DS 462, DS 463, DS 475, DS 499, DS 566, where Russia plays a respondent role; and DS 476, DS 493, DS 494, DS 521, where Russia is a complainant (Table 14.1). The above-mentioned disputes each belong to one of three groups. Firstly, the author assesses cases where the WTO panels/Appellate Body generated their reports, and one might seriously discuss whether the challenged measures were WTO consistent or inconsistent (DS 475, DS 499, DS 494).[1] Secondly, the study considers the disputes terminated at early stages of the litigation process with or without prospects of being continued (DS 494 and DS 462, DS 463 correspondingly). Finally, it assesses two recently brought cases where Russia is in the same position as some other WTO members with regard to the US trade policy actions (DS 554 and DS 566).

Table 14.1 Russia's participation in the WTO trade disputes, July 2013–December 2018

as complainant – 7 case(s)	*as respondent – 9 case(s)*
DS474 European Union – Cost Adjustment Methodologies and Certain Anti-Dumping Measures on Imports from Russia	DS462 Russian Federation – Recycling Fee on Motor Vehicles. Complainant: European Union
DS476 European Union and its Member States – Certain Measures Relating to the Energy Sector	DS463 Russian Federation – Recycling Fee on Motor Vehicles. Complainant: Japan
DS493 Ukraine – Anti-Dumping Measures on Ammonium Nitrate	DS475 Russian Federation – Measures on the Importation of Live Pigs, Pork, and Other Pig Products from the European Union. Complainant: European Union
DS494 European Union – Cost Adjustment Methodologies and Certain Anti-Dumping Measures on Imports from Russia – (Second complaint)	DS479 Russia – Anti-Dumping Duties on Light Commercial Vehicles from Germany and Italy. Complainant: European Union
DS521 European Union – Anti-Dumping Measures on Certain Cold-Rolled Flat Steel Products from Russia	DS485 Russia – Tariff Treatment of Certain Agricultural and Manufacturing Products. Complainant: European Union
DS525 Ukraine – Measures relating to Trade in Goods and Services	DS499 Russia – Measures affecting the importation of railway equipment and parts thereof. Complainant: Ukraine
DS554 United States – Certain Measures on Steel and Aluminium Products	DS512 Russia – Measures Concerning Traffic in Transit. Complainant: Ukraine
	DS532 Russia – Measures Concerning the Importation and Transit of Certain Ukrainian Products. Complainant: Ukraine
	DS566 Russian Federation – Additional Duties on Certain Products from the United States

Source: WTO (2018a).

The chapter does not intend to provide a legal analysis of panel and Appellate Body rulings. A comprehensive legal analysis requires treating every dispute with special care, and does not correlate with the purpose of the study. Also worth mentioning is that even though the basis of the study is the game-theory approach, which to a large extent requires heavy use of math, this one will concentrate on economic analysis of affected stakeholders' positions. As Breckenridge states, "[a]nalysis based on game-theoretical simulation is not simply a numerical exercise. It is, rather, the application of a rich corpus of economic theory that has evolved to explain the competitive interaction of firms in markets, and how this interaction changes as a consequence of changes to market structure and/or policy variables" (Breckenridge 2017, p. 277). Therefore, this chapter tries to see an economic background behind every case under investigation.

The WTO dispute settlement system and Russia's involvement in it

Article 3 of the Understanding on Rules and Procedures Governing the Settlement of Disputes (or the Dispute Settlement Understanding – DSU) determines that '[t]he dispute settlement of the WTO is a central element in providing security and predictability to the multilateral trading system'. And '. . . it serves to preserve the rights and obligations of Members under the covered agreements, and to clarify the existing provisions of those agreements in accordance with customary rules of interpretation of public international law' (WTO DSU 1995). In order to limit the extent to which a country's economic or political power influences whether or not it adheres to agreement with trade rules, the members of the WTO adopted a system under which each party can submit its arguments to an impartial panel of experts for a decision. Any party to the dispute can appeal the conclusions of panels in the WTO Appellate body, and its decisions become obligatory.

According to the rules, parties can reach a mutually agreed-upon solution at consultation stage or at any other stage of the dispute before the Panel issues a final report and circulates it to all WTO members.[2] Such an approach allows saving time and financial resources, and stimulates finding a compromise among parties. According to Article 11 of DSU, panels should consult regularly with the parties and give them adequate opportunity to develop a mutually satisfactory solution. A complaining party has a right to ask the panel to suspend its work for the maximum period of 12 months[3] (Article 12.12 of DSU). This is usually done to allow the parties to find a mutually agreed-upon solution. But a complainant might have other reasons behind such a decision.

It is worth mentioning that private parties (e.g. companies or business associations) do not have direct access to the WTO DS process. At the same time, they are the main beneficiaries of the challenged state trade policy measures. Therefore, the governments of the dispute parties expect to receive financial and, what is more important, information and legal support from the stakeholders interested in dispute outcomes. All information that companies and NGOs provide might figure in the litigation process.

In principle, the WTO receives complaints when a member or a group of members believes that another member applies measures that violate the law of the organization and therefore must be removed. When negotiations on bringing such measures into conformity with the country's obligation fail, the complainants might use the WTO DS mechanism as a definitive tool to force a defending party to change its policy. The country must respond to these complaints to secure its position.

After the WTO accession, the Russian Federation started to use the WTO dispute-settlement mechanism for securing its economic interests. At the same time, regardless of the rather long accession period, Russia did not manage to create a strong institutional framework for the WTO DS utilization by the accession date, for many reasons. This led to the situation of Russia receiving a first case as a respondent, rather than having initiated one as a complainant.[4] By December 2018, the Russian Federation was involved in seven cases as a complainant, nine as a respondent (Table 14.1), and 63 as a third party. Experts in international trade law always have a clear understanding of how to achieve the peculiarities of the WTO DS process by using the "learning by doing" technique. At the same time, observing attempts of other members to utilize this mechanism is always good. Therefore, it is not a surprise that Russia participates as a third party in such a substantial number of disputes.[5]

In Russia's case, the Department of International Trade Negotiations (the Ministry of Economic Development) is responsible for dealing with the WTO disputes. Specialists of the Permanent Mission of the Russian Federation in Geneva are actively involved in the ongoing disputes. The Russian government might also rely on legal support from leading international law firms that specialize in WTO law on a commercial basis.

One difficult issue at present is the source for financing the costs of Russia's participation in WTO dispute settlement, since there is no specific budget line for such litigations. The WTO appears in the budget only in the context of Russia's membership fees. Activities involving the participation of the Russian Federation in DS proceedings are carried out at the expense of the resources available to the Ministry of Economic Development (Interfax 2016).

According to expert estimates, legal support of one case with the use of the services of a foreign consultant in WTO dispute-resolution procedures requires, on average, from US$1.5 to 2 million. The involvement of Russian experts might decrease these costs, but sometimes they may not have enough experience to handle specific cases. Under the circumstances, it is important that companies become more active in initiating new disputes and financing a substantial amount of the costs.

Russia as a respondent

All in all, Russia is a responding party in nine WTO disputes. The opposing members are almost the same as in the cases when Russia plays a complainant role (with the exception of Japan). The EU initiated a maximum amount of cases – four (no surprise, as it is used to be and still is one of Russia's largest trading partners). Ukraine brought three cases, understandable as economic issues reflect ongoing political tensions.[6] Japan and the US each brought one dispute.

Even though some experts claim that the Russian Federation nowadays is experiencing a lack of lawyers who specialize in the WTO rules, one could argue that within the country there are some experts that know those provisions quite well (e.g. government officials that negotiated Russia's WTO accession, teachers of international trade law, staff of the Russian mission, etc.). At the moment of introducing and applying a certain measure, the possible reaction of other WTO members that it could affect is more or less clear.

Soon after the accession to the WTO on August 12, 2012, the Russian Federation introduced recycling fees on motor vehicles.[7] Collection started on September 1, 2012. This measure generated concerns among key exporters of automobiles to the Russian Federation, especially the European Union and Japan. The fees *per se* were not a problem; a key concern was with regard to some Russian producers receiving exemptions. Those domestic companies that have accepted voluntary warranty obligations to ensure the safe disposal of their autos did not have to pay the fee. The exemption applied to all major Russian manufacturers: AvtoVAZ, KAMAZ, and GAZ. The EU and Japan believed that the introduction of the recycling fee in this way gave advantages to Russian automakers did not comply with WTO regulations.

The topic generated concerns even before the measure went into force (European Commission 2012) and has since arisen many times in bilateral negotiations. In May 2013, the Russian government approved the draft law "On Amendments to Article 241 of the Federal Law 'On Production and Consumption Wastes'", which distributed the recycling fee to domestic producers as well. However, the spring session of the State Duma did not consider the document. By the time the Duma went on vacation, it was clear enough that the Russian Federation was not in a hurry to bring the measure into conformity with WTO law. Therefore, the EU and Japan on July 9 and July 24, 2013 initiated corresponding disputes with regard to the issue (DS 462 and DS 463).

One could argue that in the Russian Federation, here was a hope that by analogy with China and other recently acceded countries, more experienced WTO members would postpone transforming their concerns into real disputes. The author believes that Russia did not want to start its membership in the WTO with two disputes it was highly likely to lose. In October 2013, the Russian State Duma adopted amendments that satisfied complaining parties in terms of fees application, and the disputes were terminated at the stage of the panel establishment in the case of the EU claim (DS462) and at the consultation stage in Japan's case (DS463).

What was behind the way this measure was initially introduced? Domestic automobile producers historically were among those who opposed liberalization of the sector. They actively raised their fears about the future of the domestic industry after the WTO accession. The main risks announced were rapid import growth, decline of domestic production as a result of decrease in competitiveness of national industry and transformation of the Russian car market into a dump of imported old used cars. The voice of producers reached very high levels, even at the Federation Council (Terentyeva 2012). Meanwhile, the automobile industry of the Russian Federation before 2012 comprised about 1 percent of GDP, providing about 400,000 work places in companies that manufactured automobiles and component parts. Moreover, the industry created about 1 million work places in affiliated and dealer companies (Sutyrin et al. 2012). Understanding this enhanced the bargaining positions of the industry representatives with national authorities.

Traditionally, the Russian government had heavily supported car production. It used to apply all kinds of measures aimed at production and sales growth, including subsidies, demand encouragement, "industrial assembly" projects, and import duties. Before the accession to the WTO, Russia applied 35 percent import duties on vehicles (increased as a response to the economic crisis of 2008) as the Russian automobile industry and local car market turned out to be the most vulnerable during the world economic crisis (Sutyrin et al. 2012, p. 12). Such high duties used to create quite comfortable conditions for domestic manufacturers both producing in Russia/the USSR for many years and those who relatively recently had created new production facilities under the industrial assembly regime. The accession terms required a reduction of import duty rate to 25 percent and later on to 15 percent within a seven-year transition period (WTO 2011).

Obviously, such liberalization plans frightened representatives of the domestic automotive industry, and the government found a way to keep a higher level of protection regardless of the decrease of customs duties. For many, it was clear that in fact this initiative was to compensate for the reduction in import duties on new and used cars that would occur in the following years. All in all, these additional protections for domestic companies existed for about 1.5 years.

After extending recycling fees to domestic companies, the government concentrated on using other instruments of support. They included the use of subsidies (e.g. compensation of a part of interest rates on loans received for technical modernization, subsidizing the transportation of vehicles produced in the Far East to the European part of Russia, partial compensation of energy costs), leasing programmes for consumers and other measures that supported secure production and sales. The government was willing to provide that support also due to the fact that in addition to costs, measures created additional budget revenues coming from taxes and duties (Morozov 2015).

Similar behaviour – an attempt to provide greater protection to domestic industry at the expense of a foreign one – occurred with the import ban on EU pork, introduced by Russia in 2013 as a response to the threat of spreading the African swine fever (ASF). Indeed, some cases of infection turned up in Poland and Lithuania. Russia's reaction was somewhat rigid; it prohibited the supply of pork and live pigs from all EU countries and introduced a prohibition on the supply of all kinds of pork products from Poland and Lithuania. The European Union claimed that such restrictions were too tough and Russia could take less restrictive measures to protect human and animal lives. The EU argued that in fact the few minor cases of the ASF infection in wild boars near the borders with Belarus were promptly localized. At the same time, Russia decided to keep the measure as long as possible and, in this case, was ready to come through all stages of the WTO litigation process.

In April 2014, the European Union initiated consultations with Russia on the issue. They did not end up with the compromise; the domestic pressure was rather high on both members, and the EU also evaluated its chances of succeeding in the dispute as strong. On June 27, 2014, the EU requested that the WTO establish a panel, created a month later. Regardless of the fact that in some issues the WTO panel agreed with Russia's approach, it found that the measure was inconsistent with Article 5.6 of the SPS Agreement because it was significantly more trade-restrictive than required to achieve Russia's appropriate level of protection (ALOP). In principle, the Appellate Body supported the findings of the panel. At the same time, the issue is still far from resolution, as the EU is not happy with the position of the RF on implementing the DSB recommendations (DS 475).

This dispute shows the importance of applying sanitary and phytosanitary measures in accordance with WTO rules, and the need to avoid using these measures as non-tariff, restricting trade, without sufficient scientific evidence. At the same time, a brief economic analysis (see below) shows that measures the Russian government undertook allowed national pork producers to strengthen their market positions domestically and even to begin export (Ministry of Agriculture 2018). The author believes that additional costs that consumers (both households and meat-processing factories) have to bear do not count in implementing such policies.

Answering the question "*Cui prodest*?" makes obvious that the key beneficiaries of such a decision were national producers of pork. As in the case with the automotive industry, Russia's WTO membership terms facilitated its interest with regard to live pigs and pork. To regulate market access, a tariff rate quota was introduced for fresh, chilled or frozen pork. According to accession terms, a zero-duty rate should be applied in case these products come within the tariff rate quota (TRQ), and until December 31, 2019, the tariff will be bound at 65 percent for product amounts exceeding the quota. The tariff quota will be eliminated on January 1, 2020, at which point a flat bound rate of 25 percent will apply. Rates on live pigs exported to Russia decreased from 40 percent to 5 percent, from the date of Russia's accession to the WTO. The import duty on pure-bred breeding swine was established at 0 level (Schedule CLXV – The Russian Federation). The European Union traditionally had been one of the biggest exporters of pork to Russia, its share in total pork import exceeding 57 percent. Therefore, domestic producers perceived European imports as a threat. The issue was important for European producers as well. The RF was a destination country for at least 25 percent of European export of pork (Figure 14.1).

Figure 14.2 represents the development of domestic production in this sector in Russia. Starting with the USSR collapse, output decreased sharply and hit bottom in 1999 with 1,485,000 tons (Rosstat 2018d). After that point, one could observe a gradual growth of output, representing the end of the crisis in this specific sector.

Such achievements became possible due to the government's import-substitution plans and support of the sector consisting of various measures: subsidies for reimbursement of the interest on investment loans; compensation of part of the direct costs incurred for construction and modernization, as well as for the purchase of machinery and equipment; subsidies on purchases of livestock feed and other measures. Regardless of the fact that production of pork in households declined dramatically, big producers invested in modernization of their facilities and managed to fill the gap and increase production. Rapid import surge could negatively affect the sector.

Figure 14.3 clearly shows that after a gradual growth of consumer prices for pork since 2010, prices started to decline, and new price minimums were achieved by spring 2013. National producers started to lobby their interest and search for additional protection. For example, General Director of the National Union of Pork Producers Yuri Kovalev presented the concerns of the union to the government and expected development of a set of measures to reduce the risks.

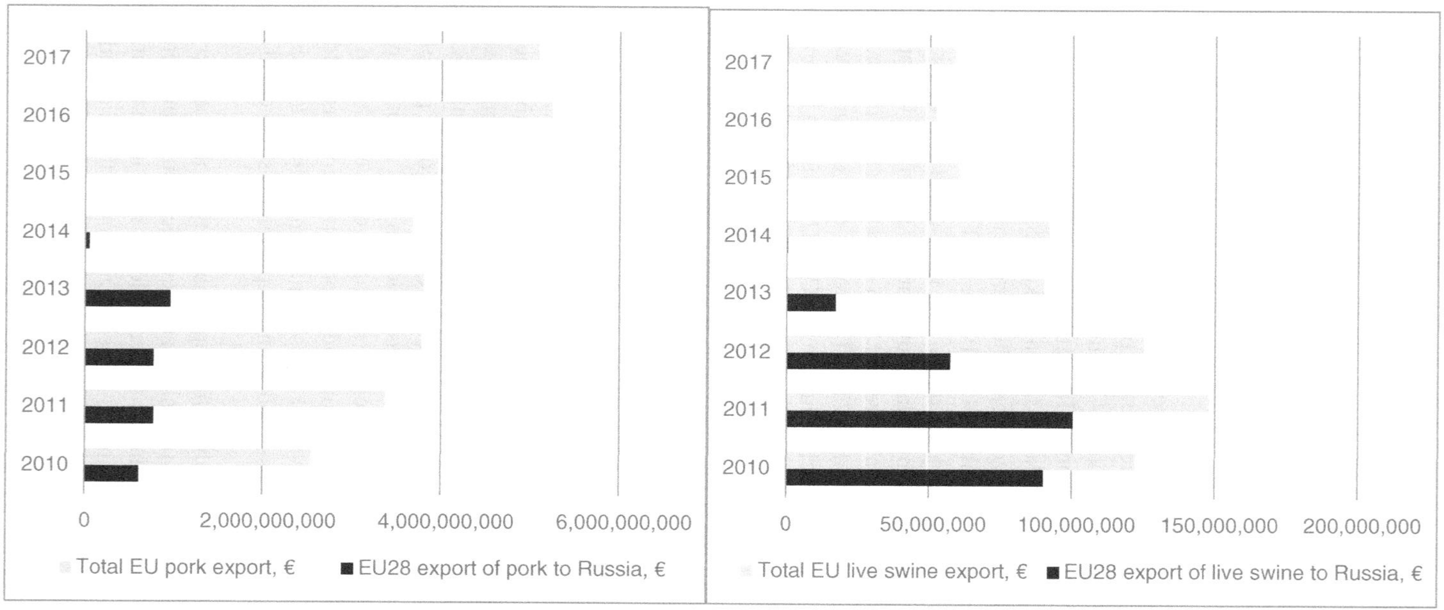

Figure 14.1 Export from EU of pork and live swine, 2010–2017

Source: EU Market Access Database (2018).

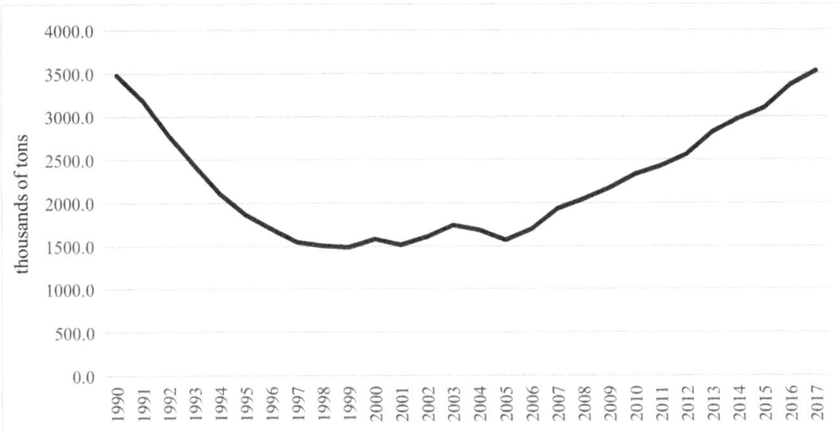

Figure 14.2 Production of pork in Russia, 1990–2017
Source: Rosstat (2018d).

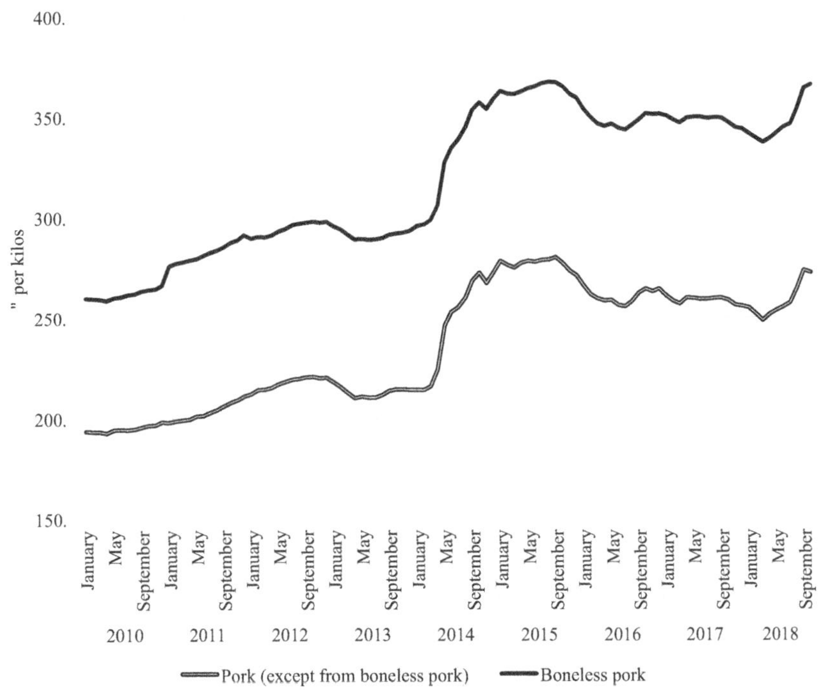

Figure 14.3 Average consumer prices for boneless pork and other pork, 2010–2018
Source: Rosstat (2018d).

One could argue that the ASF infection was a good excuse to apply sanitary and phytosanitary measures under the conditions of new market access rules.[8] As a result, import volumes declined substantially. The sharpest drop was in 2014: in 2013, the import of pork to the Russian Federation reached 1,012,100 tons, and in 2014, the volumes dipped to 427,600 tons. In 2015–2016, the trend continued, with 2016 imports decreasing to 286,400 tons (AB Center 2018). In August 2014, fresh, chilled, and frozen pork was included on the list of goods that could not be exported to Russia due to national security reasons, from countries that imposed sanctions against it. The EU was listed among them ('Postanovlenie Pravitel'stva RF' 2014').

It was no surprise that after a ban, pork prices grew dramatically: the peaks were reached in 2015 (Figure 14.3). As for the domestic industry, one could observe positive trends. By 2017, the level of pork self-sufficiency in Russia reached 74 percent, and starting in 2013, the country showed substantial export growth, after many years of having been relatively negligible (AB Center 2018).

At the same time, this dispute might have had negative consequences not only for Russian consumers, but also for national exporters of various types of products. On October 18, 2018, the European Union requested the establishment of a compliance panel, asking for an opportunity to retaliate annually for the amount of €1.39 billion. If the DSB satisfies the EU lawsuit, suppliers of other goods (e.g. metals, chemistry products) could be subject to this cross-retaliation, which might create additional tensions within the country.

An economic analysis of this case raises another question: why the Russian government, instead of imposing an import ban on European pork, did not use other instruments of domestic industry support? For example, according to the accession terms, Russia could provide support for agricultural producers within so called amber box measures.[9] Aggregate measurement of support (AMS) was established in the amount of US$9 billion in 2012 and 2013. However, the actual amounts of support did not reach the level of the total bound AMS, and the value of green box measures[10] that have no limitations for any agriculture was less than US$3 billon (WTO 2016). Moreover, support levels for specific products, as measured by the Single Commodity Transfers[11] (SCT) for pork producers, were at their minimum level in 2013, and after a peak in 2014, they started to decline again (Figure 14.4). The sub-programme "meat industry development" received less than 52 percent of the budgeted allocations in 2013 (Ministry of Agriculture 2014).

One could argue that the national pork producers lobby was probably not so well-organized and powerful as the automotive industry's, as they did not manage to secure higher bound rates and negotiate a desired level of state support. For example, in 2008 and 2011, the National Pig Farmers Union asked the government for additional subsidies to cover increased costs of livestock feeds and received what they wanted. In contrast, in 2012, only producers in six Russian regions could enjoy this subsidy. In October 2012, national agricultural associations approached the Minister of Agriculture, Nikolai Fedorov, trying to find

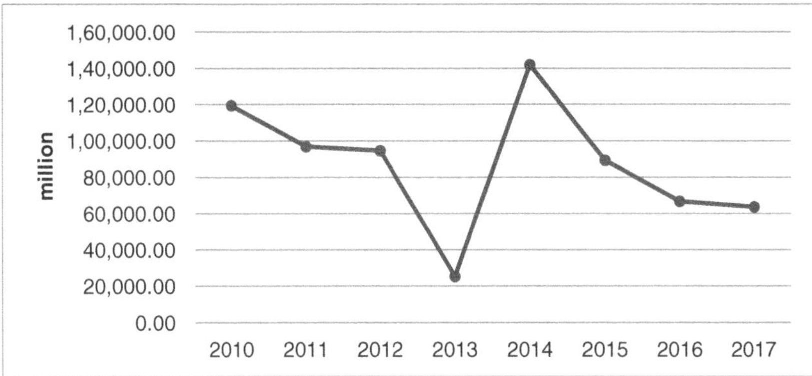

Figure 14.4 Single commodity transfers for pig meat producers, 2010–2017

Source: OECD (2018).

a way to redistribute the funds more equally. This attempt was not successful ('Sviney obdelyat rublem' 2012).

It seems that the Russian government should not have had such a straightforward reaction to the challenges that domestic pork producers faced. As already mentioned, the country elaborated measures other than bans that provide additional support. One could argue that the ban could be imposed not as a result of the national pork-producing lobby, but as a result of a wish to provide a quick and "easy" (at first glance) response to increased imports. Even though pork producers scored positive achievements, the measure created additional tensions within the country as a result of consumer losses and in relations with the EU. In addition to the lost case, the government would most probably have to react to concerns of other domestic producers in case the DSB allows the EU to retaliate, and the European Commission will use this opportunity.

The idea to support domestic producers is also not straightforward with regard to the Russian measures imposed on some Ukrainian companies. It seems they have both economic and political reasons, designed as a reaction to challenges the Ukrainian government creates for Russian companies. Undoubtedly, domestic producers of like products might benefit from these measures.

For example, starting in 2014, the Russian certification authorities began to suspend the validity of previously issued certificates of conformity for Ukrainian manufacturers of railway equipment products and limited the issuance of new certificates. Moreover, the Russian Federation has refused to recognize certificates issued to Ukrainian manufacturers in Belarus and Kazakhstan, though according to the regulations of the Eurasian Economic Union (EAEU), all of its members should recognize such certificates. The losses of Ukrainian producers are substantial; as a result of restrictions, Ukrainian exports of railway products to the Russian Federation from 2012 to 2016 decreased more than 20 times, from US$2.6 billion to US$95 million. According to the Ukrainian Ministry of Economic Development and Trade, 2013 exports of locomotives to Russia accounted for US$1.7 billion (11.8 percent of all exports of this country to Russia). In 2017, this figure declined to US$220 million, and export of passenger carriages and freight wagons declined (Popov 2018).

It is also noteworthy that Russian producers filled in gaps in imports coming from Ukraine. Figure 14.5 shows that after a decline in 2015, the domestic industry experienced production growth. Unlike the situation with pork, analysis did not discover any substantial price fluctuations for these products (Rosstat 2018a).

What could be the driving forces for such measures? Facing decline in production and sales, Russian oligarchs explored various means of increasing demand for the products. For example, Forbes (2014) reports that the company RM-Rail, part of the Russian Machines holdings of Oleg Deripaska, wrote a letter to the Russian president suggesting a prohibition of the service life of railway carriages extension. In addition, he requested imposing duties on imports coming from Ukraine. The first measure aimed at enlarging the domestic market as consumers would have to buy new carriages instead of using old ones. This idea was partly fulfilled. The second request purported to eliminate competitors. Russian authorities could not simply increase duties and most probably started to think about alternatives.[12]

As for claims by Ukraine, in principle, in "DS499: Russia – Measures affecting the importation of railway equipment and parts thereof", the Panel found that Ukraine had not demonstrated the existence of the alleged systematic prevention of imports of Ukrainian railway products into Russia. It basically supported

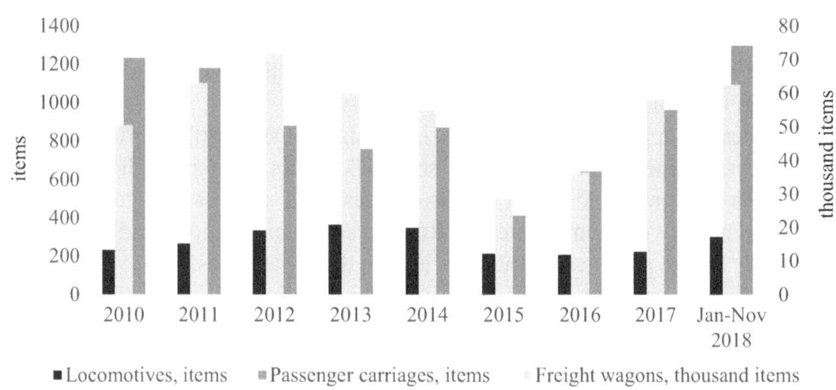

Figure 14.5 Production of railway equipment in Russian Federation, 2010 to January–November 2018

Source: Rosstat (2018b, 2018c).

concerns only with regard to Russia's refusal to recognize certificates issued by other EAEU members.

The opportunities are questionable for Ukraine to appeal in the near future. The Appellate Body announced that due to the size of the Panel record and the complex issues appealed, and in view of the backlog of appeals pending with the Appellate Body at present, Division Members can currently spend only very little time preparing for this appeal (DS499).

Other disputes that involve Russia as a complaining party have a slightly different nature and background. It goes without saying that in the latest dispute DS566, initiated by the United States, Russia is participating not due to the initial deliberate wish to provide a greater level of protection for national companies by imposing additional duties. Indeed, the Russian government applies higher than bound rates duties for some US products as a reaction to similar measures, initially introduced by the US. One could argue that this dispute is in line with some other cases recently initiated against Canada, China, the EU, Mexico, Turkey – countries that did not dare to introduce and apply measures restricting imports from the US as retaliatory measures to policies originally applied by the Trump administration.

Russia as a complainant

As of December 1, 2018, 31 countries, as well as the EU and the Gulf Cooperation Council countries, have applied restrictive measures against Russian goods. All in all, there were 162 measures, including 48 anti-dumping duties, 19 safeguards, one countervailing measure; and a set of other barriers, including technical measures, sanitary and phytosanitary measures, and excise taxes on a discriminatory basis. Not all concerns of Russian business and government end up in the WTO dispute settlement system (Ministry of Economic Development of the Russian Federation 2018).

In general, as recommended, Russia is trying to settle the problematic issues during consultations and negotiations, but sometimes they cannot solve them without requesting a formal litigation. The main driving forces for this (as in cases with all other WTO members) are national companies claiming to face discrimination by foreign governments. Also, political reasons could explain the activities of Russia as a complainant, mainly the wish to balance the amount of cases where Russia plays defensive and offensive roles. This is a general practice of most WTO members participating in the disputes.

As a complainant, the Russian Federation deals with the issues of great political and economic importance, and up to 2018 had initiated all of them against its closest neighbours, the European Union and Ukraine (four and two disputes respectively). The dispute against the United States was in line with a set of cases brought by various WTO members in response to Presidential Proclamations on adjusting imports of aluminium and steel into the United States. Worth mentioning is that Russia was one of the last in line of affected WTO members that initiated the case.

In DS474, Russia challenges certain "cost adjustment" methodologies the European Commission (EU Commission) applied when determining costs of production in anti-dumping proceedings. Basically, it rejected the domestic price of gas, as recorded in the records of producers of such products as ammonium nitrate and steel pipe. Such an approach allows determining a higher normal value of the products, and therefore applying higher anti-dumping duties.

This was the first case Russia initiated in the WTO. There were several reasons behind that, first of all a political one. By the day of the request for consultations on December 23, 2013, Russia was already a part of two disputes as a respondent without any chance of succeeding. This prompted domestic opponents of Russia's accession to the WTO to further criticize that decision. Bringing a "good" case could show that WTO participation not only leads to additional costs and obligations but creates benefits as well. In DS474, Russia tried to challenge the EU Commission's decision to reject the domestic price of gas, as stated in the records of ammonium nitrate and steel pipe producers (Bohanes and Markitanova 2015).

Minimal import volumes and significant exports to foreign markets characterize the ammonium nitrate market in Russia. At the same time, a significant increase in the production capacity of ammonium nitrate in the world raises the competition level and stimulates price volatility. This already rather negatively affects the position of Russian producers. A similar situation relates to steel and steel pipe producers. It is worth mentioning that these two industries, production of fertilizers and metallurgy, were among key proponents of Russia's accession to the WTO, as relative freedom in applying anti-dumping duties used to be a common instrument of discrimination against them. Outside the WTO system, Russia had limited opportunities to oppose those duties. The country could not challenge those measures without having WTO member status. Therefore, the appearance of this case was quite predictable.

Prior to Russia's WTO accession, Russian producers of metals and fertilizers were subjects of dozens of anti-dumping investigations. The companies could quickly provide the government with the relevant information. In addition, Russia was happy to initiate a dispute with good chances of winning.

DS474, though, ended up at the consultation stage, but Russia later generated two separate ones: DS494: European Union – Cost Adjustment Methodologies and Certain Anti-Dumping Measures on Imports from Russia (second complaint); and DS521: European Union – Anti-Dumping Measures on Certain Cold-Rolled Flat Steel Products from Russia. Even though both cases are frozen at early stages of the litigation process,[13] quite possibly Russia will defrost them (Interfax 2018), especially because there is already a decision with regard to a similar claim by Argentina, which received a ruling in its favour (DS473).

At the same time, Russia was more successful in challenging anti-dumping duties on ammonium nitrate that the Ukrainian government imposed. Like the EU, Ukraine also tried to apply cost adjustment methodologies with regard to imports of fertilizers from the RF, but the Panel upheld most of Russia's claims (DS493). The case was initiated in 2015.

Anti-dumping duties on ammonium nitrate originating from the Russian Federation and introduced in 2014 should be valid until July 2019. In July 2014, duties were raised from 11.91 percent to 36.03 percent. The Ukrainian authorities motivated their decision by the need to use cost adjustment techniques that take into account not Russian internal gas and electricity prices needed for ammonium nitrate production, but prices in third countries. In March 2018, duties on Russian ammonium nitrate were revised and their value reached 42.96 percent (for one company, 29.25 percent) (Ministry of Economic Development and Trade of Ukraine 2018).

One might wonder why Russia did not push forward juridical procedures in the case of the EU and was more active with regard to Ukraine. The answer most probably lies in political and economic rational domains. As already discussed, bilateral relations with Ukraine are very complicated, and where possible and appropriate, the RF would most probably use all kinds of trade policy instruments in order to force this country to decrease the pressure on Russian companies. Definite lack of resources for participating in several disputes at the same time can explain an economic rational domain (a complainant party has this choice, compared to a respondent). Under the circumstances, it is more efficient to concentrate on one dispute and try to win it than to distribute attention over several cases of a similar nature. The WTO panels and the Appellate Body taking into consideration previous decisions while making new rulings might be a clever strategy.

Another significant dispute Russia initiated was its second one, DS476: European Union and its Member States – Certain Measures Relating to the Energy Sector. In this case, the beneficiary is a national giant, Gazprom.

Russia challenged regulatory acts allegedly aimed at the implementation of the so-called Third Energy Package (TEP). According to Russian authorities, these acts aimed at tightening and centralizing control over the EU energy market, and TEP itself unreasonably restricts the import of Russian natural gas and is generally discriminatory. The company the TEP mainly affected is Gazprom. The company uses a comprehensive vertically integrated business model that is in line with its strategic goal as it increases business efficiency and reliability of supplies, enabling it to use accumulated production and scientific and technical potential. One of the TEP goals is a liberalization of the European energy market through ownership division for extraction, transportation, and sale of energy resources. The third package provides a set of measures for the structural reform of vertically integrated enterprises aimed at separating natural monopoly (transportation) from competitive activities (production, sales). The declared purpose of separation is to deprive the owner of the transportation system of the actual opportunities and commercial incentives to discriminate against unaffiliated companies (third parties). This idea contradicts the nature of Gazprom, which heavily invested in transportation infrastructure.

This case is a paramount issue for Russia in various dimensions. Firstly, Gazprom is one of the national economic leaders that employs almost half a million people; it is also one of the largest taxpayers in the country. Secondly, the Russian Federation is a key owner of the company. Thirdly, the Russian budget still depends heavily on exports of energy resources, and the government tries to do its best to facilitate trade in natural gas. Finally, the company has enough resources to provide support for the claim in the WTO. Therefore, obviously the Russian state would support claims of a state-owned company.

The panel upheld Russia's position with regard to several measures challenged in the case. The European Union notified the DSB of its decision to appeal to the Appellate Body certain issues of law and legal interpretations in the panel report. At the same time, with regard to the key issue of the dispute, one company cannot extract, sell, and transport gas; for all three operations, the panel took the EU's side in favour of a division at the property level. Therefore, the Russian Federation also notified the DSB of its decision to cross-appeal (DS 476). Due to challenges that the WTO Appellate Body is experiencing nowadays,[14] one should not expect a decision soon.

Policy recommendations and conclusions

Despite the fact that Russia's first steps at the WTO have not been very successful, nowadays it is trying to take full advantage of its membership in the organization. Among other instruments available for its members, Russia is learning how to use the dispute settlement mechanism for the realization of the country's commercial interests. Of course, a determination of these interests is not a simple task, and WTO must respond to the requests coming from domestic companies, set priorities wisely and take into consideration societal interests as well. At the same time, the county should not deviate from its commitments to the WTO. But it is a general task for all WTO members, and the practical implementation of this idea is a challenge.

Receiving several requests as a respondent, Russia used varying tactics for different WTO cases. It changed discriminatory measures soon after initiation of the dispute in case of the recycling fee but preferred to fight for the legitimacy of a ban with regard to European pork[15] and restrictions on import of railway equipment from Ukraine. It seems that in the dispute the US initiated, the RF will fight for the eligibility of additional duties. One might speculate that distinctions between behaviours depend on various factors: stronger lobbying opportunities of certain domestic industries asking for protection, the level of importance of the issue, the conviction concerning the applied measures, and/or experience of other WTO members.

As a complainant, Russia tries to bring cases that it has more chances to win and where it can rely on substantial support of domestic companies interested in elimination of restrictions. Industries have different lobbying powers. In case of Gazprom, a state-owned company, communications with the state should be easier than they are for pork producers. The dialogue with manufacturers of fertilizers and steel/steel products, subjects of anti-dumping regulations, is rather easy and they bring potentially winning cases. Representatives of the automotive industry are powerful enough and one can expect to maintain their support.

At the moment, Russia has managed to win two disputes out of seven in the WTO. In addition, at one dispute, the Panel upheld a part of Russia's claims. These victories create additional opportunities for domestic companies. It seems that the learning-by-doing approach proved its effectiveness and achieved one of Russia's goals behind joining the WTO. The WTO arbitration is known for its impartiality; therefore, those victories might strengthen the international prestige of Russia. They also make additional arguments against those who opposed Russia's WTO membership domestically.

It should be noted that the litigation process in the WTO was combined with supplementary domestic supportive measures of concerned industries. New initiatives that aim at providing additional support for Russian companies arose within the country. They include various types of measures that do not violate the WTO rules or have no chance of being challenged. For example, Russia gradually decreases the ceiling for duty-free purchases that domestic consumers make in foreign internet shops. The same is true with regard to products bought from abroad for personal consumption. It makes these "improvements" in response to long-lasting complaints of lobbyists; they definitely would create additional opportunities for domestic companies. Another interesting example of support is the idea to provide preferences in government procurements for certain companies. For example, the Russian Ministry of Industry and Trade generated an idea to provide priorities to the Russians Machines company (controlled by Oleg Deripaska) in government procurements (Kommersant 2018).

All in all, it seems that Russia should more intensively use the WTO dispute-settlement system as a complainant and, at the same time, apply trade policy measures in a way that would only leave infinitesimal chances of being challenged. General imperfections of the system (e.g. long-lasting procedures and current crisis with the Appellate Body) might limit Russia's participation in the WTO DS. Another limitation might reside in internal Russian problems: the lack of companies able and ready to support the government in bringing cases to the WTO and the scarcity of a political will at the national level. Russia also must improve its domestic policies in order to create a better institutional environment for doing business within the country and not to forget about societal issues in trade policy development. To achieve that requires a comprehensive public consultation process.

Notes

1 DS479 is not under investigation regardless of circulated Panel and Appellate body reports as the decision to apply challenged anti-dumping duties was taken at the level of Eurasian Economic Commission.
2 Where the parties have found a settlement of the matter, the panel issues a report in which it briefly describes the case and reports that the parties have reached a mutually agreed solution (Article 12.7 of the DSU).
3 If the work of the panel has been suspended for more than 12 months, the authority for establishment of the panel shall lapse.
4 It is worth mentionning that normally unless a newly acceded country initiates a dispute, other WTO members try not to challenge its WTO-inconsistent measures. For example, China brought the first dispute as a complainant in 2002, while receiving the first request for consultations as a respondent only in 2004.
5 The WTO rules allow its members to participate in the dispute as a third party if a county has a substantial trade interest. A similar strategy was used by China.

6 So far, the EU is more successful in challenging Russia's trade policy measures than Ukraine.

7 The base rates were ₽20,000 and ₽150,000 for cargo vehicles (approximately US$614 and US$4,600 using the exchange rate of the Central Bank of Russia for September 1, 2012). The base rates should be multiplied by coefficients depending on age and technical characteristics of cars.

8 According to Rosselkhoznadzor, in 2013 in Russia 78 and 150 cases of ASF were recorded for livestock populations and wild boars, respectively. For the period 2007–2018, 833 and 533 cases of ASF were registered in Russia (Rosselkhoznadzor 2018).

9 Nearly all domestic support measures considered to distort production and trade (with some exceptions) fall into the amber box, which is defined in Article 6 of the Agriculture Agreement as all domestic supports except those in the blue and green boxes. These include measures to support prices, or subsidies directly related to production quantities. The reduction commitments are expressed in terms of a "Total Aggregate Measurement of Support", which includes all supports for specified products together with supports that are not for specific products, in one single figure (WTO 2018b).

10 Green box subsidies must not distort trade, or at most cause minimal distortion. They must be government-funded (not by charging consumers higher prices) and must not involve price support. They tend to be programmes that are not targeted at particular products, and include direct income supports for farmers that are not related to current production levels or prices. They also include environmental protection and regional development programmes (WTO 2018b).

11 The Producer Single Commodity Transfers is the annual monetary value of gross transfers from consumers and taxpayers to agricultural producers, measured at the farm gate level, arising from policies linked to the production of a single commodity such that the producer must produce the designated commodity in order to receive the transfer. The OECD defines the Producer SCT for a commodity as the sum of market price support (MPS) for that commodity and budgetary and other transfers to producers from policy measures that have been labelled as supporting that commodity (OECD 2018). Greenville (2017) explains the difference between the PSE and the AMS. The PSE is a measure of the "current" value of transfers from consumers and taxpayers to producers, while the AMS is not. In the PSE, MPS is calculated using actual producer and border prices for commodities in a given year, while in the AMS, the MPS is calculated using the difference between annual administered prices fixed by policy-makers and world prices according to a base period (generally the three-year 1986–88 average). This results in an MPS value that is very different from what is actually being transferred from consumers to producers.

12 The author does not question findings and conclusions of the Panel in a relevant dispute. It is just a recognition that trade policy-makers all around the Globe can be very creative and apply trade-restrictive measures without violating the WTO rules.

13 Russia decided to wait for the outcomes of disputes on similar issues involving other WTO members and to concentrate on other disputes

14 At the moment there are on duty only three out of seven WTO AB body members. The United States blocked appointment of new ones. This creates delays in issuing AB reports.

15 A similar attitude could be observed in DS479 – Russian Federation – anti-dumping duties on light commercial vehicles from Germany and Italy.

Bibliography

AB Center 2018, *Rynok svininy – kljuchevye tendencii i prognozy*, 4 April, viewed 28 December 2018, http://ab-centre.ru/news/rynok-svininy- klyuchevye-tendencii-i-prognozy

Bayeva, M 2015, 'Uchastiye Rossii v sporakh VTO v 2015 godu', *Rossiyskoye predprinimatel' stvo*, no. 16 (23), pp. 4287–4396.

Bohanes, J and Markitanova, A 2015, 'A Few Reflections on DS474 and the Intersection of Russia's Domestic Energy Policies and the EU's Anti-dumping Cost Replacement Methodology', *Vestnik Sankt-Peterburgskogo universiteta. Seriya 5: Ekonomika*, no. 2, pp. 72–89.

Bown, C and Ruta, M 2010, 'The Economics of Permissible WTO Retaliation', in: C Bown and J Pauwelyn (eds.) *The Law, Economics and Politics of Retaliation in WTO Dispute Settlement*, Cambridge University Press, Cambridge.

Breckenridge, A 2017, 'The Games We Play – Simulation Models in Merger Analysis and Their Potential Use in Trade Litigation', in: T Carpenter, M Jansen and J Pauwelyn (eds.) *The Use of Economics in International Trade and Investment Disputes*, Cambridge University Press, Cambridge.

Da Conceição-Heldt, E 2013, 'Two-level Games and Trade Cooperation: What Do We Now Know?', *International Politics*, vol. 50, no. 4, pp. 579–599.

EU Market Access Database 2018, viewed 28 December 2018, http://madb.europa.eu/madb/statistical_form.htm

European Commission 2012, *EU Welcomes Russia's WTO Accession After 18 Years of Negotiations*, Press release, 22 August, viewed 28 December 2018, http://europa.eu/rapid/press-release_IP-12-906_en.htm?locale=en

Forbes 2014, 'RM-Rail Deripaski poprosil Putina zapretit' prodlenie sroka sluzhby vagonov', 2 October, viewed 28 December 2018, www.forbes.ru/news/269635-rm-rail-deripaski-poprosil-putina-zapretit-prodlenie-sroka-sluzhby-vagonov

Greenville, J 2017, *Domestic Support to Agriculture and Trade: Implications for Multilateral Reform*, ICTSD, March, viewed 28 December 2018, www.ictsd.org/sites/default/files/research/domestic_support_to_agriculture_and_trade_ictsd_issue_paper_0.pdf

Interfax 2016, *Vedeniyu RF sporov v ramkakh VTO pomeshalo otsutstviye sredstv*, viewed 28 December 2018, www.interfax.ru/business/503556

Interfax 2018, *RF poprosit VTO sozvat' panel' arbitrov po isku k ES iz-za "ehnergokorrektirovok"*, viewed 28 December 2018, www.interfax.ru/business/626156

Knobel, A, Bayeva, M and Firanchuk, A 2016, *Uchastiye Rossii v torgovykh sporakh v ramkakh VTO: analiz konkurentosposobnosti*, Izdatel'skij dom "Delo" RANHiGS, Moscow.

Kommersant 2018, *Olegu Deripaske ukorotili ruku pomoshhi*, 26 September, viewed 28 December 2018, www.kommersant.ru/doc/3752413

Lau, C and Schropp, S 2017, 'The Role of Economics in WTO Dispute Settlement and Choosing the Right Litigation Strategy – A Practitioner's View', in: M Jansen, J Pauwelyn and T Carpenter (eds.) *The Use of Economics in International Trade and Investment Disputes*, Cambridge University Press, Cambridge.

Magnus, J 2005, 'Compliance With WTO Dispute Settlement Decisions: Is There a Crisis?', in: R Yerxa and B Wilson (eds.) *Key Issues in WTO Dispute Settlement: The First Ten Years*, Cambridge University Press, Cambridge.

Ministry of Agriculture 2014, *O hode i rezul'tatah realizacii v 2013 godu Gosudarstvennoj programmy razvitija sel'skogo hozjajstva i regulirovanija rynkov sel'skohozjajstvennoj produkcii, syr'ja i prodovol'stvija na 2013–2020 gody*, viewed 28 December 2018, http://mcx.ru/upload/iblock/ecd/ecdf16896dfaf6482cc395b0522dbd52.pdf

Ministry of Agriculture 2018, *Rynok mjasa – tekushhaja situacija. Ezhenedel'nyj obzor*, 28 December, viewed 28 December 2018, http://mcx.ru/upload/iblock/05d/05db55ddc613a13e2c2f4d592727308b.pdf

Ministry of Economic Development and Trade of Ukraine 2018, viewed 28 December 2018, https://ukurier.gov.ua/uk/articles/mizhvidomcha-komisiya-z-mizhnarodnoyi-27032018/

Ministry of Economic Development of the Russian Federation 2018, *Obzor sushhestvujushhih ogranichenij v dostupe rossijskih tovarov na zarubezhnye*, viewed 28 December 2018, rynkiwww.ved.gov.ru/mdb/information/database/

Morozov, A 2015, 'Programmy gospodderzhki avtoproma v etom godu potrebuyut 27, 2 mlrd rubley', *Vedomosti*, 13 October, viewed 28 December 2018, www.vedomosti.ru/auto/blogs/2015/10/13/612547-programmi-gospodderzhki-avtoproma#/galleries/140737492462666/normal/1

OECD 2018, *Producer and Consumer Support Estimates Database*, viewed 28 December 2018, www.oecd.org/tad/agricultural-policies/producerandconsumersupportestimatesdatabase.htm#country

Perrelli, R and Grinols, E 2001, *Trade Games: The WTO's Role in Disputes – Theory and Practice*, viewed 28 December 2018, www.iatp.org/sites/default/files/Trade_Games_The_WTOs_Role_in_Disputes- Theory_.pdf

Popov, A 2018, 'Dela na milliardy: Rossija nauchilas' vyigryvat' spory v VTO', *Forbes*, 5 September, viewed 28 December 2018, www.forbes.ru/biznes/366289-dela-na-milliardy-rossiya-nauchilas-vyigryvat-spory-v-vto

Postanovlenie Pravitel'stva RF ot 7 avgusta 2014 g. N 778 "O merah po realizacii ukazov Prezidenta Rossijskoj Federacii ot 6 avgusta 2014 g. N 560, ot 24 ijunja 2015 g. N 320, ot 29 ijunja 2016 g. N 305, ot 30 ijunja 2017 g. N 293 i ot 12 ijulja 2018 g. N 420" 2014, viewed 28 December 2018, http://base.garant.ru/70712500/

Putnam, RD 1988, 'Diplomacy and Domestic Politics: The Logic of Two-Level Games', *International Organization*, vol. 42, no. 3, pp. 427–460.

Rosselkhoznadzor 2018, *Tekushhaja jepizooticheskaja situacija po Afrikanskoj chume svinej*, viewed 28 December 2018, www.fsvps.ru/fsvps/asf/chronology/

Rosstat 2018a, *Indeksy cen proizvoditelej na otdel'nye vidy promyshlennyh tovarov po sub#ektam Rossijskoj Federacii (s 2010 po 2016 gg.)*, viewed 28 December 2018, www.gks.ru/dbscripts/cbsd/DBInet.cgi?pl=1904011

Rosstat 2018b, *O promyshlennom proizvodstve v janvare-nojabre 2018 goda*, viewed 28 December 2018, www.gks.ru/bgd/free/B04_03/IssWWW.exe/Stg/d01/244.htm

Rosstat 2018c, Proizvodstvo osnovnyh vidov produkcii v natural'nom vyrazhenii, viewed 28 December 2018, www.gks.ru/free_doc/new_site/business/prom/natura/god10.htm

Rosstat 2018d, *Sel'skoe hozjajstvo, ohota i lesnoe hozjajstvo*, viewed 28 December 2018, www.gks.ru/wps/wcm/connect/rosstat_main/rosstat/ru/statistics/enterprise/economy/#

Shaffer, G 2003, *Defending Interests. Public-Private Partnerships in WTO Litigation*, Brookings Institution Press, Washington, DC.

Shaffer, G and Meléndez-Ortiz, R 2010, *Dispute Settlement at the WTO: The Developing Country Experience*, Cambridge University Press, Cambridge.

Sutyrin, SF, Lomagin, NA, Sherov-Ignatiev, VG, Trofimenko, OY, Kapustkin, VI, Nazarova, MV and Lisitsyn, NE 2012, *Russia's Accession to the WTO: Major Commitments, Possible Implications*, International Trade Centre, Geneva, viewed 28 December 2018, www.intracen.org/uploadedFiles/Russia%20WTO%20Accession%20English.pdf

Sviney obdelyat rublem 2012, *RBK daily*, no. 217. (512), November 15, www.pressreader.com/russia/rbc/20121115/281676842187012

Taşbaşı, A 2017, 'International Trade and Strategic Behaviour: A Game Theoretical Analysis of the Trade Dispute Between Turkey and Russia', *Economic Research-Ekonomska Istraživanja*, vol. 30, no. 1, pp. 581–595.

Terentyeva, A 2012, 'Proizvodstvo gruzovikov v Rossii ne uspevayet za rostom rynka', *Vedomosti*, 27 March, viewed 28 December 2018, www.vedomosti.ru/auto/articles/2012/03/27/spasenie_ot_vto

WTO 2011, *Working Party Seals the Deal on Russia's Membership Negotiations*, viewed 28 December 2018, www.wto.org/english/news_e/news11_e/acc_rus_10nov11_e.htm

WTO 2016, *Trade Policy Review Report by The Secretariat*, Russian Federation, WT/TPR/S/345, viewed 28 December 2018, www.wto.org/english/tratop_e/tpr_e/s345_e.pdf

WTO 2018a, *Dispute Settlement: Disputes by Member*, viewed 28 December 2018, www.wto.org/english/tratop_e/dispu_e/dispu_by_country_e.htm

WTO 2018b, *Domestic Support in Agriculture: The Boxes*, viewed 28 December 2018, www.wto.org/english/tratop_e/agric_e/agboxes_e.htm

WTO DSU 1995, *Understanding on Rules and Procedures Governing the Settlement of Disputes*, viewed 28 December 2018, www.wto.org/english/tratop_e/dispu_e/dsu_e.htm

15 Conclusion

Sergei F. Sutyrin

An international team of experts providing contributions to this book focused on a variety of the major aspects in two closely related issues, namely foreign trade and trade policy. In general, both of them are of an obvious importance for almost each and every national economy. At the same time, in the specific Russian case a magnitude of this importance is substantially higher than many people tend to think.

Indeed, in terms of some basic relative indicators typically used to measure the involvement of any specific country in international trade the Russian Federation is ahead of at least several leading global traders with other more or less comparable economic characteristics. Table 15.1 illustrates the situation with respect to so-called functional trade openness.

Among three countries that are ahead of Russia in this rating Germany is famous for its traditional focus and successful implementation of the export orientation growth strategy. As for Mexico and Canada, their economic performance is both substantially influenced by and dependent upon intensive interaction with the neighbouring United States. More than that, one has all the reasons to agree with Michael Hart (2002) who claimed that "Canada has always been a trading nation. From the early days of fur and fish, to the present, . . . Canadians have relied on international trade to bolster their economy".

As for Russia, a variety of factors, including its geographical peculiarities, distribution of the industrial centres across the national territory, relatively underdeveloped transport infrastructure, creates additional hurdles to foreign trade facilitation. In particular, several domestic as well as international experts tend to highlight an actual remoteness of the country from the major maritime trade routes. According to George Friedman (2018), "Russia is essentially landlocked. The ports on the Arctic Ocean are frequently frozen and the ports on the Black Sea and the Baltic Sea could have their access to the oceans blocked by enemies that control narrow straits. All of these ports are distant from most of Russia". Taking the above-mentioned into consideration one could sensibly argue that Russia in a way has more reasons to be called a "Trading Nation" than many other economies of similar or bigger size.

Meanwhile, one might perceive as a matter of certain concern the substantial imbalance of Russian foreign trade flows. Of course, a merchandise surplus as

Table 15.1 Foreign trade quotas (merchandise export + merchandise import/GDP) for selected economies in 2015 and 2017

	2015, percent	*2017, percent*
Mexico	68.7	73.2
Germany	70.9	71.0
Canada	54.5	52.2
Russian Federation	**40.3**	**38.7**
China	36.4	34.2
Indonesia	34.0	32.1
India	31.8	28.6
Japan	30.9	28.1
EU-28	23.9	24.4
United States	21.2	20.4
Brazil	20.8	18.3

Source: Author's calculations based on WTO Trade Profile (2016) and WTO Trade Profile (2018).

Table 15.2 Trade balance (merchandise export – merchandise import)/GDP ratio for selected economies in 2015 and 2017

	2015, percent	*2017, percent*
Germany	8.3	7.6
Russian Federation	**11.0**	**7.5**
Republic of Korea	6.5	6.2
India	6.0	5.7
USA	4.5	4.4
Brazil	0.7	2.9
China	5.5	3.5
Mexico	2.1	2.0
Canada	1.8	1.3
Indonesia	0.9	1.1
Japan	0.1	0.1
EU-28	0.004	0.01

Source: Author's calculations based on WTO Trade Profile (2016) and WTO Trade Profile (2018).

this country has permanently had is definitely better than a similar deficit. Nevertheless, in relative terms the aforementioned imbalance looks really excessive in comparison with the same indicators typical for many other national economies (Table 15.2). While assessing the data it is worth taking into consideration that in 1999–2004 Russian foreign trade surplus equalled to 12.3–22.0 percent of GDP.

Under the circumstances, the national trade policy naturally enough appears to be a very significant issue not only from the point of trade *per se*, but also within a context of Russian economic development in general. During the last decade at least, the latter is characterized by an active involvement of the state that (in addition to many other things) requires respective financial resources. From this perspective, Russian trade policy – in comparison with the trade policies of other countries – has appeared to be an extremely important fiscal tool (Table 15.3).

Table 15.3 Share of taxes on international trade in budget revenues for selected countries, 2008–2016 (percent)

	2008	*2009*	*2010*	*2011*	*2012*	*2013*	*2014*	*2015*	*2016*
Russian Federation	**25.2**	**25.5**	**25.6**	**25.6**	**26.5**	**25.4**	**25.1**	**13.2**	**10.1**
Brazil	2.1	2.0	1.9	2.1	2.2	2,5	2.4	2.3	1.7
Canada	1.4	1.3	1.2	1.3	1.3	1.3	1.3	1.5	1.5
China	4.8	3.7	4.4	4.7	4.7	4.1	2.8	2.4	n.a.
Japan	Between 1.4 and 1.6								
India	14.1	11.4	13.5	14.8	14.9	13.2	n.a.	n.a.	n.a.
Indonesia	3.8	2.2	2.9	4.5	3.7	3.3	2.8	2.3	2.2
Republic of Korea	3.6	3.7	4.0	3.8	2.5	2.8	2.2	2.0	1.8
USA	Between 1.0 and 1.1								
EU	0,01	0,01	0,01	n.a.	n.a.	n.a.	n.a.	n.a.	n.a.
Mexico	1.5	1.5	1.1	1.1	1.1	1.1	1.1	1.3	1.3
World average	4.6	4.4	4.3	4.1	4.2	3.9	3.5	3.6	n.a.

Source: Author's compilation using the data from World Bank (2018).

Table 15.4 Custom and other import duties for selected countries (percent of tax revenue), 2008–2016

	2008	*2009*	*2010*	*2011*	*2012*	*2013*	*2014*	*2015*	*2016*
India	16.2	13.3	17.1	16.8	17.3	15.2	N.a.	N.a.	N.a.
Russian Federation	**9.8**	**9.5**	**9.3**	**9.4**	**9.7**	**8.9**	**7.5**	**6.5**	**7.3**
Brazil	3.6	3.3	4.0	4.3	4.7	5.1	5.0	5.1	3.9
Canada	N.a.								
China	5.6	4.2	4.9	5.1	5.1	4.6	4.6	4.0	N.a.
Japan	1.9	1.8	1.8	1.9	1.9	2.0	1.8	1.7	1.6
Indonesia	3.5	2.9	2.8	2.9	2.9	2.9	2.8	2.5	2.5
Republic of Korea	5.2	5.6	6.0	5.7	4.7	5.3	4.2	3.9	3.4
USA	1.9	2.0	2.2	2.1	2.1	2.0	1.9	1.9	1.9
EU	N.a.								
Mexico	3.1	2.7	2.0	2.0	2.0	1.9	2.0	1.9	1.9

Source: Author's compilation using the data from World Bank (2018).

Of course, it is an open question whether a strong fiscal dependency is really compatible with the other goals trade policy typically tends to aim at. Table 15.4 provides certain information contributing to this type of discussion. Russia is the only country among those presented in Tables 15.3 and 15.4 with a share of taxes on international trade in budget revenues acceding a share of custom and other import duties in tax revenues. This results from an intensive use of export duties levied on hydrocarbons (the main item of Russian export) and some other natural resources.

Similarly to the majority of other countries, Russia with regards to trade policy can use three levels for its elaboration and implementation, namely unilateral, regional, and multilateral (global) ones. They interact and interrelate in an ambivalent way being partly complementary, partly alternative to each other. Under the circumstances national regulators face a dual challenge, that is to select dominant strategy and to implement it in a way to minimize the negative impact of above-mentioned alternativeness.

Theoretically speaking from several points of view, the focus on a unilateral track as the main one might be perceived as quite a reasonable (if not preferable) option. Firstly, it does not require any negotiations with international trading partners and, hence, allows economizing of valuable resources, some of which (in particular, human ones) are often extremely scarce. Secondly, according to traditional mainstream economic theory (originating from Adam Smith and David Ricardo arguments in favour of free trade) at least in the case of liberalization, it is the unilateralism that constitutes the "first-best" type of trade policy. More than that, a large number of modern publications based upon the empirical research claim that the unilateral liberalization tends to generate higher and more diverse gains from trade than any other alternative routes. On top of that, some experts argue that proliferation of global value chains (GVCs) provides additional incentives to unilateral trade liberalization.[1]

Meanwhile, one might argue that in a specific Russian case there is not that much room for unilateralism. Being together with four other economies as a member of the Eurasian Economic Union (EAEU), the country largely delegates its trade policy to the supranational regulator. In addition to the introduction of the common customs tariff the EAEU has already harmonized some other significant trade policy instruments and plans to proceed further in this direction. Nevertheless, at the moment a certain discrepancy exists. In particular, other EAEU members have not joined the Russian food import ban. Even import tariffs applied by the countries while demonstrating a convergence trend still differ (Table 15.5) with some opportunities for the unilateral manoeuvre.

Table 15.5 Particular elements of import tariff profiles for the members of Eurasian Economic Union in 2014 and 2017 (all goods)

	Simple average MFN applied (percent)		*Duty-free MFN applied (share of HS 6-digit subheadings in percent)*		*Duties > 15 percent MFN applied (share of HS 6-digit subheadings in percent)*	
	2014	*2017*	*2014*	*2017*	*2014*	*2017*
Russian Federation	8.4	6.7	14.2	15.9	8.8	3.2
Armenia	3.7	6.0	69.2	22.5	0.0	1.7
Belarus	8.4	6.8	14.3	15.9	8.7	3.1
Kazakhstan	8.6	6.5	14.3	15.5	9.7	2.1
Kyrgyz Republic	4.6	6.6	49.1	17.2	0.4	2.7

Note: The last year before establishing the EAEU was 2014. One also has to take into consideration that within the framework of Belarus-Kazakhstan-Russia customs union operating from 2010, its members officially introduced a common customs tariff.

Source: Author's compilation using WTO Tariff Profile (2015) and WTO Tariff Profile (2018).

With more than six years of full-fledged membership in the WTO Russia has good reasons to share many concerns and criticisms regarding the current state of international trading system widely expressed by politicians, business community, academia in various parts of the globe. The country, together with the other members of G-20, supports the necessity of respective reforms.[2] Nevertheless, from the Russian point of view these reforms by no means should undermine the role of the World Trade Organization as the key multilateral institution in charge of working out the international trade rules.

Within the context of the discussion above these rules could provide the binding operational framework for both regional trade agreements and unilaterally introduced trade policy measures. In contrast to that, hypothetical transition to "no WTO world" would almost inevitably mean the total absence of any commonly recognized transparent, non-discriminatory, open, and inclusive approaches to the regulation of commerce.

In terms of the focuses of its trade policy, Russia (similarly to the most of other countries) is constantly in uneasy search of an appropriate balance between pro-protectionist pressure and trade liberalization ambitions. The latter largely results from economically based believe in the positive net-effect of foreign trade growth as well as from Russian international commitments as a member of the WTO. The former has several origins. Firstly, the Great Recession of 2008–2009 gave birth in most parts of the globe to a new wave of protectionism supported by a widely shared lost of trust in trade liberalization.[3] In the Russian case these universal concerns were substantially facilitated by the economic slowdown of 2014–2016. Secondly, imperatives imposed on the respective countries by growing geopolitical tension in many instances generate extra trade-restricting measures. Thirdly, the international dimension of "Trumponomics" tends to provide a large-scale example of "beggar-thy-neighbor" policy provoking the other economies to retaliate in a similar way.

To conclude, the specific content and composition of a large variety of factors ultimately defining Russia's trade policy as well as "individual weights" of these factors are far from being stable. Under the circumstances, the book – in addition to providing some possible answers to the issues under review – also puts both explicitly and implicitly a certain number of the new questions that could hopefully stimulate further discussion among the international academic community. This discussion would become the best reward for the authors of the present manuscript.

Notes

1 It goes without saying that advantages of unilateral trade liberalization are challenged by various experts. Some of them apply to the analysis of trade policy a modified version of famous "prisoners' dilemma". As a result they come to the conclusion that unilateral liberalization not only fails to demonstrate any sufficient level of self-sustainability but in the longer run also (in the absence of properly designed international regulation) leads to expansion of mutual protectionism.

2 That idea was in particular emphasized in G20 Leaders' declaration of 2018 summit in Argentina (G20 Leaders' declaration 2018).
3 During Bloomberg New Economic Forum in Singapore (November 2018) a former EU Commissioner for Trade Peter Mandelson in particular claimed that people tend to think that international trade is "non-inclusive process that is growing the global economic pie, and in that sense is doing its job but politics is failing to divide up this pie and distribute the benefits in the way people expect". Bloomberg Economics' Stephanie Flanders added that "a part of political problem is that people feel that businesses have been too much a center-frame when it comes to trade negotiations, that these deals . . . have been done with multinational companies in mind and not people" (Bloomberg Markets and Finance 2018).

Bibliography

Bloomberg Markets and Finance 2018, *Remaking Global Trade*, YouTube video, 5 November, viewed 31 December 2018, www.youtube.com/watch?v=WDpxdrD2zTQ

Friedman, G 2018, 'Putin's Russia', *Geopolitical Futures*, March 19, viewed 31 December 2018, https://geopoliticalfutures.com/putins-russia/

G20 Leaders' declaration 2018, *Building Consensus for Fair and Sustainable Development*, viewed 31 December 2018, http://static.kremlin.ru/media/events/files/en/7Md4eDqpxxrILAUHYsyiE16g1D6xbs1C.pdf

Hart, M 2002, *Trading Nation: Canadian Trade Policy From Colonialism to Globalization*, UBC Press, Vancouver.

World Bank 2018, viewed 31 December 2018, https://data.worldbank.org/indicator/GC.TAX.INTT.RV.ZS?view=chart

WTO Tariff Profile 2015, viewed 31 December 2018, www.wto.org/english/res_e/booksp_e/tariff_profiles15_e.pdf

WTO Trade Profile 2016, viewed 31 December 2018, www.wto.org/english/res_e/booksp_e/trade_profiles16_e.pdf

WTO Trade Profile 2018, viewed 31 December 2018, www.wto.org/english/res_e/booksp_e/trade_profiles18_e.pdf

Index

Note: Page numbers in *italic* indicate figures and in **bold** indicate tables.